Sorrow Is the Only Faithful One

SORROW IS THE ONLY FAITHFUL ONE

The Life of Owen Dodson

JAMES V. HATCH

Foreword by Arnold Rampersad

UNIVERSITY OF ILLINOIS PRESS
Urbana and Chicago

This book is printed on acid-free paper.

Excerpts from *Boy at the Window* by Owen Dodson. Copyright
©1951 and renewal copyright ©1979 by Owen Dodson. Reprinted by
permission of Farrar, Straus & Giroux, Inc.

Excerpts from *Powerful Long Ladder* by Owen Dodson. Copyright
©1946 and renewal copyright ©1973 by Owen Dodson. Reprinted by
permission of Farrar, Straus & Giroux, Inc.

Letter from Jack Kerouac to Owen Dodson reprinted by permission
of Sterling Lord Literistic, Inc. Copyright by Jack Kerouac.

Letters from W. H. Auden are copyright ©1992 by The Estate of
W. H. Auden. Reprinted by permission.

Library of Congress Cataloging-in-Publication Data

Hatch, James Vernon, 1928–
    Sorrow is the only faithful one : the life of Owen Dodson / James
V. Hatch ; foreword by Arnold Rampersad.
        p. cm.
    Includes bibliographical references and index.
    ISBN 0-252-01977-6 (cl)
    1. Dodson, Owen, 1914–1983. 2. Authors, American—20th century—
Biography. 3. College teachers—United States—Biography.
4. Theatrical producers and directors—United States—Biography.
I. Title.
PS3507.0364Z64   1993
811'.54—dc20   92-18612
[B]   CIP

To Camille
Mac and Eunice
Evelyn, Susan, Dion, and Becky

Contents

Illustrations follow pages 130 and 230

Foreword

Arnold Rampersad

"Sorrow is the only faithful one" is a haunting line of poetry, one that appears to speak about an individual in constant pain, a tribute to a life attended by a final and irremediable sense of suffering, probably of failure. Certainly it captures a crucial element in the psychology and personal history of the man who composed it, Owen Vincent Dodson.

"Sorrow is the only faithful one" also seems an appropriate epigraph for a biography of Dodson, and even a fitting epitaph for a man who knew more than his share of grief and sorrow, and whose last years were marred by a chronic alcoholism that virtually nullified his talents, embarrassed his friends, and cheated his students of the full opportunity to draw on the wisdom and knowledge of one of the greatest figures in the history of the African-American stage.

And yet—as this biography confirms in splendid detail—the line "Sorrow is the only faithful one" does not report the entire, or even the major, part of the story of Owen Dodson. However unhappy his last years may have been, Dodson had lived a remarkable life to that point. As a poet and a man of the theater, and additionally as a teacher, he had epitomized vigor, imagination, and immense creativity. Thus his life represented finally not a passive surrender to sorrow but an active engagement on his part of the vicissitudes that life brought— and a triumph, ultimately, over sorrow.

In this distinctively written biography, in which nearly every paragraph is full of sinewy fact and meaning, James V. Hatch brings back to life (insofar as any biography can ever do so) something close to the full figure of Owen V. Dodson. With a virtual insider's knowledge of the various cultures that produced Dodson, Professor Hatch recreates in deft language the principal circles that swirled around and buoyed Dodson in his turbulent lifetime. Hatch leads us skillfully into the murky world of a Brooklyn of another era, the Brooklyn of Owen Dodson's birth and his fascinating early years, including his high school career there in the late 1920s and early 1930s. He takes us through the improbable but alluring, even idyllic, collegiate setting of Bates College, in Lewiston, Maine, where young Dodson, as a student there between 1932 and 1936, reached his first maturity, and wrote and dreamed of future literary and dramatic glory for himself.

We see the gentle, even pacifist Dodson in a still more improbable setting, the United States Navy during the war, between the years 1940 and 1942. We follow Dodson as he endures his various apprentice teaching positions and opportunities, which lead eventually to a professorship at the "Capstone of Negro Education" itself, Howard University. We trace the outline of his life's work there as a nurturer of the young in his position of professor of drama, from 1948 to 1970. We suffer through the details of deterioration and even ruin toward the end of his career there, when alcohol took its toll on a mind formerly of subtle inventiveness. With Dodson, we leave Howard University for the twilight years, passed in New York. There are pleasant and fruitful moments here, but this story ends on no happy note. In the last few years of Dodson's life, sorrow was indeed "the only faithful one."

Unlike his biographer James V. Hatch, who knew Dodson well and interviewed him extensively for this accomplished, sympathetic, and yet quite tough-minded portrait, I never met Owen Dodson. Nor did I ever see one of his stage productions, which were the basis of his extraordinary reputation as a creative force in the African-American theater even as his vision on the stage admitted no intrinsic limits where race or nationality was concerned. And yet the name Owen Dodson meant—and means—a great deal to me.

Deeply admired and loved by even his most gifted peers, including such towering figures as Langston Hughes and James Baldwin, Dodson stands as a figure of excellence in his world, which is the world of literature (especially poetry) and the stage. At Howard University, he

Simons, of the Amistad Research Center at Tulane University; Fritz J. Malval, director of the University Archives, Hampton University; Roger M. Dahl, of the National Bahá'í Archives; J. William Hess, associate director of the General Education Board Collection of the Rockefeller Archive Center; Beverly Guy-Sheftall, director of the Women's Research and Resource Center, Spelman College; Ann Allen Shockley, university archivist, and Beth M. Howse, special collections librarian, Fisk University; John Burt, librarian, Sussex University Library, England, for permission to use the Rosey E. Pool correspondence; Edward Mendelson, for the Estate of W. H. Auden.

For Dodson's record in the U.S. Navy, I appreciate the assistance of Richard Boylan, archivist, National Archives and Record Administration; Kenneth Shanks, archivist, National Archives–Chicago Branch; R. J. Schultz (LCDR USN), of the Naval Historical Center, Operational Archives Branch, St. Louis, Mo.; Bernard F. Cavalcante, head, Operational Archives Branch of the Naval Historical Center, Washington Navy Yard; R. L. Glass, commander, Head Directives of Naval Data Automation Command, Washington Navy Yard, Postal and Records Management.

Other scholars and writers shared their private collections of papers and letters: Anneke Schouten-Buys, Apfeldorn, Netherlands; Rod Bladel, New York City; Darryl Croxton, New York City; Michel Fabre, Paris, France; James Forsyth, Haywards Heath, England; Sallee W. Hardy, Orange City, Fla.; Gordon Heath, Paris, France; Rosemary Littledale Rieser, Norwich, Vt.; William H. Rieser, Perkasie, Pa.

Among the many, many who gave me interviews, I am especially grateful to drama department professors emeriti Anne Cooke Reid and James Butcher, of Howard University, who enabled me to reconstruct the "golden age" of Howard University's theater as well as the early years of drama at Atlanta University. In this regard, Prof. Thomas D. Pawley III was most generous in sharing his scrapbook and memories. I am also grateful to Jo Neal, who helped me reconstruct Owen's life in Ischia. And to Gordon Heath, Dodson's childhood friend, I owe a special debt for insisting I present Owen warts and all.

To the following friends, students, colleagues, and artists who had known Dodson and who gave me interviews or in other ways shared information, I acknowledge my gratitude: Gray W. Adams; Mike Alexander; Hilton Als; David Amram; Mary Ellen Andrews; Russell Atkins; Sidney E. Baker; Amiri Baraka; Floyd Barbour; Richmond Barthé; Ro-

Acknowledgments

While I was teaching school in Taiwan, Owen Dodson died. Upon my return I was able to begin research because three people had assembled papers and materials: first, Mrs. Virginia Staten, executor of Owen Dodson's estate, who was most generous and helpful in making Dodson's papers available; second, attorney-at-law Richard Barnes, who eased the legal complexities for undertaking this project; finally, Sallee W. Hardy, who had collected the many addresses, notes, and sources that were necessary for me to find my way.

The majority of Dodson's papers reside in four archives: (1) the Moorland-Spingarn Research Center at Howard University, where Thomas C. Battle, Esme E. Bhan, W. Paul Coates, Karen L. Jefferson, Marilyn Mahanand, Clifford L. Muse, Jr., Greta S. Wilson, and Michael R. Winston were most helpful; (2) the James Weldon Johnson Collection at the Beinecke Library, where Donald Gallup, Patricia Willis, and Jack A. Siggins gave me access to Dodson's correspondence with Carl Van Vechten, as well as to Dodson's manuscript notes and letters; (3) the Countee Cullen–Harold Jackman Memorial Collection at Atlanta University, where Minnie H. Clayton and Gloria Mims enabled me to read through Dodson's unprocessed files; and (4) the Hatch-Billops Collection, where Dodson had deposited manuscripts and letters for use in his biography.

Other libraries, archives, and individuals gave me access to various facets of Dodson's life: Pres. Thomas Hedley Reynolds, William Hiss, and Ruth Rowe Wilson, of Bates College; Florence Borders and Andy

belongs in the pantheon of great professorial figures—teachers and scholars—whose influence went far beyond that university and who stood for the highest ideals of intellectual commitment to African-American higher education. His peers in that pantheon are figures of almost legendary renown, including Dean Kelly Miller, the philosopher Alain Locke, the historian Rayford Logan, and the poet and literary critic Sterling A. Brown. What these men represent, in hindsight, is the pinnacle of scholastic achievement by Blacks in the face of constant and often raw segregation in America in the twentieth century.

Nothing so exemplifies the spirit of these men and their fellow teachers and scholars across the country as the grace and style and deep commitment to the highest cultural values with which they met adversity. Such grace and style and commitment Owen Dodson showed in abundance. He saw his own humanity clearly and held to it with incomparable determination. Whatever the opinions and actions of racists might have been, Dodson did not dream of questioning his right to associate—humbly but with dignity—with the great artists and writers of all races and all ages whose work stirred him. Proud of his own people and what they had achieved in spite of overwhelming odds, he saw himself, without qualification, as an authentically American artist and a citizen of the world. Not surprisingly, when the Black Power movement arrived at Howard University in the late 1960s, and threatened to destroy all that he and others of his generation had worked for, Dodson was ready to take his leave of the university— and the world.

Written with an easy, idiosyncratic elegance, with Professor Hatch's natural inflections and his own personality and style stamping his narrative from the first page to the last, this scholarly biography is a fresh, important chapter in the composite literary portrait of Black America that must be written, and that is being written now with increasing skill and determination. In addition, it breaks further new ground in its investigation of gay life in African-American intellectual and artistic circles, a topic Professor Hatch handles with frankness and freedom and, at the same time, a remarkable sense of fairness and responsibility.

In choosing James V. Hatch to write his biography, Owen Dodson chose well. Indeed, it is hard to believe that he could have done better. An engrossing book, *Sorrow Is the Only Faithful One* is a loving and memorable portrait of one of the most remarkable African-American artists and personalities of this century.

mare Bearden; Yvonne Berkelman; Marilyn Berry; Ednah Bethea; Camille Billops; William B. Branch; Paul Breman; Jerome Brooks; Alfredina Brown; Graham Brown; William T. Brown; Roscoe Lee Browne; Sadie Browne (Amparado); Cycil Bryan; Françoise Burgess; Selma Burke; Vinie Burrows; Eugene S. Callender; Dick Campbell; John Carlis; William I. M. Castleberry; Alice Childress; John Ciardi; Peggy Kelley Clark; Henry Folger Cleaveland; Richard Coe; Zaida Coles; William Corrigan; Darryl Croxton; Michael Cummings; Evelyn Cunningham; Arthur P. Davis; Clinton Turner Davis; Mike Davis; Wilva Davis (Breen); Tom Dent; Glenda Dickerson; Brenda Dixon; Millicent Dobbs (Jordan); Marion Douglas (Maranantha Quick); Richard Eberhart; James Ede; Dorothy Fax; Elton Fax; Jessie Fax; Nancy Fergussen; Robert Fish; Winona Fletcher; James Forsyth; Roger Fredland; Philoine Fried; Nancy Galbraith; Reginald Gammon; Kate Garretson; Irene Richardson Garrett; Dolly Gattozzi; Ruth Duckett Gibbs; Roscoe Gill; Joseph W. Gilliard; Sol Gordon; William Greaves; Lucy Grigsby; Nathalie F. Gross; Beverly Guy-Shiftall; Leo Hamalian; Bergit Hammer; Sallee W. Hardy; Rev. Donald S. Harrington; Oliver Harrington; Marianne Hauser; Gordon Heath; Melvyn Helstien; Abram Hill; Errol Hill; Mercie Hinton; William Hiss; Earle Hyman; Isa Isenberg; C. Bernard Jackson; Josephine Jacobsen; Joseph Janovsky; Seymour Janovsky; Sylvia Janovsky (Heimbach); Trellie Jeffers; Ruby Jewell; Helen Armstead Johnson; Robert Earl Jones; Vera Katz; Herbert Kee; Beverly Kelch; Arnold Kenseth; Alexander King; Glenngo Allen King; Fredric Kirchberger; Franklin Lafour; Joseph L. Langhorne; Whitney LeBlanc; Hal Leonard; Arnold Lerner; Harold Lewis; Hylan Lewis; Robert Lewis; Claire Leyba; Jane and Milton Lindholm; Richard A. Long; Arthur W. Ludwig, M.D.; Helen Lucas Lyles; Lloyd McNeill; Romualdo Maniere; Edward Mazique, M.D.; Ethelbert Miller; May Miller (Sullivan); Leslie G. T. Mitchell; Loften Mitchell; Carlton Molette; James Monks; Jack Morrison; Toni Morrison; Sigrun Müller; Frank Murray; Edmund Muskie; Jo Neal; Dorothy Neuman; Lottie Nickens; Bruce Nugent; Patrick O'Connor; Fredrick O'Neal; Carol Penn; Kathy Perkins; Shauneille Perry; Bernard L. Peterson, Jr.; Dorothy Porter; Peggy and William R. Reardon; Cora Reid; Lloyd Richards; Leonard Rieser, Jr.; Davis Roberts; Vivian Robinson; Roxie Roker; Susan Gardner Ross; Charles Ruas; Francesca Sacchetti; Giocondo Sacchetti; Charles Sebree; Ted Shine; Kari Skjonsberg; Vincent Smith; Terrence Spivey; Una Squires; John Stephan; Carolyn Hill Stewart; Bert Stimmel; Sara Hetman-Sutcliffe; William Swallow; Jo Tanner; Marlene Tartaglione; Thurlow Tibbs; Raimundo Torrence; Eleanor Traylor; C. James Trotman; Patrick Trujillo; Margaret Walker (Alexander); Ivory Wallace; Douglas Ward; Joe Weixlmann; Ron Welburn; Robert West; Mical Whitaker; Vantile Whitfield; Ernest Wiggins; Edna Wilson; Ruth Rowe Wilson; Michael R. Winston; Theresa Woodruff; Michael Yates; Marguerite Young; and Ruth Zwick (Goldblatt).

To Doris Abramson, Jerry Delaney, Leo Hamalian, Suzanne Noguere, Arnold Rampersad, Kathy Roe, and Ellen Simon, who read the manuscript and suggested changes, I give my heartfelt appreciation.

For encouragement to keep on keeping on I thank Camille Billops, Judy Blum, Meryl Burre, Gail Cohen, Bill Dutterer, Leo and Linda Hamalian, Gary Ingamells, Jamie Johnson, Barbara Lekatsas, Cora and Stanford Myers, Guillermo Noriega, Teófilo Ruiz, Ralph Scholl, Noriko Sengoku, Nancy Stillians, and Victoria Sullivan. For insights into psychoanalytic literature, I thank Ruth Helfrich. For sound advice, literary and legal, my gratitude to Ellen Simon, attorney, and to Joe Weixlmann, editor of *Black American Literature Forum*. For enabling me to successfully use a computer and word-processing program, I thank O. Vernon Matisse, of DPL Los Angeles.

For permission to use photographs, I thank Mary Ellen Andrews, Camille Billops, Jeanie Black, Bruce Kellner, Alexander King, Robert McNeill, and Joseph Solomon; and to Gregory Miroslav a special thank-you for his drawing of Dodson.

I wish to thank the following publishers and libraries for permission to quote from published and unpublished materials: Farrar, Straus & Giroux for *Boy at the Window* and *Powerful Long Ladder; Black American Literature Forum* for "All Our Farewells Cry to Thee" and "The Alchemy of Owen Dodson"; Sterling Lord Literistic for Jack Kerouac's letter to Dodson; the Moorland-Spingarn Research Center for Dodson's correspondence with Rosey E. Pool and Alain Locke; the Countee Cullen–Harold Jackman Memorial Collection, Atlanta University Center Woodruff Library, Division of Archives and Special Collections, for Dodson's papers and correspondence; the Special Collections of Fisk University for the Rosenwald Fund papers; the James Weldon Johnson Collection, Yale Collection of American Literature, Beinecke Rare Book and Manuscript Library, Yale University, for Dodson's papers and letters, as well as those from Carl Van Vechten; the Amistad Research Center, Tulane University, for Dodson's correspondence with Countee Cullen; the Hampton University Archives for Dodson's correspondence with Malcolm S. MacLean and Robert J. Sailstad; the Rockefeller Archive Center for the records of the American Film Society and the General Education Board; the Estate of W. H. Auden for Auden's letters to Dodson; and Paul Breman Ltd. for *The Confession Stone.*

Finally, my appreciation to the National Endowment for the Humanities for the award of a research fellowship in 1983 and a travel grant, and to the City University of New York for providing three Faculty Research Awards. These grants enabled me to complete this book.

—James V. Hatch

1

From Boydton to Berriman, 1870–1921

A baby born of a woman at forty, as an old wives' tale has it, will be a bright, gifted, and peculiar child, in some ways born already old. On the evening of November 28, 1914, in the Flatbush section of Brooklyn, Sarah Goode Dodson gave birth to her ninth and last — a Saturday's child. At age seven Owen asked his father where he, Owen, had come from, and his father replied, "Dr. Owen Wallah rushed up the stairs of our apartment in Brooklyn with a little black satchel, and he sat beside your mother and opened it and there you were." When relating this anecdote, Owen would look up out of the top of his eyes and add, "That was my first taste of sex; I was little and they all loved me."

Perhaps the talisman of the doctor's good name ensured Owen's survival. In this family, a boy and a girl, twins, had already died; before Owen would reach ten, two more would succumb, one to tuberculosis, the other to meningitis. Said Owen, "There was a great scent of death in the garden when I was born."

For Owen's birth, the wood stove had surely been fired, warming a floor cruelly bare of furniture (the young children sat on the ironing board suspended between two chairs). But when recalling their childhood, neither Owen nor his sister Edith ever used the word "poor"; nonetheless, in the winter's hungry days, the family wore their coats in the house while Sarah prepared oatcakes for breakfast, rice for lunch, and lima beans for dinner. No matter how parsimonious the servings, Sarah always held back a spoonful for Papa to take a second helping. Elevator operator, "college" graduate,[1] syndicated columnist, Sunday school superintendent at the Concord Baptist Church: Nathaniel Dodson wore his decorum clean and starched. His neighbors, privately, called him Reverend Dodson; children on the block tagged him "the preacher." Seated at the head of the table, Papa would read from the Bible and then call out, "Momps, where are the napkins?" Momps would reply, "They're in the same place, Papa."

"Edith, fetch the napkins," and Owen's sister would go to the buffet and take nothing out of the top drawer and hand each person an air-shaped napkin; the children would giggle and clap hands.

Nathaniel referred to his two youngest sons as "his Chesterfields," after Lord Chesterfield, the epitome of a gentleman. Although inconvenienced by poverty, on Saturday and Sunday the boys wore freshly laundered sailor suits. An old acquaintance would later refer to the immaculate family as "those damnable Dodsons."

The father served Booker T. Washington and Dr. James Sheppard[2] as press agent. Owen recalled with glee, "Once Dr. Sheppard came to our house. My father told us that he was bringing a great man to see us and wanted Kenneth and me both outside when they arrived. My mother had fixed the house up and we'd done the best we could. My father came up the street with Dr. Sheppard, and he introduced us, and he said, 'After you, sir,' and when he opened the door, the knob came off in his hand; without hesitating, he handed the knob to me, saying, 'Son, tend to this.' I was eight, so I handed the knob to my brother, who put it in his pocket. When we got to the dinner table, my father said in a loud voice that wasn't pompous, 'Momps, where are the napkins?' My mother said, very quietly, 'Papa, they didn't dry in time.'"

The Dodsons' Baptist devotion to the Bible embodied their reverence for literacy. Born to parents only five years out of slavery, Owen's father and mother made little distinction between their passion for Christ and their burning love for education. Before each meal, his father asked the Lord's blessing as if praying before the whole Sunday school; and after dinner his mother or father read aloud from the Bible. Their children, Owen in particular, were ordained to a life sonorous in language and resonant with literature.

All of this began, as it must, long before Dr. Wallah trudged up those creaking stairs to pluck Owen from his satchel. Nathaniel Barnett Dodson was born March 11, 1870, to William Armstead Dodson and Lucy Cannard Boyd on a farm near Boydton, Virginia, a village of 400 near the North Carolina border and more than 100 miles in from the coast. Here Nathaniel absorbed an elementary education at the New Liberty and Shiloh schools of Mecklenburg County. In those black schools, with their make-do buildings, few books, and painfully underschooled teachers, Nathaniel learned commitment, devotion, and prayer.[3] Anyone who could read, write, and cipher had a duty to the race,[4] so at age sixteen Nathaniel himself became a teacher, but after one year he joined the flight from rural poverty.[5]

In the spring of 1887, Nathaniel, five feet six, a precocious seventeen and wearing his round rimless glasses and a high starched collar, stepped onto the wharf in New York City. (Almost daily, ships sailed from Charleston, South Carolina, to Boston, pausing at Norfolk to take on passengers—the fare under five dollars if one slept on deck, where life preservers were carefully labeled "colored" and "white.") In his pocket Dodson fingered an address of a fraternal organization, the Sons of Virginia, to assist him in securing work and lodging.[6] In Pierrepont House, one of Brooklyn Heights's most elegant hostelries, he became an elevator "boy."[7] At first glance, it might seem happenstance or peculiar fortune that he found his way to Brooklyn, but the "better classes" lived there. Blacks on the island of Manhattan were confined to a midtown ghetto called the Tenderloin, a few noisy blocks of ragtime and theaters. (The Dutch, Jewish, and Italian enclaves of Harlem [Haarlem] real estate had not yet been unlocked to Blacks.) By contrast, Brooklyn boasted a pre–Revolutionary War history of black communities.[8]

Young Dodson rented a single room, worked hard, saved his money, and, when he could, returned to his hometown for more schooling at the Boydton Virginia Institute. The attraction of shuttling between New York and Virginia involved more than homesickness: Sarah Goode taught school in Boydton, and, further, an opportunity to matriculate into the senior class at Wayland Seminary had presented itself. For a young black man in the South, the ministry, subsidized by northern missionaries, provided the only low-cost education.[9]

Wayland Seminary rigorously imposed upon its Negroes reading, writing, oratory, Bible study, and ethics, as well as Latin, Greek, and other foreign languages. Nearly every graduate became a schoolteacher or a minister. At the end of a year, Nathaniel graduated salutatorian, and his education produced a quick profit: at Pierrepont House he was summoned from the elevator and placed behind the desk as night clerk.

In 1897, the year before he married, Nathaniel took a position with the American Press Association at 225 West Thirty-ninth Street in Manhattan, a syndicate of country newspapers founded by Major Orlando Jay Smith (a white man). Nathaniel served as general inside messenger, telephone operator, and confidential man to the president.[10] "Confidential man" suggests everything and nothing. Certainly Nathaniel served as contact with the National Negro Press Association, over which, for a time, he presided as chairman.

Knowing all about the financial instability of southern black schools and how desperately they depended upon Negroes in the North to send money back home, Nathaniel convinced Dr. James Sheppard of North Carolina College and Booker T. Washington of Tuskegee Institute that he should be their press agent: they would send him news; he would print it (for a commission) in his own hoped-for syndicated column,[11] and that would increase donations to their colleges. Nathaniel's syndication idea had to wait two years for his boss, Major Smith, to die; then, Smith's son, Courtland, allowed Dodson to edit his column. The enterprise took off: on January 4, 1909, Dodson, as the editor and manager of the *Afro-American Page,* syndicated his six-column, illustrated weekly news service to "colored papers in twenty-eight states,"[12] an American first.

After securing his position with the American Press Association, Nathaniel furnished an apartment with a bed, a table, and chairs, and then wrote to Sarah Goode in Boydton:

My dear Sarah:

Your dear letter bearing its ripe fruit of thought came on the 10:00 o'clock mail on Wednesday. I was busy waiting on a customer, and afterward came the postman. I immediately grew anxious as well as expectant. I was not disappointed, for at a mere glance I saw it was from you.

Your promptness is love, and your expression charms. I was very much animated by your wit in reference to the storm and my being blown away. I wonder does the same apply to my friend (laughter).

The poet Saxe says: "To be a good woman is better than to be a fine lady," and the proper study of mankind is man, but the most perplexing one, no doubt is woman (laughter).

I want to ask you to think over the subject of coming to visit your cousin in Newark during the coming summer. If you will come, then I shall make a proposition to you whereby releasing you of all the expense that would tend to hinder you from so doing.

You know I want to see you very bad, and as it is perhaps easy for you to comply with this request, I hope you will give it your most careful consideration.

"I live for those who love me, whose hearts are kind and true for the Heaven that smiles above me, and awaits my spirit too."

God be with you always, Amen

Yours sincerely and faithfully,
Nathaniel[13]

In 1898, the year that New York City annexed Brooklyn, Nathaniel returned to Boydton, and on May 4 married the short, nut-brown schoolteacher with dimples. In July of the next year, he brought his bride to East New York, an area much like adjacent Brownsville though still sparsely populated. (At this time the Dutch dairy farmers in New Lots still sold milk by the jar or pail.)

The newlyweds joined a diverse Brooklyn—a city of churches but also a city of forty-five breweries supplying every man, woman, and child in Brooklyn with close to two barrels of beer a year.[14] Nathaniel chose a second-story apartment in a block of two-story homes and contiguous brick apartments pocked with occasional vacant lots, an integrated neighborhood[15] of Italians, Jews, West Indians, and southern Blacks.

For Nathaniel and Sarah, 309 Berriman offered cheap rent, space for a vegetable garden, and an elevated-train station at Pitkin Avenue and Montauk Avenue, a four-block walk. A grocer occupied the first floor; to the right, a stairway ascended to the Dodson floor-through; on the third floor lived an Italian widow who spoke no English, but who shared her Italian pantry with Sarah. This Berriman Street block become the setting for Owen's first novel, *Boy at the Window*. Here, his mother gave birth to eight of her children. The neighbors remembered her as a stout woman who did not easily linger at the stoop for gossip. All recalled that later in her life she had a limp, her left leg and arm paralyzed by a stroke. Owen's sister Edith remembered that "Mama was head of the Mothers' Club in Brooklyn. She served as president of the Society of the Daughters of Virginia and of the East New York Community Club. These colored women all considered themselves superior to New York City people."[16]

Although Owen remembered many anecdotes about his father, about his mother's background he had only this to say: "I don't know when she was born. I don't know much about my mother at all, if she went to high school or not." However, on a plain white card in ornate penmanship she left her name, dated "June 5, 1891, Boydton Inst., Boydton, Va.," possibly the day of her graduation. (Her obituary reported that Sarah had taught school in Virginia.)

To bear her first child, Sarah traveled home to Boydton; on February 8, 1899, she gave birth to Lillian Cunnard, named for Nathaniel's mother. As the eldest, Lillian later cared for her brothers and sisters: Nathaniel, Jr., born October 31, 1901, an All Hallow E'en's child, and one destined to be an object of Owen's scorn; Harold, born in 1902, who died of spinal meningitis at age seventeen; the twins, Ralph and Ethel, who died shortly after birth, around 1904; Evelyn, born circa 1908, who succumbed to tuberculosis; Owen's favorite sister, Edith Katherine, born August 12, 1909; Kenneth, July 3, 1913; and finally Owen, who was born November 28, 1914. Of nine Dodson children, only five survived adolescence — the scent of death in the garden.

The children's father himself barely survived the great flu epidemic of 1918. During the siege, he wrote Joel E. Spingarn in an unsteady hand, "I have been seriously ill for a month and am just able to get to business again." With six children, two boarders, and a wife to provide for, he dared not die.

On twenty-five dollars a week, the Dodson family eked by. Then in 1921, the election of Warren G. Harding to the presidency promised to bring to the Dodson table, if not bounty, at least sufficiency. Courtland Smith's brother-in-law (the editor-in-chief of Hearst publications) had actively supported Harding, and the spoils of the Republican victory trickled down to Nathaniel's boss: Smith moved to Washington as assistant postmaster general. From there, he became vice-president of the Motion Picture Producers and Distributors of America. With a view from the top, Smith then founded Fox Movietone News, and in the 1930s organized the Trans-Lux Theaters and became president of Pathé News, all very high cotton for Nathaniel Dodson, Smith's "confidential man."

Smith's successes didn't exactly translate into luxury for the family of his trusted confidant. According to Owen, "My father came home proudly one day and said, 'Momps, Courtland Smith is really going to do something big for us this Christmas!' The family was very excited by the prospect of a gift from a rich man. Guess what my father brought home, hang-dogged and ashamed? A dozen linen handkerchiefs. That was the present he got for Christmas from the vice-president of the Motion Picture Producers and Distributors of America."

Smith had two sons, Archie and Orlando. They were just a little older than Owen and Kenneth, and Nathaniel would bring home their old clothes, which Sarah would make over to fit her boys. Owen recalled one winter when Smith sent his father way out to Long Island to a hothouse to bring him back strawberries: "I guess Smith loved my father because he was a good and faithful servant."

Owen cast Smith as Scrooge, but laced into his anecdotes is a subtle anger with his father; nonetheless, Owen did respect him. How could he not? His father, under constant economic pressure, did not abuse or abandon his family, did not turn to alcohol, drugs, or gambling. What if he did sometimes hustle Owen under the subway turnstile, or secretly smoke cigars, or bestow upon Owen's female cousins kisses that they found "long and juicy"? These were venial sins. Nathaniel's day-by-day heroism kept bread on the table.

In his later years, Owen wrote a series of vignettes, which he intended to publish as *The Gossip Book,* to strip away the masks of those he had known; this constituted his style. But when he spoke about his mother, his father, and even his neighborhood, he insisted on a perfect rose. In the entry entitled "The Family," he wrote:

> Now speaking about my mother's and father's relationship, it was the calmest and most tender. I was home so much of the time that I am sure there couldn't have been any friction whatsoever between them. My mother was concerned for my father's every little wish. For instance, during the last few years of her life, she was paralyzed in one arm and leg, and yet with all that, she took the household in her hands and made it charming,

livable—a place of peace for us children. She always served the dishes for dinner from the kitchen, and I was one of the children to carry them out. In taking my father's dish in [to him], as she handed it to me, she made sure the vegetables were arranged with what little meat we had, and she always wiped anything that spilled aside, and she did have that clean housedress on when he came home every night, and she found time in the day to take a bath, so her disposition as well as her body was sweet.[17]

If one presumes Sarah's marriage to have been made in heaven, one should remember that this woman, over sixteen years, bore nine children, four dying in her lifetime; she watched her husband and her eldest son locked in classic struggle (the boy spent time in a reformatory); she supervised or did herself the shopping, cooking, laundry, and ironing; she suffered a series of strokes. Her husband "liked women," and her children *needed* the secondhand clothes friends passed down to them. Was this also the woman who must bathe each afternoon, put on a clean dress, and hold back a spoonful of food from a meager meal so that her husband might have a second helping? Owen hid his sensitivity behind the fable of perfect parents, but in his art one hears his muffled rage.

2

309 Berriman, 1921–27

With the same goldleaf memories with which Owen had gilded the portraits of Sarah and Nathaniel, he gilded Berriman Street as a "Grover's Corners, New Hampshire" in Brooklyn where on a summer afternoon Joe and Seymour Janovsky slammed away at punch ball, striving for a two-sewer hit; their sister Sylvia, her glasses fixed purposefully on her nose, would read as she walked the long distance from the Arlington Library. In their backyard, the Richardson and Marston boys would pound a stick into the ground for a game of mumble-the-peg, forcing the loser to retrieve the peg with his teeth, while Cyril Bryan, who had converted his roller skates into a push-mobile, worried that his West Indian father would spot the wear on his ragged right sneaker. On those warm summer afternoons, West Indian mothers dressed up to sit under their awnings on the stoop. Mrs. Richardson taught her daughter Irene that "you either have a book or you crochet or do needlework."[1] With the coming of autumn, Abie Fox would stuff potatoes into a tin can punctured by a wire and set them ablaze with leaves; then, in pubescent ecstasy, he would whirl the baked "mickie" over his head, spewing out rings of fire. When winter arrived, snowballs smacked against walls and trees, while sleds bounced down the hill near the "goat lady's" shack. Berriman—an enclave of humanity in a sea of weeds.

The police periodically raided the pool hall on the corner where the gang hung out. The older boys initiated the neighborhood kids into crime by sending them to the market to clip a purse with scissors and leave the woman with the handles. The gangsters of the Amboy Dukes and Murder Incorporated grew up nearby. When Owen was ten, an Italian called Jew Boy marched into Halpern's drugstore and held a gun on Halpern, who knew him from a kid. Jew Boy said, "Give me your money or I'll shoot you." Halpern said, "I'll tell your mother." The kid said, "Don't tell my mother." Halpern told her, and she was furious with Jew Boy. "Don't rob your own people!" she rebuked him. "Go to the next block if you want to rob people."[2]

Sociologist Harold Lewis recalled that when he, working as a paperboy, delivered the Brooklyn *Eagle* in a German neighborhood, "the Germans would stone me because I was Jewish, but on the Berriman block, we had Germans who were no problem."[3] Irene Richardson recalled that sometimes the "American people" called the West Indians "ringtails" and "monkey chasers," and some of the mean boys would chant, "Nigger!"

The Dodsons lived in East New York for thirty years, twenty-seven of them at 309 Berriman, between Sutter Avenue and Blake Avenue, a block where kids still learned their values from church, school, and home. On Sunday, Owen absorbed God: Sunday school in the morning, church in the afternoon, and Baptist youth meetings at night. The family rose early (baths had been taken on Saturday night) and assembled in the living room, where the father, dressed in his cutaway, would ask everyone to read Scripture. Next they filed into the dining room for a long, long prayer before breakfast, after which everyone quoted a verse from the Bible.[4] The children then lined up to pass inspection. One morning Sarah caught Owen concealing a hole in his stocking by dabbing shoe polish on his heel.

With a nickel for Jesus tied in the corner of a clean handkerchief and a nickel for the "El" at Montauk Station, Owen and his family rode toward the Concord Baptist Church in downtown Brooklyn, near Fort Greene Park. In half an hour, the steeple with its clock tower rose into view, the one that would explode so dramatically in Owen's second novel.[5]

Concord Baptist enjoyed an elitism,[6] believing that the better class of colored people moved to Brooklyn to flee the vicious conditions in the colored sections of Manhattan. The Dodsons concurred. Edith recalled, "We weren't anxious to go to Harlem; there were all black people there! Don't go up there! And we didn't until we got older."[7]

A few blocks from Concord Baptist, the Dodson boys sold newspapers after the Sunday service to those who attended Holy Trinity Church. Owen loved Trinity, for there he found a Jeremiah in the person of the athletic Thomas S. Harten, whose sermons, some of which lasted over two hours, ended in a frenzy with "men and women shouting for joy." Dodson recalled Harten's creation of the world:

> He said the usual things at first: "God made the oceans, and the earth, and the sun to light them, and the moon to shade them." There was very little response from the congregation, and he liked yells and screams because it was like applause and appreciation of his art of preaching, and I guess he thought he had better get *man* in there somewhere, so he made the elaborate description. He must have taken it from James Weldon Johnson. He said: "Then God knelt down and shaped a ball of clay in his own image, then he blew into it the breath of life." It still didn't get the great response he was used to. He waited a little while, then he shinnied up one of those firemen's poles that supported the ceiling, and he threw one hand up in the air with a large gesture and said in a ringing voice: "And then He hung out the Au-ro-ra Bor-e-al-is!" The church was on fire. Sister Webster, whom my brother and I knew, began to jump "Ah . . . Ah . . . Ah . . . Ah!" and the other old sisters caught the spirit. Then he slid down and strutted as they shouted and said: "Yeah! Yeah! Yeah!" Reverend Harten had won again.[8]

Church one day, but school five. Two blocks from home, school at P.S. 64 became for Owen a passionate experience. Clean every day. Everyone. Hair trimmed close to the scalp by his father, who sat Owen on a pile of books and cut the part into his son's hair. School began at 8:00 A.M., and not until 3:00 P.M. did the children fly out. Class began with a prayer that Miss Binatree had made up herself, followed by a reading from the Bible, and then the students stood facing the front of the room, where the alphabet, bold as the Old Testament, stared down on them. At attention, they saluted the flag with a pledge that did not yet contain the phrase "one nation under God." Large classes spent the entire day in one room with one teacher.

The assistant principal, a natty dresser with pinstriped suits, pressed shirts, and ties, Albert V. Blum became a model for Owen. In moments nostalgic for P.S. 64, Owen would point to a copy of *The Mystery of Edwin Drood* that Blum had inscribed to him for "greatest proficiency in declamation." Owen confessed, "To this day, I have never read beyond the inscription he wrote in his neat, clear hand, which was a model for us all."

The men and women who taught the children of the European, West Indian, and southern black migrants earned their students' devotion. Miss Elizabeth Taylor was a woman with ruddy, unattractive skin, crooked teeth, and a large, sharp nose. When her classes studied for the Regents Exams, she took those weak in one subject to her home on Arlington Avenue, an elite area of East New York; at the end of the lesson she served her students lemonade and cookies. At the end of the term she had a gift for those who had very good grades; for those who had lesser grades she still had a gift, almost always books. She once wrote a letter inviting Owen's father to open house, asking him to come "even if you have to take the day off." After commending Owen's manners, she pointed out that he wrote with his left hand, and advised that "we ought to correct that." The father replied, "We will not. If he is left-handed, he is left-handed." When Owen's father died, she came to the house and hugged and kissed the boys in her shared sorrow. Miss Elizabeth Taylor became for Owen the model of the devoted teacher.[9]

At the end of the sixth grade, P.S. 64 separated the children into the industrial course and the general. Few needed a high school diploma to find work. In the industrial course the boys learned carpentry, printing, and mechanics; the girls, home economics and secretarial and business skills. Owen, with small talent for numbers and none for manual training, entered the general course to parlez-vous a bit of French.

On June 26, 1927, thirteen-year-old Owen, with 180 classmates, passed into the ninth grade. The ceremony included a Scripture reading, a salute to the flag, two choral selections—Mendelssohn and Schubert—and "Swing Along Chillun," a Negro spiritual.

Education! By the time Owen and Kenneth were born, their father had understood not only the imperative for learning to write with a clear, round hand, but also the necessity for mastering middle-class manners: for those who wielded power in the black community held college degrees; those who traveled abroad possessed decorum and eloquence; those with tuxedos wore clean socks.[10]

Owen's eldest brother, Nat, Jr., did not wear clean socks. Said Owen, "His feet stank; that's what I remember most." Born October 31, 1901, he became the family's black sheep.[11] The Dodsons' neighbors, the Bryans, remembered Nat, Jr.: "We used to sit out on the stoop, and the front of the fence by the gate had a big ball on it which was loose, and Nat would come by and say, 'There's the Bryan house,' and flex his muscles like a strongman, and say, 'Aaaaah, Nathaniel!' Then he would pick up the ball like he was a Sampson, because he knew it was loose, and then he would put it back."[12] One can speculate that Nat, Jr.'s gift of dramatic self-presentation may have been too vibrant to be sealed into the mold of the Lord Chesterfield his father wished him to be. In any case, Nat, Jr.'s adolescence tossed him into full rebellion against authority.

"That boy caused one of the saddest moments of my father's life," recalled Owen. "Mme. Walker, the first Negro millionaire, had built a house on the Hudson called Villa Lewaro. In it she had built an organ [$8000 in 1918]. She couldn't play it but she had it because she wanted the best of everything in the world. My father had been invited to the christening, where Enrico Caruso was to smash a bottle of champagne against the golden pipes. All black men had tuxedos then, and my father got all dressed in his, and the last thing, his slippers— patent leather. My brother Nat had stolen his slippers! He had only one other pair of shoes, his everyday working shoes, and my father had to polish his ordinary shoes to go to the christening of her organ. That boy was that nasty."

"Your feet stink and you don't love Jesus!" summed up Owen's anger. Here, the youngest child—Owen could not have been more than five years old—assumed a paternal role, furiously condemning his brother for a moderate misdeed. But the misdeed as defined by the Dodson canon was not moderate. Mr. Dodson wanted for his sons the world of elegance and power, and, for a poor man, the road into that world lay mined with dinner napkins, carefully matched verbs and nouns, patent-leather slippers, and socks that didn't stink—a hard road for a farm boy up from Virginia. Somehow the family's righteous anger with Nat, Jr.'s styling out in his father's shoes smashed like a cosmic ray into Owen's five-year-old soul and left a dark mole of hatred.

Edith, the more objective, said of her eldest brother, "He did many things that weren't considered kosher; there was a girl who was pregnant, and he was supposedly responsible. After the baby was born, she used to parade in front of the house with a baby carriage, rolling it up and down."[13]

Nat, Jr., smoked cigarettes, did number one in the alley, "knocked up" a girl, and stole his father's dress slippers. Yet his crimes do not seem particularly lurid for the American adolescent of his day. Why, then, were Owen's outbursts so vituperative? (He even refused — fifty years later — to attend his brother's funeral.) Owen's sibling spite may have been a displacement of his own anger, a rage he dared not openly express against his father.

Hints about his father's autocracy are scattered throughout Owen's writings. It should be noted that Nat, Jr., early on filled his father's shoes and forced his severance from that tightly knotted family. In retrospect, it seems clear that Nat, Jr., was fighting to have his own life, and won. Of all the nine brothers and sisters, only he procreated and left progeny.

Whatever the mysteries surrounding the diverse fortunes of the Dodson brothers, there can be no question that Nat, Sr.'s failure with his firstborn reinforced his determination to sculpt Kenneth and Owen into little Lords Chesterfield. Every Saturday, Mr. Dodson would take off work to escort his sons to something educational — to Grant's tomb, to Bedloe's Island to see the Statue of Liberty, once to a baseball game at Prospect Park, where, after the first inning, he asked them, "How do you like it, boys?" The sons didn't, and so they left.

Initially a shy child, Owen spent much time in the house. He recalled a practical "nurse" climbing the stairs twice a week to rub his mother's withered arm with "alcohol, musteroll, gossip, and Jesus Christ."

Lillian, sixteen years Owen's senior, became his second mother, father, and teacher; yet, in spite of these duties, she matriculated at Hunter College (the only black girl in her class) with a scholastic average over ninety. (Hunter's high scholastic standards forced nearly one-third of an entering class to drop out before graduation.) When, on June 16, 1921, Lillian received her B.A. (in a dress her Aunt Mary had sewn for her), she brought her education and her salary as a fourth-grade teacher to her family.

At the turn of the century, nieces, uncles, cousins, aunts, and orphans concurred with Robert Frost that "*home* is where when you have to go there, they have to take you in." The house at 309 Berriman became home for an extended family. The children of Aunt Mary — Beatrice and Leroy (the father of Flip Wilson) — put their feet under the Dodson table while their mother worked in domestic service. In 1914, Edna Wilson, a fourteen-year-old cousin, came to live with and to help Sarah.

Even before Edna arrived, another girl, Louise "Lef" Leftwich, had already moved in.

Roughly the same age as Lillian, Lef came up from Boydton prior to Owen's birth. Not a blood relative, Lef nevertheless joined the family. Edith wasn't thrilled about this: "Leftwich, who was one of the young women who belonged to the church and to whom my mother was a sort of guide, became a great influence and in a sense forced herself upon us; she lived with us without being invited."[14] All of the time, she wasn't mean, but she couldn't accept your friendship; she always thought you had ulterior motives. My father never liked the idea of her being around."[15] Neighbors remember Lef as "acid and bossy." When both Dodson parents died within a year of each other, Lillian and Lef became the mother and father of the family. No woman in Owen's life ever gave him such pain and bitterness as his live-in "sister."

Evelyn, Owen's older sister, possessed the family talent for recitation, carrying off first honors in the declamatory contest at the Nazarene Congregational Church. Shortly after this small triumph, she was confined to a tubercular home, probably Sea View, located on Staten Island. Owen recalled, "When she died, Evelyn dressed in white, lay in a white casket; when everything was set in place, they called the family in, and the last was my mother. She saw her girl lying there, an open casket (you saw them from head to toe). They sang, 'God will take care of you through every day all the way, God will take care of you.'" Evelyn's death may have been too much for her mother—she suffered a third stroke, which paralyzed her speech.

The next blow to Owen's faith in God came on February 11, 1926, when, despite his having prayed for the healing of his mother's paralysis, Sarah Goode Dodson died. Owen built a love altar in his heart, and on it he tended the flame of guilt. In his first novel, *Boy at the Window,* his mother's funeral stands as an elaborate memorial. The youngest son [Owen] refuses to acknowledge his mother's body in the coffin; when he is forced to look, "his tears would never stop."[16] Fifty years later he wrote in *The Harlem Book of the Dead:*

> The dead are the signs
> Of our cross;
> The bury-hour
> Our living crucifixion.[17]

In June of 1927, a year after Sarah's death, the family moved four blocks to an old house at 450 Shepherd, between Sutter and Belmont. On the porch of this gray brownstone were pots but no flowers. A quiet street, with fewer children—gloomy.

Nathaniel Barnett Dodson, Sr., after being attended by Dr. Benjamin Kojat for five days, died of lumbar pneumonia on October 18, 1927, just nineteen months after his wife. The funeral director from Lewis and Goldblatt came and nailed crepe to the door. Relatives and neighbors offered condolences in the front parlor where his body had been laid out.

For her father's funeral, Lillian attempted to notify Nat, Jr., whom they had not seen since March 4, 1926, when his own baby boy, also named Nathaniel, had died after a life of only twenty days. Lillian could not locate her brother. "We advertised on the radio," said Edith, "a practice in those days, but we didn't reach him. As the funeral procession traveled to Concord Baptist, it passed his wife, Margaret, and she was saying, 'I wonder whose funeral that is,' not realizing that was her father-in-law."[18]

When Virginia Staten, Nat, Jr.'s daughter, related this same story, her memory placed her father on the street, wondering who the funeral was for. Whatever the case, this father and son never managed to connect in life or in death.

At ages eleven and twelve, Owen lost his mother and father. In his poetry, novels, and stories, death and funerals became a threnody.

> Death always happens
> To somebody else
> Not the dead.
> Somebody—friends
> Somebody—aunts
> Cousins, nephews, mothers,
> Fathers, sisters, brothers—
> Not the dead.[19]

3

Thomas Jefferson High, 1928–32

[To the tune of the Cornell Alma Mater]
"Lift our banner, lift it skyward
Loud our song renew
Jefferson, our Alma Mater
The orange and the blue."

With father and mother buried in Mt. Olivet Cemetery, Lillian, now thirty, moved her family from the old neighborhood to an integrated block at 422 Quincy Street. From their home on Shepherd Avenue, Kenneth and Edith had been able to walk the mile to Thomas Jefferson High School, located in mostly immigrant-Jewish Brownsville, in fifteen minutes. From their new home, the walking time to school tripled, but their reward was to study under Thomas Jefferson High's principal, Elias Lieberman, who taught his students "how to behave in good society and how to make a favorable impression on people whose opinions count. We want you all to speak well in the manner of refined and educated men and women."[1] With folded arms and piercing brown eyes, he transmuted Peck's Bad Boys into Horatio Algers. Those who would not or could not transmute dropped out. Lieberman was the very principled reincarnation of Nathaniel Dodson, Sr.

"Jeff" opened its doors in 1924 (the cornerstone is engraved "1923"). Although the class of 1926 had only twenty-five graduates, the school soon burst its seams with both commercial and academic students, enrolling in shifts of nearly 6,000, mostly children of refugees who had fled the tenements of Lower East Side Manhattan. The principal enforced a dress code: boys wore shirts and ties; girls, skirts and blouses. A social-forms class taught "conduct" at dances and teas held by the principal. The weekly assembly began with a salute to the flag and the singing of "The Star-Spangled Banner." A full symphony orchestra and a large chorus performed classical music. Short plays or scenes could be part of the program. Fifteen hundred people would attend an interschool debate and between rounds listen attentively to a student string quartet. Contestants read poetry, sometimes verse written by their principal.

Lieberman loved poetry, wrote poetry, required his students to memorize poetry, and admired the Dodsons' recitation of poetry. He had won a prize for his poem "I Am an American," which boosted him into the Poetry Society of America (he later became its president). In truth, this principal was more rhymester than poet; nonetheless, his appreciation of the real thing was the real thing. Several times a week Lieberman assembled his students and talked to them like a father and a counselor. One day he said, "I would like to have on either side of the auditorium some lines of Keats just to remind us every time we come here, 'A thing of beauty is a joy forever,' and on the other side, 'Its loveliness increases; it will never pass into nothingness.' "[2] From this time forth young Owen knew that art held dominion over death.

Fifteen speech teachers did all they could to "correct" immigrant phonetics. One, Marian Millstein, who came from the tenements herself, set the example by speaking with an English accent.[3] This emphasis on proper diction Owen passed on to his own students at Howard, going so far as to bring professionals into the department for purposes of removing "mush-mouthed diction." Declamation (memorized recital of poetry or drama) and elocution (original oration) entertained and inspired assembly audiences. Owen and Kenneth so dominated the speech contests that their classmates unanimously praised their talents and confused their performances. Their repertoire included Edna St. Vincent Millay's "The Suicide" and John Masefield's "Dauber," but the Dodson strength lay in black poetry, a genre that their competitors did not know, or even if they did, that left them uncertain about the propriety of reciting "Go Down Death" with Baptist zeal. On the wings of his triumphs, Owen penned this letter to black poet James Weldon Johnson:

> I am a student in the Thomas Jefferson High School. Every term the Elocution Department gives a Poetry Reading Contest in which a number of students participate; out of about fifty,

from eight to twelve are chosen. These are considered to be the best of the students of speech. Each selects a poem and memorizes and interprets it. Both my brother and I have had the good fortune to be in several of these contests. In two of the contests in which we participated we chose two of your poems in your *God's Trombones*—"The Creation" and "Go Down Death" and won first and second prizes respectively.

I thought that you might be interested in this. I am sending you the programs of those contests. Perhaps you will remember my father, N. B. Dodson, who was active in civic and newspaper work in Brooklyn.

Sincerely,
Owen Dodson[4]

Johnson's response arrived in three days.

My dear Mr. Dodson:

I appreciate very much your letter and your kindness in sending me the two programs. . . . I think it is quite a remarkable accomplishment on the part of you and your brother to have won first prize last spring and second prize this spring. It must have been quite a thrilling experience for both of you. I need not tell you how pleased I was to see that you won with two of my poems. My only regret is that I did not have the pleasure of being present and witnessing your achievement. I knew your father and admired him very much.

I wish for you and your brother the fullest success. I shall be glad to hear of your progress.

Sincerely yours,
James Weldon Johnson[5]

A school day at "Jeff" started at 8:15 A.M. and ended at 2:30 P.M. with boys and girls integrated in class but separated by a wall at lunchtime. Owen, along with most of his classmates, carried his lunch and used this time to read his Latin pony, or to receive coaching in French from his buddy Milton Fried, or to seek help with his math, where his grades ranged in the 60s and 70s. (His grades in elocution ranged from 90 to 95.)[6]

Although Owen grew up without knowing his grandparents, he was presented with a god/grandmother—Mrs. Enoch H. Wells, whose birth name had been Mary Folger (her brother Henry was president of Standard Oil). Grandmother Wells lived at 140 Quincy, a short walk from the Dodsons at 422. She had been widowed early, and traditionally her three daughters and their families gathered at her house for dinner. Her daughter Lydia, active in social-outreach programs, had met Edith at the YWCA and brought her home. Subsequently, Grandmother Wells came to know Lillian, Kenneth, Owen, and "Lef" Leftwich, and when she needed help with the sumptuous family dinners, the Dodsons served her table and babysat the grandchildren, with the exception of Lillian, whose position as a teacher kept her from menial employment. "One Sunday," Owen recalled, "they would have chicken, the next roast beef, and always we got the leftovers. We would have enough to have good eatings for a week. We had little white coats. They didn't treat us like servants but only like we were only helping them out."

As further recompense, Owen and Kenneth accompanied Grandmother Wells to plays. Because of her poor sight and hearing, they always sat in the first five rows, where they enjoyed performances of Maurice Evans and Judith Anderson in *Macbeth* and in *Romeo and Juliet* (1934). They loved Katharine Cornell and Basil Rathbone, with Blanche Yurka playing the nurse, and a young and slim Orson Welles, who had just returned from the Abbey Theatre.

The Folger family had a membership at the Brooklyn Academy of Music, where Owen attended movies, lectures, and music programs.[7] The Wells's grandson, Henry Cleaveland, though younger than the Dodson boys, became a running buddy of Kenneth's and took Edith and Owen to the Brooklyn's Majestic Theatre, where they watched Walter Hamden play Cyrano with a live horse onstage.

All these performances served Owen's apprenticeship in theater. "I learned from Ethel Barrymore, who played in *L'Aiglon,* a lesson I'll never forget: onstage, you never do anything you don't have to do. We saw her as Lady Teasdale; she was a little bit tipsy; they were taking their curtain calls in the manner of the period. Miss Barrymore came forward to the footlights and made a curtsy and fell on her face, then the curtain came down." When Jeanne Eagles died (Oct. 3, 1929), Kenneth and Owen, bright and cute in their sailor suits and without a chaperone, attended her funeral at Campbell's on Eighty-first Street. Gazing into her coffin, they looked upon death and whispered about her life, her art, and her sins.

Owen recalled: "My first gold medal was for 'The Highwayman.'

When I got it, the Folgers gave me a big treat of vanilla ice cream and ginger ale! I was so proud. That whole Wells family influenced us more than anyone except my sister and the church because they were calm, quiet, and unpretentious." While the nation lay mired in its greatest economic disaster, Nazimova, Barrymore, Hamden, Le Gallienne, Schildkraut, and Cornell all performed for Owen, who sat in the orchestra, fifth row.

The Wells family served for theater and culture, but for heart-to-heart talks, Owen's real buddy lived at 374 Bradford Street, an hour's walk from Quincy but no distance at all for adolescents. Recalled Owen: "Sometimes, when I stayed late at his house, he would walk home with me, and then I would walk him back to his house and he would walk back to my house, and we couldn't get enough of each other's knowledge. With Milton Fried I had the most beautiful friendship that I ever had in my life."

After school, they would go to Fried's house and Owen would eat from a box of cherries (he had never seen anything like boxes of cherries), and while they spit out the pits they read *The Return of the Native* or *The Mill on the Floss*. Remembered Owen: "His parents, who owned a store, would call and ask if I could stay with Milton for the night because they wouldn't be home until late. Milton had a heart condition [rheumatic fever]. One night Milton didn't seem so good, so I said: 'What's the matter?' He said: 'I don't know — something must be wrong with my heart.' I said: 'Dear heart!' He said: 'My heart!' I called his parents and said: 'Milton seems ill.' They said: 'Wait there! Stay there. We will be home soon.' So I waited and I thought Milton would die, but of course he didn't."[8]

In Owen's recounting one can hear the voice of Owen the child, and later, pulsing through many of his poems, one hears that same innocent, ingenuous, plaintive heart murmur. He emphasized that "the love that Milton and I had was not an abnormal love, but just the love of two boys who helped each other." Milton was Owen's one good childhood friend, and Owen searched for that relationship the rest of his life. His search for a companion to share his secret visions, a silent partner in whom he could have total trust, his knighting of Kenneth, then Milton to be his forever-true friend — this winsome but desperate note in his art — made disasters of Owen's intimate male affairs. No single earthbound heart could serve two souls.[9]

At fifteen, adolescence thrust upon Owen an awareness of his blackness. One day, in the Fried home, Owen enacted Desdemona's deathbed scene with Esther, Milton's sister. He placed his hands about her white throat and thundered Othello's line: "Out, strumpet! . . . Being done, there is no pause." There was a pause. Esther's father had arrived home and had entered the room, and, according to Owen, who oft told the tale, her father said, "Choke her just enough for the play but not too hard." The moral, to Owen's mind: the strong trust the father held him in. Yet in his notes to *Boy at the Window* he wrote: "What was before to Esther and Owen illusion [and] make-believe in the truest sense became to Owen the first revelation of the truth of being a Negro."[10]

Owen and Kenneth spent summers at the YMCA camp for African-American boys, a ten-acre site located on a lake near Poughkeepsie, New York. Both Dodsons attended camp on "kitchen" scholarships, arranged for them by Robert Elzy, who had founded the Urban League in Brooklyn. Part of each day they acted like "mothers" to the other boys—they had a sewing box, and they mended the clothing of the other lads when needed; they also directed the camp evenings with songs, recitals, stories, and reenactments from the plays they had seen.[11]

Owen remembered: "At camp, I was not aware that I wasn't big and muscular or anything. I had never really looked at myself. The kids called me 'Crisco, fat in the can.' You know, I don't have a great behind, but I almost always backed out of a room rather than show my behind. One day, I looked in one of those three-way mirrors and said, 'My behind is normal.' It was not strictly beautiful, but a normal behind."

On a July evening in 1930, the camp director, Mr. Dotson, stood before the campfire to introduce a special program—recitations by the Dodson boys. With all the assurance of a prize winner, Kenneth, echoing the round Sunday-school tones of his father, marched Shackelford's black regiment down Fifth Avenue:

> Go on Three Hundred Sixty-Eighth,
> Go prove your loyalty,
> And do your bit to make the world
> Safe for Democracy.[12]

Then Kenneth changed pace, wooing his audience to the soft southern sounds of Dunbar's "When Malindy Sings":

Let me listen, I can hyeah it,
    Th'oo de bresh of angel's wings,
Sof' n' sweet, "Swing Low, Sweet Chariot,"
    Ez Malindy sings.

Kenneth was a hard act to follow, but Owen, fresh from gold medals at Jefferson High, began, "The highwayman came riding, riding—the highwayman came riding, up to the old inn-door." The crickets in the grass and the frogs at lake's edge seemed stilled as the flames from the campfire flickered over the young faces envisioning "Bess, the landlord's daughter, plaiting a dark red love knot, into her long black hair." As the terrible climax of the highwayman's doom approached, their eyes grew round when Bess fired the warning shot that took her own life. A terrible pain had gripped the boys. From that moment, twelve-year-old Gordon Heath knew that he wanted more than anything to recite poetry, to be an actor. Owen became his lifetime mentor.[13]

When Owen graduated from Jefferson High, his general scholastic average was 76.85—in today's grading, a "B." His average in elocution, though, was 95. On April 8, he triumphed over David Wrubel to enter the finals of the *New York Times* Oratorical Contest. "I consider," thundered young Dodson, "the power to annul a law of the United States assumed by one state incompatible with the existence of the Union." He received ten dollars and a medal. That Saturday, the Poetry Reading Contest attracted 1,300 people to Thomas Jefferson auditorium. The evening began, as it always did, with an organ solo played by the head of the music department, Louis F. West. Owen, number five on the program, recited James Weldon Johnson's "Go Down Death, A Funeral Sermon."

    Weep not, weep not,
    She is not dead;
    She's resting in the bosom of Jesus.
    Heart-broken husband—weep no more;
    Grief-stricken son—weep no more;
    She's only just gone home.

The three judges decided unanimously to give Owen a silver medal, second place. Perhaps he missed first place because he didn't truly believe "weep no more."

The yearbook *Vista* ribbed the graduating seniors: "Owen Dodson, well-known ventriloquist just closed his new starring vehicle, 'Bells in the Pawnshop,' which enjoyed a success of two and a half performances; and Beatrice Rosen received a prize for the worst sonnet ever written."

On Tuesday morning, June 28, 1932, Owen joined 600 classmates at the Brooklyn Academy of Music in their recessional to the "American Legion March." Beatrice, Lady of the Worst Sonnet, also excelled as Lady of the Grade Point; she delivered the class of '32's valedictory address. Apparently she gave a copy of her speech to Owen for suggestions, for on a copy in his files he wrote: "1). Despairing tone improper. 2). Correct the quotation. [He replaces "still" with "all" and "passing" with "parting."] 3). Length, too short. 4). Preachiness is to be avoided. 5). Parents. [She had neglected to include them in the salutation.]" Owen's preservation of this speech may indicate the degree of pleasure he received in being the director behind the Lady of the Brains.

Immediately following his graduation, Owen reported to Quogue, Long Island, where he served at an inn as glass and silverware boy, hoping to earn enough money to attend the City College of New York, the next step for many Jefferson graduates.[14] He never matriculated. Ad astra, per aspera—fate carried him off to Maine.

4

Here's to Bates, 1932–36

Leaving *had seemed the happiest word he knew.*
Leaving *was a word you could stretch when you said it.*
It wasn't like don't.
                                            —*Boy at the Window*

Owen owed his escape from East New York to a proud black family with a fancy house at 366A Grand Avenue, the Taylors of Brooklyn. They had three children: two boys, Councill and Walter (nicknamed Robin), and a girl, Grace, who had fallen in love with Owen. Robert Elzy,[1] founder of Brooklyn's Urban League, asked Robin Taylor where he wished to attend college. Robin replied, "Harvard." When Elzy said he thought he could get Robin scholarship money, Robin's father intervened: "We don't need any help from anybody!" With his jocular laugh, Elzy then turned and offered the scholarship to Owen, who promptly dumped his plans for CCNY and sat down with Alexander Miller (boys' work secretary at the YMCA) to run over a list of New England colleges founded by the Free Will Baptists— Bates, Colby, Dartmouth. Owen soon divined that he should be on the banks of the Androscoggin River, in Lewiston, Maine, a textile center and home to the seventy-five-acre Bates campus. Benjamin Mays, a Baptist and a black scholar, had graduated from there in 1920. Owen liked the academic plan, and he liked the tuition—room and board for $750.

Wet with kisses and aching with hugs from Edith, Kenneth, Lillian, and his mother's sister, Aunt Mary, Owen boarded a packet for Boston, and from there went by bus to Portland, where on Saturday, September 23, 1932, the electric interurban carried him thirty-five miles to Lewiston, a mill town of two- and three-story houses occupied by French

Canadians and immigrant Lithuanians. In a separate area, the mill owners lived in the big houses. When Owen arrived at Bates College he felt that he was where he should be.

The campus, a gem set near farms, mustard fields, and woodlands, had wrapped itself in autumn flame, the full glory of its hardwoods—maple, oak, elm[2]—and crowning the autumn silence, an English Gothic chapel.[3] Sweaters, strange accents—in the cool afternoon nearly 200 freshmen milled about Hathorn Hall for registration. Over two-thirds listed Maine as their native state. Many worked off campus at the hospital or restaurants and lived at home; the Bates student during the Depression was "one with a patch on the seat of his pants."[4] Owen claimed he felt suddenly and sharply all the tradition of New England. "I knew why they said two years of Latin in high school and two years of Latin here. I knew why they had clipped, sharp speech. I knew by the no nonsense agony all those people had, an agony for learning."

Annually, Bates enrolled at least two Blacks, a quota system regarded as a liberal policy, a remnant of abolition days. The even-numbered quota made Owen's roommate assignment predictable. The son of a railway porter in Portland, Emerson Cummings joined Owen on the third floor of Roger Williams Hall. The lad from Brooklyn had little enthusiasm for a fellow nicknamed "Goosey" who drove a taxi part time, liked math and football, and thought "poetry the bunk and only knew Gray's 'Elegy.'" Owen branded Cummings a dully, the dullyest of them all, and declared he would not room with him another year. Added Owen: "This, of course, is not mutual. He thinks I'm great."[5]

In the dormitory, Owen—five feet six inches tall, 135 pounds, a handsome, smooth-skinned seventeen-year-old—decorated the wall above his desk with a small Navajo rug; he also placed small candle holders about the room, making it, if not luxurious, mysterious. One day Owen returned from class—he never locked his room—and found it decorated with toilet paper—a racial incident? Dean Rowe called him in and asked, "What do you feel?" Owen said that he didn't know. The dean said, "Just don't speak about it; let it go." Other pranks followed—his neckties tied into knots, his bed dismantled and reassembled in the hall—but fellow student Milton Lindholm, who also lived in Roger Williams, interpreted these incidents as hazing—"not necessarily an act of discrimination, because Owen would read Shakespeare aloud in front of candles on his bureau and the freshmen kids didn't understand Shakespeare and candles."⁶ Some Maine lads did write poetry. On his dorm's second floor, Dodson discovered a poet whose verses he liked, Edmund Muskie (later U.S. senator and vice-presidential candidate).

Freshman week: rising bell at 7:00 A.M.; breakfast followed by chapel; assembly of men, assembly of women (each had their own dorms, deans, and dining halls). Speeches of welcome, lectures of caution, sermons of inspiration; examinations for French, for physicals, for psychology. Library conferences, YMCA and YWCA conferences, registration (bring fountain pens). They learned a Bates tradition: when you walked across campus, you had to say hello whether you met a stranger or a friend. Saturday night "I-Am-You-Are" dance where Jack met Jill, and then suddenly, Monday morning—the first day of classes.

At precisely the ring of the bell, Prof. Robert George Berkelman closed the classroom door. (On some occasions he locked it against a late student.) He was a small man with a slight frame, maybe 132 pounds with his shoes on. At thirty-two, he was prematurely bald; he had a clipped moustache, and brown eyes so intense that when he stared at his students, they dropped their gaze. He did not smile, but asked the thirty of them to stand, one by one, and say their names. Then he said, "Sit down." He turned his back for a few moments, then faced them and addressed each by name. It was a thing that frightened and delighted Owen.⁷

One day, from Keats's sonnet "On First Looking into Chapman's Homer" Berkelman read aloud, "Much have I traveled in the realms of gold," then asked Owen what he thought of it. Young Dodson allowed that the sonnet was OK, but said he could write one as good himself. The little ball of saliva that rolled perpetually on Berkelman's lower lip glistened in still wonderment; then he spoke: "Mr. Dodson, you will write a sonnet every week and bring it to me each Monday"— he paused—"until you write one as fine as Keats, or until you graduate, whichever comes first."

At this forge Owen labored, writing sonnets for four years until he had a stack of them; some he destroyed, some he published in *Crisis* and *New Masses*. Berkelman had pushed Owen off into another world, one he might never have seen or known. A hard man, a cold man, a man who had headaches, Berkelman had no laughter. Once he got a hold on someone who he thought had talent, he was merciless. Not only would he correct the first draft, he would say, "You keep working on it until you get it the way you want it to be, and the way I want it to be." Said Owen, "I have heard of no teachers since that time."

Owen mastered the Shakespearean sonnet, a skill more a blessing than a curse. It taught him how form enslaves the novice but serves the professional. He worked his way through the clank of forced rhymes and heavy meter toward his own voice, toward lines that flowed by submerging their rhymes as a river does its fish. To achieve his craft, Owen left on the margins of his papers hundreds of pencil strokes, meter scansions — iambs, dactyls, and trochees. Here is an early struggle:

> Sick am I of your staid love, go your way.
> I care no more to list to songs which cling
> To your empty threat or take gifts you bring
> To my impoverished door. I will not stay
> With thee who map my path of woe each day
> And make me wear a mask of clay and sing.

The distance between this first plodding and those sonnets composed near his graduation is mensurable. In his senior year, he published a collection of eight sonnets, entitled *Jungle Stars;* dedicated to his father, the poems traversed the black experience from Africa to Harlem. "Post Emancipation" is the best of these:

> Rescind the hope that we may walk again
> Without the heavy chains of servitude
> That bind our flesh to soil and heartless men
> Who mold our lives to fit each fickle mood.
> Rescind the hope although it was decreed
> That freedom would be ours to wear and keep
> For centuries, aye, for eons till the seed
> Of freedom died or earth was drowned in sleep.
> The parchment that declared that we were free
> Is now collecting dust in some dark spot
> Despite the promise and the certainty
> We thought its words would give, but gave them not.
> "Distrust all words that echo to the stars
> When earth is bound with unrelenting bars."

After the sonnet's publication in the left-wing magazine *New Masses,* Berkelman ordered Owen to rewrite the final couplet. Owen did: "Beware the serpent with its patterned skin; / the twisted greed, the venom lies within."

With the publication of eight sonnets, the young poet felt he had little left to master; his mentor seized the moment to tell him otherwise: "You have made one big mistake in choosing your subject. The sonnet is a cool, formalized form. Your subject of slavery is too fiery."

Owen winced. "But you let me go on for four years!"

"You were learning your lessons and your craft, but now I want to tell you that form and content go together, and they cannot be separated. For what you were writing about, you need a kind of Walt Whitman style. You can't write a Shakespearean sonnet about slavery." (Berkelman hadn't read Claude McKay.)

Owen later admitted that his slavery poems lacked vitality. "I had not gone through slavery; I had not read Frederick Douglass; it was all imaginary. It was not until I was in the Navy, when I wrote 'Black Mother Praying,' that I began to be conscious of race in a deep kind of way."

Twenty years after he had met Berkelman, Owen assembled a collection of poems entitled *Cages,* which he dedicated, "For Robert Berkelman, who put me on the train, and then was there to meet me at the station." Any speculation about what might have happened to Owen's poetry if Langston Hughes had put him on the train is fruitless. Owen had read Hughes, admired Hughes, borrowed Hughes's style for a number of poor poems, and dedicated at least two poems to the black laureate, but Owen remained a mandarin. His family had firmly placed his feet on a powerful long ladder that led him away from the speech patterns and dialects of black folk, although genteel poverty remained a problem.

Weekly he sent his soiled laundry home to Edith and she mailed it back. To Robert Elzy went anxious inquiries about budget and paying fees, but Elzy sent no assurance the scholarship would be continued. Lillian, a fourth-grade teacher, supported the family; she sent Owen small amounts of money when she could. Edith worked in the employment agency of the YWCA, and Lef worked in practical nursing, but doctor bills for Lillian, Edith, and Kenneth mounted. (In his last semester at Thomas Jefferson, Kenneth won the presidency of his class; he then enrolled at Brooklyn College, a free-tuition school.)

The semester rolled on. The Bates and Yale football teams tied 0–0. Owen watched from his third-floor room, trying to be enthusiastic about sports, but the rituals of the marching band and the bonfire rallies pleased him more. His distaste for athletics, or even physical exercise, lasted a lifetime.

On October 19 in a straw vote, the college approved Prohibition and elected President Hoover to another term. On November 9, Roosevelt surprised them. That same month, William Butler Yeats lectured at chapel. Owen reported to Quincy Street: "Last week we heard his bloomin' Majesty, tall, refined, distinguished looking. Every inch a poet. As he came on the stage in Chapel, he tripped (well, I nearly died laughing, it was so funny). When he started talking one could hardly hear him. He was all in all quite a disappointment."

Owen saved his most venomous attack, though, for a YMCA worker named Sue Bailey Thurman: "Do you remember my writing about a Negro woman who was to speak here on Negro Culture as seen through music? Well she came (late mind you). Quite a dashing looking 'snip,' but Oh! I never in all my life was more embarrassed. She was putrid! Putrid! Terrible! Horrible! A disgrace! I came away more ashamed of our race than ever."

He tried out for debate. "If I win," he said, "I will be on the Bates Varsity Debating Team which means a tux and 'tout les garnitures.' Of course, if I do, I'll be quite a big shot up here." The Dodson family was spared the tuxedo's expense, although "everyone said I was the best."

Science and biology bored him; he postponed the twelve credit requirements until his last year and worried whether he would be able to graduate. A classmate, Roger Fredland, endeavored to tutor Owen: "I remember the painful process of my trying to teach him—then a college senior—how to do long division."[8] For his part, Owen introduced Fredland to W. H. Hudson's *Green Mansions,* Norman Douglas's *South Wind,* and Theodore Dreiser's *An American Tragedy.* Owen lived for literature, for drama. In the one month of November, he devoured the stories of Edith Wharton, W. E. B. Du Bois's *Souls of Black Folk,* Erich Maria Remarque's *All Quiet on the Western Front,* E. A. Robinson's *Tristram,* a biography of Euripides, and "a few plays by John Synge"; not one of these works was required for his coursework.

Owen won the freshman prize in speech, which netted him a welcome twenty-five dollars. Elected to the staff of the *Garnet,* the college's biannual literary magazine, he published a prize story and two small poems, all forgettable. Nominated to the Spofford Club, he met and made his closest friends, poets of the soul: Arnold Kenseth, Glidden Parker, Priscilla Heath, William Swallow, Roger Fredland, Gray Adams, Betty Winston, Edmund Muskie, John Ciardi, Robert Fish, Nils Lennartson, Frank Murray, and John Kenny.

The eccentric black boy who read Shakespeare aloud by candlelight had found allies. His grades, passable — Bs in English, sociology, and history; a C in Latin; and in French, his bête noire, a D (in the spring he failed French the second semester). His strength remained in public speaking, where he earned an A. In the stress of his first term, he gained fourteen pounds.

Always he wanted, needed more pleasures than he could afford. He raked leaves; he cleaned house for Mrs. Ross, the richest Negro in the area, making money to buy books or to go to a play in Boston. He learned to wash his own underwear and to use his shirts sparingly. For his spring vacation, Owen wheedled a ride to Boston, where he met Walter Robin Taylor (who had indeed gone to Harvard, making way for Owen at Bates). Owen was hurt when Robin pointedly refused to introduce him to his Harvard friends, but on Saturday, April 1, they stepped off the bus together in Brooklyn, Owen with a secondhand typewriter that he promptly handed over to Edith so that she might have it repaired in time for his return. Money for his next year's tuition dominated the family discussion. Elzy had not confirmed the scholarship.

Owen approached the United Baptist pastor in Lewiston about working for his room and board, and on April 21 accompanied the reverend to Portland, where Owen spoke on Negro culture, read poetry, and discussed "our attitude toward the whites in general." Apparently he did not resent being *the* Negro-in-residence; his appearances before white church groups, like New England itself, gradually "darkened" him, increasing his awareness of negritude and forcing him, as he neared graduation, toward a painful birth of racial consciousness.

Disappointed but not discouraged by Edith's failure to provide him with a summer job at a YWCA camp, Owen prepared to send his trunk home. At 1:30 A.M. as he packed his gray trousers so worn in the seat, male marchers "in their night clothes with bugles, drums, saxophones, paper flags, rolls of toilet paper, sang lewd songs in front of the girls' dorms: 'We'll sit on the steps of Parker Hall and shout till break of day. To hell with Harry Rowe [dean] and Clifton Dagget Gray [president].' " Owen did not venture into this Dionysian shower of vernal hormones, but watched from his third-story window. Indeed, judging from the number of books he consumed and the pile of poems he wrote, his freshman year had been monastic.

Summer found Owen at Quogue House on Long Island, serving as glass and silverware boy. As late as August 20, Elzy could not assure Owen of a scholarship. It had rained for five days straight, and Owen wrote "a poem about Mussolini's invasion of Africa (it's one of my best I think)." At this point his pacifism muted his anticolonial stance. The magazine *Opportunity* published "Desert in Ethiopia," which reads in part:

> I know that hope alone is not release
> from scintillating swords that catch the sun;
> I know that peace must some day bleed for peace
> If stars in nights to come will shine again
> Upon this husk inhabited by men.[9]

The summer ended, and Elzy had still sent no word about Owen's scholarship. The family decided Owen should start the semester and pray. To be on the safe side, he again applied to City College, a free-tuition school, and wrote Edith, "Tell them [family] not to borrow any money to keep me; Lillian has to have all she gets for herself. Don't be depressed any of you for depression makes life harsh and quite hollow." Brave Owen.

He threw himself into his sophomore courses—French literature of the seventeenth and eighteenth centuries, public speaking, English poets, classical civilization, psychology, and geology. He passed them all, receiving a D in French because he depended on Kenneth in Brooklyn to do his translations. On Thursday evening, November 9, in Hathorn's Little Theatre, he and two other "salts" walked on as crew members in O'Neill's sea drama *Ile*. Still the scholarship money did not materialize. Owen wrote his sisters, "I had a very charming tête-à-tête with the bursar who very acidly and delightfully informed me that my bill had not been paid in full. 'Really,' I answered sarcastically (to myself). I rushed about to send a special [delivery] to Mr. Elzy—he [the bursar] rushed about to send a telegram (going me one better). Everything is like 'delphiniums blue and geraniums red' as A. A. Milne would wistfully exclaim. Well, now that this semester is cleared up, what about next, I say tearfully to myself."[10] The tide of the Great Depression lapped at the very edge of Owen's toes.

In January 1934, Carl Sandburg, who the next year would publish *The People, Yes,* lectured at chapel. Owen reported the poet to be "cordial, witty, ingenuous. I liked especially one of his definitions: 'Poetry is an echo dancing, asking a shadow to be its partner.' He sang bizarre western and Negro (pronounced nee-gro) songs."

Owen sent two poems off to the *Literary Workshop,* "the national organ for student expression," a publication based in New York City. For gentle Owen, this introduction to "professional" criticism must have aroused the urge to kill. They wrote him, "All the pieces here contain minor imperfections, trite images and irrelevancies. These would be excusable in a poet with less talent than you obviously have. So let us see more of your work." The letter was unsigned, but terminated with "The Critical Staff."[11]

In February, cast as the Old Man in *Macbeth,* he promised to steal the scene with his twelve lines; no record, however, of his coup de théâtre has survived. On one of his regular runs to the library, Owen met a great tall New Englander in a white sweater, Glidden Parker, who lived with his parents in Lewiston. Odd, sensitive, temperamental, he wrote short stories and published one in a literary magazine that began with a line Owen loved: "It's a long way to Trinkle and a longer way from Trinkle to Trelleen." In Glidden's old broken-down Buick the pair would drive to Saint's Rest outside of Portland. There lived a friend, a woman who had a pear tree, and every autumn they would shake the fruit down. Owen transmuted those harvests into "Sickle Pears," a nostalgic lyric dedicated to Glidden. Owen had found someone he could talk to, a soul mate. Together they formally organized a poetry society: "Several boys and girls who are particularly interested in creative work meet, eat supper, and discuss their works. I am head of it. I hope to make it a name up here. I have written loads of poetry, mostly in sonnet and blank verse form. It is better than anything I have written up to date."[12]

The Bates poets "worshipped beauty, truth, and read *Hedda Gabler* aloud. They thought the play shocking, Hedda shooting herself— 'Merciful God! People don't do such things!' "[13] But like Judge Brack in that drama, Owen learned that people do: years later, Glidden killed himself.

Another poet, Arnold Kenseth, who lived on the same dormitory floor, saw "Owen coming out of his room with a white stone that appeared like a stone from the ocean that had been smoothed by the waves. He had a cloth, polishing it. And I found it very strange and I said, 'What are you doing?' and he said, 'Polishing my stone.' The stone would appear from his pockets from time to time."[14]

"The White Stone," a poem dated April 29, 1934, moved Kenseth's trivial observation toward mystery. Enigmatic, composed of seventeen rhymed couplets typed as quatrains, the poem seems to be translucent and suggests a sexual initiation. The poet finds a slim white stone in the woods that he presses against his cheek. Another speaker, male, asks where he may find his love. Exchanges of muddied moon, shadows, and wave images follow. The final quatrain: "Deep in the woods / where the leaves make a bed / I found the lover / peacefully dead." Owen may have consciously obfuscated a sexual initiation. At the top of the page, he had typed an epigraph from the Book of Revelation: ". . . and I will give him a white stone with a new name written upon it which no one knows except the man who receives it." That man may have been Glidden Parker, who in later years acknowledged his homosexuality. "It's a long way to Trinkle and a longer way from Trinkle to Trelleen."

"The Poet's Caprice," Owen's second literary sexual fantasy, appeared in the winter issue of the *Garnet,* and represented a major effort. This one-act play, composed in unrhymed pentameter, evoked the evening that Lord Byron returned home to find his sister, Augusta, pregnant with his child. Gordon confesses his love for his sister and the depth of their passion that created the child, then demands she abort it. Augusta refuses, and her brother declares he cannot remain with her: "Here I would be hard and unkind because the earth is calling me to come and watch its rivers swell in spring." He leaves her. The moonlight falls through the damask drapery, silhouetting Augusta. Although romantic fervor cloys and smothers the play, Lord Byron's passion to leave his sister for a life of poetry cuts through like ice. Owen's marriage would not be to a woman but to art.

With his name embossed in garnet red upon rag stationery, Owen jubilantly welcomed his junior year and flagrantly demonstrated that Elzy had persuaded a Mrs. Daboll, widow of a shipbuilder, to renew Owen's scholarship. (She paid not only for his last two years at Bates, but for three more at Yale.)[15]

Bates had blackened up—six Negroes enrolled. To Owen's delight, Jimmy Carter[16] became his roommate—he smoked a pipe, drove his own car, played on the tennis team, sang pop concerts, and was invariably associated with Kay Craft, granddaughter of Ellen Craft, author of a famous slave narrative.

Owen kept a diary: "One day he [Carter] came in and told me that he had been to the bar in the Dewitt Hotel. I asked him what he did and he said, 'I had a couple of martinis. Smoked a cigarette.' I wrote in my diary that night: 'Jimmy told me that he had a martini and smoked cigarettes. I hope I will never descend to that.'" Virtue untested. Later Owen wrote, "My roommate, Jimmy Carter, came into $90,000, the first payment of his father's estate. He had a party for all the black students. Five of us went to a hotel. I had my first martini, two of them. My eyes became slits . . . kind of fun."

That same fall, Owen and Priscilla Heath (his future fiancée) became assistant co-editors of the *Garnet*. In the November issue, perhaps as a birthday present to himself, Owen published "Brittle Wings, Four Sonnets on Beauty." A fair criticism might have been, "Someday, this emerging talent will achieve." By welcome contrast, in the same issue Owen reviewed Edna St. Vincent Millay's book of sonnets, *Wine from These Grapes*. He admired her craft, and offered his purview: "Whereas formerly her work was gay and lifting, now her poems are tinged with the melancholy of the world—this melancholy is not personal, but classic." Years later, Owen commented, "At eighteen, one is not really sad. You feel sad, you make sad, but the joy and beauty of life, the sun coming up every day in Maine, the nip of all those winters when we wore thick sweaters and a scarf around our necks; there was only a little sadness."

For Christmas, Owen treated himself to Broadway. He sent money home for theater tickets: *Romeo and Juliet* with Katharine Cornell; Maxwell Anderson's *Dark Victory;* Kaufman and Hart's *Merrily We Roll Along* and *The Distaff Side;* and Lillian Hellman's *The Children's Hour.* (The cheaper seats cost $1.10.) When he returned to Bates, his friends heralded his reviews, complete with impersonations of Tallulah Bankhead half-soused, swearing and striding and talking in deep swelling tones. Owen's declamatory training made his performances delightful, but at the same time his burlesques locked him further into the role of raconteur, a prison whose walls grew higher as the years passed.

On February 20, the first streamlined train purred into Lewiston, a steel stallion, progressive as a world's fair poster, pretty as an airmail stamp. Modern women smoked cigarettes (clandestinely) at fifteen cents a pack. Owen smoked a pipe. The guys drank home brew costing thirty-five cents a quart, or at Stickinos's a nickel a glass; Owen sipped wine. Twentieth-century fever swept over Bates College: they allowed men and women to eat dinner in the same hall. Coed dorms hovered a generation away. The changing world brought twenty-year-old Mr. Kazushige Hirasawa from Tokyo Imperial University to Bates for "a first-hand acquaintance with actual American people." He went on to say that "Americans as a people have an exaggerated notion of the militaristic character of the Nipponese government."

Owen struggled to write *The School,* a play about a white school-teacher in Georgia, her reverend husband, and a young Negro. The wife of the wealthy minister opens a school for black children and hires a black man she met while in the North to run it; the black teacher narrowly escapes lynching. (When it was produced at Brooklyn College in May 1936, the title had become *Including Laughter.* Kenneth, the producer/director, plastered posters about the campus proclaiming, "Black plus white equals dynamite!")

At the end of March, Owen, home on spring vacation, bid good-bye to a favorite poet, Edwin Arlington Robinson: "I went to that little church on the East Side the day before his funeral. The sexton greeted me and led me down the aisle past the altar. The director had stuffed the greatest poet of our times into a little corner in the Anglican Church. And there he lay, silence around him like a shawl, his trimmed mustache, his precise collar, the grayness of his hands, one on the other. I waited. Far off the children playing before their parents called them in to supper, and the dim cough of the sexton. To myself I recited his poem, 'If years had been the children of his wishes / Mathias would have wished and been immortal.' I was a young man looking at the Master—dead. I took the book and signed my name. And no one else was there."[17] This rather studied, self-conscious portrait throbs with romantic loneliness, probably just right for Owen at twenty.

He rattled back to Bates on the bus and called the poets of the soul into celebrated mourning: John Ciardi wrote a tribute for the *Bates Student,* and, on April 16, Owen eulogized Robinson for the Spofford Club, reading from *Tristram* and describing the funeral procession "led by Robert Frost and Carl Sandburg—what a wonder! They rocked down the aisle, the poets of America to say 'hello' and 'goodbye,' and there were [*sic*] I, Owen Dodson." Owen enjoyed funerals, enjoyed the spectacle, and he certainly took pleasure in being the only Negro there.

He also enjoyed a good resurrection. On Easter morning, April 21, "four trumpeters summoned the college to sunrise worship on the gaunt rocky hill." That evening at United Baptist Church he presented his own Easter pageant, *The Terrible Meek*. He had built three twisted crosses onstage to convey the torment. The main one, up on the rocky hill, was eleven feet high. (The cross that would dominate the Yale stage for his *Divine Comedy* would be thirty-two feet high!) Owen was gearing up for the main drama of his life: the suffering Jesus versus an indifferent, if not malevolent, father.

Was young Dodson devout? He attended the Baptist church on Sundays and compulsory chapel the other six days. A fellow student, Frank Murray, later ordained a minister, recalled that he invited Owen to his mother's home in Lewiston for dinner, and Owen knelt down to pray with them. But devout? Well-mannered, certainly—and a college boy did have to eat.

May sunshine warmed the cold stones of New England, showering the landscape with lilacs and violets; boys and girls shed heavy coats and planned their Ivy Hop. With an impressive display of talents the poets of the soul brought out the spring edition of the *Garnet*. Owen published a short play, *Sonata,* a drama about a boy who commits suicide because his father demands that he sacrifice his nascent if jejune career as a pianist to join the family business. This portrait of a teenage suicide borrowed its sensitive adolescent from Willa Cather's young hero in "Paul's Case"; however, Owen's boy aesthete remained not only unconvincing but unsympathetic. In the same issue, Owen published three sonnets, revealing in "Claustrophobia One" his rapid mastery of the form to passionately express his desire to escape his flesh. Was Owen's longing to abandon his claustrophobic flesh merely a romantic pose, or the genuine yearning of a spirit to soar toward the stars, a yearning shaped by idealism and fueled by the hormonal thrashings of a twenty-year-old with no lover? Probably the latter. How else could he have produced a magazine, two plays, and publishable sonnets while carrying a full courseload?

Summer came, and with it a change of work venue. Edith secured Owen a position at Camp Robin Hood on Upper Twin Lake near Central Valley, New York, where he lay out naked on his cot, the sweat dripping, while he completed a sonnet sequence, *Jungle Stars,* and felt free to start a novel. Then Edith wrote that Lillian had bought a house! How she and Lef had scraped and saved and borrowed and mortgaged can only be speculation. Perhaps Grandmother Wells. . . .

The classic three-story brownstone at 469 Quincy, two blocks from where they had been renting, made Owen ecstatic. "Thrilling—your letters—it must look perfectly enchanting—or will look after everything gets up. Of course, I have had plenty of time to think—this is my plan for our room," and he drew a floor plan that included the location of furniture, the bookcases, the shoe cabinet, the mirrors, his bed and Kenneth's (side by side), and two bars (incorporated, no doubt, for the slitty-eyed pleasure of martinis). The house at 469 Quincy became the Dodsons' castle, a palace whose windows winked with real venetian blinds.

At the beginning of Owen's senior year, paddles smacked smartly on freshman bottoms. Owen eschewed the pranks for his own writing, which by this time had developed into a serious avocation. Elmer Carter, editor of the magazine *Opportunity,* accepted two poems and asked Owen to submit short stories or a play on a Christmas theme, but all Owen's stories concerned death.

Owen's senior year yielded a crucial insight: he confessed to Lillian, "I was made for creative writing and not scholarly research. I know that—it's no use for me to go into honors work and not make a fine showing. I would do better to stay in a field where I am more at home—it's no good trying to glean amid alien corn. You understand, I hope."

Nonetheless, his senior grades surpassed those of his other terms. He threw himself into fine arts, English survey, and elementary German, which he liked for "its masculine swing." He translated small poems of Goethe and Heine, and for the first time in any foreign language he received an A. But his forte remained drama, his pride and joy.

Grosvenor Robinson, nearing his fortieth year of teaching speech and drama, encouraged Owen's bent for theater. Professor "Rob," he of the puffy cheeks, bulbous nose, and clothes that seemed to have borrowed a body, recognized Owen's genius for spectacle and ordered him to direct a one-act costume drama, *Allison's Lad.* The play, set during the war between the Cavaliers and the Roundheads in Caroline England, pleased even the persnickety Berkelman: "Much of the success belongs to the director. Good as individuals were, the best feature was the harmonizing of all its appeals. If the play left anything to be desired, it was that the enunciation was unclearly mumbled." He mentioned nothing of the performance by John Ciardi, who may have been one of the mumblers.[18]

Owen's triumph gave him the opportunity to direct Shaw's *Candida.*

His biggest challenges were posed by the little theater, which occupied the rear half of Hathorn Hall, the oldest building on campus. Its limitations forced creativity: no sewing room, no makeup room, no storage place for costumes, and no room for an entire cast backstage at the same time. No room at all in the wings, and no way to get from one side of the stage to the other except across the stage. (Actually, there was one other option: an actor exiting stage left could climb out the second-floor window, descend a ladder placed against the building for this purpose, circle the rear of the building, ascend a similar ladder on the other side, climb through a window, and make an entrance, being careful not to appear breathless.)

Candida played two evenings. Berkelman praised its "subtly modulated character interpretations and the expressive stage business." Owen personally identified with the play's poet, Marchbanks, who gives up his love of a woman to pursue a greater secret. With this production, Owen engaged his new love—theater.

The winter of '36 settled in with record snowfalls; Harold Bailey, chairman of the winter carnival, one night romped through the snow—nude! The senior girls won the snow-sculpture contest with "Puritan Lady." And that winter, another Puritan lady, of flesh and blood, fell deeply in love with Owen. Her name was Priscilla Heath.

Born in Manchester, New Hampshire, raised in the First Congregational Church where the Heath family sat in their own pew, Priscilla looked as WASP-y as her name. About Owen's height, blond, she wore her hair short. Her classmates described her as brilliant, sensitive, talented, conscientious, quiet, not one to socialize much. During the three years of her friendship with Owen, they had cooperated at the Spofford Club, competed in the *Garnet,* both entered the speaking contests, both carried off honors, and both wrote poetry. Two shy souls hiding behind public faces had discovered each other.

Recalled Owen: "We'd just go for walks, that's all we'd do. We would sit down by the river and talk. I still have a picture of her sitting there like a proper New England girl; she read about half of the book *The Prophet,* by Gibran. It has stayed with me. Another day, she read *The Devil and Daniel Webster.* She always had something, something working."

Owen had blossomed into handsome manhood; his hair clipped short above a high forehead, his skin without blemish, he cut a dashing figure as he strode across campus, his great black coat open, a scarf flying; he wore his broad-brimmed hat with a wide band pulled low enough to be fashionable but not unfriendly. One might assume that Priscilla had noticed him from the first. In their shared passion for poetry, she had found a male who more than matched her own creativity. Owen had found a Candida, who, like his mother, possessed virtues priced beyond rubies.

"I wanted to make a life mask of her and she was willing. I got the plaster of Paris and I put it on her face, but I had gotten the wrong mixture: I had gotten slow-drying plaster. I waited for it to dry and it didn't. Then came the trying to get it off her face. I said, 'Keep your eyes closed, keep your eyes closed,' and finally we removed all that plaster, but love is such a thing. She said, 'Well, I can see you again.' That was the only thing she said about my mistake. I guess in a way, we must have fallen in love with each other; anyway, she fell in love with me; I know that because every time she came from the dorm when I said we'd go for a walk, she had Listerine on her breath, which meant she wanted me to kiss her. I don't know whether we kissed or anything, but anyway, there we were."[19]

Priscilla's faith in mouthwash persisted into the spring; yet Owen's shyness, or his uncertainty about how Bates would take the liaison of a black poet with a white flower, kept his lips platonic; no banns were published. But then, suddenly, as Owen recalled, "We became engaged: I don't know what I gave her for the engagement ring, but then she said, 'Now is the time for us to go to Manchester, New Hampshire, and see my mother, my father, and my sister, and introduce you.' I was in a bind."

Owen arranged to stay for the weekend in Manchester at the home of a classmate, William Swallow, a fellow *Garnet* staffer. On the first day, Swallow, Priscilla, and Owen hiked to a little cabin owned by the Heaths called Pinecrest. That evening, Owen reported to her family's modest dwelling. Her parents were maybe in their sixties. Her father resembled Prince Albert of England: tall, slender, rather elegant and serious. He held a middle-level position in the Amoskeag Savings Bank. Mrs. Heath was softer, a motherly type. Priscilla had one sister, who kept her distance.

The house had style: New England immaculate. Priscilla's parents surveyed Owen as if they had binoculars, peering into his heart, into his mind. Priscilla told Owen afterward that they approved of him, but her sister, who once had fallen in love with an Armenian, said, "I don't think that you should make the same mistake." Priscilla, a sociology and economics major, with intentions of becoming a caseworker, certainly was not deterred by race. Quite the opposite: she believed that if she allied herself with Owen, both their lives would be enhanced.

In the draft of his play *Including Laughter*, written the summer after their engagement was broken, Owen wrote of two young lovers in a New England college: a black boy, Leslie Brown, and a white girl, Demeter Eveing. In scene 1, they meet, recite Shakespeare together in the maple grove beside the river, and she asks him, "Why don't you write about your people, the dusky dream, the low Christ song, the flashing Harlemite? They would be your poems then."

Leslie replies: "I never thought of that. All my life has been spent in white schools, among white people. My thoughts are like their thoughts. Why should I love the dark?"

In scene 2, a jealous white boy threatens violence if Leslie does not stop seeing Demeter. By scene 3, Demeter is ready to flee with Leslie, even if he goes south to teach school. Leslie tells her it would be impossible. She persists: "Deep, deep down in my heart, Leslie, I know this life I lead (or will lead) is pale, diluted, worthless as a yen. I give up nothing really. This is love, love, Leslie. I know what I must face. I see clearly the road's ending, but first I love you, and secondly, in me beats a tune that will not let me waste my life." Leslie refuses her, and the play ends predictably. The love between Priscilla and Owen, however, did not end so quickly, nor so buried in resignation, for Priscilla fought not "to waste her life."

With the melting of winter's deep snows, the lowlands of Lewiston vanished under record floods, while Owen's last semester cascaded on; Priscilla stood aside so that Owen might be editor-in-chief for the final issue of the *Garnet*. Louis Untermeyer visited the campus and reviewed the magazine; he pronounced the poetry of Heath, Richardson, Dodson, and Kenseth to be well above the level of the ordinary college magazine—noting particularly the excellence of Miss Heath's sonnets.

On March 20, Priscilla, now a member of Delta Sigma Rho, the prestigious National Honorary Forensic Society, privately pledged her Delta key to Owen, but unlike the river, his ice did not melt. On March 30, Priscilla delivered the keynote address for the Phi Beta Kappa initiation.[20]

Something in Owen disturbed Priscilla, who approached her high school classmate Bill Swallow for advice. Recalled Swallow: "She was very troubled because someone had told her that Owen was a homosexual, and she turned to me as a mutual friend to see whether I could affirm or deny the allegation. I told her honestly that I had no direct knowledge whatsoever that Owen was gay, and that I had not even heard a rumor to that effect. Actually, I suppose I was pretty naive. Had I had more knowledge of the gay world, I probably would have attached more significance to some of Owen's remarks about his brother Kenneth, his Brooklyn friends, and some of his Bates friends about whom I knew very little. At any rate, whatever comfort I could offer to Priscilla was most likely misleading."[21]

In the mid-1930s at a Christian college in deep Maine, homosexuality was not a subject for public discussion. (At the very most, a worn copy of Radclyffe Hall's *The Well of Loneliness* might have secretly crept around the dorm.) The term "homosexual" would not become current until Kinsey published his studies in the forties, a decade when the term "gay" still meant lighthearted. At Bates a boy who preferred to behave like a girl might have been called a "sissy," which in no way described Owen. Priscilla was puzzled.

Owen, the more sophisticated, at twenty knew in his bones that Priscilla's embrace could never warm him. He simply "froze" her out until she had to admit that she could not share his life, even to save her own. She wrote him a poem, "Masks On!," veiling but revealing:

> I tried experiments with truth
> To test if truth be wise;
> Yet all the while, I think I knew
> That proof would favor lies.
> A final hour precedes the mask;
> Then glances dare not meet
> Lest truth should recognize itself
> And guise begin retreat.
> I did not want a blindfold game.
> I did not want to know
> That counterfeited fact is true
> When wisdom wills it so.

Formally their engagement had ended. Priscilla grappled with her disappointment eighteen years before she published a story of two college lovers, entitled "Farewell, Sweet Love"; it was selected for *The*

Best Short Stories of 1954. Even a casual reading will reveal Owen and Priscilla caught in the very subtle death throes of love.[22]

In their *Garnet* photo, Owen and Priscilla sat side by side, he in his dark suit, she in her white wool, topped by a mantle worn over her shoulders; she wore her glasses and looked deep into the camera lens. As "personal editors" for the senior annual, *Mirror,* they had collected the benchmark qualities of the class of '36: "Jimmy Carter, the best dressed; Edmund Muskie, the most respected, best scholar, most likely to succeed; Priscilla Heath, most efficient, outstanding, respected, most likely to succeed (female); Owen Dodson, the most talented."

On Friday, April 3, Owen escaped the mad pace by hurrying home for spring vacation to see Broadway productions of *Idiot's Delight, End of the Summer, St. Joan,* and *Ethan Frome.* He brought with him two brothers, both professors at Bates—Angelo and Peter Bertocci. Peter taught psychology and philosophy; Angelo, French and classical civilization. Angelo, with a panache of black, wavy hair and animated speech and gestures, belonged to Owen's dinner club (a group of young men who pooled their resources for an evening meal). Angelo frequently had invited the Negro poet, along with other students, to his rooms over a drugstore for literary discussions. Owen had trusted Bertocci's friendship, but soon after he and Priscilla had broken their engagement, Angelo proposed to Priscilla, and she on the rebound accepted him; then Priscilla called it off. When Angelo informed his brother, Peter responded, "Don't worry about that because after all she was engaged to a nigger." This remark was repeated to Owen. Arnold Kenseth recalled signs left on Owen's door calling him "nigger," and that he had no business going with white girls.[23] This was a great hurt.

On the last evening in April, Owen starred as a "Nameless Man" in a one-act, *Granite;* the part required a grim and haunting laugh, which he practiced until "when I laugh now, it seems false." At the same time, he and Louise Geer, also from Priscilla's hometown, began to co-direct the Class Day (June 13) play, *Trojan Women,* on the front steps of Coram Library, using its columns, steps, and ornate door to suggest a Greek stage. Owen performed the prologue; Priscilla led the chorus. By selecting the world's most ancient antiwar tragedy, Owen reasserted his pacifist stance, a position he had become identified with after a brilliant reading of three antiwar poems in chapel.

Owen wrote and read the class poem, and with Dalie Nigro composed the final chapel hymn. His "Ode to the Class of 1936 Everywhere" appeared on the editorial page of the *New York Herald Tribune*. Then he won the Maine State Poetry Contest. Professors Berkelman and Robinson composed lyric encomiums about his talents. The Yale School of Fine Arts, School of Drama invited Owen to enroll—a blessed time for great exultation, except for a thing or two.

June swept the seniors out. The seventieth commencement awarded 144 sheepskins. Edith and Lillian, in new taffeta dresses, Aunt Mary, in great hat and beads, and Kenneth, in a white double-breasted suit, all came to the Dodson triumph. In four years, Bates had groomed Owen's talent for poetry and wedded him to the humanities and to Thespis. He had turned his back upon marriage and upon an extraordinary woman. Like Hippolytus, he chose to ride horses in the company of males. Bates had forced Owen to see his negritude, and what it meant in a white world. Owen might have agreed with Benjamin E. Mays, who wrote in his autobiography: "Bates College did not 'emancipate' me; it did the far greater service of making it possible for me to emancipate myself, to accept with dignity my own worth as a free man. Small wonder that I love Bates College!"[24]

5

Divine Comedy, 1936–38

Summer at Quogue again. Owen polished silver and glass from 6:30 A.M. to 9:15 P.M., with two hours free from the wailing and shouting of the West Indian chef. On July 3, he escaped home to the garden behind 469 Quincy to celebrate the balloon-and-banner ritual of Kenneth's twenty-fourth birthday. Owen admonished Edith, who was recuperating from a stay in Jewish Hospital, to rest, contemplate the flowers, and read Edith Olivier's *Dwarf's Blood*.

That fall, Kenneth did not return to tuition-free Brooklyn College but to Lincoln University in Pennsylvania. Edith, Lillian, and even Lef sacrificed for the boys to attend private schools. Edith, at twenty-seven, and Lef, at forty, in and out of hospitals with various "female maladies," remained single. Lillian had refused her only marriage proposal to head the family. Now, at age thirty-eight, her heart began to refuse its duty. While the men climbed the powerful long ladder, the women's dreams shriveled — raisins in the sun.

Owen settled into Yale for three years. He occupied the front chamber of a small apartment at 152 Grove, near a cemetery with an Egyptian gate carved in stone legend: "The Dead Shall Be Raised." At the beginning of the term, a handsome, firm-jawed black man peered through Owen's front window, then rapped on the door. When he introduced himself, Owen exclaimed, "Ollie Harrington! You draw 'Bootsie?'" Harrington said, "Yes, I draw that cartoon; that's what I will be living on at Yale." Harrington moved into the back room[1] and soon was inviting Owen to spend evenings at the Green Lantern, a bar where noisy people told tall tales and lies, a stimulating source for a cartoonist or playwright, but Owen preferred to hear Ollie's adventures second-hand.[2] He remained a mandarin, a hostage to grandparents born in slavery and to their children's fierce flight from illiteracy and those loud, noisy people.

In New Haven, the black community lived on two sides of the university: to the south and east, the working class; to the north and west, the professionals who gathered near the Dixwell Avenue Congregational Church, pastored for thirty-five years by the Reverend Edward Franklin Goin. On his first Sunday, Owen roused himself and walked the few blocks to meet the reverend, his charming wife, Viola, a graduate of Oberlin, their daughter, Vi, and their son, Edward, who had lost his arm in a streetcar accident but continued to drive his car with an abandon that frightened Owen.

On the top floor of the Goins' home at 573 Orchard Street roomed Anne Margaret Cooke, a tall, slim, light-complexioned woman with a hint of a melancholy pout. Cooke, Owen's senior by a decade, had attended Oberlin at age sixteen, had founded the first black summer theater in America, and had enrolled at Yale for a Ph.D. The afternoon that the Drama School gave its introductory tour of the theater, Owen's ear caught her precise stage diction, with its clip of culture, of worldliness. When Owen "ooooohed" over the fly space and kept repeating, "Think of all the magic, all the wonderful things we can do here!" Cooke, regal in her green velvet dress, arched her plucked eyebrows and wondered if Owen were capable of coming out of the clouds. In retrospect she commented, "He had always kept a bit of the child about him. If he didn't have wonderment naturally, it was always easy for him to create it."[3]

Together they attended the drama productions and she listened while he tore them apart. Together they attended dance class, where Owen's dance movement consisted mostly of rubbing cream on his ashy legs. Assigned to a crew to construct flats and paint scenery, Owen reported at 7:00 P.M. and went home at midnight, assuming his duty had been met. Three days later, his name appeared on the spindle: why hadn't he reported to crew every night? (Crew worked *every* evening until the show went up.) He wrote Edith, "I didn't know a director or a playwright had to know about scenery. You have to know something about everything. That is an allegory for life."

His first-term teachers showed no mercy. The British scholar Allardyce Nicoll, who chaired the school, offered an introduction to and survey of theater history; Alexander Dean and Halstead Wells taught directing; Walter Pritchard Eaton, a tweedy, balding American from Sheffield, Massachusetts, taught play writing. They rewarded Owen's talents with Bs; Constance Welch, the voice-and-diction coach, gave him a C, along with an enduring passion to "speak the speech trippingly on the tongue." Cooke didn't take diction at all; hers was perfect.[4]

Recalled Owen: "I sat through one whole year in play writing without knowing what they were talking about." For his first play, he adapted Langston Hughes's short story "Red-Headed Baby," a bitter tale of miscegenation. Professor Eaton thought Owen's adaptation to be "effective, powerful, Faulknerish." Owen retitled it *Gargoyles in Florida*[5] and pondered sending Hughes a copy for permission to copyright. He never did, but on November 13, 1941, he won the first annual playwriting contest conducted by the Department of Drama of the School of Education at Tuskegee Institute, and pocketed $100.

Owen's second one-act, *The Shining Town*, a solid advancement in craft and character (he never learned to invent plot), dealt with the "domestic slave market" in the Bronx near the Jerome Avenue and 167th Street subway stop; here, black women auctioned themselves to white women for day work. These black women, trying desperately to support their families in the Depression, undercut each other brutally, working for ten or fifteen cents an hour. Though Owen hadn't witnessed these auctions, he had heard Blacks tell of them, and he did know the bitterness of those who toiled in domestic service. The play, now published, remains unproduced.[6]

For his next assignment, Owen chose to adapt Thornton Wilder's novel *Woman of Andros*. He carried the novel everywhere, one day to a performance at the Yale theater, where he noticed a man looking at the book. The man asked how he liked it, and Owen replied that he loved it. The man asked him what he planned to do with the novel, and like all young people Owen babbled in great detail about his plans. Then the buzzer rang, curtain going up. Afterwards, Owen asked the man his name. He said, "Thornton Wilder." (Wilder lived with his sister in nearby Hamden.) Years later Owen again met Wilder, who asked about his adaptation. Owen confessed he had never done it. Wilder replied: "You never finished it because you talked about it a great deal. If you talk about it enough, you will think that you have done it."

For Easter, Owen announced a miracle: "Mr. Nicoll sent my work down to the Rockefeller Foundation, and the Head, Mr. Stevens, came up to interview me. Me! Owen!! Imagine!!! Fancy!!! Well, don't fancy then, but at least be amazed!" Owen raved on: "The brother of Lillian and Edith *may—may* I repeat, receive a two year scholarship to Yale in play writing. Well that's an earful for you all. But keep it under your bonnets, me girls, for I ain't-a-tellin' Mr. Elzy—or if it doesn't pan out I will be still a stepchild of Mrs. Daboll. All this means, Anne Cooke says, a permanent job when I graduate for what is the Foundation for anyway?"[7]

Anne Cooke, familiar with the Rockefeller General Education Board policies, advised Owen to fill out the section entitled "Future Prospects" with an expressed desire to teach in the South. In his application, Owen presented his own dream of teaching and writing plays and poetry: "I should like to be instrumental in forming a Negro Theatre where Negroes may have plays presented where the Negro will be able to speak in his own language and thereby add to his race and the American Theatre." The Rockefeller Foundation noted on Owen's application summary that he "will probably have work in a Southern College."[8]

Owen's ecstasy added up to $3,200; the family kept his secret (if it was that) and he "lived in the lap of luxury," buying books, attending the theater, and enjoying his own record player, an Ainsley Dynaphone floor model.

In the flush of affluence, Ollie and Owen donned their sport jackets, polished their white bucks, folded the top down on "Nimrod," Harrington's 1929 Ford, and sped nonstop to Philly, supposedly to cheer the Penn Relays but really to consume eggnog, salad, olives, cheese at open bars. A Mrs. Norwood, learning that Owen attended Yale, introduced her daughter Vashti as "unmarried." Owen simply left for another party where there were "plenty of drinks, close dancing music, red lights duly dimmed." They started home at six in the morning, hauling in the rumble seat a pixilated young man who agreed to pay for the gas but who, when the car sputtered for fuel, claimed bankruptcy; they frisked his pockets, found nothing. In desperation, according to Owen, Ollie poured water in the tank, and Nimrod took off for home.

Owen had hung in his room portraits of Kenneth and himself painted in oil by a black artist from Brooklyn, Walter Simon (later a career diplomat for the United States Information Agency). Although the work of a novice, the paintings displayed an intrinsic talent and bore a likeness to the brothers. One day, Owen found them missing. Oliver confessed that he had painted them over because he needed the canvas, and besides, they were "bad pictures anyway."

Owen recouped payment. Harrington had sketched the palace of Negro dancing, the Savoy Ballroom. Disgusted with his effort, Harrington threw it into the wastebasket, and Owen snatched it out. At age twenty-three, Owen was honing his taste. In May 1937, he and Ollie visited Richmond Barthé's studio on Fourteenth Street in Manhattan; they found Helen Mencken sitting for a portrait, and a bust of black baritone Roland Hayes awaiting completion. On that day Owen fell in love with Barthé's unfinished pietà, "Mother and Son — After the Lynching," a sculptural group replete with a selfless world sorrow. Barthé thought it the best thing he had done.[9] A year later, the Contemporary Arts Exhibit displayed the pietà at the World's Fair.

Inspired by Barthé's work, Dodson composed a sonnet, "Lynching," challenging Berkelman's admonitions and nearly succeeding in wedding the bitter, passionate cry of race to the sonnet form. Roger Starr, editor of "the oldest monthly magazine in America" (1836), wrote Owen, "Your first sonnet is one of the finest pieces of poetry the *Yale Literary Magazine* has ever published."[10] "Lynching" appeared in the May issue:

> Swaying in the shadows of a tree,
> A long, thin noose of wire hangs alone
> Above the after-silence. Hauntingly
> Below a skull and by its side a bone
> Lie in a heap of ashes: this is all
> The restless eyes and passionate hands have left
> For flies' and swamp mosquitoes' sting ball.
> And this is all: The mother is bereft.
> In rain upon a hill with morning light
> She kneels and fingers dust and rubs her eyes:
> She cannot rub the orgy of the night
> Away, nor can she hope that God is wise,
> When in her crusty hands lie years of pain,
> When all her dreams run down-hill with the rain.

Owen continued pulling older sonnets out of the drawer and refurbishing them; he also wrote new ones. *Opportunity* accepted two, published one — "Metaphor for Negroes." In December, the *New York*

Herald Tribune on its editorial page reprinted "Desert in Ethiopia." The *Yale Literary Magazine* published three sonnets.

Owen's pivotal publication came in *Challenge*, a small monthly magazine founded in March 1934 by Dorothy West to establish a new movement in African-American writing for young voices; the periodical, after sporadic appearances, death, and a revival as *New Challenge*, collapsed for good in 1937, but not before printing Owen's "New England Color Scheme," followed by "From Those Shores We Have Come." He received no payment, but something more precious — recognition from the associate editor, Harold Jackman, a major Medici of the Harlem Renaissance.[11] While the Depression still raged, Owen and Ollie ate well. Ollie discovered that he could make good money washing dishes in the Chi Psi House, an exclusive fraternity whose members included "Henry Ford who owned all the cars in the world, somebody Grace who owned all the steam ships in the world, and another somebody who owned all the pineapples in the world." As Harrington worked there, he began to put on weight, especially after he discovered that he could take delicacies home — such as quail from Scotland stuffed with strawberries and cream.

On June 21, 1937, Ollie persuaded Owen to help him serve at the Chi Psi reunion for the class of 1897. Owen's letter home acidly reported the dinner: "Old flabby cocks, free of their hens: they stand for fascism, anti-Rooseveltism, anti-lynching [*sic*], anti-Negro, pro-scotch and soda, pro-champagne vintage '97. They were drunk as cardinals over their communion wine and sat on their soft haunches like contented hens on eggs; the cigars were at least fifty cents per and they spent money as if it were free rain, only we don't get very much of it." Owen, the poet, saw in their prodigality his own bitter penury, whereas Ollie saw in their golden flatulence a subject for cartoons and lamb chops for his lunch.

Owen did enjoy intimate dinner with Thurgood Jones, a valet to one of the important professors. Harrington recalled, "I took Owen up to Jones's apartment for classic meals. Thurgood was gay, but I didn't know it. I did know that he was very gentle and different. He had that strange twinkle in his eye, that I learned later that many gays have, that they were aware of something that escaped everyone else. But then, most Blacks had that twinkle, too. Now I realize that Owen was gay at Yale; in retrospect, when I analyze the atmosphere that I no way understood, I realize that most of the people in Owen's group, in the Drama School, were gay, for the provincial lug, like myself, would not have known. Another friend of mine told me once later that Owen had told him to never let me know that he, Owen, was gay. It wouldn't have made any difference."[12]

The Thursday after his serving stint, Owen returned home to serve again at Quogue, but this time he did not feel chained to the job. In two months, the Rockefeller scholarship would begin, and further, his year of creative freedom at Yale made polishing glassware more odious. He wrote Lillian for permission to quit, come home, take care of the garden and write. She consented. As he sat in the backyard with the flowers and grass, he remembered that Frances Gunner[13] had driven Kenneth and him as boys to Sayville, Long Island, to meet Father and Mother Divine.

At a banquet table when Father Divine kept pouring milk from the spigot that never ran dry, Kenneth had looked askance; after everyone left the dining room, he looked under the tablecloth, and there a little Negro boy pumped milk from a large cask. With the return of these memories came his feelings about Father Divine. "I was very impressed with that little man, how happy all the people seemed. As soon as I began to write, suddenly my first year at Yale, the talks, the lectures, all came into focus. I wrote for hours at a time. I have never been so conscientious. I finished *Divine Comedy* in about a month, and Edith typed it. I wondered how I had done it, got it all down on paper."

The late 1930s favored Owen's play: fascism, religion, and poverty held the public eye; the esteem of *Green Pastures* and *Porgy and Bess* had opened the way for serious plays on Negro themes; the drama's high literary quality gave the script academic chic while at the same time capitalizing on Father Divine's notoriety in the newspapers; and finally the play pleased Yale because *Divine Comedy* presented a black man as exploiter of black people.

Who was this Divine Messenger? In 1915, a small-statured preacher named George Baker had left Valdosta, Georgia, with his wife for the North. He preached that we should worship and rely upon God in each of us. Later, he preached we should rely upon God in the Divine Messenger; finally, he preached that George Baker *was* God, and his true name, Father Divine. His slogan, "Jesus will lead me and welfare will feed me," expressed hope to nourish both body and soul.

The plot of Owen's play: the full terror of the Depression is on; people are hungry; children die of TB; the traditional churches offer salvation through prayer. Cora, an old woman who has earned her living by day work, joins the Apostle of Light (Father Divine), and urges her friend Rachel to join, too. It is Christmastime, and a mother tells her child that Santa Claus has starved to death. In the bars, street-life characters drink, play the numbers, and fight. Rachel's son, Cyril, moves away to Virginia to teach school. After a struggle, Rachel in her loneliness accepts the Apostle of Light. The first act climaxes with the Apostle's sermon — "Ain't you glad!"

In act 2, Cyril returns to find that his mother is going to deed over her house to the Apostle; his mother refuses now to call him "son" because the Apostle says she has no family except her brothers and sisters in his temple. Cyril in frustrated anger shoots and kills "God." We are taken to the bars to hear and see the low-life versions of what has happened, a kind of satyr parody. The play ends with the people recognizing that "we still thrive. Christ is the power in you, not in prayer. We need no miracles, we are the miracles." (A triumphal choral music rises up like a prayer and the curtain descends like a benediction.)

When Owen returned to Yale in the fall, he read the play aloud in Eaton's class, and they all got quiet because so many of the students there could write but had little experience to write about. Then Owen got a note from Allardyce Nicoll, who asked to read the script, and two days later the faculty said that in the spring during Alumni Week, they would give the play a major production. They asked him to read the whole play through so they could record it and get an idea of his interpretation. Owen made a few changes for transitions, not many. They asked him to leave the auditorium, and they did not call Owen back until they began dress rehearsals.

Remembered Owen: "The play had a cast of twenty-nine characters plus a chorus. With only four blacks in drama, the school said it would use white students and teach them how to speak and to dance. The rehearsals went beautifully, but Frank Bevin, in charge of costumes and makeup, at the first dress rehearsal painted the white actors with cork and thick lips. I said, 'Mr. Bevin, black people do not look like that. Do I look like that? We Negroes range from bright mulatto to eggplant.' He said, 'You are the playwright and I am doing the makeup. Shut up and go sit down.' But do you know, he got that makeup together because my comment made him walk the streets and look at Blacks in all their magnificent colors."[14] Dick Campbell, who saw Owen's play, recalled no black makeup; however, Peggy Clark, who designed the lighting, reported that the whites did all have a base to darken them into different shades because she used lavender gels to favor their darkness.[15]

When Owen saw the magnificent set that Clark had designed, he wrote Lillian: "Tonight rehearsal for my play begins. From now on we shall go with seven league boot speed. The music has all been written, and the set definitely selected. The design is right for the play, very right. The stained glass window towers thirty-six feet in the air, dominating all. There are steps and platforms that would warm Bel Geddes's heart. With all, simple but tremendously effective."[16]

Constance Welch, the speech teacher, directed the chorus; Frank McMullan, the actors. They got someone to teach them trucking (popular black dance) and to sing the music of Morris Mamorsky, which had a Gershwin sound. Owen reported that "the white actors played the spirit and the humanity of the play. They learned that dialect is not only broken words, but an essential rhythm of the language. It built up into a great evening of ecstasy and death and resurrection and hope. When *Divine Comedy* opened February 16, 1938, *Variety* reviewed it favorably. Everyone expected something big to happen to it." Owen wrote his sister: "Perhaps *Divine Comedy* shall burst on Broadway, but it is too early to think about that now. Too early and too bewildering."

Paul Robeson and his wife, Essie, took a copy of the play to England; after a few months, Essie wrote to Owen, "All of the producers have returned the play, saying they hadn't the vaguest notion what it was about, and didn't understand it anywhere from beginning to end! This did not surprise me because we American Negroes are always forgetting that people outside of America do not know the most obvious details about the Negro problem."[17]

Owen sent a copy of his script to the white playwright Ridgley Torrence, who was then working with the Gilpin Players at Karamu Playhouse in Cleveland.[18] Torrence responded, "It is a brave and ambitious attempt to scale a high peak in dramatic expression. The texture of the verse does not, as poetry, equal the quality of your concept." Despite Torrence's reservations, Dodson believed the play would be done at Karamu. It never was. Even years later, it seemed *Divine Comedy* might see Broadway. The original stage manager of the Yale production, Bo Wilder, gave a script to a Broadway producer, whose voice one day came over the telephone to Owen: "This is Eddie Dowling and I have just finished the first act of your play. It is magnificent! If the second act is as good I will put it on as soon as *The Glass Menagerie* is over."

"I had become the chief writer of the world," said Owen. "Dowling had said, 'I'll be in touch with you in a week or two.' Over a month went by. Finally, I went to the matinee to see that man: just as I entered the backstage area, he had just started up the backstage steps. I called him by his name: 'Mr. Dowling, I'm the author of the *Divine Comedy,* that play you said you liked so much.' 'Oh,' he said, 'Magnificent! Oh my God, what a play!' and he kept on going up the stairs. I never heard from him again." A half-dozen productions in colleges and small theaters followed. (Later, in the mid-forties, Owen rewrote his script in the militant tone of the labor movement of the thirties—a tighter, better version that was never performed.)

When Owen sat in his backyard in Brooklyn that summer, and the play "came to him" he knew not how, the spirit of his own family had descended on him, descended with all its paradoxes. Owen had fired a booming volley in his war with God the Father. He dramatized the oedipal murder of the Father by the Son, as punishment for God's seducing the Mother. (This would become a major theme of his plays and poems.) His verse play had further significance. Black American theater history, until Owen, had no poetic drama. William Easton and Joseph S. Cotter, Sr., had written verse plays, but in truth, *Dessalines, Christophe,* and *Caleb the Degenerate* march along in stilted rhetoric rendered in ragged Jacobean similes; they never saw production. Owen's modern tragedy not only was the first true poetic play for the black theater, but, along with Edna St. Vincent Millay's verse plays, stands as one of America's better early poetic dramas, certainly superior in verse to Maxwell Anderson's *Winterset,* a play the young Dodson much admired. The name "Miriamne" often formed on Owen's lips, but no other word, phrase, or line in *Winterset* is as memorable as "I am black, I am black. I am dangerously black. They call me 'Nighttime,' and when I pass by they look for stars."

6

Garden of Time, 1938–39

In April 1938, Anne Cooke challenged Owen: "Can you really do anything but talk? Do you want to help me at Atlanta this summer?"

"I don't have a job," replied Owen. "I'll do anything."

Cooke proposed a brutal schedule: five plays in eight weeks. She promised Owen sixty-five dollars plus room and board to direct one play, act in others as needed, work properties, and build scenery. His response: "We'll produce *Medea!*" Her response, "You're off into the wings with no sense of theater or what it is about." Nonetheless, the combination of Owen's flights of fancy and Anne's solid administration produced the best theater that Atlanta, and later Howard University, would come to know.

In her small car Cooke drove from New Haven. Owen didn't know how to drive (he never learned). While Cooke concentrated on the road, Owen asked, "What is that? Can we stop here? Can we see that?" He started off with a tie but soon got rid of it. No air-conditioning. For a time, he sat in the back, his head wrapped in a scarf, and complained about the heat. Then he said to Anne, "Why don't you move around a little bit? You keep your foot in the same place all the time." She replied, "It helps to accelerate the car." Her sarcasm didn't register. Owen, sweating and fanning, griped and griped. The highway ran along the railway track, with a depot in each little town. Cooke drove up to one of them and said, "Get out and get your bag and wait over there and a train will come along sometime and take you to Atlanta, and you will have the experience of sitting in a Jim Crow car; then you'll have something to write about." Contrite, he suffered in silence the rest of the way.[1]

Owen, with a wicked head cold that he blamed on Jim Crow, was given a room in the faculty dormitory and introduced to a charming southern girl, Ednah Bethea. Cooke asked her to show Owen around. Ednah took Owen's hand and led him off to see the campus. She recalled, "I was rather naive myself, but I think he was more naive than I. We had a wonderful time." In the flush of the meeting, Owen probably did not notice Ednah's round, pretty face or her southern speech, which resembled his mother's. He should have.

In the mornings, Owen taught an advanced speech class; then came rehearsals, which lasted from 1:00 P.M. to 5:00 P.M.; after supper, from 6:30 to 7:30 P.M. (his only free hour), he went to the music room and listened to recordings;[2] then, from 7:30 to 10:00 P.M., they rehearsed the next play on the bill. After that they built sets, pausing to go out and drink ale on Ashby or Fair Street, never getting to bed before three or four in the morning. Owen loved it.

The first show, George S. Kaufmann and Marc Connelly's comedy *Dulcy*, opened June 21, directed by a black Yale Drama School graduate, John "Mac" Ross. Owen wrote home that "Negroes look very foolish doing *Dulcy*—talking about big corporation mergers and golf and all sorts of rich ju-jitsu. Once in awhile they come down from their high horses of speech and become utterly Negroid. Then it is a scream." Cooke's production of *Outward Bound* opened the next week. In this Sutton Vane mystery-of-death drama, Owen played the lover opposite Ednah Bethea.

One of the five plays each summer had to be about Negro life. For their third show, Owen directed *Divine Comedy*. Few in Atlanta knew about Father Divine. The audience applauded but didn't understand the play; they understood the pain but not the poetry. Bethea recalled, "Owen was onstage, all over it, directing the bodies, the places, the timing, a strong disciplinarian. Occasionally, he would rage if things were not done as he said they should be."[3]

Following a mystery, *Three Faces East*, Cooke closed the season with Maxwell Anderson's *Mary of Scotland*. In the role made famous by Helen Hayes, Cooke cast the head of the Department of French, Billie Geter Thomas, a woman who became a good friend to Owen. When the last show closed, Owen and his new friends drove down to Tuskegee, "where they teach our folks to make bricks without straw."

On July 28 outside of Atlanta, he visited Stone Mountain, the largest solid stone in the world, where at night, on its bald dome, KKK crosses flamed.

Cooke decided not to drive back to New York and turned the task over to James Butcher, who recalled that "Owen sang spirituals in the car the whole time. I said, 'Owen, will you shut up!' He acted like he lived in a different world: a young college kid, very bright, but in some ways very naive."[4]

Back in New York, Owen received a letter from George W. Crawford, a prominent black lawyer in New Haven, inviting Owen to write a play for the 100th anniversary of the Amistad mutiny. The play would be performed at Talladega College in Alabama.

Owen began research. The incident involved a slave ship, the *Amistad*, carrying fifty-four Africans, who in 1839 were to be sold as slaves in Cuba by the Spanish. Under the leadership of Cinque, the slaves overpowered the crew, murdering all but two, who were to navigate the ship back to Mendi, the West African homeland. Instead, the sailors landed the Africans at Montauk, Long Island, where after lengthy trials they were returned to Africa as free people. The defense of the Africans by abolitionists led to the founding of the American Missionary Association, which in 1939 wished to celebrate the trial's centennial with the dedication of the Savery Library at Talladega College; the occasion would feature a performance of Dodson's play, followed by the unveiling of Hale Aspacio Woodruff's "Amistad Murals."

When Owen returned to Yale in September to begin writing, he found that a storm had mauled New Haven. Crippled oaks, maples, and elms had fallen everywhere, some lying on roofs of houses, some fallen across power lines, leaving only red lanterns to light the street. "Where there should have been a riot of color like a young Joseph's coat, the leaves shriveled, the branches bare."

Owen and Ollie moved into 74 Lake Place, a university house, and with them, an international ménage of housemates. Three lived on ground floor: Ollie had the front room; then, beyond a sliding door, Owen had the middle room; in the back lived Peter Katz from Holland. Katz's impersonations of Napoleon and Hitler delighted everyone, except for the German lad who lived upstairs. Owen confessed to Harold Jackman that the German "keeps reminding me that he is not Jewish. He looks it tho'." Above Owen lived a Japanese fellow and a Puerto Rican, and across the hall, off the bath, roomed Michael Yates, an eighteen-year-old English lad whom Allardyce Nicoll had invited to the Drama School.

Initially reserved and somewhat shy, Yates entered Owen's room one day to show him a book, *Letters from Iceland,* written by W. H. Auden and Louis MacNeice. There in a photo, as a boy of fourteen, sat Yates on horseback; Auden called him Tinker. Owen admired Auden, even to the point of having borrowed for his *Divine Comedy* the structure of Auden's *The Ascent of F6,* with its dramatic episodes alternating with choral scenes. Responding to Owen's enthusiasm, Yates showed him a proof copy of *Dog beneath the Skin* and several poems that Auden had dictated to him.

A short time later, Auden himself appeared. Yates recalled, "He had come for the publication of his first book of poetry in America. I introduced Owen, and before he left the theater, Auden asked me, 'Can you come to breakfast with us at the Taft Hotel? And see if you can persuade your Negro friend to come along, too.' This was in the spring of 1939, and I can remember the occasion, and those actual words quite clearly. I also remember the eyebrows of the waiter at the Taft Hotel the next morning."[5]

Owen related the meeting differently: "One day, Michael rushed in and said that Auden was coming that day, and would I take Auden and show him around the campus until he could get back. I rushed out and bought Auden's book. Then Michael brought Auden over and ran off. In came this tall, blond, exquisitely dressed Englishman in his double-breasted, pinstriped suit. He came in and stretched out his long legs and took off his shoes. I learned later that he had the biggest bunions and corns. His face, unlined, looked just as you would expect a young poet to look. A blond Byron, or Tennyson in his youth with a mole on his right cheek. What do I say to this man? To someone who has published a book? I had just written my verse play, *Garden of Time,* so I spent two hours reading it to him. Later he said, 'What a bore it was,' but he was pleasant and nice about it."[6]

Yale had thrown Owen into a gay ocean of talents where he swam like a porpoise. Dearest among his friends was Siefield Gordon Heath, Owen's childhood companion from Camp Carlton, who visited Owen on weekends when Harrington left for Harlem. At age twenty, Gordon possessed a resonant baritone and a Barbadian profile that resembled the stone heads on Easter Island. He had graduated from the New York High School of Commerce, but while halfheartedly pursuing nine

credits at City College, he turned his attention to his true love, theater.
"Come, Owen," he asked, "see me perform in *The Merchant of Venice*
in Harlem."

A Scots director, Hamish Cochrane, had come to Harlem, with a
mission similar to that of German choreographer Baron Eugene Van
Grona, who the previous year had founded the Negro American Ballet
to provide an outlet for "the deeper and more intellectual resources
of the race."

On Saturday, October 8, Ollie and Owen piled into Nimrod for a
mad weekend. First, they drove directly to a morning wedding where
"the Rev. Adams grinned his sultan-in-the-harem grin; the groom kissed
the bride and then wiped his mouth with a healthy swing of his hand."
Dashing out of the reception, they hurried to a Broadway matinee of
Sing Out the News: "This was to *Pins and Needles* what domestic
caviar is to Russian." That evening at 6:30, Owen escorted Edith in
her blue dress to Maurice Evans's uncut *Hamlet.* Sunday afternoon,
Owen and Edith managed to squeeze into a buffet supper at Dorothy
Peterson's, an attractive actress whom Carl Van Vechten used as a
model for his heroine in *Nigger Heaven.* That evening in Harlem's
Grace Congregational Church, Owen surveyed Gordon as Antonio in
The Merchant of Venice;[7] he thought that his vocal technique still came
through too much, and that the director was hammy and pompous.
As though in compensation for missing the glorious weekend, Owen
bought and mailed Kenneth a maroon lumber jacket.

> *I sing in praise of college*
> *Of M.A.'s and Ph.D.'s*
> *But in pursuit of knowledge,*
> *We are starving by degrees.*
> "Ode to Higher Education"

Owen wrote Lillian that when he came home for Christmas, he
would be able to supply cigarettes and decorations but no liquor. He
sent Kenneth six dollars and told him that was that for Christmas.
Owen's additional Rockefeller money evaporated because the Dodson
men were living in style. Kenneth's invitation to Edith to attend the
Alpha Glee Club's formal ("the best affair at Lincoln") read like an
F. Scott Fitzgerald party: "I want you to ask Thelma Carter to come
as my escort. She looks good, dresses well, and is excellent company.
Wear your best and look good—bring a sport suit and shoes, and

afternoon frock, a traveling dress and two evening gowns at least. Just about the whole campus is participating, and you must come. Thank you very much for the money. I don't have to go into a long discourse about how much I appreciated and needed it. Merci."[8]

Owen penned his periodic mea culpas for spending his sisters' hard-earned wages: "Edith, I hope you plan to do some resting this summer. You've been so good to Kenneth and me. You have done all you could to make us happy and to help us get where we want to go. I want you to have what you want too. More than I want it for myself because I've had the breaks all along the way, and if I don't get any place I have no one to blame but myself. If I can find a job so that I can help Lillian's load, I'd be more content. I've thought a long time about this and very often when I'm writing or watching a play or just walking or sometimes I wake up in the middle of the night and wonder how much all of us at 469 will get what we want."[9]

Harrington recalled that the college students of Owen's generation were terribly involved with themselves: "On the campus at Yale, I knew several rich students who carried racing cars to Europe every summer for the races, and some had Nazi flags hanging outside the windows. Not a serious thing. The trains ran on time; the men handsome; hotels wonderful. The only ones that I knew who understood were the ones who had been in Spain in the war, two or three, and the conscientious objectors, but as a nation, we had not grown up yet."[10]

A tall, lanky friend of Owen's, Joel Durlam, who looked like a young Abe Lincoln, would drop by the house to argue politics. When these discussions arose, Owen's close friend, Wilson Lehr, who was a quarter Jewish, would get up and walk out. From Bates, Owen had carried away the conviction that war with its mass death was unacceptable. These men would soon face that decision, forced by the Selective Training and Service Act of 1940.

Owen worked furiously on the play commissioned by Talladega, scribbling ideas on backs of dining-hall menus while he ate dinner, writing late at night while others slept. By Thanksgiving, he had created *Amistad,* a pageant with sixty-eight characters. Owen's passion for A. E. Housman served him well in choral lines short, simple, and lucid.

Just after the New Year of 1939 he mailed the play off to Lillian Voorhees, the white director at Talladega, with a caveat not to make any changes that would affect the drift of the play. When Owen viewed her production on April 15 in the DeForest Chapel, Voorhees had reduced the cast of sixty-eight to fifty; she used the chapel organ, which, with the drums and singers, pulled the production together. Owen was pleased. The next morning, Sunday, he attended chapel and met Frances Gunner (the woman who had taken him to see Father Divine). As a memorial to her grandfather, the founder of the Savery Library, Gunner unveiled the "Amistad Murals" painted by Hale Aspacio Woodruff.

Owen returned to New Haven three weeks before his new verse play, *From This Darkness,* was to open on the main stage. He first changed the title to *The Golden Fleece,* then settled on *Garden of Time.* A reworking of the Medea story, the plot had a gimmick: The traditional characters of Colchis at midplay abruptly reincarnated themselves in the postbellum South; Jason, now John, a white son of a plantation owner, had married Medea, now Miranda, in Haiti. As in the original, their destiny sealed, the theme brilliantly caught in a choral refrain:

> Nothing happens only once,
> Nothing happens only here,
> Every love that lies asleep,
> Wakes today another year.

> Why we sailed and how we prosper
> Will be sung and lived again;
> All the lands repeat themselves
> Shore for shore and men for men.[11]

"Bone," a staff reviewer reporting for *Variety* (a publication that in 1948 was reluctant to support the integration of theater audiences), declared the play "the best major production in a somewhat uneventful season." He went on to say that it had been written by a Negro student "who plans to aid in the establishment of a Negro theatre especially adapted to his race. As an instrument for this purpose, *Garden* is excellent, showing the outcome of intermarriage of whites and blacks in ancient and modern times."[12] Directed by Frank McMullan, the cast included Owen's friend Wilson Lehr as the Orphic singer; the only Black in the play, Shirley Graham, wrote the music, which Owen did not like, but "the powers that be seem to think it is hot shot."[13]

Owen felt he had arrived. Yale radio interviewed him as "one of the most promising personalities at Yale." Race did not seem to stand in his way; indeed, it seemed his asset. In his sonnet "Metaphor for Negroes," Owen affirmed his negritude:

Cease to regret dark pigments of the skin,
the tightness of the hair, the ample jaw
Each flower holds its pollen deep within
And beauty blooms where darkness slept before.

If critics noticed that *Garden of Time* suffered from being more lyric than dramatic, they ignored it by overpraising the play's future. On May 8, 1942, Margery Bailey, the proctor of the Maxwell Anderson Verse Drama Award at Stanford University, penned Owen a lyric response: "Your beautifully conceived and highly poetic play has reached the group of first honors, and has every chance at present of winning first place under the Anderson Award." She then asked him for a statement about verse drama, a biographical sketch, and a photograph for public notices. Her letter bubbled on: "We hope to send your play to such publishers and producers as French, NBC, MGM, Pasadena Playhouse. Its excellence is such that we shall try to engage the attention of the Lunts or Theatre Guild through Miss Helburn." Bailey advised Owen to copyright his work, and then closed the letter: "Felicitations upon your thoughtful, sensitive, and passionate work, and thanks for allowing us to read it. The Alliance sends to you its best-wishes for success among the Judges [Norman Corwin, George Altman, Helen Hicks].[14]

Margery Bailey's rhapsody reflected her 1942 taste for high art as represented by Maxwell Anderson's *Winterset,* the apogee of American verse plays — romantic, idealistic, socially conscious. Owen responded that no, he had not committed his play to anyone. Yes, she could give MGM a copy. "The Lunts! What a coup!" He enclosed a short personal history, a statement concerning his thoughts upon the place of verse drama in American theater, and a photograph — the last, an error, for he received second prize and no invitations for production. In an appeal, Dr. Allison Davis of the University of Chicago, who had seen the Yale production, forwarded the script and the Stanford letter to the head of the Rosenwald Fund, Edwin R. Embree, who responded: "In spite of the expansive gesture of this letter [Bailey's], I cannot believe that his play was turned down because he was discovered to be a Negro." But all was not wasted: Owen Dodson had come to the attention of the Rosenwald Fund.

And to the attention of British poet Edith Sitwell. Geoffrey Gorer, an English anthropologist, had sent her a copy of *Divine Comedy*. Her response to Gorer:

> I do think that Mr. Dodson has real talent and considerable poignancy. He has obviously got a real gift for compassion, and I think should produce some very fine work. I don't think he has broken through (cast off his husks) yet, except in the first page and a half of the ms. you sent me. You and he will probably want to hit me, but if it has not yet been published, I strongly advise him to publish *that* passage *alone*. If he would like it done, if he will send it to me, I'll pass it on to *Life and Letters*.[15] That passage is most deeply moving. Why I suggest his publishing that alone is that he is so young, has (I hope and pray) much time ahead of him in which to work, and I don't want him to run any risk of giving people the idea that he has less power than that which is obviously in him.

The time had come for the poet to earn a living for himself and for those at 469 Quincy who had invested in him. Anne Cooke, who decided to complete her Ph.D. at Yale, recommended Owen to Spelman College as her substitute. On May 28, 1939, Pres. Florence Mathilda Read sent a telegram offering him $1,500 ($125 a month) and a place to live in the dormitory if he would teach three classes and help with the dramatics. He must begin in June by directing in the Summer Theatre. He could not attend graduation ceremonies.

At twenty-four, Owen had made important friends—Auden, Jackman, Van Vechten—all eager to help him with his career. Edith Sitwell had praised him. If he sensed that the world had begun to burn, the flames burned far away in Spain, China, Ethiopia, and Poland. Pearl Harbor lay more than two years distant. "Yale had passed like a dream."

7

Southern Exposure, 1939–40

Don't lower me in Georgia clay,
Don't bury me in Georgia Pine—
You gotta seek some other frame,
Some other case for this flesh o' mine.

After staying only two days at 469 Quincy, Owen boarded the train for Washington, D.C., arriving at nine that evening. Unable to contact Alain Locke, who had no telephone, Dodson boarded a Jim Crow car early the next morning with two ladies who wore hats and gloves. He asked if they minded that he smoked. They said they did mind, so he went to the back of the car by himself and rode eighteen hours. After the train left Durham, North Carolina, he fell asleep, and just on the outskirts of Atlanta, the conductor touched his knee and said, "Wake up, little nigger boy. You almost there. Wake up."[1] Yale Drama School's "most promising personality" had arrived in Georgia.

Anne Cooke stood waiting in the bright sunlight, dressed up so everyone would know that she knew about good deportment. They embraced and Dodson started out the front door. She said, "Owen, it says, 'White only.'" He shrugged, "What about it?" and went on out the front door. No one stopped him. James Butcher considered Owen a naïf, a nice guy who simply did not realize consequences. Cooke saw Owen as a mock child: "Around Atlanta, he was the favorite little boy who kept that little-boy presence toward life. It intrigued people."

The complete segregation of Atlanta startled Owen. "I had been to Harlem and seen black people, but as we approached the college, I had never seen such a coverage of black people—not one white person! My whole life had been with white people. So I understand how white people are amazed when they see black people in a mass, and so many poor. Just off the center of town, they had shanties, dilapidated, looking like the thieves who hung beside Christ. When we reached the campus, I felt like I had come into an oasis."

Founded in 1877, when three million black women could not read or write, one-third of them under twenty-one, Spelman College had depended upon the Women's American Baptist Home Mission Society. Sophia Packard and Harriet Giles, two New England missionary women, by begging, borrowing, and sacrificing had started the school in a church coal cellar, which became an institution that sent hundreds of women into nursing and the teaching profession.[2]

Owen lived in the faculty dorm at Chestnut and Beckwith, a three-story replication of the ubiquitous college dorm: red brick with white gables. A bower builder, Owen set about decorating his small basement room, arranging his few clothes, unpacking his most precious books and a small portable record player. (He would have his Ainsley Dynaphone shipped later.) He had been assigned two roommates—John "Mac" Ross, a theater director who had attended Yale, and actor-playwright Thomas Pawley, a recent graduate from the University of Iowa.

At Yale Owen had partied, but he had not bent elbows with the members of the black bourgeoisie of Atlanta who had partied in the wider world. Heading the hierarchy at seventy was W. E. B. Du Bois, who taught graduate students at Atlanta University and edited *Phylon*. From Paris, two black artists had been lured home to build an art department—Hale Woodruff and Elizabeth Prophet. Next door to Owen, William Stanley Braithwaite, Boston literary lion and a founding member of the American Poetry Society, shared quarters with another poet, Sterling Brown. Braithwaite wore spats and carried a cane; Brown carried an appreciative eye for the women.

The white desert of self-segregation that ringed the university had created a rich intellectual black oasis. Educated in the best northern and European universities, the faculty could find jobs only in southern black colleges. Worldly but denied the world, they turned in upon themselves with a proud, insouciant anger. To quote Richard Long, "when there were no whites around, they practiced on each other."[3]

These sometimes-caustic "worldlies" chafed under the discipline of Pres. Florence Mathilda Read,[4] spiritual "daughter" of the missionary founders.

President Read parted her flaxen hair on the right side and pulled it into a small bun, thereby enlarging her strong, rather broad Teutonic face. She opposed smoking, even out of doors, and drinking was absolutely forbidden. Once, when the KKK marched to the campus and placed a burning cross on her lawn, she strode onto her porch and stood immobile in the flaming shadows of Satan's henchmen; they never returned. Her softer side she reserved for John Hope, the president of Morehouse College for men, a black man with blue eyes and blond curls that blew in the wind.

As Rockefeller's right hand, President Read initiated changes. Prior to her tenure, the Morehouse men had been able to visit the Spelman women only once a month for twenty minutes and then chaperoned; Read allowed them two hours on Saturday. She liberalized the old curriculum, with its Booker T. Washington emphasis on practical training, to one concerned with liberal arts, and she hired the faculty to teach them.[5] Anne Cooke proposed a summer theater; Read endorsed her idea, and in May 1934, Atlanta Summer Theater premiered. It became the longest continuing summer theater in America.[6]

Howe Memorial Hall had a raised stage twenty-five feet in width with fringed curtains; its scenery was built in the basement or out on the lawn. Already initiated at Bates into how to transform an unsuitable stage, Owen Dodson turned Howe Hall into a silk purse. Beginning on June 20 with a modern melodrama, *Kind Lady,* he mounted five plays in six weeks; the annual summer play of black life turned out to be three one-acts: Langston Hughes's *Don't You Want to Be Free?,* a proletarian collage calling for racial unity: "White worker, here is my hand." The cast, short on whites, used fair-skinned Blacks to accept the gesture of brotherhood. When they joined hands and the piano struck the first note of "Lift Every Voice and Sing," the audience rose to join in. *Little David,* by white writer Marc Connelly, featured Owen in the lead. *Smokey,* an anti-lynching drama written and acted by Tom Pawley, closed the bill.

On the Fourth of July, Rufus Clement, president of Atlanta University, invited the faculty to his hilltop home. Owen won a crocus-sack race, did a good lap in the relay, played softball, and—most important—conquered the vittles.[7] Then the actors excused themselves to perform in *The Nervous Wreck,* a farce that left them wet with Georgia perspiration. Owen wrote Alain Locke: "I must talk to you about Negro audiences sometime. They are so fundamental and primitive: Food and sex! Bananas and lust."[8]

In his late hours, he penned home the night sounds—dogs barking, howling, the lonesome wail of the six-stringed guitar, the cottonseed oil that "smells like medicine made from kerosene and then molded in a damp place." He clung to the campus, but even there fear pushed its dirty edges into his life: the tales of the KKK; the rumor of twenty-five police who surrounded a black boy in a field, and "after they killed him, continued to pump bullets into his body until there was blood over all."

And things happened. Rough House Haynes, a fullback on the Morehouse team, enjoyed acting for two summers. One night during rehearsal, he told Butcher that "as I walked along the street the squad car pulled up and these guys jumped out and pulled a gun and said, 'Nigger, where you going?' and backed me up against the wall, and they questioned me and threatened me, and I almost cried because here were these little guys that I could have torn apart, and I had to stand there and take all that. I finally convinced them that I was a student at Morehouse."[9]

During performance, the doors of the second-floor Howe Memorial Hall had to be left open, but the summer heat did not faze an audience desperate for escape. At thirty-five cents a ticket, performances sold out. Thornton Wilder's *Our Town,* with Owen playing the town drunk, closed the season, and no one thought it strange that only Blacks occupied Grover's Corners, New Hampshire. The summer had "shot by like Ex-Lax." Before leaving for Brooklyn, Owen spoke with President Read to negotiate a salary increase of $100, making the total $1,600 for the nine months, and perhaps $50 more if the budget could stand it. Then he traveled home to touch base with the art world, to write his "Negro Miracle Play," one he would eventually entitle *Doomsday Tale,* "a play that more or less concerned the Dodsons."

At home, he plodded through an August day at the New York World's Fair. When he finally trudged to the Art Center, perhaps too tired from seeing too much, he paused at the entrance, gazing upon a sculpture by Augusta Savage, "Lift Every Voice and Sing." Owen pronounced this great plaster-cast harp with a dozen Negro heads singing from its top rail "a pile of chocolate [that] sets the tone for the pieces inside. I don't deny that there is much that has merit but also there is too much from seventh rate paletters and chippers."[10] In the arts, Owen never bowed to racial chauvinism.

To work on his new play, Owen fled Brooklyn for Alfred, New York, a small upstate village. Here his college buddy Glidden Parker had founded his own ceramic company and taught at Alfred University. Owen slept in a remodeled barn, swam several times a day, but his "Negro Miracle Play" did not move beyond notes; perhaps the drama cut too close to the Dodson family for him to write. Instead he pontificated to Carl Van Vechten about his theory of theater—anything to avoid writing the new play.[11]

In Manhattan Owen attended a reading by a black writer whose play *Big White Fog* had shaken the Federal Theater Project in Chicago. Theodore Ward had grown up poor in Thibodaux, Louisiana, and as a boy had literally walked the railroad tracks north to self-education. Fourteen years Owen's senior, Ward perceived class and race as the determining forces in American society and instinctively shied away from middle-class Blacks like Owen who had visions of joining mainstream America. Nonetheless, Ward, shrewd enough to realize that if he hoped to establish a Negro theater he needed allies in the very class he mistrusted, invited Owen to be an active member of the Negro Playwrights Company, adding his name to those of Langston Hughes, Paul Robeson, Edna Thomas, Richard Wright, and others. Owen wrote Alain Locke that Ward's adaptation of Richard Wright's *Bright and Morning Star* "is an impressive piece of playwriting: simplicity, restraint, suggestiveness, a brutal fierceness that can be checked by a good director."[12] Dodson did not participate in the Negro Playwrights Company. Lillian's bad heart caused her to miss more and more school days. Edith had passed a social-service exam, but her salary was meager. Kenneth had no job at all. Owen's $150 a month supported the family.

In the men's dormitory, Owen sat on the edge of his bed. The summer students had vanished; the fall term had not begun. He studied the bleak walls of his room and conjured memories of Van Vechten's chic apartment at 101 Central Park West, with its silver ceiling and stars in the wallpaper. He opened his suitcase and placed Glidden's ceramic candle holders on his bookcase. Room 144 had assets: three large windows looked out on great oaks, weeping willows, and the long green carpet of the athletic mall rising up a hill of clover to the president's home. He uncrated his Ainsley Dynaphone, which had

arrived with a fresh package of cactus needles, and selected Ravel's
Bolero.

He heard sounds outside, so he cracked his door a bit and saw
people going upstairs: Negroes with Negroes dressed for Negroes—
women in long gowns and men in tuxedos! He could hear them upstairs
and he was so lonely and angry at the sound of their rejoicing. Above
him lived W. E. B. Du Bois, who had a suite of rooms (Owen had a
single). Recalled Owen: "I saw Mr. and Mrs. Ira De A. Reid, the great
sociologist. (When his wife died many years later, Anne [Cooke] married
him.) There was the poet William Stanley Braithwaite; Frank Snowden
and his wife; Mercer Cook and his wife, Vashti (Negroes really get
names). The 'Moonlight Sonata' played in the background. Everyone
had been invited except me. I turned up Ravel's 'Bolero' little by little
until it drowned out the 'Sonata.' I could hear Du Bois turning his up,
but you know the 'Moonlight Sonata' can't drown out the 'Bolero.'
For about five minutes we had a battle, and then he clicked off and
so I turned mine off too—my first brush with W. E. B. Du Bois and
the niggeratti of Atlanta society."

As the first week passed, he noted that during the dinner hour
between five and seven, the dining tables were always full except for
that of Dr. Du Bois. Owen took courage and sat down with the famous
scholar, something that no one dared to do unless invited. "He was
so distant and stiff, and he knew more about everything than you did.
If you talked of literature, he knew more than you did; if you were a
musician, he knew more; and so, all the fields of science and culture.
The faculty down there hadn't studied in Berlin, traveled to Africa,
and they feared him. At twenty-six, I wasn't afraid of anything except
loneliness. I discovered his distance, his stiffness, to be a mask."

That autumn, Du Bois attended the first play under Owen's direction,
Susan Glaspell's *Alison's House*. The drama, built around Emily Dick-
inson's legend, so impressed Du Bois that he wrote Owen: "Your play
last night was one of the best, if not the very best, ever given at Atlanta
University. I congratulate you especially in the light of the difficulties
which you have had."[13]

The "difficulties" remain unknown, but on Sunday mornings the
good doctor entertained, inviting Owen and half a dozen people to
his suite. The coffee, blended, ground, and shipped from New York,
he served in a splendid silver set. For common palates, the mixture
was much too strong, but no one complained. From his silver cigarette

case, Du Bois offered to both men and women Benson and Hedges, the prestige cigarette. Conversation followed and then everyone was dismissed. The day following that brunch, one might meet Du Bois on campus and be ignored entirely.

In 1934, determined to build an art department, Pres. John Hope of Morehouse had lured sculptor Elizabeth Prophet from Paris. Whether to isolate herself from mundane campus life or to retain her own sense of well-being, Prophet had clung to her eccentricities. She loved costume and dressed formally for dinner.

Owen liked her intense dark eyes and her hair sweeping back from her thin, classic face, and he adored her cape as she glided across the campus. Prophet invited Owen to her studio, part of a complex of buildings and grounds that adjoined the boilers, a seemingly infinite distance from the rooftops of Paris. Outside her studio stood her statue, a snake-haired Medusa. A staircase led one down toward a lower level. Dressed as a Greek Sibyl in a long, flowing robe, she awaited Owen there. The studio, well below ground, had an earthy smell, not unpleasant. Prophet had furnished it exquisitely with her own work and several Holbeins—what an artist's European apartment should be. He asked, "Do you invite people over?" She said, "No. I'm rather lonely here." (She spoke in whispers and Owen found himself whispering, too.) He replied that many of the faculty appreciated art. She responded that if they are not your kind, "you can still be lonely."[14]

The cultural chasm between Owen and his southern coeds was not easily crossed, although he boasted to Harold Jackman that he would sock any student who called him "professor." But when he mentioned a name like Edith Wharton or Henry James, their faces looked blank. Said Owen, "I didn't look down on them, but all my high-flown ideas had to be adjusted." Lucy Grigsby, at that time a young graduate student, saw Professor Dodson every day in the dining room. "He would say hello to me but little else. I remember sitting at the table when he chatted with his friends and the conversation had to do with living in New York and Yale. He didn't mistreat us, he ignored us."[15]

Owen appreciated the sophisticated Atlantans—like the Dobbs sisters, who all spoke French and sang beautifully. (Mattiwilda, the youngest, became the first African-American to sing at La Scala in Italy.) Another worldly, pretty seventeen-year-old, Marion Douglas, sat in the back of his speech class; she was the granddaughter of Abbie Mitchell and Will Marion Cook, black performers who at the turn of the century had appeared before Prince Edward at Buckingham Palace. Raised in Europe, Marion had traveled with her father as an acrobatic dancer. Then Hitler had closed Germany's borders to gypsies of all kinds, and Mussolini with his invasion of Ethiopia had decreed that no person of African descent could work in Italy as a bartender, a domestic, or a theatrical performer. Marion's father, reading the signs of the times, sent his daughter to Spelman to speak English and to learn to be "Negro."

With a very special anticipation, Owen called upon this grandchild of theatrical greatness to read aloud her assigned poem. Marion rose slowly from her throne and with an insouciant teenager's regality moseyed to the front of the class; carefully opening her book, she turned her back upon the class and began to read to the blank wall. The class sat in embarrassed silence; they already knew how Marion had been humiliated by her previous speech teacher, "Mac" Ross, when she had read her first English poem one syllable at a time: "To . . . be . . . or . . . not . . . to . . . be." The class was convulsed with laughter, but Ross had insisted she finish the speech. From that moment, Marion had elected "not to be."

Owen allowed her to finish, then asked her to remain after class. Fifty years later, Douglas remembered, "Owen asked me, 'You are Abbie Mitchell's granddaughter? Will Marion Cook's granddaughter and you can't look at an audience?' I broke into tears. Owen made some adjustment which I don't remember and told me that I would be all right, although he wouldn't let me turn my back. He talked about how I had been on the stage and how people had applauded me and loved me, and he made it so simple and so loving. Owen had one gift — he understood without taking sides. I don't know if he ever spoke to the class about it. The class accepted me; he was the first person who had been nice to me."

Professor Dodson invited Marion to auditions. She responded like a broken Cinderella: " 'Do you really want me to come?' 'Yes, chile, come on, be brave.' So I went and received the part of an angel, a switchboard angel. I lived that part. I improvised chewing gum. The night of the play I mugged; people were hysterical. From that time on, I worked in the Atlanta University Players. Owen changed my life."

Within a year of that quiet encounter Marion triumphed as Lady Teasdale in *School for Scandal*, as Mme. Ranevsky in Owen's *The Cherry Orchard*, and later as Ophelia with Gordon Heath in *Hamlet*. The rebellion of Marion Douglas might be interpreted as the loneliness of a teenager far from home, but as an "outsider" she saw the black elite in jagged relief, the horror of segregation that they pretended to ignore.[16] The black college bourgeoisie, easy targets for Franklin Frazier and Ralph Ellison, had frozen themselves into a colored museum. Dodson, too, mocked them, mocked their thin fair skins and thinner masks, their tests that required a girl to speak French and to pass an ironing examination before graduation. If Owen remained less frozen than his colleagues, it was periodical escapes to his family in New York that freed him.

Determined to bring world theater to Spelman and inspired by Hitler's invasion of Poland, Owen directed *No More Peace,* a German antiwar satire. W. H. Auden had translated the play from *Nie Wieder Friede!* by Ernst Toller, who had committed suicide in New York City earlier that spring—the despair of a young talent on the eve of World War II, a despair that Owen and Kenneth shared. The magazine *Theater Arts* published a full-page picture of the production, but the play slipped quietly in and out of Atlanta's consciousness. To reaffirm the spirit of beauty, Owen turned to Christmas.

The most holy and joyful hour of the year came annually in mid-December at the Sisters Chapel, when Kemper Harreld conducted the Christmas Carol Concerts. In front of the six Doric columns a living pine tree rippled with lights. Two hours before the evening concert began, people who had traveled great distances—from Arkansas, Mississippi, Tennessee, and the Carolinas—crowded to stand on the steps. By eight o'clock, hundreds who could not get seats lined the walls. The service opened by the traditional lighting of candles by two robed students while the unseen Morehouse Brass Quartet softly played three Old English chorales. Before entering the chapel, the chorus sang as a prologue the spiritual "Rise Up, Shepherd and Follow." Twenty-six carols followed, sung in French, Russian, Ukrainian, Spanish, German, Slovak, Polish, and English. The program closed with five Negro spirituals, with the audience invited to join with the chorus in singing the recessional. Hosanna, hosanna! Owen floated off into the evening, reborn.

When he composed his own Christmas lyrics, however, Owen heard another angel, a torn bird. He decorated his Christmas cards with a woodcut—a pope wearing a gas mask while he raises his right hand in blessing—and a poem inside: "Christ never will consent / to another

Christmas Eve / until the killing iron stars are spent." For the next thirty years Dodson caroled variations on this theme. For a holiday of peace and joy, a festival he loved, his Christmas poems howled with grim and brutal irony.

Secure together again at 469 Quincy, the Dodson clan celebrated — the boys sleeping again in their twin beds, Edith and Lillian wrapping gifts, and Lef baking cookies. Owen gave Kenneth a fashionable felt hat he had purchased in Atlanta. Kenneth presented Owen with a brown satchel whose sides ballooned out, very like the one from which the doctor had delivered Owen. The gift tag read: "Ye must be born again." Everyone enjoyed the humor. Kenneth, always "imperially slim," now appeared to be delicate, in a fevered way. With only a semester or two to go before he would graduate from Lincoln — where he had become the *Lincolnian*'s editor-in-chief, an accomplished actor, a polished speaker, and a formidable debater — Kenneth had dropped out. He did this ostensibly to find a job, but in truth school no longer promised a future. Kenneth had taken on mankind's pain. He spoke to Owen about the slaughter in Europe, racism, the death of the Jews. His personal angst had wrapped itself in the black winding sheet of the world's despair.[17]

The holidays swept furiously past, and Owen returned to the South and his duties. A short time later, one evening after rehearsal, as the shadows of mid-February began to lengthen over Atlanta's red clay, a message came: "Kenneth seriously ill . . . come home." His brother for several days had been walking around with pneumonia. Owen packed his doctor's satchel and left.

8

Kenneth, 1940

As the train from Atlanta crawled its way north, memories of Kenneth flooded Owen. He and his brother had cleaned floors and baseboard moldings for neighbors, who had thought them fraternal twins. Together they had sold the *Amsterdam News* and the Pittsburgh *Courier* to the big-bosomed sisters as they left church; to earn five cents, they had run messages from Kotek's drugstore to families without telephones.

The Dodson boys had exuded cuteness. In the book-cover photo of *Boy at the Window* with Cousin Edna, her arms pulling both lads to her, the boys' eyes glow from the adoration of parents, sisters, cousins; Edith's devotion lasted a lifetime: "We felt that Owen and Kenneth were just what the doctor ordered: bright, attractive; Owen the more serious; Kenneth looser, more gregarious."

They had shared a love of self-presentation: singing, reciting, and finally an egg-crate theater at 309 Berriman, where the Jewish grocer, Mr. Altar, permitted the boys to use his basement for a stage. Said Owen: "I remember my mother had a long gold chain—pure gold—that my father had given her. We needed it for a prop in a play, but it was too long, so we just cut it and tied the ends together. They found sheets missing. They asked us where they were, and we said we had to use them as curtains. We charged two cents, but to our parents' friends a nickel to see Kenneth sing 'Yes Sir, That's My Baby,' while I at age nine walked along dressed as a girl—sometimes raking in as much as sixty-five cents."

Some acquaintances were jealous of the brothers' intimacy. Once at Sunday school, a fellow said to Kenneth, "I have known your brother in the biblical sense," and Kenneth and he fought with fists over that. Owen bridged that anecdote with a memory of Kenneth and him singing *The Lost Chord:* "While seated one day at the organ, I was weary and ill at ease, and my fingers wandered idly. . . ." Owen stated explicitly that he never engaged in sex with his brother, but the fantasy had engaged his mind.

"I remember the first time I had a wet dream. I told Kenneth, 'I don't know what's happened to me. I haven't done anything with anyone. I haven't even kissed anybody. You think I have syphilis or gonorrhea?' He said, 'Owen, you've had a wet dream.' All I ever knew about was Yeats and things."

At twelve or thirteen, he and Kenneth gave their last duo performance, possibly shortly before their father's death. Kenneth had reached puberty and didn't want Owen tagging along, dogging his street adventures, too shy to initiate his own.[1]

Kenneth loved young people; he made them laugh. Henry Cleaveland would go with him to after-hours places in Harlem. Their late-night carousing caused trouble. Lef left a six-page letter on Kenneth's breakfast plate:

> The subject of my discussion is not new, but a matter which you have failed to give proper consideration—gangs and continuous traffic. I do not receive anything for the upkeep of the property, but my check. Lillian is ill and cannot do much physical labor. I use but one room, but clean up for the rest of the family. "If the old fool wants the work done, let her do it, she is servile." Yes, I have been a servant, but not necessarily servile.
>
> When that Lincoln [College] and Communist gang start this way, show them the way to the YMCA or the Hudson Boys Club. Last, but not forgotten, Greenwich Village. I thought I would let your conscience be your guide, but I find there is no boundary.[2]

Kenneth, as reformist editor of the *Lincolnian,* had written editorials chastising the university for its failure to insist upon integrated seating at local concerts; he ridiculed the Lincoln fraternities. He supported the loyalist cause in Spain and hosted Langston Hughes when he returned to Lincoln to speak about the Spanish Civil War. Once he crashed the midtown Feagin School of Dramatic Art because he believed he was cracking down the gates of the Confederacy. Mike Alexander (who was one of two Jews enrolled—all the others were southerners who looked upon their acting classes as a finishing school) arrived with Kenneth at Feagin's graduation ceremonies, and a terrible hush descended over the little theater. People formed a line to greet Lucy Feagin, the director, a southern woman in her fifties. As Kenneth and Mike came upon the stage, they could see her shriveling. Kenneth bowed over her hand, told her how lovely the commencement had been, and chatted away. They left with euphoria. The next day Feagin dismissed Alexander from the school.[3]

Owen adored Kenneth for his courage, and with equal passion he despised Nat; when the train arrived in New York, Nat, Jr., met Owen at the station. Said Owen: "I was a schoolteacher. I didn't have to be met, not by him!" Owen's fury grew from knowing that Nat's coming to meet him meant that Kenneth was dying.

On the second floor of 469 Quincy, the doctor had interred Kenneth in an oxygen tent; on the floor, with the tubes snaking in, a cold metal cylinder monitored his breathing. A night nurse had been hired. (Lillian's heart did not permit her to take lengthy duty; Edith and Lef had to work to pay the expenses.) The house had an air of exhaustion. Owen slept in the bed next to his brother and sat beside the tent all day while Cousin Ruby Jewell came to wash Kenneth's pajamas and sheets soaked with sweat.[4]

By February 19 only the oxygen insisted he live. Recalled Owen: "It was a sad time. At 1:30 in the morning, the nurse woke me up, but happened to poke her finger in my eye. The sadness of the time and the great pain in my eye complemented each other. She said, 'I think you better come and see your brother; he's going.' The ritual of death. I remember opening the oxygen tent, and the last thing he said was 'I love you.' I locked myself in the closet and wouldn't come out until Lillian and Edith made me come out."

Kenneth died of lumbar pneumonia at 6 A.M. Owen wrote a threnody for his brother, entitling it "Six O'Clock."

> I have a river in my mind
> Where I have drowned myself
> So many times I feel sharp flesh
> Of water underneath

My eyelids; and between my toes
The minnows smuggle time
And heard it where all shells begin
To grow what children on the shore
Will beg to listen to.
Horizon, water, land
For me at six o'clock:
A scarlet time of sky
That drinks your rim, horizon;
Turns your blue to blood,
Oh sea; absorbs your green,
Oh land: in scarlet time
I'll see the wave,
The quicksand arm ascend
To master and control
All teeth, death-growing hair,
(Goodbye) Each cell that loves.
(Goodbye my dear goodbye).[5]

On Thursday, February 22, Baptist Concord Church overflowed with young men from Lincoln; friends came from Bates; families from Berriman and Quincy streets. Ednah Bethea comforted Owen. The Reverend James Adams of Concord Baptist conducted the ceremony. There was poetry of Shakespeare, Housman, Keats—"to cease upon the midnight with no pain. . . ." Music from Bach, Franck, Tchaikovsky, Sibelius; also "Lil' David Play on Yo' Harp." Scripture from Ecclesiastes, the Lord's Prayer, the Twenty-third Psalm. And a self-portrait Kenneth had written.

Before the body was driven to Evergreen Cemetery, Owen buried the maple coffin beneath armfuls of heather. That night and the next day it snowed. On Saturday, Owen packed his satchel; his sisters reserved a sleeping birth for Owen's journey to Atlanta. From Spelman, he wrote them, "Pullman is more than a Jim Crow car. It's Porterhouse to hamburger. After Washington, I had a drawing room. I set up house right away. Hung up my coats, put up Kenneth's pictures, took out a book and ordered coffee."

Every two or three days, in spite of rehearsals and classes, Owen sent eulogies to Quincy. In part they exorcised the death, in part they confirmed Owen as head of the family. He began to write the *Kenneth*

Poems, something akin to Tennyson's *In Memoriam.* Was not Kenneth his Hallam? And would he not mourn Kenneth's passing with each recurring spring? To pay for the printing, he borrowed thirty dollars from Thomas Pawley, who never expected to see the money again. (Owen repaid the sum but neglected to give Tom a copy.) The booklet, on heavy rag paper, contained six poems and a photograph in profile, as well as Kenneth's self-portrait. Owen's poems issued no challenge to an evil God, no call for a reunion in green pastures. The forceful last lines squarely pronounce his brother dead except in memory.

> That body in the ground
> With the chin set hard against the neck
> Expanding the face,
> The rigid shoulders,
> The hands posed artificially.
> (He had beautiful hands)
> Is awaiting nothing—
> It has its final—horizontal home.
> Even though the sun comes only through the roots
> Like vitamins, it does not matter.
> There will be no resurrection:
> No eager Gabriel trumpet.
> The resurrection is now, in Memory,
> Ringing all her jester bells;
> Is now and for the ever of all my days.[6]

Revised by addition and deletion, and sprinkled with startling images, the *Kenneth Poems,* said Owen, "were the most deeply felt things I have written. I had to write them. I couldn't leave his memory go unnoticed." Six years after Kenneth's death, Owen published the poems in *Powerful Long Ladder* (1946). That same year, Thomas Pawley visited 469 Quincy. The family had prepared dinner with six place settings. Pawley asked, "Is someone else coming?" He was told, "No, it is for Kenneth." Pawley was embarrassed.[7]

After the first death, there is no other? With his mother's death, Owen had declared he no longer believed in God. His lines to Kenneth affirm "there will be no resurrection." This he maintained to the end of his days, and yet . . . and yet, he carried on a lifetime argument with God in much the same way he continued to talk with Kenneth. Sometimes, while drinking alone in his bedroom, he might be heard to say,

"Get out of here. Leave." If one of Edith's guests chanced to hear him, she might confess that her brother talked with Kenneth. Owen affirmed it: "The dead forget the living, but the living cannot forget the dead. They are still here to haunt us. I've tried to erase Kenneth from my mind by writing poems to get him out of my system, but every year the same mourning is there, the same anguish. I want Kenneth to leave. I just don't want to hear his voice anymore."

The 1940 winter faded; spring rushed in. Owen's production of *Medea* went up Saturday, March 15. For the opening, Owen wore one of Kenneth's ties, a pair of his socks, and his hat; he also carried his brother's wallet. The efficacy of the talisman!

Home for Christmas in 1941, Owen wove a holly wreath and took it out to Evergreen Cemetery to place on Kenneth's grave. "I had written a poem, 'Here is holly, for you brother, here is mistletoe ... / But woven in these blanket wreaths is sorrow, pared and wild.' " It had been snowing, and the family had placed no tombstone. Owen couldn't find the grave; he just left the wreath on the snow. The old year turned its corner, and on February 20, Owen mourned the anniversary: "It's nearly the same day, ready for rain and darkness, listening to Tchaikovsky's first concerto ('None but the Lonely Heart')."

As head of the family, Owen provided: He sent ten dollars a month for the grave, five toward the flowers until the bills had been met. By the end of March, thoughts of death and illness brought Owen to pay $2.50 a month for health insurance and to contemplate purchase of a death policy of $2,000.

Death had ridden the Dodsons with a hard saddle, chafing them raw but also cinching them tight to one another. Edith sent gifts, including a pair of trousers that fit beautifully. She clipped items from two or three papers and sent them regularly. She sustained Owen with letters, with gossip, with love. With Kenneth gone, he had her all to himself; he would be her Kenneth. For Edith's birthday, August 12, Owen composed a poem, wooing Edith's affections from Kenneth to himself, and sealed it in three places with purple wax. In part, it reads,

> My sister who stood with me
> When our brother leaned on Death
> And at the apple drop and break in our grief,
> Be that brother in your sisterhood,
> Load my arms with memories

And be a shelter to the breaking heart.
In this frantic year.
You were born in an uneven time:
Close to the first disaster of these years
And now in a new disaster
You are born again with grief and happiness
Standing with each other holding hands
Like naked children in a naked wind.
Before, I was young enough to judge,
Now I am too old to say:
This or that should be
In this or that way.
My pride is for you and her,
We have made plenitude of home,
And just as the tide goes out
It will come again to home.
Let us be here on many days like this,
Weeping or laughing at some commonly remembered jest
Let us be always looking to another star
And re-seeing that last: that is best.

Owen

469[8]

"Be that brother in your sisterhood" a classic likely-unlikely Dodson image. As the head of the house, Owen addressed a major family distress: finding a husband for Edith, who now had passed the magic age. For her thirty-first birthday, Owen, like Tom Winfield in *The Glass Menagerie,* invited an eligible gentleman caller to meet his sister. And Edith, like Laura, discovered that her gentleman caller, Joe Jenkins, an instructor at Spelman, was already engaged to marry a "swell" girl. Owen, a swell sport, wrote an epithalamium for their wedding, which he later published in *Powerful Long Ladder.* As the years passed, Owen and Edith attended more and more functions together; some people who did not know them thought them married.

9

Farewell Atlanta, 1940–41

Within three weeks of Kenneth's funeral, Owen transmuted the storm of his feelings into theatrical splendor. Owen had discovered Dorothy Ateca, statuesque as an opera singer, with a voice pitched thunderously low—a perfect Medea.

Owen began designing, searching for the right fabrics, the perfect colors—the chorus in tones of green; Jason, yellow and white; Creon, rust and green; Medea, blood-red and gold. Spectacle, Owen's hallmark, drained his budget, but each time the great center doors rolled open and the human heart burst onto the stage, insisting upon its arrogance and suffering, something in Owen opened to say "Amen." During his career, Owen unleashed Medea's proud spirit in six productions, including his own *Garden of Time*.

He wrote Countee Cullen, whose translation[1] he had staged: "Before the curtains opened you heard a gong and after that low rumble of drums that built up to a climax of rumbling drums (we had tympany); out of the drum rhythm came a harp, trumpet and organ music which continued as the curtains opened on a black stage. Then a spot came on slowly revealing Medea in a blood red cape that dripped from her shoulders. You saw only her back, but her shadow was huge against the great brazen doors. As the music faded out, drums rolled and from them came Medea's voice (a speech of about fifteen lines that I added), and with her back to the audience still and her cape trailing effectively, she went into the house, her shadow becoming larger as she approached the doors. The music came up and died again. The doors closed on

Medea and the lights came up coldly on the set. Two chorus women passed. The nurse came out and began, 'Those Greeks. . . .' "

Owen's grasp of the essence of theater enabled him to take a dreary adaptation by Cullen and through the magic of spectacle make it live. At the end of the play, after Jason—bowed and broken by grief— had left the stage, "the lights went down, only great green shadows were left on the great doors and quietly at first and then louder and louder the drums came up. The green lights faded out slowly. Only the shine of the doors could be seen, all else was black; the drums faded out and the curtain closed in blackness and silence."[2] As the years passed and he directed Cullen's play again, Owen added and changed more, until finally, after Cullen died in 1948, Owen placed his name beside Cullen's, and renamed the play *Medea in Africa*.[3]

In conjunction with the production, Owen secured Richmond Barthé's statue of Rose McClendon in the role of Serena (*Porgy*)—an eighteen-inch bronze patina. Although McClendon's death had prevented her from playing the role, she would be present at the premiere with her head tilted back in fervor and her hands clasped tight as if enclosing her faith. From the moment of uncrating, Owen loved her. Insolvent or no, when the show closed, Owen carried his bride home.

As spring caressed the lawns of Spelman, Owen, rose in hand, read the "Rubaiyat" to Billie Geter Thomas. A natural aristocrat of the Department of French, Professor Thomas (a close friend of Anne Cooke's) in 1928 had traveled to the Moscow Art Theatre, had seen the tears in the eyes of Alain Locke as he wept in the opera at Leningrad. A trifle bored with provincial Atlanta, Thomas had for each dress, suit, and sweater a pair of matching shoes; when she passed in the hall, her perfume, like her insouciance, lingered. That day on the lawn, as Thomas sprinkled French phrases into the salad of her conversation, she allowed Owen to glimpse the fear that sifted down like bone ash upon the campus.

Driving alone one evening, Thomas made a wide turn (she was known to enjoy a cocktail or two); the police stopped her. Thomas, who might have passed for Asian or white, let them know she was Negro. On the pretext of booking her, the two white cops forced her into the back of the squad car. To stem their advances, Thomas, ever the actress, became old, old enough to be their mother. From which plays she took her lines it is not known, but she talked her way out of the squad car and, trembling, drove home, perhaps for a drink. Owen wrote Countee Cullen, "The South on the whole is one big stink."

On May 22, Owen closed the Atlanta season with *Mary Rose,* a fantasy, recognized as J. M. Barrie's quintessential oedipal wish. In the summer, Cooke returned to direct *What a Life.* (The British school farce had become a popular radio serial, "Henry Aldridge.") Ednah Bethea, who had been away teaching in Edison, Georgia, returned to help Owen stage *RUR,* and then to admire him as Benjamin Backbite in *School for Scandal,* but Owen's need for a helpmate did not translate into a marriage proposal.

Instead, Owen at twenty-six had announced, declared, asserted his passion for perfection of his art. During the rehearsal of the church scene for *Mamba's Daughters,* when the gunman entered, the preacher, played by Ira De A. Reid, attempted in comic overstatement to "climb the wall." With a director's righteous rage, Owen seized a stepladder from the apron and threw it crashing into the auditorium, a dramatic assertion that laid a heavy blanket of silence over the cast. He refused to compromise his art — except for Pres. Florence Read, who read all scripts before production to ascertain their moral fitness for her girls. The president held tight rein on the budget. Dodson had seen the Group Theatre's production of William Saroyan's *My Heart's in the Highlands;* the director, Robert Lewis, had employed a Hammond organ for special effects — the sounds of the sun rising, the gurgling of water, etc. Owen insisted upon an organ for his production, but Read denied him the twenty-five dollars for rental. Counting on the organ to unify the loosely structured play, Owen charged the organ rental to the college anyway. Read attended the performance and congratulated Owen, never mentioning his misdemeanor, but four years later, when Spelman produced Owen's play *Everybody Join Hands* (a spectacle concerning Chiang Kai-shek's struggle against the Japanese), in place of royalties Read sent Owen a note: "You will notice that twenty-five dollars has been deducted from your royalties for organ rental."[4]

Puritan closeness fortified by hard work permeated the history of Spelman. God had sent missionaries to rescue the souls of the poor and the black, and no frivolity, no lack of decorum, no idleness would stand in His way. The faculty bitched about Read's penny-pinching (a second towel in the faculty dorm could not be obtained without the president's approval), yet Spelman could not function without parsimony, even unto stinginess.

The annual Founder's Day celebration, mocked in genre by Ralph Ellison's *Invisible Man,* elicited Owen's serious attention. Invited to write a Founder's Day poem, he composed the encomium "Miss Packard and Miss Giles," certainly the best of several occasion poems he composed during his career. The founders, he wrote,

> . . . made their crucifix far more
> Than ornament; they wrestled with denial
> And pinned him to the floor. . . .[5]

No scandal ever threatened funding. Youth was still a time of innocence. One day, a girl came to the dean of women, weeping over a self-diagnosed pregnancy. Mrs. Lyons asked her how she knew, and the girl told her that she had walked down the lane at night, and her boyfriend had put his arm around her. The dean replied that there had been no conception in that embrace. The girl rushed on, "But he kissed me and put his tongue in my mouth!"

For Christmas presents, Owen ordered Cullen's *The Lost Zoo,* a children's book with illustrations by Charles Sebree. The previous summer at Harold Jackman's apartment Owen had briefly shaken the artist's hand, and Sebree's touch had lingered. Owen wrote: "Charles entered the room like an angel full of grace. His large black soft eyes compelled you. He had a smile like half the sunshine of Florida. He gave me the impression that he was shy and forward at the same time, as if he were doing a cake walk with his emotions. I wanted to talk to him, but he excused himself." Sebree recalled Owen less romantically: "Owen talked well about theater. Sort of an enthused boy or little bald man. He was quite young, I think twenty-something [26]."[6] But whatever the two men's first impressions, their careers and passions soon interlocked, and Owen would take Charles home to meet his family.

Owen worried for Lillian's heart: "All we can do is the best for her. We all might as well grab all the sensible happiness we can because there's a cloud forming over America." In August, Owen returned to Brooklyn. Only during his vacations could Edith take time off from nursing Lillian, now chronically ill.

The fall of 1941, Owen's last year in Atlanta, had a bright side— the Dodson debts were paid off. Beginning in October, he told Edith, there would be some money for saving. And recognition still whispered at his door: the editor of *Theatre Arts,* Rosamond Gilder, had selected his poem "Guitar."

For their swan songs, Cooke and Dodson mounted three demanding plays. With Raphael McIver as Thomas à Becket, *Murder in the Ca-*

thedral became an accessibly lucid production. Years later, at a reception in Washington, D.C., Owen met the poet: "I sat next to T. S. Eliot, and we just looked at each other, English-fashion. Finally, I said, 'Mr. Eliot, I think you might like to know that we produced your play in Georgia, before an audience who had not even seen a play before; some were deeply moved and some wept.' And he said, 'Indeed.' That captured the whole spirit of T. S. Eliot." Nonetheless, Eliot's play indeed had an influence on Owen's writing.

The second production, Coffin and Cowen's *Family Portrait,* the drama of Jesus, Joseph, and Mary, portrayed the Holy Family as intimately human. Owen played young Judas, and his exposure to this play became an inspiration twenty-five years later for his song cycle *The Confession Stone,* wherein the Holy Family (including God) is portrayed in the most human terms.

From the over 100 plays that Owen directed, the single surviving director's prompt script[7] is for Anton Chekhov's *The Cherry Orchard.* The script confirmed the testimony of actors: Owen's training at Yale had emphasized the writer's need to rewrite, so Owen rewrote Euripides and Chekhov to fit his stage. In his cast, Marion Douglas played Mme. Ranevsky and the young Louis Peterson (who in 1954 would write *Take a Giant Step* for Broadway) played Marion, an officer. The remarkable production premiered in three weeks, just before Thanksgiving. After the play closed, no sooner was the set taken down, and costumes put away, than *Life* magazine arrived and asked that the whole be reassembled for pictures. Owen did it, but the photos were never published.

In the summer of 1940, France fell, and the Battle of Britain began. President Read, to strengthen the fiber of the youth so that they might be better able to face war, hardship, and destruction, initiated knitting lessons among the girls coupled with a program to pick up papers on the campus.[8] Owen mocked her war effort but never questioned the rising tide of war. When the head of the student council at Morehouse approached him to speak to the Morehouse men about the impending crisis, Owen wrote a poem, "Iphigenia," a reference to Agamemnon's daughter who was sacrificed so the Argive fleet could sail to its death and glory. Owen said of the poem, "No one has ever reprinted it, but I like it as much as any poem I have written. I wanted to say that the world is corroded, and the idea that fighting for an ideal will not make it any better."

Out of the sin of man
Comes the sin of mankind,
And we are corroded,
We are corroded, O my dear.

. . . .

We are on the altar,
Sacrificial and elect
To feel the steady knife:
The knife unshaped by us, but the knife:
The final spilling, O my dear.

. . . .

We will die but we are innocent.
Go to the records, read the cause,
Sandpaper the sky to erase the blood.
Doomsday will shed doomsday
On those who deal another destruction
From another sky:
O my dear, O my dear, O my dear.[9]

The men of Morehouse must have sat in silence; their teacher, their leader had not played "Stars and Stripes Forever," but had instead laid upon their hearts the slaughter of innocents: those who rain death from the skies will receive death from the skies. And indeed, one of Owen's own beloved actors, Walter Westmoreland, who joined the air cadets at Tuskegee, was shot down on the Italian front.

Owen published "Iphigenia" in *Powerful Long Ladder* and dedicated it to Ednah Bethea. At first glance it hardly seems a poem one might give to a loved one, but, as we shall see, he later "sacrificed" Ednah to the war, and perhaps Owen also viewed himself as Iphigenia. For the first time in history, Americans in their local cinemas experienced the high whine of the Stuka dive-bombers, a sight and sound that pierced fear into the heart. Like Kenneth, Owen had begun to internalize the world's pain, to mingle his own anxieties with those abroad; the personal reference "O my dear" places the poem in the tradition of Matthew Arnold's "Dover Beach."

The suffering poured out in poem after poem. "Pain Is a Monument" wailed with a lyric that anticipated Bob Dylan:

I saw a boy lynched once; he did not resist
I saw a man sing while his wife was raped

> and now a new war is brazen
> and my color is my monument.

The local draft board classified Dodson 3A (temporarily deferred). His anger, so savage in the poems, in his life remained amorphous and inarticulate. To his sister he wrote, "Somehow, Edith, I feel lonely. I don't know exactly for what, but the feeling is there. Perhaps it's just the distance from home and all the things I love. Anyway, I'm working on my writing and before I go into the army, if I have to go soon, I ought to have several plays and poems in the market. Perhaps it's living with the people and poems I create that makes me draw into myself. Well, I suppose everyone feels alone sometimes."[10]

He plunged desperately into Christmas revelry. He asked Edith for records—Brahms, Brahms, Brahms—and planned a post-Christmas breakfast for twenty-six friends, including Braithwaite, Cullen, Jackman, Barthé, Heath, and Du Bois. They would have waffles, Canadian bacon, fish cakes (Lef's specialty), orange juice and coffee on Sunday, December 28, at 11:00 A.M. "Do you think Lillian's too sick to have the breakfast?" he asked. He bought gifts of toilet water, powder, and a grand nightgown to placate Lillian; perhaps he would also have her antique watch repaired and the family copy of *Pilgrim's Progress* rebound for her. He told Edith, "I have another small gift for her [Lillian]: Ednah! I had a letter from her—a long and swell letter. I think we'll have to pay her fare up—I just don't have the money and you need yours. Her mother's sending us the usual greens. I bought her a handsome, soft sweater." He wrote this letter on Sunday, December 7, 1941, the day that was to "live in infamy."

Owen's fondness for Ednah stemmed from her devotion to him, and from her sensitivity to poetry and other art (she herself had considerable talent); this affection remained somewhat dormant until Lillian, the pillar of the family, collapsed, perhaps dying. A new, strong female presence would stabilize the house—a nurse for Lillian, a companion for Edith, a wife for himself. Why not? His friend Countee Cullen had found Ida; Carl Van Vechten had Fania; Glidden Parker had found Harriet, even fathered a son. Ednah loved him, admired him, wished to care for him; she even resembled his mother. Like Priscilla before her, Ednah, if she noticed Owen's true sexual preference, first brushed it aside, perhaps believing that Owen needed only a good woman to love him enough. Owen sent down roots: he asked Ednah to marry him.

10

Anchors Aweigh, 1940–42

Ednah accepted Owen's ring, a curious ivory band, with the understanding that until the war ended the couple would not march to the altar. She took a new job in Washington, D.C., working on Series E savings bonds, and Owen moved from Atlanta to Hampton Institute in Virginia, where in September 1940 he had delivered an address on theater, radio, and film. The institute's new president, Malcolm S. MacLean, liked what he heard, and in November traveled to Atlanta to see Owen's production of *The Cherry Orchard*. MacLean found Owen's show "swell." Owen responded: "I hasten to answer your swell letter." MacLean then invited Owen to visit the newly formed Department of Communications at Hampton. Owen met the president's wife and wrote that "She is really swell." MacLean responded: "Your letter of April 3 was swell." And on the swelling of mutual enthusiasm, Hampton hired Owen with a telegram dated, improbably enough, February 30, 1941. His new position paid $2,000, a raise of $500—really swell.

Hampton Institute lay between the York and the James rivers, eighteen miles from the U.S. Naval Station at Newport News, Virginia. Hampton, an old settlement of mixed Indian, white, and black population, had been burned early in the Civil War. At the war's close, General Samuel Chapman Armstrong, the son of an Irish-Scots missionary—with help from the American Missionary Society, the blessings of General Howard, and funds from the Freedmen's Bureau—founded a training school for freedmen.

From 1868 to 1940, the school had changed little. Booker T. Washington, Hampton's most prestigious alumnus, preached the gospel of hard work, and the institute had trained hundreds to read, write, and cipher, giving them the skills to earn a livelihood. Christian and consecrated, hundreds graduated. By 1940, agriculture, carpentry, and bricklaying had sustained the curriculum and careers for seventy-three years, but future graduates would need radio, film, and television.

With some prodding from the Julius Rosenwald Fund, Hampton hired a liberal white Minnesotan to propel the institute into the twentieth century—not an easy task, for neither the alumni nor the local gentry approved of MacLean, who permitted faculty members to smoke in their offices. It was whispered that he served alcohol in the presidential manor, and that he even had asked the faculty to call him "Prexie." The new regime lasted two years before MacLean fled to the military. But in the meantime, who better to head the Department of Communications than the rising bright star from the Yale Drama School?

On arrival, the grandson of Virginia slaves paused at the edge of the quiet summer campus to acknowledge the Emancipation Oak, where Blacks had first heard freedom. (Today, timbered beams, like crutches under old and weary arms, support the oak's branches.) The brief and sinuous campus streets were named for the school's founders: Shore, Armstrong, Frissell. At the campus's center sat the theater auditorium, Robert Curtis Ogden Hall, with its three Roman arches facing the central maidan. At its sides were the chapel and the dorms—an accumulation of Gothic nightmares, gracious Victorian homes, and "modern" Georgian brick. Platoons of petunias beneath spiny branches of crape myrtle guarded the president's home. Holly Inn Dining Hall fronted the faculty dorm, named without irony "The Monastery." Owen had written MacLean, "For the past ten years I have lived in one room and haven't been able to spread my pictures or my books or myself or entertain students and friends at all. I would like something like the apartment Mr. Apter has."[1] (He had a grand piano.) Owen had to settle for a single, Monastery 101. He later secured a private room in the house of Prof. Collis Davis.

The students liked their bouncy, pipe-smoking professor. (In his room, Owen kept Pall Malls because they looked so elegant on the table.) He taught his beginners how to sit and move onstage, then plunged into summer production with *Divine Comedy,* a choice that impressed the locals that they did indeed have a famous playwright on campus. The play opened in three weeks, using twenty-five technicians and seventy-five actors.

Owen soon discovered Hilda Moses Simms. At age twenty-four, five feet four inches tall, weighing 108 pounds, Simms had come to Hampton as part of the MacLean team. Although Simms's theater experience had been confined to the Phillis Wheatley House and the Homewood Theatre in Minneapolis, Owen promptly cast her as Hedda Gabler, describing the actress as a "restrained bobcat." When Simms announced that she intended to be a Broadway star, Prof. Arthur Davis replied, "Miss Simms, you are beautiful, but you don't sing and you don't dance and you are too white."[2] Two years and two months later she starred in *Anna Lucasta* at the Mansfield Theatre at 47th Street and Broadway.

Keenly conscious that he had left his cadre of skilled actors behind at Spelman, Owen invited Gordon Heath to Hampton, awarding him a stipend of $125. Tall and lean, his Shakespearean voice resonant with "brown bread and butter" diction, Heath inspired respect and admiration for his portrayal of *Pygmalion*'s Professor Higgins, who pointedly asked the Tidewater folk, "Why can't the English teach their children how to speak?"

Owen had announced a schedule of plays for the season that included Maxwell Anderson's *Winterset;* his own uncompleted play *Eaters of the Dust,* a Hampton "Self-Portrait"; and *Arsenic and Old Lace.* However, when the curtain came down on October 31, the cast sang "Anchors Aweigh." Owen had unexpectedly enlisted![3]

Hampton had initiated a naval training program under the command of Lieutenant Commander E. H. Downes, an officer who had come through the Naval Academy, then dropped out of the service to become a school superintendent. When the hostilities began, he returned to Hampton. Downes combined two rare qualities: as part of the naval brass hierarchy, he could obtain special equipment, programs, and dispensations for his men; at the same time, he was an educator with humanist proclivities. In June 1942, the Navy began accepting Blacks for general service in the reserve components, 277 each week. The previous policy had limited people of color to the sole position of "messman."[4] On September 8, Owen signed up for the V-6, a reserve unit that could lead to an officer program but not an officer-training program per se.

Why had Owen changed his mind? Barely six months earlier, he had read a poem to the men about to be inducted:

> We are on the altar,
> Sacrificial and elect
> To feel the steady knife:
> The knife unshaped by us. . . .

Had he abandoned pacifism? Certainly he had no motive to leave teaching: "Some of the happiest days in my teaching career were at Hampton, a serene place, a quiet place." That same summer, Owen wrote Carl Van Vechten, "I saw today a sign reading 'Air Raid Shelter.' The sign pointed straight to the entrance of the National Cemetery."[5]

How then did Owen come to enlist?

Several factors: The draft board had ranked Owen as 3A; at any time, his status could be changed to 1A. Then, too, the naval training center on campus, with its black men brisk in their middies, may have made the military appear benign, more of the spectacle Owen loved in theater. And perhaps his engagement to Ednah? No date was set, but military service would put distance between Owen and the event, even though he himself had courted that embrace. He may have also hoped that by enlisting, he would be kept at Hampton. Finally, the Nazis' victories had altered his politics.

In March 1941, the journalist Hans Habe published in *The Nation* an eyewitness account of Nazi racism: "The Germans' hatred of the colored people seemed deeply rooted. Dozens of current German periodicals, pamphlets, and newspapers portrayed the Negroes as cannibals. They tried to convince the German soldiers that if they did not kill the Negroes [French African colonials], they risked having their throats cut. Black prisoners told me that the German soldiers fought them much more bitterly than they did us."

The four-page, double-column article detailed the cruel treatment the Africans received in the camps. No doubt remained about the destiny the master race had planned for the darker peoples of the world.[6] Owen composed "The Decision," and in his book placed it immediately following the "sacrifice" poem he had read to the men at Morehouse. The final three verses:

> If your final home will be
> Where brother knows brother,
> Chews meat, breaks bread
> Together with his brother;

> Or where a man will trample again
> His neighbor, shake no hands,
> Scorn fellowship, light fires
> Of dark bones and flesh to warm his hands.
>
> Who are these among you
> Longing for peace among all men,
> Longing for each homesick heart
> To make a pilgrimage among all men?[7]

According to Owen, "There was a great fear that we would be overrun by Germany, and I was going to do anything I could." Like other patriots, Owen looked about for a branch of the military where he might both serve his country and safely pass the dangerous night. At the age of twenty-eight, he enlisted as an electrician's mate, even though S2c (seaman second class) Dodson had no interest in and small talent for technology of any kind.

Enlisting was simple, induction a mess. On October 31, as the last chords of "Anchors Aweigh" faded, Owen packed his books and clothes, paid all his debts, and, expecting to go directly to Great Lakes Naval Training Station near Chicago, reported for duty at Newport News. When Dodson showed them his papers, they told him that he had the wrong date. Intending to enter the service, he had brought almost no money. His friend John Hall found him a room in Williamsburg, where segregation prevented him from attending the historical concerts.

The day after Armistice Day, Owen received his physical. Vision: 15/20; height: 5 ft. 7¼ in.; weight: 167 lbs.; chest expansion: 2½ in.; ½-in. birthmark on the left thigh; complexion: Negro; hair: Negro; eyes: Negro. The doctor did not ascertain his pulse or his blood pressure or if Owen had sugar or albumen in his Negro blood, but scored his form with an 85 percent and summarily stamped it *"ACCEPTED."*[8]

Recalled Owen: "We boarded the train for Great Lakes Naval Training Center. They got out the oldest, the messiest, the funkiest, the shoddiest train — filled with white and black but segregated because we were going to a segregated camp. The food was bad. There was nothing to drink, nothing to alleviate the fear and the tension but talk of hospitals and dying. The word was going around that to be sent to the South Pacific was certain death. So these young men talked about fucking [half were under nineteen], began to tell all the dirty jokes, and then they had cock raising contests. Someone had a tape measure that appeared from somewhere and they measured their hard-ons. I said, 'What have I gotten into?' Are these the black people that I am going to be associated with? Almost all of them came from southern states and there was a general air of ignorance."

Suddenly Owen found himself submerged (to borrow a phrase of the sixties) in the "black experience." All were enlisted men, many of whom had joined for the luxury of eating three solid meals a day while earning fifty dollars a month. After spending a miserable day and night on the miserable train, on November 13 they stumbled off at Great Lakes to join the Eighteenth Regiment in a camp that had but three months earlier been named Camp Morrow, but was now called Camp Robert Smalls.[9] As Owen's eyes traveled over the camp's high fence with barbed wire on top, he felt his commitment to save the world for democracy withering: "They are putting us in a concentration camp."

Lt. Comdr. Daniel W. Armstrong, USNR (reputedly a good friend of Eleanor Roosevelt's) welcomed the men. Armstrong, son of the founder of Hampton Institute, had grown up in Summerville, South Carolina, and shared its white values. All officers, including petty officers, were white. Owen commented, "I guess they thought because Armstrong was the son of the founder of a black college, he would know Negroes better than anybody."

Armstrong did not appreciate the reforms that President MacLean had introduced at Hampton, so Owen didn't mention MacLean. Owen determined that he would pass through basic training by distinguishing himself from the 40 percent of the men whose literacy skills tested below fourth grade.[10] He was not an intellectual alone; segregation had amassed university professors, artists, and musicians: Frank Silvera, the resonant-voiced actor; Harlan Jackson, the painter; Herman Hill, the musical director. Said Owen: "We had some of the best minds — teachers. We had the best band, the best choir; we had so much talent because segregation had brought us all together." These middle-class intellectuals became the troublemakers, the malcontents. Of them, none exhibited more independence than Charles Sebree. Slight of stature and braving a bit of a mustache, for seven years in Chicago (1933–39) he had danced, designed, and toured with Katherine Dunham, but Sebree's major talent was as a visual artist — painting and drawing.[11]

The first day of basic training, Sebree and Dodson were marching at the end of the line. A man named Lear marched at the head, and he never turned back to see who was and was not there. When they got to the obstacle course, there was a great high wall they were supposed to climb over. As soon as Sebree and Dodson saw the wall, they did a hup right and a hup right and turned to the left and marched behind some barracks. Dodson claimed they never went through any of that basic training. "I guess there were so many of us there that they didn't notice."

Sebree, "a taffy-colored Icarus," held faithful to his astrological sign—secretive, sexual, creative, capable of deep friendship, sensitive to the fragility of human nature—a Scorpio. But he also had become watchful, manipulative, as an artist must to survive in the courts of the Medicis, and on occasion he would lash out with a deadly sting.[12] At a later date, John Carlis, a Chicago artist, recalled several scorpion episodes: "He once went into a fancy restaurant, Henrici's, without money to pay for the dinner. When finished, he flicked some cigarette ashes onto the dessert and began screaming, 'You're trying to serve me food that had cigarette ashes in it!' "[13] Sebree, just the Scorpio for Sagittarius Owen to fall in and out of love with.

Within a week of Owen's arrival, the *Great Lakes Bulletin* announced: "Leading Negro Playwright in Navy as 'Boot.' " Lieutenant Commander Armstrong summoned the playwright to his office. A fifty-year-old white man with a widow's peak of graying hair, he spoke with a Carolina accent. He asked Owen, "What will we do with you? I know we don't want to pay you to go to cook and baker's school. What would you like to do while you are here?"

"I want to direct a drama group," replied Owen. Armstrong consented. He said, "How about every week, a fifteen-minute show, showing the lives of the great naval heroes?" And that's exactly what Owen did.

On December 8, he submitted a proposal for a Department of Drama, himself as head. He suggested seven items: a company talent competition "just as they have athletic competition"; a standing dramatic club to present skits or plays once every eight weeks; plays written for Great Lakes Radio; a speech choir; a writing laboratory; a vespers program each Sunday; and the idea Armstrong saluted, "a series of skits on military heroism as well as outstanding events from Negro life

(Robert Smalls, General Armstrong [*sic*], Dr. George Carver), will be presented every Wednesday as a part of the Happy Hour."[14]

Dodson and Sebree (whom Owen requested help him) had lucked out. With an entire barracks to themselves, all they had to do was to march to breakfast; then Owen was supposed to write the play; then they would march to lunch; then they would work on the play and march to dinner; and at 6 P.M., Mr. Lear would march the sailors over to rehearse.

Eight days after receiving permission, Owen presented "Robert Smalls," a fifteen-minute radio documentary on the Civil War's black naval hero. It became the prototype for his other Navy plays—*John P. Jones, Lord Nelson, Old Ironsides,* and *Don't Give Up the Ship*—which interwove song and choral speech with tableau and minimal movement. Every week, a new production.[15]

Three days before Christmas, Carl Van Vechten sent Owen a harmonica. (He never learned to play a lick.) The Navy took Owen's mustache, and then took more. For the first Christmas ever in his life, there would be no family ritual. "I never liked Bing Crosby, but one night they played 'I'm Dreaming of a White Christmas' and I was all in tears."[16] His '42 Christmas poem reflected his mood:

> Now we go to make a present for the Lord
> of the liberty and peace and strength stored
> in our young dark bodies. These we give
> that our children, this earth, the mystic
> child again may live.

With a production every week, January evaporated. The end of boot camp coincided with Negro History Week, and on February 7, Sunday vesper hour, Owen climaxed his series with *The Ballad of Dorrie Miller,* which premiered in the drill hall. With music by E. Hathcock and movement by Charles Sebree, the program listed "The Speakers, The Singers, The Movers." The Movers belonged to Sebree who had taken the boys from Georgia and from the South Side of Chicago and taught them to dance. Sebree knew that if the men realized they were dancing, they wouldn't and couldn't do it, so he told his seamen they were doing extended drill programs.

In real life, the black hero of Dodson's choral ballad, a messman named Dorrie Miller, in the face of serious fire on the USS *West Virginia* during the Japanese attack on Pearl Harbor, had seized a machine gun and shot down four enemy planes; for this he was awarded the Navy Cross. Miller's bravery fortuitously served the Blacks who were struggling to change the Navy policy of restricting them to ships' galleys ("waiters and bellboys going to sea"), and, at the same time, served the Navy in its propaganda efforts to enlist black patriotism. In his theater ballad, Owen came down on the side of we-too-sing-America:

> There are millions of Dorrie Millers living
> And millions of Dorrie Millers dead.
> They are signs, signals, tokens, that free men
> Will rise and claim this earth again.

Ironically, five months following his citation, Miller died in the torpedoing of the escort carrier *Liscome Bay,* on which he still served white officers as a messman. Owen's piece received national recognition when the magazine *Theatre Arts* printed part of the text with a Sebree illustration.

At the end of basic training, given a nine-day furlough, Owen raced home to 469 Quincy, pulling with him Charles, who remembered: "Lillian and Edith were keeping the house. I didn't feel comfortable there at all. It was so clean, well-appointed, and the dishes and the silver, and there was a lady named Lef who had a wicked kind of control. It wasn't a happy place."[17]

Van Vechten agreed to show *Garden of Time* to Judith Anderson for the star role of Miranda (Medea). His mentor also introduced him to Mme. Chiang Kai-shek, then touring America drumming up money and support for the Nationalist cause. When Mme. Chiang said that Mao and the Communists were atheistic savages burning the gentle Chinese Christians from their homes, Congress believed it. Dodson too. He wrote Carl, "She is really a great person. The kind you follow and who makes a great halo light about the future."[18]

Mme. Chiang had fired Owen's poetic imagination; he immediately began *Everybody Join Hands,* a short play about China to let "the boys here know more about this people who have bled for six years, who scratched the Burma Road out with their fingernails."

Writing plays for the Navy could not distract Owen from his poems, and when his friends Arthur Davis and Sterling Brown edited their anthology *The Negro Caravan* with Ulysses Lee, they included two by Owen — "Miss Packard and Miss Giles" and "Cradle Song." The editors noted that Margaret Walker and Owen were the most recent newcomers to "the ranks of poets who are socially aware." The inclusion of Owen's poems in *The Negro Caravan,* the largest and most representative anthology of black writing ever published until then (1941), moved Owen into the official canon of black literature, and periodicals began to request his work.[19]

Dodson's long poem "mocking" the anniversary of the Emancipation Proclamation, "Seventy-five Years Is a Long Stretch of Land," appeared in the University of Chicago's *Trend.* Using a freedom of line and image, Dodson varied the line lengths and employed unexpected, unannounced, and even bizarre conceits that linger in the memory:

> This is a rusty time to sing in:
> A rusty broken hingeless time:
> The temperamental doors of liberty undone,
> Undone and lying before the lintels
> of the doorway in this winter,
> Like dead gangsters.
> . . . .
> Stop the baritone notes of time:
> Time who has one foot stamped in the past,
> The other pressed in the belly of the future:
> . . . .
> From this present
> Will the future be sent
> Like a trained pigeon
> Flying from tomorrow
> To now and this sorrow:
> A terrible message waving from his neck.

In the middle of the poem, Owen introduces an abrupt change, switching to a blues ballad about Mary mourning for the death of her baby Jesus, a theme that he would develop twenty years later in *The Confession Stone:*

> Mary, sweet Mary
> Moaning by the cross tree,
> Never really understood
> The tricks of Galilee
> The valley so silent

An' the mountain so tall;
I don't reckon ma baby
Comin' back at all.

Hard upon the ballad's ending, which leaves Mary standing at the grave with a handful of dirt, Dodson concluded with a virulent attack on white racists:

Look!
There are more dogs in Georgia
Than cats, in fifty years in the catacombs of Rome.
Mangy, terror-large-eyed, vicious, inferiority-
complexed, singing, pleading, elemental as Georgia clay.
They bark in the listening night,
They run in packs through the rays of the lantern
Georgia-Moon: lesser wolves;
Their direction not mapped.

When Dodson returned to Great Lakes, a new assignment to a special training school should have been waiting. Those who qualified (about one-third) would become gunners' mates, radiomen, quartermasters, signalmen, yeomen, storekeepers, aviation machinists and metalsmiths, shore patrolmen, and cooks and bakers. The others would serve as messmen or in labor battalions, loading ammunition onto ships. Lieutenant Commander Armstrong, however, retained Dodson, Sebree, and Silvera on base to perform more "morale" plays. Once a month they must produce one longer piece on the allies and the enemy, and they would do the shorter hero pieces in between. Owen wrote six more plays—producing five of them before he was discharged.

To mount *Everybody Join Hands*,[20] the Chinese play, Owen initiated a search for properties and costumes. "Once Sebree and I went to Waukegan to shop. Charles said, 'Let's get us some rum.' I said, 'You know we are not supposed to drink on the base.' (I should have known what he was like, but I hadn't really listened to people.) So we had this rum at the bottom of the bag and he said, 'Owen, you know I have been carrying this stuff all the way, and you haven't even offered to carry it.' When we got to the gate, if the guard found it, I would be chastised. The guard said, 'What have you got in there?' I said, 'Some things for the play.' He said, 'Let me see them.' Sebree said, 'Don't you dare touch the commander's things,' and he snatched them away and strode through the gate. He got us out of many scrapes, and he got us out of the Navy."

The anecdote reflects the rift that was already growing between the two artists, a rift that widened over the years, and about which both men, like an old married couple, kept account books. Sebree's version of smuggling liquor claimed that Owen had hidden a bottle of vodka in the prop basket and given it to Sebree to carry. When the guard began a search, Charles told him, "Go ahead and look through the commander's things; he'd be delighted to know you went through his things," and the guard stopped.

In any case, liberal passes from the commander—to Chicago, an hour's train ride on the North Shore Line—encouraged Owen and Charles's absence from the base. They attended the American Ballet Theatre, which featured Nora Kaye and Hugh Laing. (The latter, with his famous pelvis-thrust-forward walk, thrilled Owen in *Pillar of Fire;* Owen began collecting Laing photographs from Van Vechten.) At the Chicago Opera House Owen saw *Aida.* For lighter evenings he and Sebree bar-hopped nightclubs on the South Side: the De Lisa and the Rhumboogie.

With Sol Gordon,[21] an Army air cadet, he saw Ben Hecht's pageant *We Shall Never Die:* "Sol was not only bright and educated, but he knew how to get tickets to the opera, all the machinations to enjoying himself in Chicago. At the climax of the pageant there must have been a thousand in this great auditorium of men and women with candles, dressed in costumes of all ages in which Jews had existed; they called off the names of the great ones: Moses and Jeremiah. The whole place glittered with candlelight, and it was tremendously moving, and I realized that we were not the only people who had suffered. So I wrote the poem for Sol, "Jonathan's Song, a Negro Saw the Jewish Pageant, 'We Will Never Die.' "

> I am a part of this:
> Four million starving
> And six million dead:
> I am flesh and bone of this.
>
> I have starved
> In the secret alleys of my heart
> And died in my soul
> Like Ahab at the white whale's mouth.

The twisted cross desire
For final annihilation
Of my race of sufferers:
I am Abel, too.

Because my flesh is whole
Do not think that it signifies life.
I am the husk, believe me.
The rest is dead, remember.

I am part of this
Memorial to suffering
Militant strength:
I am a Jew.

Jew is not a race
Any longer—but a condition.
All the desert flowers have thorns;
I am bleeding in the sand.

Take me for your own David:
My father was not cruel,
I will sing your psalms,
I have learned them by heart.

I have loved you as a child,
We pledged in blood together.
The union is not strange.
My brother and my lover.

There was a great scent of death
In the garden when I was born.
Now it is certain.
Love me while you can.

The wedding is powerful as battle,
Singular, dread, passionate, loud,
Ahab screaming and the screaming whale
And the destination among thorns.

Love is a triple desire:
Flesh, freedom, hope:
No wanton thing is allowed.

I will sing thy psalms, all thy psalms,
Take me while you can.

Owen scavenged several of his best lines and embroidered them into later poems; nonetheless, "Jonathan's Song" remains an aroused river that flows from the suffering of the two races into the rapids of a personal passion, at once sacred and sensual. In Othello's words, "She lov'd me for the dangers I had pass'd / And I lov'd her that she did pity them."

Meanwhile, his monthly dramas marched forward. For April, *He Planted Freedom,* an encomium to the commander's father, Gen. Samuel Chapman Armstrong, became the camp's documentary. For Owen, celebrating the commander's father was more than apple polishing. The fact that a white Moses had led Blacks out of the bondage of illiteracy could never be a debate about color; the literacy bestowed was not an internal colonialist policy, but one of racial progress.

By the summer of 1943, visitors from other regiments and guests from Chicago were calling for reservations to see performances of the reruns. On June 6, Owen launched his best but most politically dangerous production, *Freedom the Banner,* a dramatic hymn to the struggle of the Russian people against the Nazis. With a blast of music and drums, sailors dressed as Soviet soldiers burst through the six doors of the hall. As an air-raid siren sounded, ten flag bearers marched across the stage, singing; their red banners, as large as bedsheets, waved over them like hot breath. Some, with rifles aloft, suggested the tomb of Lenin. A vivid red light shone on Soviet citizens singing:

> Russia is always.
> Red is our color,
> The blood of martyrs,
> These, no other.
> . . . .
> Nothing can stop us,
> Our endless people
> Moving forward
> Tidal wave [against] evil
>
> (While the people sing, the announcer speaks)
> . . . .
> Russia! Whoever shall ascend into her vastness

> Shall have a pure heart and a clean mind:
> Whoever shall love her people
> Shall love the bright wilderness of the human spirit!
> Nothing can avail against these comrade crusaders
> Who drove the money changers from the temple
> Whose dream is rooted in granite and steel
> Whose reality is a sermon on the mount.[22]

Then the Nazis appear. Women and children die; guerrilla fighters emerge through the snows; Natashya, the flower, falls, but the people keep coming and coming: "The people move off as in procession — banners by their sides waving red and the music swells up wonderfully."

The production, triumphant; the commander, furious: "What the hell did you think you were doing, Dodson?" Owen replied, "You told me to write about the allies." Armstrong said, "I didn't tell you to include Russia!" Probably Owen knew as little about Stalin as he knew about Mme. Chiang. True, Sebree and Silvera had attended meetings of the leftist John Reed Club, and Owen may well have tagged along, but a communist, or even a sympathizer, Owen was not. A poet, he saw no reason not to put his words in service of the Chinese and Russian people.

Outside the camp, forces contributed to the tension inside, and the Detroit race riot spilled into Camp Robert Smalls. The summer of '43 had initiated race rebellions in a number of American cities, including Los Angeles; Beaumont, Texas; Newark, New Jersey; and Mobile, Alabama. After a decade of depression, high wages in the war industries had lured hundreds of thousands of poor Blacks and whites to the North. In Detroit, 50,000 Blacks competed with nearly a half-million whites for jobs and housing in the "Arsenal for Democracy." As inevitable as summer, trouble erupted. On a Sunday afternoon, fights broke out between teenagers. Rumors of atrocities followed. After thirty-four citizens had died, Mayor Jeffries called in the National Guard. As one old black woman said, "There ain't no North anymore. Everything now is South."

The Navy reacted to the news by denying the black men access to all newspapers and by confiscating all radios. In the barracks, ugly fears and rumors suppurated. Many had mothers, fathers, and friends in Detroit. Sebree recalled, "They sent special people out to talk to us. Some of the men threw rocks. It was quite a shock. It depressed Owen greatly." Confined to barracks, Sebree chewed on his bitterness: "We had no black officers; some of the men tried to climb over the fence, but they fell back with their hands bleeding like stigmata. To see them in corners weeping, and to see how little the officers cared! It was one of those times I felt a real fear in the camp. I felt the officers and the commander were as bad as the Nazis."

In the midst of this turmoil, Owen began, and in two days completed, almost without revision, "Black Mother Praying in the Summer of 1943" (later he shortened the title for publication). He stated that even the most illiterate listeners, no matter their color, knew exactly what he was talking about. The first two stanzas show why the poem has been so popular in programs of oral poetry:

> My great God, You been a tenderness to me,
> Through the thick and through the thin;
> You been a pilla to my soul;
> You been like the shinin light a mornin in the black dark,
> A elevator to my spirit.
>
> Now there's a fire in this land like a last judgment,
> And I done sat down by the rivers of Babylon
> And wept deep when I remembered Zion,
> Seein the water that can't quench fire
> And the fire that burns up rivers.
> Lord, I'm gonna say my say real quick and simple: . . .

Black people loved it. White liberals needed it. Owen read it on radio, and it was printed and reprinted. "Black Mother Praying" became the most popular poem he ever wrote. Not everyone, though, thought it his best. W. H. Auden gave him sound criticism: "I feel you should beware of exploiting 'dialect'; the immediate emotional appeal, as in Synge, is always in danger of becoming too easy a trick. It would be all right if you were a naif writer who naturally spoke in it, but you aren't. Above all, I think it is a mistake when your theme is specifically racial conflict because it sounds 'stagey' and the subject is much too serious for that."[23]

Owen never wrote in dialect again.[24]

In July, Owen mounted *A Tropical Fable,* "a musical about the American tropics" in which Charles leapt through a paper wall of painted flowers as the legendary Babalu. Sebree had borrowed heavily from Katherine Dunham's *L'Ag'Ya* (1938), a piece he knew very well; nonetheless, he credited himself on the program as having conceived this dance drama. This apolitical fable played as Owen's swan song; immediately after the production he was assigned to the South Pacific, where the casualties were fearsomely high. Sebree, however, working in the office, forged a change in the orders, and Dodson was sent back to Hampton Institute to study electricity.

Sebree's and Dodson's falsifications deserve comment in context of the double and triple binds of racism of that era. Had Lieutenant Commander Armstrong deliberately ordered Owen to a distant war? Or had his name fallen on that list routinely? An answer demands an inquiry into the policies and politics at Great Lakes and into the commander's life as well.

The military needed men, and the Navy felt the pressure to do what the Army had done: admit Blacks in segregated units. Because the Navy had never commissioned any black officers, the appointment of a white paternalist seemed appropriate ("a man who understood Negroes"). On May 29, 1942, Armstrong, a 1915 Annapolis graduate, was assigned "to supervise and direct the training of Negro recruits." He received this appointment because the Navy assumed that Armstrong would be "dedicated to the principle of enabling Negroes to become self-reliant and set examples of industry for their own people." They promptly promoted Armstrong to commander.

In an address delivered on Armistice Day, 1942, to DuSable High School students, the commander told the Negro youth that he had recommended to the secretary of Navy that Negroes be commissioned; however, "for him [the Negro] to assume undue responsibilities of rank before he was properly trained would have been a grave injustice to him, and yet there are those who clamored for this very thing."

Dodson, if he had not clamored, had dreamed of donning the ensign's cap, and Sebree delighted in telling about how naïve Owen went down-town and chose a pinkish beige for his uniform: "When he asked me which color I wanted, I said, 'gingham.' " In September 1942, Armstrong promoted a few career messmen and others to the rank of chief petty officer, but the rank and file refused their leadership. Then, before Armstrong could bring Dodson and his friends to the point of nomination for ensign, the Detroit riots postponed commissions until March 1944, long after Dodson's discharge.

Armstrong, caught between hard-line Navy racists who wanted no black officers and his own go-slow policy, had few allies to support his directives. The Navy's own administrative report stated that at the time of his appointment, "rightly or wrongly, other officers formed the impression that Armstrong was 'trying to make a job for himself,' " an impression that did not encourage cooperation. Several of his officers believed he was not tough enough. An investigative report written by the Navy in 1946 stated that the officers "believed that there were many stabbings and barracks fights among Negro recruits that could have been avoided," and consequently some of the white officers took discipline into their own hands, "taking a recalcitrant recruit into a room where there were no witnesses and beating him."

Officers who worked with Armstrong did not accept his basic philosophy that the Blacks should have special treatment, such as "having the Negro recruits learn and recite a creed dealing with the advancement of the Negro race, and having them sing spirituals on Sunday nights." (White liberals and middle-class Blacks at this time viewed singing spirituals as a symbol of slavery, that is, something that should be abandoned.) Silvera and Dodson agreed, and so informed the Rosenwald Fund.

Most controversial among the commander's special-treatment policies was his decision that "Negroes [were] unable to compete with white recruits in some departments; therefore should not be required to compete with whites for rosters and in school selection." With 75 percent of his recruits coming from the South, where 90 percent did not know how to swim and 40 percent did not know how to read, the commander may have had a point.[25] But Lt. Comdr. R. C. Southworth, Jr., in a report blasted Armstrong's literacy program. "The amount of time and effort required to train these recruits is admittedly much greater than is necessary for normal men. It is exceedingly doubtful whether this expenditure is justified."[26]

The year Owen served at Great Lakes, the number of Blacks in special schools more than doubled. However, the attacks on Armstrong's programs continued. Lower selection standards were assumed to be an integral part of his segregation policy. In sum, the Navy's approach was to segregate the Blacks, then complain that they were receiving special treatment. (Affirmative action?) This disastrous policy ended on June 11, 1945, when the Bureau of Naval Personnel recommended that "all Recruit Training commands assimilate Negro and White enlisted personnel alike."[27]

That remained two years away. In the summer of 1943, doubts about the Negro's loyalty to America persisted; according to Sebree, "station intelligence watched the Negro regiments carefully." In August 1942, an inflammatory leaflet issued by the Colored Americans National Organization was found in Camp Robert Smalls. In June 1943, when there were race riots in Detroit, the commanding officer ordered special vigilance. In the next six months several Blacks were investigated for doubtful loyalty and for communism. One was found to be "intensely interested" in problems of Blacks; others were interested in "elevating the status of the Negro race." One yeoman third class was "extremely dissatisfied with the inability of Negroes to advance in the Navy." Investigation led to the transfer of a few Blacks. Was Owen one? His available records do not show it, but a shadow of suspicion may have fallen on him. The evidence is provocative but circumstantial.

After the production of *Freedom the Banner,* naval intelligence summoned Sebree. "There was an extension of the John Reed Club (communist) where Frank Silvera and I used to go all the time. They'd have little parties. When intelligence questioned me I said to them I didn't know what it was about. I just went because I was invited. They wanted to know if I was a member; I told them, 'only of the Negro race.' They gave me a rough time. I got discharged on a kind of mental disaffection."

Owen related an entirely different story, one he repeated often and one that, in part at least, was either a confusion or a lie: "Sebree told me, 'I am sick of this. I want out [of the Navy].' I said, 'You have signed up and if you get out, you will get a dishonorable discharge that will follow you.' He said, 'I don't care. I'm going to get out. You go see the commander's yeoman and sit down, and I will leave the door open a crack because I have made an appointment to see the commander.' I said to myself, 'I have to see how he is going to deal with this.' He went in and said, 'I want out.' The commander got so red and replied, 'How dare you talk to me that way!' Sebree said, 'I want out. I want it within the week.' The commander said, 'I am afraid that can't be done.' 'Oh,' Sebree said, 'it can be done. I'll tell you about the officers around here and what they are doing with the colored boys.' And he was out within the week. It was a big, bold gesture, and he didn't know anything about the officers, but he made it seem as if there were sexual scenes. They got him out in less than a week. When I would go into Chicago on weekends, I would see him."

That Sebree would dare such a ploy need not be questioned, but the truth of the matter is that Owen was not at Great Lakes when Sebree was discharged. Sebree may have informed Owen that he did it, but Owen never witnessed it.

There is no question, however, that Sebree did change Dodson's order to be shipped out. Reported Sebree: "I was always around the regimental offices. I took Owen's name off the list to go to the South Pacific. They had checked some names off already; I couldn't find the right kind of ink they had used, so I took some black crayon so probably when they looked, the black crayon looked like ink. Some of the fellows did go to Guam and places like that."

Said Owen: "I really appreciated what Charles did because the South Pacific was certain death, and I hadn't practiced jumping over ponds and climbing over walls or anything like that."

Had Lieutenant Commander Armstrong decided—perhaps with some encouragement from naval intelligence—to break up the pinko gay team? Did Armstrong, when he learned that Owen had escaped to Hampton, pursue him there? (He did make a trip immediately after Owen's transfer.) In any case, in the face of necessity, military segregation eventually collapsed, and hindsight did not fail to comment. Said Captain Bond of Great Lakes: "Segregation was an egregious error. It was un-American and inefficient. Armstrong was an evil influence." And even Armstrong was quoted by a Great Lakes officer as saying at the close of the war that "integration should have been instituted at the beginning."[28]

The Navy's later condemnation of Armstrong as "an evil influence" because of his special-treatment policies is hypocritical. Armstrong did what he was promoted to commander to do: use the Negro to serve the war while keeping him in his place.

Lt. Comdr. Daniel W. Armstrong died on July 16, 1947, at the age of fifty-four, himself a lifelong victim of the racial madness he had sought to direct, while two Negroes he had sought to control escaped the Navy altogether.

Were Dodson and Sebree morally culpable for ducking out? The question is impertinent. They were not bound by a social contract from which they were excluded.

11

Angels on His Shoulder, 1942–43

He borrowed money from her. He dedicated his first novel to her and her husband Leonard, as well as the poem "The Precedent" in *Powerful Long Ladder.* He remembered her birthday. He sent her a Mother's Day card and signed it, "Another Son, Owen." Owen chose Peggy Rieser as his second mother.

They met in 1943 when the Riesers, along with Edwin Embree of the Rosenwald Fund, visited Camp Robert Smalls to see *Freedom the Banner.* The next day, Owen wrote Mrs. Rieser, "Swell of you to come here to see the play and invite us to your lovely fresh home. It's seldom that one meets good people, really good people."[1] On July 16, Owen wrote her again: "Today is your birthday although you won't get this until tomorrow. Happy Birthday to you for many reasons beginning with your husband and children [they had four], ending with the garden, the rafters in the living room, the fire, the scotch, the piano you play and the woods along the road." For a sailor lad living on a naval base, Owen had discovered paradise, and every weekend they could, he and Sebree slipped away to the Rieser home.

The Riesers waved their wands over Owen and for a time raised him up amid the constellations of influence for social change. Leonard Rieser, a graduate of Michigan and then Harvard Law School, served on the board of the Rosenwald Fund. Peggy, a graduate of the University of Chicago, had worked at Jane Addams's Hull-House and demonstrated a passionate distaste for segregation. Their son Leonard, Jr., recalled, "Our home was one of the few places in Chicago where Blacks and whites met together."

The Riesers had purchased property about twenty-five miles north of the Loop, at 1525 Dean Avenue in Highland Park, near the edge of a wooded ravine two blocks from Lake Michigan. In 1924 they had moved into "Ravinia," a two-story brick structure with the downstairs designed as one large L-shaped room with a fireplace. Interested in childhood education, Peggy ran the Rieser Nursery School in the basement. A screened-in back porch served throughout the summer as a cool oasis where Owen heard the Chicago Symphony play Mozart. (The adjacent thirty-six-acre Ravinia Park served the patricians of the North Shore.)

Only two blocks from the interurban electric train, Ravinia lay less than an hour from Great Lakes. On Sunday mornings the children might come down to find refugees from bootcamp who had arrived Saturday night stretched out on the couches.[2]

The Riesers lived by a simple belief that good-hearted people could make a better world. Their major instrument for turning this dream into reality lay with the Rosenwald Fund, for which Leonard served as legal adviser. The late Julius Rosenwald (1862–1932), president and chairman of the board of Sears, Roebuck, and Company, had diverted a part of his fortune from a mail-order business to philanthropy. He saw the twentieth century as a canvas for three great struggles: technology against agrarianism; wealth against poverty and ignorance; and race against race. The African-American has been the underdog in all three.[3]

Just before enlisting in the service, Owen had been awarded a Rosenwald Fellowship to write a series of "Negro plays" for black colleges, but had postponed it for the duration. His productions at Great Lakes Naval Training Station confirmed the foundation's opinion that he would be a distinguished leader in communication arts, and Owen proposed to Embree, the director of the fund, an ethnic pageant of gigantic proportions to cure the racial problems of Chicago.[4] (The city's black population had tripled during the war.) Embree mothballed the pageant.

Owen's social contacts now began to include the wealthy. He met heiress and poet Inez Stark, who placed African sculptures in her bathroom. All his future bathrooms would pay homage to that inspiration. On another weekend Sebree took him to 459 Longwood Avenue in Glencoe, to the seventeen-acre estate where in the 1880s the MacLeish family had built a limestone mansion that looked down on Lake Michigan. The father had made his money as manager of Carson Pirie Scott and Company. His son Archibald had become poet laureate at the Library of Congress. Mrs. MacLeish (Martha, née Hilliard), almost ninety, took Owen's "Black Mother Praying" and sent it to Archibald, who passed it on to the editor of *Common Ground,* M. Margaret Anderson, who in August 1944 published that poem and another of Dodson's, "The Decision."

Summer came, and the trees, flowers, and weeds of the North Shore stirred up a fury of pollen. Although in previous years Owen had never suffered from allergies, that season the hay fever swam in his eyes and bloated his sinuses — suffocation by mucus ("all roses lead to ruin").

Dodson spent his last days at Great Lakes as camp librarian, blowing his nose and writing friends to solicit books on black culture.[5] He implored his friends to catch John T. Frederick's radio program "Men and Books" on September 4, a coast-to-coast CBS hookup featuring Owen Dodson.

From the distance of a thousand miles, Owen ignored the Harlem riot of August 3 and, except for six postcards admonishing Ednah "to take care of yourself and be happy," he pretty much ignored his fiancée, too.[6]

On September 8 Owen boarded "a twenty- or thirty-year-old box-shaped railway car with gas lighting and soot aplenty," and arrived at Hampton, Virginia, two nights later to begin his study of electricity. "I thought I might learn something about stage lighting. The first day we all gathered in the laboratory and each of us had a large table with a complicated machine because they wished to learn our aptitude for things mechanical. As soon as I saw that, I raised my hand, 'May I go to the head, please?' I went to Anne Cooke's [in charge of communications there], and we had martinis the rest of the afternoon." Ten days following the martinis, he was transferred to Norfolk Naval Hospital, having suffered a virulent attack of hay fever. He couldn't eat; his eyes watered; he vomited; he coughed all night. The fellows in his barracks couldn't sleep — "Goddammit, shut up!" He told them to keep on complaining. Finally, to get rid of him, the doctors sent him to the naval hospital at Portsmouth.

For the next six weeks, he read books[7] and wrote letters. To Carl

Van Vechten he sent a joke: "It seems that a boy went to his friend all upset. He stamped his pretty toe and pouted and little tears ran down his cheek and he said, 'I can't stand it. I just can't. Oh, I'm so unhappy and miserable. Nobody loves me. Oh dear.' His friend replied, 'Don't worry, honey. Take your troubles to Jesus. She'll take care of them.' " Owen considered this "delightfully sacrilegious," and, in 1943, it was.

To Edwin Embree, he complained:

> I am in the South again and it comes back to me with putrid and terrible vividness—this whole race question. I am having a fresh experience because always I have been in a school, academically clothed, now I am naked. I am in a ward with white and black boys, surrounded by boils, swollen feet, heart murmur and heart burn, men with no legs, and I know they have seen not the glory but the Solomons: those here for mental observation, those here who hate the Navy, those here who wet the bed. There's a Filipino who swats flies all day; an old chief who shuffles down the aisles, touching each bed, murmuring to himself like an old parrot with all his colors faded. No one ever talks of the aims of the war, freedom or anything. These men will go out to breed, work, look for a nickel on the pavement and die with all their prejudices clinging to them to the grave for God, devil or worm.[8]

On October 29, the news came: "Good discharge this date by reason of physical disability. Not misconduct [*sic*]. You are not qualified for reenlistment in the U.S. Navy." They gave him $58.87 of his monthly stipend, five cents a mile to travel home, and $200 discharge pay; and, for two years following, he received a disability pension.[9] One week after Owen's discharge, Sebree received his—medical, 1C—and, in the spirit of "I can do anything better than you can," Sebree applied for a Rosenwald to paint twenty illustrations for Negro poems, and asked Owen to recommend him.

To celebrate Owen's twenty-ninth birthday, Ednah traveled to Brooklyn. At the party, Countee Cullen and Owen announced that they were undertaking the writing of a ballet together. Owen wrote "Ma" Rieser, "I feel clean again—clean to fight with my weapons—small as they are—perhaps they will serve a little."[10]

12

New World A-Coming, 1944

"They got pictures of V stamped on letter stamps
Miss Eagle wear one in her lapel to her Red Cross suit.
Mr. Bigful, the bank president, got one in his lapel too;
. . . .
Now let's get this straight: what do them V's mean?"
"V stands for Victory?"
"It what we get when we fight for it."
"Ought to be Freedom, God do know that!"
— "Conversation on V"

The Pittsburgh *Courier* and the *People's Voice* sported double V's on their mastheads (one for victory over fascism abroad, the other for victory over racism at home). Remembering the broken promises made during World War I, in the summer of 1943 Harlem Congressman Adam Clayton Powell organized a successful "For This We Fight" rally in Madison Square Garden. The next year, his public-relations arm, the Negro Labor Victory Committee, sent a telegram to Owen: "Are you available to write script for pageant at Negro Freedom Rally Madison Square Garden June 26th. Your presence required here immediately if available."[1] On Saturday, April 22, Owen met with Howard Fast, Frank D. Griffin, and Peter Lyon in Powell's home on St. Nicholas Avenue. Dodson would write and direct the pageant.

Most inspired when he had costumes to design, dancers to direct, crowds to move, Owen set to work, borrowing the title (with permission) from Roi Ottley's book *New World A-Coming*, subtitling it "An original pageant of hope." Three weeks later, on Wednesday evening, May 17, actors Leigh Whipper and Will Geer read the script aloud to a select audience assembled at 23 West Twenty-sixth Street in the Library of the Institute for International Democracy. Conceived to play less than an hour (it would be preceded by two hours and twenty minutes of speeches), the pageant had to be rousing. It was. They approved the twenty-seven-page script.

When the day arrived, Lillian shared her brother's triumph: "The skies have cleared and are an azure blue. Tomorrow night the jungle stars will be shining, your dream stars. They are smiling down upon you with great hope and expectation. June 26, 1944 is the unfolding of the dream of your life and the fulfillment of mine. I'm supremely happy and shall live it fully with you."[2] The "damnable Dodsons" from Berriman had returned to Madison Square Garden, where once Owen's father had spoken at the Baptist Concord Church rally.

In the center of the stadium, a gigantic red star-shaped platform rested on a huge blue stage.[3] The unions had given Owen access to the big names—Langston Hughes, Canada Lee, Abbie Mitchell, Josh White, Marie Young, and Will Geer. Pearl Primus danced and Duke Ellington's orchestra played. For his walk-ons, Owen used seventy-six "lesser" bodies. Gordon Heath directed the "voice crew" and James Gelb the lighting. Ray Elliott and Evelyn Araumburo wrote original music for Owen's theme song, designed for the audience to sing along:

> There's a new world a-coming, come on
> We've buried Jim Crow, We'll keep him down
> White supremacy has no crown
> Come on, come on
> and on and on and on!"

The play was written in eight scenes; the opening one set the tone of the whole:

[THE HOUSE LIGHTS DIM. ORGAN MUSIC SWELLS UP WITH THE THEME SONG AND OUT OF IT A GREAT ROLLING OF DRUMS. A SPOT COMES UP IN THE CENTER OF THE STAR REVEALING A LONE SENTRY PACING WITH A GUN ON HIS SHOULDER. THE DRUMS BEAT LOW. THE SENTRY POISES HIS GUN.]

    SENTRY
Halt! Who goes there?
    VOICE
[FROM THE DARKNESS] China against the enemy! [THE DRUMS ROLL

UP AND THREE CHINESE SOLDIERS CARRYING HUGE CHINESE FLAGS
RUN THROUGH THE SPOT. THE DRUM GOES LOW.]
    SENTRY
[CONTINUES PACING. THEN THE DRUMS UP] Halt! Who runs there?
    VOICE
Great Britain against the enemy!
    SENTRY
Pass on, Great Britain against the enemy!
[THE DRUMS ROLL UP AND THREE BRITISH SOLDIERS CARRYING THREE
HUGE FLAGS: CANADA, AUSTRALIA, SOUTH AFRICA RUN THROUGH
THE SPOT. THE DRUMS GO DOWN.]
    SENTRY
Halt! Who goes there?
    VOICE
Russia against the enemy!
    SENTRY
Pass on, Comrades against the enemy.

[THE DRUMS AND THREE RUSSIAN SOLDIERS WITH FLAGS RUN
THROUGH.]

    SENTRY
Halt! Who goes there?
    VOICE
America against the enemy. [ONE NEGRO, ONE WHITE AND ONE
MEXICAN WITH AMERICAN AND MEXICAN FLAGS RUN THROUGH THE
SPOT. THE SENTRY RELAXES, LEANING ON HIS GUN AND A CONTIN-
UOUS PROCESSION OF ALLIED FLAGS RUN THROUGH.]

From the international front against fascism, the pageant quickly
narrowed its focus to the injustices suffered by the Blacks and the
Jews. Sojourner Truth, Dorrie Miller, Tom Paine in cameo proclaimed
freedom. Owen inserted, in its entirety, his poem "Black Mother Praying." The tension mounted when "Mr. Speaker" (Congressman Rankin
of Alabama) spat out a poem composed by Countee Cullen:

        Before I'd let a nigger vote
        Or match me place for place
        With my own hands I'd slash my throat
        To spite that nigger's face.
        I'd raise my hand in holy heil,

March with the Germans knee for knee.
Niggers may be American
But Hitler's white like me!

But a united front of workers rose up against the fascists and, joined by the audience, sang "There's a new world a-coming." A large section of the Negro Freedom Rally had focused on the Jewish struggle in Europe and America. This occurred in part because Owen believed in the alliance, and in part because Congressman Powell courted the trade unions as important allies for his program of change in New York City.[4] The *People's Voice* reported that "New York City demonstrated its interest in fuller democracy for the Negro people throughout the world Monday night when 25,000 [Owen reported 22,000] representing nearly every race, faith and political belief jammed Madison Square Garden and thousands more clamored outside to attend the second annual Negro Freedom Rally. Mayor LaGuardia had the highest praise for Owen Dodson's brilliantly written pageant."[5]

W. H. Auden had noted in his recommendation of Owen to Rosenwald that Dodson's "sense of language is at the same time both poetic and suited to the theatre." *New World A-Coming* used all of Owen's talents and all he had learned at Great Lakes; he would write and direct other pageants, but never would he command so much attention for his democratic ideals. As he had confided to Peggy Rieser, he was free to fight with his own weapons, and he began signing letters with Congressman Powell's slogan, "Keep the faith."

Since their initial meeting at Yale, Auden continued as a bright thread throughout Owen's career. In October 1940, the English poet, along with writer-editor George Davis, had taken up residency on Middagh Street in Brooklyn Heights in a house he had labeled "the menagerie" because of the bohemian character of its inhabitants. At one time or other, the menagerie sheltered Carson McCullers, Benjamin Britten, Peter Pears, Erika and Golo Mann, Paul Bowles, Stephen Spender, Louis MacNeice, and Oliver Smith.[6]

Gordon Heath invited Owen to Middagh Street to to meet George Davis, feature editor of *Mademoiselle* and author of a novel, *The Opening of a Door.* Owen recalled, "We became good friends. The next time we went to his house I took a friend of mine, Frank Harriott. We were two of the very young people amid a rare group of artists. One evening Frank was talking to Carson McCullers—she was sitting on the staircase leading downstairs, and he was talking very earnestly like only a twenty-two-year-old man can, she answering briefly. Then she said, 'I can't answer that,' and she fell off this chair and fell down the steps; nothing happened to her because she was stoned."

In 1942, Auden left Brooklyn to teach at Swarthmore College, about sixty minutes from Philadelphia. When Owen received his discharge, Auden invited Dodson to the school: "Do come and see me and stay a weekend. I have been working quite a lot which I'll show you when we meet."[7] As Swarthmore was "a dump without either a bar or a movie house,"[8] Auden brought his wine by suitcase from Philadelphia, and one may speculate that the men were thrown upon one another's resources for entertainment. In any case, Owen showed Auden his rewrite of *Divine Comedy*.

The time went well, for indeed they shared many qualities: Both thought of poetry as something to be read aloud (both in childhood had loved Poe's "Raven" and Tennyson's "In Memoriam"); both were accustomed to believe that in any company "I am the youngest person present,"[9] because both had been the youngest and brightest child in their families; and alas, both had been adored by mothers whose love had imprisoned them. Neither was athletic, and both were gay.

Recalled Owen: "The first day, Auden read my play and asked me to read *For the Time Being,* which he had just finished. [It would be published in September 1944.] He said, 'I'll be in a faculty meeting and then we can talk about yours and mine.' He said that he liked the way I read aloud, and if they did his oratorio at Town Hall, he wanted me to do the narration.[10] He told me that *Divine Comedy* made him think that I should write libretti. This was a new idea to me; I had not thought that a libretto had any literary value, and I said that I knew nothing about it. He offered to teach me.

"The next day after lunch, he played *Rosenkavalier* right straight through and then began to tell me about the elements and balance of voices and music and choral poems. He was brilliant and there was hardly anything I could say, or anyone could say, and that is one reason that he was so lonely, because he knew so much more. He talked until dinnertime, then we traveled into Philadelphia to a restaurant that played opera. Auden requested *Norma* and again analyzed it for me. He was a teacher as well as a great poet, and I have never known anyone like him."[11]

In a city dimmed in wartime brownout, the winter had been slushy, nasty. In February 1944, Owen wrote Peggy Rieser, "I do three things: write, scrub, dust and see shows at a minimum price." Even though Lillian's night nurse had been dismissed, money remained tight. ("Sixty-five dollars every week for a practical nurse who also did the shopping and who bought the best cuts of meat and sliced off a little bit for herself.") Finally, Lillian was "creeping about," and Owen removed her oxygen tanks from the bedroom.

To escape for an hour in gloomy February, Owen passed into the mirror of Jean Cocteau's film *The Blood of a Poet*. When the surreal film ended, a part of Owen had metamorphosed; in his imagination he would be Orphée forever; on the corners of letters, postcards, and poems, he drew Cocteauesque stars. From another Cocteau film, *Orphée*, Owen borrowed "Heurtebise" as a byword for "handsome male companion," a sobriquet by which he sometimes addressed Earle Hyman. To Peggy he sent postcards with orphic verse:

> Today is winter
> the pure white colt
> lean and cruel
> bow and arrow
> wounding and beautiful
> the blind animal.[12]

In April, as Persephone emerged from Hades, Owen courted a new friend, Karl Priebe, a painter who at the age of twenty-seven had been appointed director of the Kalamazoo Art Institute. Priebe and Dodson were born the same year and shared similar statures, oval heads, widow's peaks, full lips, and a naughty sense of playing at Peter Pan—twins in "high vibration," to borrow a phrase of Father Divine's that Owen favored.

Black friends described Priebe's skin as "porcelain," and they gave him that affectionate nickname. Priebe painted, befriended, loved black people. The Kalamazoo *Gazette* noted that "his professional interests are reflected largely in his painting as will be seen in his pictures of animals and Negro subjects. He has found in these colored people an imagination and fantasy that has inspired some of his best and most popular works."[13] Priebe seems to have been openly and unabashedly a negrophile, belonging to a cadre of white artists—Jean Cocteau,

Ronald Firbank, Charles Cullen—whose attraction to "darkness" racists labeled "exoticism."[14]

At the opening of Priebe's exhibition in Kalamazoo, Owen danced, played Billie Holiday records, drank Kalamazoo's version of intoxicating liquor, sang, and talked "like bell clappers all night long." The previous year, Priebe had won a Prix de Rome; he would soon be featured in *Life,* along with two other rising stars, writer James Purdy and sculptor George Dickey. The exhibition itself boasted of the "largest carved rhinoceros horn in the world," just the kind of believe-it-or-not item that might bring a wispy smile from Owen: "Largest horn in the world! I think that's kinda nice, don't you?"

Owen's most important spring sojourn he announced as a visit to the Riesers at Ravinia, but its primary purpose was to lobby Edwin Embree at the Rosenwald Fund. Owen's fellowship (postponed when he enlisted) had been reinstated—$1,650 for nine months, but after that, what? Eleven dollars a month from the Navy's hay-fever pension combined with his pocket money from writing reviews for the *People's Voice* would not keep the wolf from the door, and the wolf could be heard. Lillian had retired and her heart condition periodically required a nurse. Edith, in social services, earned little; Lef contributed, although with her jaws and her purse clamped tight.

Owen's visit to Edwin Embree was fortuitous because the Rosenwald Fund and the Rockefeller Foundation were about to launch an experiment in "social control" through film.[15] The impact of both the Farm Security Administration's documentary films of the Depression in the thirties and the compelling British war documentaries of the forties had impressed the foundations: cinema would dominate and define culture. In 1939, the Rockefeller Foundation funded the American Film Center through the Institute of Public Administration (Luther Gulick served as its president and Herbert Hoover as a trustee), with the sole objective "to develop the use of films for educational and public purposes."[16]

On February 17, 1944, the Board of AFC (American Film Committee) declared it would establish a wing for research. The board created the Committee for Negro Mass Education. Among the nine basic problems to be explored was that of "film and unlearning (here we were concerned with the use of films in breaking down thought patterns and in performing a sort of mass psychoanalysis, separating irrelevant emotions from the symbols or events which evoke them)."[17] In layman's terms, film could change the way a "cracker" perceived a "nigger" and vice versa, a heady idea that quite possibly had been motivated by the four major race riots in the summer of 1943.[18] The American Film Committee recorded that it was not reasonable to expect any single foundation to meet a budget that would support activities on the scale demanded by the problems of the times. Enter the Rosenwald Fund; on Saturday, May 13, Owen attended a meeting at Rockefeller Center to discuss ideas for "a series of educational pictures [films] dealing with a Negro theme."[19]

Dodson wrote Leonard Rieser: "Don Slesinger [director of AFC] remembered you with great vividness and said he thought you two [Peggy and Leonard] plus and very plus. I like him. He's honest and clear. Big things will come of that Committee."[20] As it turned out, Owen's comment, like the prologue to a Greek tragedy, was at once both prophetic and ironic.

13

Democratic Vistas on Film, 1944–46

Owen never fulfilled his "contract" with the Rosenwald Fund to write plays for Negro theater. Instead, he spent his summer directing O'Neill's *Homecoming* for Howard University's summer school, billing it as "the first non-professional production of any part of the trilogy, *Mourning Becomes Electra*." Unwilling after Madison Square Garden to play to a small house, he staged it on the columned portico of Douglass Hall and persuaded James Braxton of the School of Engineering to devise and install outdoor lighting.

The exterior location meant that they could rehearse only after school hours, and that the actors must shout. Owen pulled in Gordon Heath for the lead as Adam Brant. For Lavinia he got Patricia Harris, née Roberts, the leading player from Howard. (She later became head of Housing and Urban Development for the Carter administration.) For the third major role, Owen chose a woman he had seen act with Gordon in the Harlem production of *The Merchant of Venice*, Sadie Brown. The minor roles he filled with students, and he played the Gardener walk-on himself, singing "Oh Shenandoah, I long to see you." Owen enjoyed Howard, but, as he wrote Edith, "I went to the National Gallery to hear a concert and have lunch. Air-cooled and no prejudice there at least."[1]

Ednah Bethea had moved to Washington, D.C., to work in the Bureau of Engraving. By the opening of *Homecoming*, the couple realized the emptiness of their engagement, now two years old. Edith had warned Ednah: "My brother needs a husband to look after him." Owen suggested they hold a disengagement party. They did, inviting family and friends. Like Priscilla Heath's, Ednah's anger found its way into poetry:

> Forget my tears, not that the winter in my heart
> forgets its snows that drifted in so quietly.
> How could I know that warm and unprotected dreams
> nursed for years could ice and shatter brittlely with rage?
> . . . .
> Forget the promises.
> Although there is hope for another spring,
> no buds appear on last year's frozen flowers.
> I really do not care any more, my love
> I really do not care.[2]

She never sent Owen the poem. For his part, Owen never gave her "Engagement" (perhaps not about her), which he published in *Powerful Long Ladder*:

> If there must be elaborate favors
> For this simple partnership of years
> Elaborate whisperings in the fragrant ear,
> Kissing by the hour and by the letter,
> Accounts of how the evening went
> When I went out alone,
> Where this dollar disappeared and where the small affection
> Like the ear kiss
> If each time you catch my eye mine must twinkle back:
> "I love you and will through thick and thin,
> Especially through the thick, my dear, especially then."
> If I must arrange my letters so that I can tell
> Which have been touched or re-arranged by kettle steam,
> If I must thread my needle with the camel
> Of your curiosity, explore the haystack,
> Unload the woodpile . . .
> Then no and no and no.
> I have other fish to fry over other fires
> In the meadows of another country.

Ednah's pain festered from a deep commitment, a hope that she had nursed for their marriage. Owen's anger proceeded not from the souring of deep love but from a man trapped. Had he, like Cullen or Van Vechten, married a woman dedicated to his art—as Ednah had been—perhaps he might have ameliorated the loneliness of his last days. Or perhaps a marriage would only have made it worse. His sister Edith, who finally played out the role, did all she could to love her brother but nothing sufficed.

In late August, Owen hurried back to New York to attend Canada Lee's first-night party for the Broadway opening of *Anna Lucasta* (1944). In the forties, Negro actors had burst onto Broadway stages in serious drama. Canada Lee played Bigger Thomas in *Native Son* (1941). Paul Robeson opened in Margaret Webster's *Othello* (1943) and broke the Broadway record with 296 performances. The musical *Carmen Jones* (1943) ran two years. Gordon Heath starred in *Deep Are the Roots* (1945), directed by Elia Kazan; this was followed by Theodore Ward's *Our Lan'* (1947). In the Negro theater the feeling was "yes, we can."

Abram Hill invited Owen to direct *Divine Comedy* at the American Negro Theatre, but Owen opted for *Garden of Time*. Hill argued that a Harlem audience knew about Father Divine and would attend out of curiosity, but how could he sell *Garden of Time* (about the mythic Greeks) to an audience of union members in the Bronx? Hill lost that fight and lost the battle to have ANT members cast in the production.[3] Loyal to his friends, Dodson cast Gordon Heath and Sadie Brown. Sebree designed the costumes and created a masterful unit in a closet of a space that served as four sets. For secondary roles, Austin Briggs-Hall and Elsie Benjamin proved more than adequate. For the role of the orphic singer Owen discovered an eighteen-year-old in Pearl Primus's African Dance Company. Although William Greaves did not play the guitar (Gordon played it backstage while Greaves faked it), he had the homey quality that Owen wanted. Greaves had never acted before, and Dodson hovered like a mother hen.[4] When the critics taxied up to Harlem for *Garden*'s opening on March 7, 1945, they basked in Greaves's warmth and thought Sadie Brown had raw power, but they found the play itself slumbering, remote, and too poetic. Gordon agreed: "The production was a failure because the script is two-thirds poetry and not dramatic." Van Vechten spared Owen by complaining that his seat had been behind a post where he couldn't see the play.

Offstage, Gordon was conducting his first heterosexual affair, perhaps inspiring Owen to begin courting Sadie Brown, who recalled, "After *Garden* closed, Owen invited me and my sister to see Ethel Waters in *Blue Holiday*. During intermission, Owen leaned over to me and said, 'I took my ring back from Ednah.' This was almost a year after it happened. He said, 'I'll be over to take you to the park on Sunday.' He came over and we went walking. We talked and he indicated he wanted a closer relationship. He was the sort of person who would not push. He had to be sure the thing was acceptable on both sides before he would pursue it. I looked upon him as a force, an extremely brilliant man, but I knew that Frank Harriott had a case on Owen. I couldn't understand what Owen was saying to me because Frank was there and obviously there. There was no way there could be any relationship between Owen and me."[5] Brown assessed Owen's proposal accurately: two years later, Harriott moved to 469 Quincy to live with Owen.

In May 1944, Hampton offered Owen an assistant professorship at $2,500. On June 7 he asked for $3,000. Pres. Ralph P. Bridgman hesitated two weeks, then raised his offer to an associate professorship at $2,700. The next week *New World A-Coming* climaxed the Freedom Rally, and Donald Slesinger of the American Film Center offered Owen $3,500 plus $1,000 travel expenses to take office September 1 as the executive secretary of the the Committee for Negro Mass Education. His primary task: to raise money for films that would change the ethnic images of minorities in America![6] Owen leapt at the chance.

Two weeks after he took office, he changed the group's name to the Committee for Mass Education in Race Relations (CMERR). The Rosenwald Fund appropriated $12,000 for a two-year budget. Owen took the $1,660 set aside for a secretary, hired Gordon (a graduate from a commercial high school) as a research assistant, and set to work. Owen's job was to influence people who had money or access to influence. At that time, he gained about fifty pounds taking the wealthy to lunch. ("We would have several cocktails, lobster, filet mignon and brandy. The richer they are, the greedier they are.")

Peggy Rieser introduced Dodson to Julius Rosenwald's daughter Marion Ascoli, who had married the Italian refugee and owner/editor of the *Reporter*, Max Ascoli. When the family returned from their summer place, they invited Owen to 23 Gramercy Park South. It was Halloween evening, and dinner would be at eight. With two hours to kill, Dodson walked from his office on Fifty-first Street. As he passed by Bryant Park he saw a boy with a pumpkin and thought, "Why don't I carve out a jack-o'-lantern for the Ascolis three-year-old son Peter?" When the Ascolis' butler opened the door, he saw a black man holding a jack-o'-lantern with the candle burning. Mrs. Ascoli came running. Owen held out the pumpkin. "This is for your son." She smiled. "I will go and wake him up." The child loved it and took the pumpkin to bed. Mrs. Ascoli returned with a look of ecstasy, and told Owen, "My father left me and my sisters a great deal of money and all this time we had never thought of buying my son a real pumpkin." Owen left their house with a check, he said, for $30,000. He called the jack-o'-lantern a "$30,000 pumpkin." (In fact, the figure was probably $3,000.)[7]

Dodson approached his boss Donald Slesinger with a proposal to establish four fellowships (set design, photography, directing, and writing) in film for Negroes because "they had no opportunity to get in 'downstairs' on making pictures." He approached the producer for the "March of Time" series, Mr. Woods, who would take on apprentices but would not provide money. Owen turned to Rosenwald, but the fund gave fellowships to individuals, not to organizations. The foundations professed a desire to change racial images but refused to disturb the lily-white Hollywood unions. Not until the Watts riot in 1965 did minority-training programs blossom.

Owen wrote letters to motion-picture personalities asking for endorsement of CMERR. Margaret Sullavan, Edward G. Robinson, and Fredric March said, "No." Frank Capra said the Army wouldn't allow him. Norman Corwin, Edward Weston, and John Dos Passos all said, "Yes, but. . . ." Lillian Smith, Herman Shumlin, Arch Obler, and Ansel Adams gave an enthusiastic "Yes." Owen decided to go to Hollywood himself and see if he could convince Tinseltown to support CMERR with production skills and money.

Before leaving, he attended the all-out-for-Roosevelt rally in Madison Square Garden: "Dorothy Maynor stood on one side and Helen Keller on the other with Henry Wallace smiling in the middle; the audience surged forward with applause, an applause for an attitude in life of justice and hope."[8] The party dumped Henry Wallace and nominated Harry Truman for vice-president; FDR was elected to a fourth term. On November 9, Owen stepped off the train in Chicago to enjoy four days with the Riesers. On the 13th he reboarded the Challenger for a two-day panorama of the American West.

Owen's mission: to persuade influential stars and moguls to change the "Coon 'n' Mammy" images to more realistic portrayals. Walter White, the head of the NAACP, twice had undertaken the same mission (once accompanied by Wendell Willkie), and twice failed. Owen had the advantages of innocence, the confidence of his $3,000 jack-o'-lantern, and the names and phone numbers given to him by Walter White. And he had a few contacts of his own. A hat designer (unnamed by Owen) gathered a group of "people who later came to be censored by the House Un-American Activities Committee, people like Dalton Trumbo." Dodson did get interviews with Walter Wanger and Joan Bennett, both acquaintances of White. Orson Welles, who was then married to Rita Hayworth, invited Dodson to dinner:

> Rita was having their first child, the largest pregnancy I had ever seen; she sat at a glass table, so you could see this great thing under the glass. When I explained my plan, Orson Welles said, "My God, what an idea! You know what I would like to do for free? The story of Toussaint L'Ouverture, Henri Christophe and Dessalines! I would like to do a trilogy, all in color. And show how the first Negro republic of Haiti was founded." He knew the history of these three men. Anyway, he said, "I will be in New York lecturing at Mecca Temple [now City Center]. You come after the lecture and we will make some more concrete plans." Very cordial. He gave me his telephone number where he would be staying. About two weeks later, we had a meeting with the committee, and I reported on the check from Mrs. Ascoli and Orson Welles's commitment to do the film for free! Well, they loved me. I have books, almost all of them signed, "To Owen, with admiration for his great work for our committee." I also got a raise, but when I spoke to Welles later, he said, "We can do this for several million." I said, "That's fine." He said, "You can raise that money, can't you?" I said, "You said it wouldn't cost us anything." He replied, "I meant my fee; my fee wouldn't be anything." When I reported back to the committee, they didn't take their books back, but it was a very defeating moment.

In sum, Dodson's Hollywood flirtation appeared to have produced little more than a pad of writer's observations noting that he had seen his first bubble dancer, and that in a bar named the Lyon's Den he drank a concoction called a "Hollywood Wet Dream."

Clearly, Owen believed that film could change racial hatred to tolerance, ignorance to understanding, and that he, Owen, now commanded artists funded to create those films. If Hollywood refused to help, why shouldn't he write the script himself? His first forty-page effort, "Where You From?"[9] had almost no narration or dialogue, which is to say that his maiden effort was totally visual—filled with details and images only a poet sees. Read today, it is still a fine cinematic script. Its thesis—that there exists a bond, an American brotherhood of all races—offered a vision far ahead of its time. The tortuous tale of Owen's struggle to get it produced is a classic one: a man with good intentions is never given authority by those in power to make the project happen.

Owen's original script, typed on cheap yellow paper, may never have been duplicated, indicating CMERR's less-than-enthusiastic response. Even the committee's black members cast a chill over Dodson's democratic vistas. Langston Hughes, who hoped to see his own script "The Negro Speaks of Rivers" produced, wrote Arna Bontemps, "Why don't you talk up another meeting of the Film Committee with Owen so that I'll have an excuse to get back to New York?"[10] Both had been involved in white-money-will-change-the-racial-world projects before. Bontemps responded to Hughes, "We must not forget the 9th of December, because that is the day on which each of us collects $$$ from the American Film Center—providing we do our home work."[11] Both poets had their own projects, and neither supported Dodson's script.

Charles Johnson, a nationally known black sociologist from Fisk University who sat on the board of the Rosenwald Fund as well as on CMERR, joined the equivocators, writing Embree, "I have some reservations about the story. They are, as might be expected, mostly sociological in essence." Johnson's comment in translation: dramatic images must be changed to didactic ones.

A skeptical Richard Wright doubted that the committee could produce a film, and he told Dodson that the only way he could make any serious film was to buy a camera and put it in front of people, which was exactly what he intended to do with *Native Son.*[12]

Because no one fathomed or admitted that Owen had written a superior film script, CMERR hired two professionals, John Bright and Herbert Kline, both white and leftist, to rewrite; they did, changing the name to "Journey to Paradise" but leaving the script mostly intact; Owen's name was retained as third writer. Not all the committee members had read the script. Bontemps, unhappy not to have been consulted, wrote Hughes, "I've now seen Owen's *Journey to Paradise,* also Charles's [Johnson] extended comments on it. . . . I get the impression there isn't enough money in the cash register to call Committee meetings anymore."[13]

Chairman Johnson became cautious. After a meeting in early September, the committee voted to have the script rewritten again (by Dodson), this time built around one black family, the Carters, and their migration from the rural South to the urban North. It would be called "They Seek a City," run twenty-five or thirty minutes, "be appropriate for both theatrical and non-theatrical distribution," cost about $50,000, and "would not be a documentary in the usual sense of that word, but would in every way be comparable to a short Hollywood feature."[14]

Johnson's assignment was to secure $60,000 for the production— $30,000 from Rosenwald and $30,000 from Marshall Field. When the script reached the Rosenwald Fund, Will Alexander, formerly with the documentary division of the Farm Security Administration, read it and told Embree, "I fail to get out of the reading any of the great lift which came when I read the script of Pare Lorenz's *The River* or *The Plow That Broke the Plains.*"[15] The head of AFC, Donald Slesinger, picked up the challenge, generously assuring Embree that the film would make $25,000 from black theaters in the South and would be seen by unions, maybe six to ten million people in the North. Embree, reluctant but eager to secure some fruition after a weary year of committees, awarded them $30,000 on the condition that it be spent only for production expenses.

Slesinger agreed to the terms but at the same time had his own reservations about the script. Owen rewrote the script again, but with each rewrite "by committee," it became less visual and more weighted down by narration. At one point, they hired Josh White to sing the narrative bridges. Then Slesinger called in, to write evaluations, Kenneth MacGowan, major producer at Paramount; Herman Shumlim, producer-director of *The Little Foxes;* Kenneth MacKenna, head of MGM's story department; Archer Winsten, *New York Post* film critic; John Gassner, former head of script department at Columbia Pictures; and John McManus, film critic of *PM.* Predictably, they disagreed about the quality of the story and the art of the film, and, equally predictably, everyone voted for racial harmony. All that remained: to persuade Marshall Field to cough up his $30,000.

In the meantime, Owen wisely converted his script into a half-hour radio drama. Produced on WMCA in New York as a public-service drama, "Hot Spots USA,"[16] starring the Broadway actor Frank Wilson, apparently left Charles Johnson feeling that Owen didn't know his material. The group "creative" process had reached its nadir; the committee had destroyed the original concept, introduced outside writers, and undermined Owen to the point that he no longer could find his original vision. Conclusion: send Dodson to do research, send him on a tour through the South. Frank Harriott reported in *PM*: "A Negro and a white man from the North made a trip together through Tennessee, Mississippi, and Georgia studying Jim Crow to find more than the mere facts. They wanted to catch the way people glanced over their shoulders, to hear how they talked, maybe to learn what they thought about themselves and each other."

Slesinger paid for the trip from AFC production funds. Owen's traveling companion, Rudolf Carlson, tall, blond, and looking like an FBI agent, received $3,150 for a six-month salary, plus $800 for travel expenses. If the trip were justified as gathering firsthand impressions of Jim Crow, why send a white and a black man together? Was Carlson along to protect Owen? True, Owen had lived in the South, but he had not traveled the back roads. The only productive result of this expenditure was that Richard Wright arranged the publication of Owen's notes in Dorothy Norman's journal *Twice a Year*.[17]

By the summer of 1946, film shooting had not yet begun, and Dodson informed Embree that he was worried. He could not report more without appearing to be talking behind Slesinger's back. Then the bad news broke. Slesinger, in a private letter on July 22, 1946, confessed to Embree that Marshall Field would not contribute to the film, and worse, nearly all of the $30,000 that Embree had awarded them for production had been spent on administrative salaries and travel.[18] Embree fired a telegram back: "Terribly distressed for you and shocked at situation. Have reported to our Executive Committee who ask for immediate audit and conference with you and Rockefeller people concerning recovery of remaining funds and salvaging of the movie project. Make books and records available."[19]

Slesinger, filled with mea culpas, explained that he had intended to recoup the funds from other projects, and that the misappropriation of the money was misjudgment, not fraud. (He had once been a professor of law.) Given some time, he pleaded, he could still recoup the money if they didn't close down the office. But those conservatives at the top of the pyramid did not tolerate spending other people's money. When Luther Gulick, director of the Institute of Public Administration and chair of the Board of Directors of AFC, learned of Slesinger's misappropriations, he became righteous: "I have never before been even remotely connected with the misapplication of the grants of any foundation, though I have administered several million dollars of such funds over the years. I shall go after this matter with energy." He closed the books, rented the office space, and froze all funds, including Owen's salary. A total of $12,674.44 had been lost forever; after the sale of all assets, $21,025.56 was returned to Rosenwald.

To Embree's credit, he wrote Owen, "I can assure you that we will not allow you to be dropped without fair warning and without a chance to turn around and get yourself properly placed." Embree paid Owen's salary for the remainder of 1946, a total of $875 — money Owen desperately needed, for Lillian had fallen ill again.

Dodson, partly from politics, partly from respect for Embree, wrote a poem, "For Edwin R. Embree," which he read aloud at a dinner honoring the director at the Gramercy Park Hotel. In no wise worse than other occasion poems, it concluded:

> Because there are still men whose hearts
> Bear the large optimistic burden of freedom and peace:
> Men who rise up early
> And labor through the day for other men.
> Time bleeds, shadows shift
> But there is a time of healing coming
> Because these men of strength are with us.[20]

From a retrospection of thirty-five years, Owen summed up his experience: "Child, I went to Hollywood and met them all, the top writers. But they didn't pick up our cause because there were so many things going on in the government — Joseph McCarthy — and they were afraid. In my time, I was a very eloquent and good-looking young man. I should have had rays to pull them into our cause. But the commercial world had sucked them in, and they would not let their careers go away with a black cause even though they believed in the whole damn thing. And finally, liberal people are not always liberal with their money, so we folded up."[21] Owen wrote Leonard Rieser, "The AFC has gone down not 'with a bang but a whimper,' and I am here like 'an old man in a dry month.' It has been a great disappointment to all of us."

So the Committee for Mass Education in Race Relations came to its end. Clearly Dodson was not responsible for the financial debacle, nor was he remiss in providing quality scripts and ideas. Equally clear is the fact that CMERR had never been structured to succeed. If it had been, knowledgeable production people would have been in charge with realistic budgets in place. A generous interpretation would be that fuzzy thinking from well-intentioned white paternalists and self-serving cynicism from black intelligentsia killed a splendid idea. A less-generous interpretation would be to quote from Ellison's *Invisible Man*: "Keep the nigger boy running."

Nathaniel Dodson, Sr., ca. 1920.

Owen and Kenneth at ages seven and eight with cousin Edna Wilson at the beach, Brooklyn, ca. 1921.

Kenneth Dodson, high-school
graduation, 1933.

Kay Craft, Jimmy Carter, Owen, and John Kenny (standing), drinking
"slitty-eyed martinis," Bates College, 1936.

Priscilla Heath, Bates College graduation, 1936.

Production of *Divine Comedy,* Yale School of Drama, 1938.

Owen in double-breasted suit at
Spelman College, Atlanta, summer
1938.

Owen, Gordon Heath,
Edith, and Lillian at 469
Quincy Street, Brooklyn,
September 1940.

Thomas Pawley, actor, playwright, and dean of humanities at Lincoln University.

Owen in the Navy, December 1942. Photograph by Carl Van Vechten. Used by permission of Joseph Solomon.

Ednah Bethea, Owen's fiancée, ca. 1950.

Louise Leftwich, Lillian, Edith, and Owen at 469 Quincy Street, Brooklyn, birthday party, 1945.

Nathaniel Dodson, Jr.

Edith Dodson's wedding to Arthur Taylor, September 3, 1948. Photograph by Alexander King.

Owen Dodson and Claire Leyba at bon voyage party on SS
Stavangerfjord, August 1949.

Edith Kate Dodson, ca.
1955.

Owen and Earle Hyman in rehearsal for *Hamlet*, Howard University, 1951. Photograph by Robert McNeill.

14

Powerful Long Ladder, 1946–49

When Countee Cullen died on January 10, 1946, his wife Ida asked Owen to write an epitaph to appear in the newspaper. The poem begins:

> Now begins the sleep, my friend:
> You showed us that men could see
> Deep into the cause of Lazarus,
> Believe in resurrection.
> You come back to us
> Not unwinding a shroud and blinking at known light
> But singing like all the famed birds,
> Nightingale, lark and nightjar.

Eleven years Cullen's junior, Owen appreciated a model who could write sonnets and perfect quatrains, and his death brought a "terrible sense of loss." The morning before the funeral, Ida Cullen asked Dodson to come to their home in Tuckahoe, New York, to help pack the years of accumulated books, manuscripts and memorabilia; and on his way, would he drop by the undertaker's to make sure that Countee had on a fresh shirt, that his hair was combed right? The three-story brownstone funeral home in Harlem was, said Owen,

> the tackiest place I had ever seen. I went down the steps and rang the bell and I rang the bell. Finally, a woman stuck her head out of the third-story window. She had on an old kimono, and

those great pink curlers in her hair. "What do you want?" she said. I replied that I would like to see Mr. Cullen. She disappeared for a second, then poked her head out and called down to me, "He ain't ready yet." Somehow it seemed obscene—in the face of a man who had written about grace, and God, and who had spoken French.

Anyway, I had planned the funeral for a poet. Looking back on it now the plans seemed exquisite and right, but the next day, I found his father, Pastor of the Salem Methodist Episcopal Church, had turned the whole thing around. Instead of the pure voice of Dorothy Maynor, he substituted the stubby, wobbly voice of an old sister. Most of Countee's poems had been left out. And there were eulogies, and telegrams to be read. The only telegram from a prominent writer was one from Clifford Odets. The others all sounded like "Inasmuch as it has pleased Almighty God. . . ."

The funeral lasted three hours. (Some of the old honorary pallbearers had to slip away.) It was sad to see his students weeping for the death of their teacher. When they wheeled the coffin along the front row, the relatives screamed. Alain Locke came up to the casket dressed in his usual gray—his gray hair, his gray eyes, his gray suit, his gray shoes. He was such a small man and he stood by the casket and looked into Countee Cullen for a long time. Those of us who knew Countee and Alain had a tingle as the dead lay still and the living looked on. He saluted Countee as though he were his son. Raising his right hand, he brought it to his forehead and made a sharp distance between life and death.

When we got to the grave, there seemed to be mud everywhere; Arna Bontemps, Langston Hughes, Harold Jackman, myself, and two others almost slipped carrying Countee home. To have dropped his body would have meant desecration of the new age of crafts-manship, lyricism, and raised consciousness.[1]

In 1945, Dodson and Cullen had been asked by Mura Dehn (Mrs. Erwin Piscator) to write a poem for a modern-dance performance at the New School of Social Work, so every week and sometimes more, Owen had gone up to Countee's home in Tuckahoe to discuss and write *The Third Fourth of July*.[2] At that time Owen learned that Cullen's father was in fact his foster father. His mother was somewhere in the "aches of Tennessee or Arkansas." Owen speculated that Countee married twice just to get away from his stepfather, the Reverend Cullen: "To hear his father say to him, 'Countee, where's your spiritual poem this week?' Countee would get nervous because he had to write a spiritual poem. Religion and race kept him from becoming one of the greatest poets of our time, but because he was Black he felt compelled to write poems about race. He didn't feel them like Langston Hughes to his marrow bones. He liked to escape the turmoil of Harlem, go up to Tuckahoe where they had a beautiful home with Jacob Lawrence pictures in it. As a poet, he died inside because he wasn't able to do what he wanted to do without feeling guilty. I understand now what W. H. Auden meant at the end of *For the Time Being* when he talks about the Holy Family moving into Egypt: 'Safe in Egypt, we shall sigh for lost insecurity. / Only when its terrors come, shall our flesh feel quite at home.' "

Cullen died two months before his collaboration with Arna Bontemps, the musical *St. Louis Woman,* opened at the Martin Beck Theatre. Walter White, then head of the NAACP, had bad-mouthed the pre-production for perpetuating stereotypes (prostitutes and gamblers). Lena Horne had been invited to star, but, sensitive to White's criticism, she had refused. As executive secretary of CEMRR, Owen wrote Ms. Horne, introducing himself as one who had known her from Brooklyn days: "There is nothing in any of the works of Countee Cullen and Arna Bontemps to indicate that they would permit a production to go forward that would put the Negro in a shameful light. I hope you will continue with your plans in regard to *St. Louis Woman.*"[3] His appeal failed, and Ruby Hill sang Harold Arlen's music in the role of Della. The show ran 113 performances.

Gordon Heath, staff announcer on WMCA (one of the first black announcers in radio), arranged two slots for Owen to write radio dramas for "New World A-Coming," a weekly public-service series devoted to "vivid programs on Negro life based on the theme of Roi Ottley's book."[4] Heath also asked Pearl Primus to use Owen's poetry in her Broadway show. She did — for one night only; then she cut it. Part of that sound track appears in *Powerful Long Ladder* as "Poem for Pearl's Dancers." Owen dismissed his disappointment as vanity; however, his failure to be on Broadway as either a director or playwright saddened his later years.[5]

In the summer of '45, Owen wrote, "If you are Negro you want to be in the arts now." Perhaps as a way to lure Owen back to the South, Robert Salestad, his old boss at Hampton Institute, invited him to direct two plays for their summer festival. Owen began rehearsals in New York for *Outward Bound* and *Hamlet,* with Gordon in both leads; all major roles he cast with actors he knew.[6] The "spear carriers" he picked up at Hampton. Rehearsals held at the Equity Library Theatre went well, but Gordon "sawed the air" and filled the auditorium with round tones of "brown bread and butter," for which he received a thirteen-page criticism. For nine pages Owen reviewed Gordon's previous roles, finding him graced with talents, sound of body and voice; then the director zeroed in with his own "speech to the players": "Now we come to the weakest and the strongest consideration in you: your voice, your diction and your manner. He [Hamlet] has no rolling speech, no round accent, no syllable uttered in studiedness. He is plain and hero as sky is. Don't attitudinize him or lift him. Let him be mortal."[7] Owen's passion and his clear director's vision to propel Gordon's Hamlet into a human reality became his manifesto: classic drama must be rooted in common sense available to all.

Two days before the cast departed for Hampton, Owen handed out the train tickets. P. J. Sidney, cast as Claudius, said, "You mean Hampton, Virginia? I thought we were going to East Hampton." Owen said, "No, Virginia." The king replied, "I won't play in the South." And he didn't. Owen himself had to assume the role of Claudius, and did so with the actor's traditional pseudonym, adding Sidney's initials: P. J. Spelvin. His *Hamlet,* considerably cut down from its nearly four hours' playing time, succeeded. So strongly did the play appeal to the audience of nearly 2,000 that, at one performance, when Gordon picked up the poisoned cup, a voice shouted from the audience, "Don't drink that!"

A brief two months later, Elia Kazan cast Gordon Heath in *Deep Are the Roots* as Brent, a black veteran returning home to the South. Opening on October 7, the play ran fourteen months on Broadway before traveling to the London stage. In looking back, Gordon testified that "the two main influences on my acting were Kazan and Owen. Kazan gave me the underpinning, and Owen the confidence to fly. Kazan, the gas; Owen, the flame."[8]

Even with his theater assignments and a full-time job at American Film Center, Owen did not neglect his first love. He placed poems in *Common Ground, Phylon, Theatre Arts, Christendom, Opportunity,* the *Crisis,* and *Tomorrow.* He assembled poems, old and new, for a book tentatively entitled *Poems for the Intolerant,* a misnomer that reflected his anger more than the content of his verse. He sent the collection to John Farrar, who on January 24 sent him a telegram: "Would like to publish your poetry when we both consider the volume ready. Excited by possibilities of your writing. We will discuss everything when you return." (Owen was visiting with Charles Johnson at Fisk.) Farrar didn't think the poems "tough enough. I hope you don't mind my saying so, but I am keeping them by me and going over them again."⁹ Nonetheless, he sent a contract giving Owen a 10 percent royalty—twenty-five cents a book. Inside the publisher's office, a "mole" scribbled a note to Owen: "Your book is ready—it smells of glue and print, it has weight, texture, a price inconspicuously in the upper right corner of the front flap [$2.50]. It meets the eye; it is something to heft in the hand. You are lucky."¹⁰

On August 1, the postman delivered an advance copy of *Powerful Long Ladder,* a not-so-slim volume of 103 pages. On the cover, a naked black man reached for the stars, but at least no broken shackles dangled from his wrists. On the back cover the poet in tweed jacket and plaid tie seriously contemplated love, death, and race. In the year 1946, the publisher found it necessary to inscribe on the book jacket, "In this first volume of poems by a young Negro writer, you will find rhythms and a simplicity of structure essentially primitive." Yet, all in all, Owen was "lucky."

Its contents—thirty-six poems, three choruses excerpted from the *Divine Comedy,* the nine-poem requiem for Kenneth, and two sonnets—were sweet with melancholy and sorrow. Some of Owen's quatrains echoed Cullen and Housman ("rhythms and a simplicity of structure essentially primitive"), as in "Circle One," written "For Gordon Heath":

> Nothing happens only once,
> Nothing happens only here,
> Every love that lies asleep
> Wakes today another year.
>
> Why we sailed and how we prosper
> Will be sung and lived again;
> All the lands repeat themselves,
> Shore for shore and men for men.

Reviewers praised. No doubt *Powerful Long Ladder*'s sales benefited from the success of Gwendolyn Brooks's volume of verse *A Street in Bronzeville* (1945), for which she received an American Academy of Arts and Letters award. (In 1950, she would receive a Pulitzer.) While Langston Hughes remained *the* black poet, white America wished to acknowledge others, particularly those not too far politically left. Jessica Nelson North, in her review for *Poetry,* noted that

> every good Negro poet has a double allegiance. He belongs to a nation where publishers look eagerly for manuscripts by Negroes, and where the public will read his poetry with interest because of his race. He belongs to the great spiritual brotherhood of sensitive intellectuals and is more closely akin to them than to the downtrodden sharecroppers of the south; but he can not and should not forget that he is a Negro and that in this same nation cruelty and injustice are allowed to exist. All the more because he is privileged and articulate, he must speak for those who are not. Owen Dodson celebrates the wrongs of his special minority, not with bitterness but with sorrow.[11]

M. L. Rosenthal, in the *New York Herald Tribune Weekly Book Review,*[12] placed Owen in the tradition of

> that large group of modern "social" poets who seek to fuse ideological conviction with personal emotion that is the traditional basis of lyric poetry. With this effort, in our time, have been associated such varied talents as Auden, Kreymborg, Aragon; and in other directions, Williams, Tate, Eliot, Pound. These are writers each of whom has, in his way, achieved a certain maturity and perfection. Dodson, however, aside from his persistent, and frequently successful, attempt to speak realistically and angrily for the American Negro, is still young enough to be looking for just the right vocabulary and viewpoint to suit his special abilities. He does many things excellently.

After praising several poems individually, Rosenthal concluded, "It remains to be seen whether, in this medium and in his future work, he will display that mastery of structure and intellectual control in a really sustained work which are needed to fulfill the promise of the present volume."

Alfred Kreymborg[13] correctly perceived that "even his lyrical poems have a dramatic tendency," much as his theater critics noted that

Dodson's plays had a lyrical tendency. Jessica Nelson North observed that Dodson's poems "remind us again of the difficulties of combining drama with poetry." The critics had discovered the betwixt-lyric-and-drama tenor of his verse, the same insight that spurred Auden to suggest that Owen write libretti. Nonetheless, the political left discovered enough militant verse to satisfy, while those who worshipped the well-wrought urn detected enough form to appease. Altogether, he received fair and just appraisal as a talented, creative young man with promises of a mature greatness.

From his peers Owen received deference. He had sent galleys to Richard Wright in Paris, who responded, "I liked the book lots and will send you a blurb which you can use for it." Owen then asked Wright for a review in the *New York Herald Tribune Weekly Book Review,* but Wright either didn't submit one or was rejected.[14] Alain Locke wrote Owen a personal letter: "What puzzles me most is how racial is it or isn't it? I know the blurbists have to have raciality for public bait, but then that is only a passing phase of our culture. Though few believe it, I have never advocated that all Negroes who write poetry be Negro poets."[15] Not all praised the book: "One Negro paper blasted hell out of me as if I were a criminal and at least Edgar Guest. I understand Negro papers but think they stink in many ways because they go for the same kind of easy catch philosophy as the Hearst papers."[16]

In eleven months the book went into a second edition. By October 1946, Farrar, Straus & Giroux offered Owen a contract for a novel, which he had barely begun. Indeed, the novel wasn't on his first mind; Ibsen's *Peer Gynt* was. While lunching with two classmates from Yale, Wilson Lehr and Blevins Davis, Owen related seeing Gordon Heath in a production of *Peer Gynt.* His friends asked him, why not a Black American version? Owen placed the play in the bayous of Louisiana, and it became its own thing. Blevins suggested some rewriting for authenticity and offered Owen some money if he would go down to New Orleans. Owen said he would. But then Morgan Farley, who had played in *An American Tragedy* (1926), offered Owen the use of his cottage in Vermont, and Owen decided he could create Louisiana just as well up there.

On July 22, 1946, before leaving Brooklyn, Owen painted 469 Quincy's garden furniture blue, hoping to distract or appease Lillian, who had shown an alarming tendency to become ill whenever he left town.

Farley's rural haven in South Dorset turned out to be a one-room cabin, complete with an oil lamp, a potbellied stove, and with a hound dog whose ears made "that dry flapping sound when he walked." Never really a loner, Owen found that neither the mountain stream whispering beside the cabin nor the dry flap of the dog's ears sated his need for conviviality. Hungry for conversation, he called his patron in New York. Blevins Davis asked, "Where are you calling from?" "Vermont," he replied. Davis said, "You get your ass to Louisiana. That's what I gave you the money for." Dodson left for New Orleans and toured the bayous and heard the patois of the people; the play took a deeper and warmer shape in his mind. The Cajun exposure lasted two weeks; then heat, hay fever, and Lillian's stroke pulled him back, but not before he had discovered a title—*Bayou Legend*.

Davis sent the play to Katherine Dunham, who invited Dodson and Davis to her office, which was decorated like a South Seas island— bamboo and exotic plants. Said Owen: "Katherine was looking cool and beautiful, and she introduced us to her designer-husband, John Pratt. She said she liked the play, and asked for the part of Hethabella, the mean one, to be expanded because she wished to play it. She suggested that the part of the heroine could be played down, and John Pratt would do the scenery and the costume. As she spoke she had a letter opener in her hand fixed against the palm of her other hand, and she was rolling it around. She knew that Blevins had all that money he had inherited from his wife.[17] Blevins got redder and redder. Finally, he said, 'In other words, Miss Dunham, I will not be the producer, but I will be working for you and providing the money.' Dunham took the letter opener and drove it into the desk and said, 'That's right!' That was the end of that production. She had treated him as another property she could exploit—greedy."

By April 1947, publicity appearances for his poetry book swept Owen on a tour of readings as far as Cornell College in Iowa and Lincoln University in Missouri. Stopping in Chicago, he read at the Southside Community Center and visited the Riesers. Then Lillian suffered another stroke, and he borrowed money to fly home. She did not die.

Much of Lillian's care fell to Owen. (Edith worked for social services and attended Baruch College at night.) Although he was able to write at home, little time and no money remained for the parties, the theater, the comradeship he loved. His only surviving joy lived upstairs—Frank

Harriott, handsome in the image of Harry Belafonte. To him Owen dedicated the poem "Rag Doll and Summer Birds." The two men would play records and drink sherry and wait for Lillian's bell to ring, then go downstairs to answer it. After a time Frank got bored, and he began partying with a set of people whom he had met through Karl Priebe. In the spring Rosenwald awarded Harriott a fellowship to write a novel based on his interviews with Billie Holiday, and on January 30, 1948, he left Owen and moved to Milwaukee to be with "porcelain Karl." Owen loved the young man; several times over the following years he hurried to Milwaukee because Harriott had become seriously ill. He died September 6, 1955, from a disease Owen couldn't name. The loss was serious: "Frank was one of the best friends I ever had."

Owen sacrificed his lover to remain with Lillian, the very sacrifice that she had made for him when he was a child. With no more salary after January 1947 from AFC, Dodson had applied to Rosenwald for another fellowship. His recommendations glowed: Auden and John Farrar praised him; Karl Shapiro called Dodson the best Negro poet since Langston Hughes—but no Rosenwald. In February, Owen wrote Peggy: "I don't think you can imagine how long it took for me to decide to wire you. I had just about spent the last scrap I could get together. Our doctor stayed about an hour yesterday. All is mixed up with physical and [her] psyche. Lillian had just told us to ask the Board of Ed to let her resign. I went out to school to get her things. When I brought them back, she was dismayed. Then she had the attack. On her birthday, the 8th [February], she said she wouldn't see another. I think you understand why I had to have some money on hand."[18]

The next week Owen told Peggy "I could begin to teach again or go into other work, but I feel that I can get the novel and the play on the docket and so in the interim, I must sacrifice. Besides, I can't leave Lillian in her present state. Peggy, I'd like to talk to your friend at the mental hygiene clinic. Every time I go away, even overnight, something happens. I'm not discouraged tho—I just want to do my best since I'm the titular male of the house."[19]

By April Owen had spoken to a psychiatrist who suggested that Lillian would do better to leave 469 Quincy for three or four summer months by the sea. Owen told Peggy that "if she doesn't, the psychiatrist can't tell what will happen. I've rented a floor of a summer place in Nyack. I don't know how I'll pay for it. For this period I'll need six hundred dollars. Peggy, you once wrote me a letter saying if I needed anything don't hesitate to ask and that it wouldn't spoil our friendship. I know it won't. In the fall I'll either have that job or at any rate the nurse won't be needed, and what we've been paying her can go toward paying back any part of this total amount that you could possibly help me with. I feel deeply about writing a letter of this kind but I have to do it."[20]

The Riesers advanced the money. Lillian, with Nurse Lewis, moved to Nyack, New York, for the summer. Edith graduated from Baruch College in business administration, and on June 2, Owen fled to Yaddo, New York. To keep Owen writing, John Farrar had arranged for a six-week fellowship. Having three times left Lillian and three times been called to hurry to her bedside, Owen feared to leave but did.

Located near Saratoga Springs on the wooded estate of Katina and Spencer Trask, Yaddo was founded in 1926 as a haven for creative artists. No artist would pay. Yaddo would provide each writer, composer, painter, sculptor, or photographer a studio and three meals a day. During his six weeks, with no trace of proletarian disdain, Owen strolled through the oval gardens, admired the trees, the stone mansion—an American fantasy of European royal estates. Here he shared time with Arna Bontemps, Marianne Hauser (novelist), Ulysses Kay (composer), Robert Lowell (poet), Bucklin Moon (novelist), Theodore Roethke (poet), Agnes Smedley (writer), Marguerite Young (novelist), and Thomas E. Doremus (novelist).[21] Said Owen: "Yaddo is a cross between Proust and Thoreau. I'm crazy about it all. So many angels and ministers of grace to defend us. Dinner times are the best—in sight of mountains. We discuss everything from beards to beer, from Episcopal chairs to bogs, from ragweed sauce to night shades seen in ditches to bullfrogs. Work is going well."[22]

From 9:30 A.M. to 4:00 P.M. he worked on his novel. After talking it through with Arna Bontemps, he realized that his book was a trilogy—*Boy at the Window* would be part 1. On one of many long walks with novelist Marianne Hauser, Owen confessed he wanted to write a libretto, and toward that end he engaged black composer Ulysses Kay to write an opera about Willie Francis, who had been "tickled by Alabama's electric chair" but refused to die, and had to go back a second time to meet death. The opera would cover the year between Francis's executions, presenting his growth from a hysterical delinquent to a man who is ready to live just as he must die. They never wrote it.

Yaddo gave Owen his last chance for the next dozen years to write poetry. Mrs. Katherine Biddle, a poet and the wife of Roosevelt's attorney general, had seen Owen's first productions at Howard, met the young poet, liked him,[23] and invited him to send some "Negro" poems to her. Owen sassed her by saying he hadn't felt like a Negro in years, but sent poems. Biddle sent "Crystal Us the Future" to her sister, a countess in Rome, who published the poem in *Botteghe Oscure*.[24] Finding himself in an issue with W. H. Auden, Edith Sitwell, Conrad Aiken, e. e. cummings, Theodore Roethke, and William Carlos Williams made Owen feel it "is kinda important because there are so many plus people." All well and good, but Owen needed money. Completing the novel could free him.

In March 1947, Ruth and John Stephan invited Owen to submit poems to their new literary journal, the *Tiger's Eye*. In June, they accepted "Six O'Clock,"[25] the threnody on Kenneth's death, and "Crazy Woman to the Virgin,"[26] a short poem presaging the monologues of *The Confession Stone* (1970). Said Owen: "I got more money for two poems than I had gotten ever—over one hundred dollars. Wonderful magazine. No names at the end of the poems so you would read them for the poem itself."[27]

At Yaddo that summer, Owen wrote an elegy, "Funeral Sermon for a Poet." He dedicated it to Marguerite Young, "a sister, a poet who dreams of a new harmony where purposeful fire burned the land black." Arna Bontemps wrote Owen, "Your concluding lines for Marguerite's funeral are stirring. You have never written more beautifully, and she should feel more than complimented. That's going to be your best poem, and I think we should have it for the Anthology" (Hughes and Bontemps's 1949 collection *The Poetry of the Negro*).[28]

Owen neither finished nor abandoned the poem, but kept adding a verse here, moving a section there, changing lines. As the years went by, he began to cannibalize images and verses for other poems. It's a pity, for Bontemps had correctly assessed its merit. The work begins when the poet's friends see her dead and laid out for the first time:

> When we looked your face had gone
> to childhood; there might have been
> a ribbon in your hair and at
> your breast an abstract doll
> sucking the shroud. We might

> have known you were not what
> you were. Girlhood caresses
> your dead age.

The first part concludes with, "We juggled days and waited for exhaustion / This is the way we are." The second section is the voice of a man "who loved the woman in the coffin but never expressed it to her even when she declared her love for him":

> The nightingales of my disposition
> have changed to the raw sounds of crows,
> the lost flat sounds of sparrows in snow,
> birds without summer or summer songs:
> nightjars and the caw caw of ratbirds
> flying over the rotted wharves of my dreams.
> I would descend to you without dying and beg
> peace from the passion I stored up
> and never spent with you. How shall
> I walk within the halls of your body now?
> . . . .
>
> Shut in her dying she died with sins
> uncommitted but felt. Alone and the racing miles
> dark of winter and fresh of spring and she alone
> coffined in the unpredicted death of death-love.
> Who says: sweetheart through a tight mouth?
> Who says: love me now in a dirt blanket that was
> to be burned and scattered?

In love with corrupting death, the poem moves through images of the undertaker's preparations and the grave's decay. Then from the dust the final section arises like an Easter hymn, one that Owen published as the coda to his *Harlem Book of the Dead*:

> Oh let it be the wheel of resurrection
> Upturning blooming waters from her soul;
> Oh let them splash flat-vertical and high
> To arc a rainbow in that triumph time
> When startled angels graduate cum laude,
> From adoration to the bright Divine;

Marguerite Young[29] may have been the vehicle, but the immediate prickings for the poem sprang from Lillian's long illness and from Owen's knowledge that his sister had sacrificed her chance for love and children for him. Just as he would press down into the pages of his novel his unconsummated grief for his mother, Lillian's dying electrified the images he dedicated to Young. Although Owen made several attempts at completing the poem (he had selected sections for an unpublished collection, "Cages of Loneliness"), the passing of his sister on December 31, 1950, left his threnody incomplete. The passion that thundered from his pen at Yaddo never stormed into his consciousness again.

Even as he discarded poetry for prose, evidence poured in that he had been accepted into the Negro canon by his seniors. He read in Howard's chapel with Hughes, Bontemps, and Brown.[30] His poems appeared in the major black texts of the fifties.[31] In October 1952, during the seventy-fifth anniversary of Jackson State College, he appeared with Bontemps, Tolson, Redick, Hayden, Brown, Hurston, Walker, and Hughes in the now-famous photograph. All this during the decade he had stopped writing poetry.

15

Howard University, 1948

In the spring of 1947, Howard University's dean, St. Clair Price, offered Owen an associate professorship in English beginning "*immediately if necessary,* but certainly by September."[1] Dodson wrote Peggy, "Somehow I feel the R[osenwald] Fund was instrumental in my going to Howard. They perhaps thought a fellowship wasn't enough cash or enough future for me. They probably were right." His friends never considered that the life preserver they threw him might drown the poet. The surrender of his "bohemian" life for that of a salaried professional made Gordon's announcement that he would sail for France most painful; Heath's first letter home must have cut like a knife: "Paris is full of perception, liveliness, vitality and a hovering joy. The air is free and flecked with quick alert intelligence. The streets are named after artists and they are with honor in their own country. It is a beautiful city—you feel suddenly that there is nothing to look at in our part of America. Paris was made for lovers if ever I saw a city so framed and made capable."[2]

Gordon had no Lillian to care for.

For a final fling at bohemia, Owen spent August at Alfred, New York, living in Glidden Parker's barn/studio, which gave Owen the vision of converting a stable in Washington, D.C.: "If I can persuade the owner to put in a chemical toilet and a spigot, I'll move in with a potbellied stove."[3] But by September 15, homeless Owen found himself living in Carver Hall for Men. (Small comfort that Gordon, too, had to share a *salle de bains.*) Then Miss Elsie Austin, a disciple of Bahá'í who planned to spend a year in a "communion center," offered Owen her apartment. A lonely Owen moved in: "No one realized what I could do. I just taught speech in the English department. I felt annihilated." Once again Anne Cooke rescued him, inviting him into her newly created drama department.

Since 1907 the students at Howard had read Shakespeare in performance, but the university had not considered it necessary to devote an academic department to Thespis. Suddenly, Howard hired three teachers: "Queen Anne" and "Mr. D." from Yale, "Beanie" Butcher from E. C. Mabie's rigorous department at the University of Iowa.[4] Cooke's strength lay in the classics and in administration; Butcher's in acting and set design; Dodson's in directing and spectacle. Each possessed ambition and talent; all knew and respected world theater; all had had ten to fifteen years of experience in their arts. James W. Butcher, who had returned from the service, undertook to renovate the second floor of Spaulding Hall (the ROTC's "shooting gallery"). The narrow stage allowed no space for actors to pass behind the scenery, but the building had windows that enabled an actor coming up from the dressing room on stage left to exit, climb a ladder, cross the roof, climb down into another window, then saunter in from stage right. No air-conditioning, one dressing room on the first floor, one telephone for all offices, three pipes holding all the lights, controlled from a tiny booth located over the offices at the entrance. The auditorium could pack 200 into wooden office chairs. To Owen, Spaulding replicated Hathorn Hall at Bates or the drill room at Great Lakes. However, he produced his best work when most restricted.

In the faculty's salad days, even philosophical disputes had produced excitement: Should Blacks be trained only to teach in black colleges? Should they aspire to professional jobs? Should they produce only black plays? In 1948, these questions seemed moot. Anne Cooke declared that her mission was to make a department that would be not commercial but professional. Although there seemed no future in majoring in drama, she trained students to enter that world. When in 1950 Roxie Roker asked Cooke where she would find work as an actor, Cooke told her to get her training and be ready. The next year the Royal Academy in London announced a summer program and Roker was accepted.[5]

James Butcher, who for a time had attempted professional acting, told his students that if they planned to become actors, they should also train themselves to teach: "It was a poor way to talk to students, but when we started, there was nothing for us in professional theater."⁶ The department did not restrict itself to Negro themes and plays. Within four years, a student who came to the theater could see a Greek play, an Elizabethan play, a modern play, and a new play. They premiered dramas by Kaj Munk, Mario Fratti, Albert Camus, James Baldwin. Howard tried to say that there would come a time when the students would be called upon to play any role, and they would not be prepared if they had mush in their mouths, only wore jeans, and had no instinct for costumes.

The students built scenery. Majors took turns in the box office and makeup. The department insisted on "total theater." Black youngsters who barely understood the portent of their dreams enrolled. In 1949, Roxie Roker, who lived in Brooklyn, enrolled because she had heard that Owen had come from Brooklyn.⁷ White students enrolled; Catholic University sent its graduate students to direct laboratory productions. For those who dared dream, the ensemble of Cooke, Butcher, and Dodson conjured magic. From 1948 to 1957 the Howard drama department instilled into its students a respect for quality. With dedication and a Spartan budget, Howard rose to a first rank position in college drama.

In February 1948 Dodson directed his premiere production—Arthur Miller's *All My Sons*. For the first time white drama critics came to see a Howard play. The novelty of seeing *All My Sons* as a black family impressed Richard Coe of the *Washington Post,* who began to review Howard regularly: "I came to know Owen and believed in him, one of those people who is so good that you know that immediately he's an innocent, a pure soul. His productions had a sense of assurance, one expected intensity in the performance, and he had a passion for literate speech."⁸

For the last production slot in May, Owen persuaded Cooke to direct his new script, *Bayou Legend,* and he insisted that Charles Sebree be brought to Washington to design the set and costumes. Cooke agreed, but she had no budget. Owen asserted that *Legend* would not be legend without Sebree.

Owen owed Sebree money for a painting, "The Dwarf Clown." For two months, Sebree had dunned him: "I would appreciate something. I am broke."⁹ Then, a month later, "I hate to ask you for the money just now with the holidays so near but I am real broke. I live by my painting but since I've made my choice that's that. I am holding on like death." A week after that, "I spent my rent money expecting your check. I spent it for frames. The landlord. . . ." Owen himself was borrowing money from Peggy and from Alain Locke, and yet he held onto the painting, perhaps rationalizing Sebree's suffering as the price the artist must pay for his freedom.

By mid-February, Sebree had Cooke's permission to design *Bayou Legend,* and he moved into Owen's apartment to work and presumably to eat and drink up the "Dwarf Clown" money that he could not wrest from his patron. While Owen's friendship to Sebree might flag, his dedication to Sebree's art did not. He spent hours helping him write a play entitled "My Mother Came Crying Most Pitifully"; this romantic fantasy later appeared on Broadway as *Mrs. Patterson.* Owen confessed that "Sebree's dialogue is so rich and funny and pathetic that I hate to change or even suggest commas. Really brilliant."[10]

In April, Owen threw himself into the production of *Bayou Legend,* even importing real Spanish moss to hang from the stage trees. Cooke choreographed forty actors in and around the vest-pocket stage. Sebree's set and costumes delighted the *Evening Star*'s Jay Carmody, who pronounced it the "most elaborate production staged in campus theatre history. . . . Dodson's conception is more that of the poet than of the dramatist. He is an author who sees visions and loves words and whose blending of the two stimulates the imagination more than it satisfies any audience demand for the tidy or the terse."[11] Alas, too true. Owen possessed two great talents—one for words, the other for spectacle. His talents melded in pageantry but never into a tightly constructed play. The inherent opposition between the luxury that poetry afforded the inner stage of personality and the cinematic pressure that modern drama demanded for external action stymied him.

Bayou Legend did well, extending its run two days. At that time, Owen didn't deny his debt to Ibsen; indeed, the Howard program noted that his play was "based on Ibsen's *Peer Gynt.*" As the years went by, however, he began to resent those who referred to his play as an adaptation; he felt that, except for the story line, "the play is my own as much as Anouilh's *Antigone* is attached to Sophocles." In any case, many who saw the play in 1949 did not know he had written it—his name had been omitted from the program.[12]

Amid all of his production work, Austin returned from Bahá'í and reclaimed her apartment. Owen settled into a third-floor walk-up at

1715 Fourteenth Street, N.W. Below were a barber, a tailor, and a laundry; on the sidewalk outside, ladies of the night. With a monthly salary of $360, Owen felt $83 to be too much for an unfurnished apartment.

To his new nest he invited two Navy buddies as houseguests: Sebree came to stay during production, and then painter Harlan Jackson joined them. Just before the end of November, the two artists announced they would give Owen a birthday party and asked him to give them a list of his friends. He did. Then the artists hung his walls with their paintings, asking, "Dodson, you think that Anne Cooke would like a Calder?" When Owen said yes, Jackson made some mobiles like Calder's. They asked Owen what kind of pictures Jimmy Whyte liked (he owned the Book Gallery on Connecticut Avenue). When Owen answered "Miro," Sebree put a little string and some balls into his picture. They went down the guest list, entitling each picture to entice the special interests of Owen's birthday guests. When it was over they had sold everything. Dodson recalled it as "a lesson to me, but I never learned that lesson."

Poet and playwright May Miller attended that birthday party (her name then was Mrs. John Sullivan). She took Owen aside, asking, "How much do you pay for this apartment? Eighty-three dollars! Much too much. I have an apartment on Sixteenth Street right across from the Universalist Church. It's only sixty dollars a month. The living room is more than twenty by twenty. The dining room is at least as large. There's a small bedroom and a small kitchen, and a large hall where you could put all of your books, and a patio."

Owen seized it. Then the tenant above Owen moved out and he seized that one, too, connecting the apartments with a spiral staircase. For $120 a month he had two apartments—one with a working fireplace. For nearly twenty years, Owen held court at 1813 Sixteenth Street. There, students saw a home with original paintings, with shelf upon shelf of theater, art, and poetry books, with stacks of classical records; and there they marveled at the two carved carousel horses that held up the round glass table.

In January Owen sent John Farrar the first three chapters of *Boy at the Window;* the publisher pronounced them good and urged Dodson to complete the book by September, but Owen had no summer to write. (Howard paid his salary for only ten months of the year, making summer-school teaching obligatory.) In June, academic penury encouraged Owen to join Cooke at Atlanta University Summer Theatre, to celebrate its fifteenth anniversary by producing *RUR*, *Oedipus Rex*, *The Glass Menagerie*, and *Camille*—hardly a schedule that allowed Owen to complete his novel.

For $300 Cooke persuaded Lee Simonson, designer and director of the New York Theatre Guild, Louis Kronenberger, drama critic for *Time* and *P.M.*, and Elmer Rice, playwright, to come to Atlanta, each for one week. Owen, in charge of their lodging, their comfort, their shopping, made each his friend. Simonson carried away a copy of *Bayou Legend* and gave it to a producer. Rice invited Owen to visit him in his home. And after searching all of Peach Street for Kronenberger's special brand of rum, Owen traded poetry with the critic.

Lillian's illness hovered over Owen's career. Hardly had he arrived at Howard when Edith rushed Lillian to the hospital for oxygen. Nonetheless, by April she had recovered enough to visit him for two weeks, viewing the National Art Gallery, cooking for his friends, and attending her brother's play. But the big news from 469 Quincy: Edith planned to marry!

Her choice, if it was that, for it seemed as if she had been sentenced to wedlock for being found thirty-nine, was Arthur Taylor. Tall in his dark double-breasted suit, he arrived at the house on September 3 to claim his bride. A family friend, Alexander King, took nuptial photos: Edith, in a simple silk crepe dress with a cummerbund tied in back and graced with several strands of pearls and four white carnations, stood with her chin high, her hair combed back and carefully rolled at the edges. Like a jolly giant, her husband smiled down on his bride; he held her hand to cut the cake; he placed the fork to her lips. But his wife never smiled, never looked up at him; her arms hung to her sides. In a solo shot, Edith stood alone before the mirror, her tiny earrings casting a delicate shadow on her neck, her eyes hard around the edges, staring into the mirror and beyond.

Owen, in his bow tie, his hair freshly clipped, stuffed his hands into his pockets, showed his teeth. Garlanded in gardenias, Lillian sat in her chair, the official mother, too ill to stand. The happiest face was the eight-year-old boy from next door, the one Owen "adopted" because he saw resemblances to himself at that age. Lef, nowhere visible, no doubt prepared more orange-sherbet punch in the kitchen. Was it for this the morning stars sang?

Arthur and Edith moved into their apartment at 720 Marcy Avenue in Brooklyn. Within two years, Edith had moved to 270 St. Nicholas in Harlem, and Owen no longer addressed letters to Mrs. Taylor but to Edith Dodson. The gossips had their day. Some whispered that Edith had met Arthur while working at her social-service office; he had been a client, and she had dated him against professional rules. Her investigation had been incomplete, for she discovered later that he was already married with children. Some of Owen's friends preferred a variant rumor that Arthur was gay and Edith had discovered him in flagrante delicto. A better conjecture is that Arthur Taylor did not have the class to ascend into the Dodson phalanx. Those who met Edith after 1950 never knew she had been married, and when in the 1970s an old friend brought up the memory, Edith appeared startled, exclaiming, "I had forgotten all about it." In any case, Mr. Taylor went away, and Edith walked free to care for her brother, whom *Ebony* had just designated as one of the most eligible bachelors of the year. When Sebree saw the article, he wrote Owen, "I just saw your picture in *Ebony*. I knew you were a bachelor, but I never guessed you were eligible."[13]

16

Wild Duck Flies Home, 1949

On Saturday morning, November 20, 1948, Fredrik Haslund, then Norway's delegate to the United Nations, searched through the *Washington Post* for a theater performance to brighten his evening. As of August 1, a strike by Actors Equity had withdrawn all performers from Washington's only major commercial house, the National Theater, until it dropped its 112–year-old policy of excluding Negroes. Marcus Heiman, a New Yorker and president of the corporation operating the National, refused to lower the color bar, and the strike lasted eighteen months, indirectly encouraging theatergoers and drama critics to attend performances at Catholic and Howard universities.

Amazed that there was no live theater in the capital of the United States, Haslund's eye caught a one-inch announcement: *The Wild Duck*—final performance 8:30 at Howard University. The novelty of a Negro Ibsen intrigued him. He phoned for six tickets, and, fortunately for theater history, the Norwegians were admitted at curtain time.

After the performance, Haslund approached the director and inquired casually if she would like to bring her *Duck* to Norway. Dr. Anne Cooke responded, "When would you like us to come?" He thought a moment. "Perhaps next September. Could you provide me with some photos and a recording?" He was not joking.[1] Haslund showed the documents to theater producer Hans Nilssen. Together they persuaded the Norwegian Parliament to commit $4,500 to bring twenty-four people to Scandinavia for ten weeks. Local citizens would provide room and board for the Americans, keeping the cost down.

An additional $4,500 remained to be raised. Howard University had no funds, nor could the State Department finance the students under the Fulbright Act, which was reserved for individual scholars. After three months no angel had emerged, but, unknown to Howard, help was on its ironic way from Paul Robeson.

In April 1948, Robeson had spoken in Paris at a Conference for World Peace and declared that if there were a war with the Soviet Union, the American Negro would not fight the former U.S. ally. After provoking America with this headline, Robeson then toured Stockholm, Copenhagen, and Oslo in a series of standing-room-only concerts, commanding more headlines by announcing that "only in Russia could the Negro artist straighten his shoulders and raise his head high." When Robeson returned home, a mob of American patriots stoned him at the Peekskill concert. The next summer, the advent of the McCarthy Era saw Congress pass the Mundt/Nixon Bill, which required all Communists to register and to surrender their passports.

Pres. Harry S Truman's chum Blevins Davis, when he heard Robeson's denunciation in Paris of American racism, countered by giving Howard the additional $4,500. (That same summer Davis also had financed the production of *Hamlet* at Elsinore with actor Robert Breen, a man who, as it turned out, also benefited from the Howard tour.) What had begun as a Haslund-Cooke cultural handshake across the seas now emerged as an East/West propaganda tilt. Drew Pearson headlined his syndicated column "Negro Actors to Trail Robeson," and wrote that "the appearance of these American Negro student players in Scandinavia will be testimony to the fact that it is not only in Russia (as Robeson alleges) that the Negro artist can breathe easily and freely."[2] And to sweeten the package, the United States High Command in Europe invited the Howard Players to perform at six bases in occupied Germany.

Cooke, Butcher, and Dodson did not plan a tour as representative American Free World Negroes, but they did plan to present the best productions possible. The Norwegians wanted two shows, one an American play. Owen suggested *Bayou Legend*. Cooke turned it down because it was too Ibsen-like and not "Negro folk" enough. Dodson accused Cooke of denying him international fame, but in truth, *Legend* was too long and its cast too large and not congruent with that of *The Wild Duck*. However, when it was announced that Dodson would direct *Mamba's Daughters,* by the white playwrights of *Porgy and Bess,* black critics envisioned images of gospel-singing, dialect-sprouting, knife-wielding Negroes being sown across Europe. Black playwright Theodore Browne expressed his fury about the choice of play. "Instead of fostering the culture of its own people, [Howard] is making it quite plain that it is not interested in the culture of its own people."[3]

On August 31 in New York harbor, Eleanor Roosevelt, as a trustee of Howard University, boarded the SS *Stavangerfjord*, bidding the Howard troupe bon voyage, but Cooke and many of her cast had not yet arrived—their Washington train had been delayed two hours. When they rushed to the pier, they discovered that Secretary of State Dean Acheson had sent a representative; Clarence Derwent, president of Equity, had also come; so had a representative from ANTA. The press, the relatives crowded around; everybody had come except Mordecai Johnson, president of Howard University. In retrospect, Dr. Cooke thought Johnson's failure to attend the official farewell connoted no lack of interest or even administrative snub; Johnson simply had failed to see the significance of Howard's Department of Drama being the first undergraduate group in America with State Department sponsorship to be honored with an invitation to perform abroad.

If there was naïveté in Howard's administration, innocence also prevailed among the players: an innocence about being Truman's countermove to Robeson; an innocence about bringing *The Wild Duck* to a culture that had a strict tradition for the performance of Ibsen, who "had cast such a great shadow, there has been no light in Norway ever since."

If the *Stavangerfjord* went down, down would go the entire faculty of Howard's drama department, along with twenty black students and Ronald Weider, a white boy. The first day out of harbor, the actors ran line rehearsals for three plays. (The Swedes had requested that Howard perform *Miss Julie*, the one-act by Strindberg, but Butcher, who was playing the servant role opposite Zaida Coles, judged the play underrehearsed and refused to perform it before Swedish audiences.)

Aboard the clinically white steamer, her double stacks billowing clouds into the autumn air, Owen, tucked into a chair on the upper deck, leisurely read Gwendolyn Brooks's recently published *Annie Allen*, which won the Pulitzer in 1950. He also wrote Lillian, thanking her for the gift of handkerchiefs, and Edith and Arthur, who had presented him with a new pipe; someone else had sent a carton of cigarettes and three pairs of socks. The nine-day crossing allowed time for seasickness, cold catching, line rehearsals, and letter writing.

To present a more intimate account of this odyssey, a first-person "community diary," constructed from letters, journals, and interviews, begins here on the evening of the captain's dinner.[4]

September 8, Thursday. Everyone dressed to the nines—the women in their black dresses and heels. Professor Dodson presented Dr. Cooke with four flowers kept eight days in the refrigerator, still so fresh, so bright! The pièce de résistance of our banquet: venison; but in spite of Dr. Cooke's admonitions on cross-cultural etiquette, some of us couldn't devour Bambi.

Our first glimpse of Norway—strange rock formations like old sleepy trolls rising out of the sea. As we steamed into Bergen, we were entirely surrounded by mountains with houses built tier on tier, their orange slate roofs disappearing in mist.[5] A band played "The Star-Spangled Banner," and I was surprised at myself—I was so stirred. During our six rainy hours ashore, fourteen of us braved the rain to the Bristol Inn, where the waiters speak perfect English! The toilet paper—rough! Then back on the ship and up the coast to the town of Stavanger, where the peasants stared, not hostile but curious. We stared back at their knickerbockers. Edwin Ellick eased our tension. He smiled at the children and talked between his teeth, "What the hell are you looking at? Never seen a black person before?" We laughed, and they, not knowing why, laughed too. In our two hours ashore, we learned to "skål." Zaida says that their pronunciation of "negger" [black] is too close to "nigger."

September 10, Saturday. We disembarked in Oslo and were met with flowers and speeches. All of us were assigned families to live with. Somehow Zaida Coles's host family knew it was her twenty-first birthday and brought her flowers. A restaurant owner had volunteered to house Edwin Ellick and Roxie Roker because he thought Roxie was a boy's name. Edwin had to sleep on the couch. Weather—dreary and wet.

September 12, Monday. The American embassy gave a reception for us to meet the royal family. The girls were instructed that Americans on embassy soil do not curtsy to royalty, but on the street, we do; the boys may accept a handshake if offered but must not presume. The

American cultural attaché asked us, "Have you ever drunk champagne?" His paternalism engendered an embarrassed silence until Mr. D. assured the diplomat, "Yes, chile, Negroes do drink champagne."

The king was ill, but Crown Prince Olaf, his wife, Marta, and their two daughters attended. American ambassador Charles U. Bay hosted. Dr. Cooke, regal in her hat and silver hair, made us fearless; we all lined up to shake hands and to introduce each Norwegian to the student on our left. Well, the names are jawbreakers, and halfway down the line when the crown prince shook Edmere Windfield's hand and said, *"Welkommen til Norge"* (welcome to Norway), Edmere, thinking he had not gotten the name straight, asked in the friendliest manner, "Mr. Who?" The prince had a silly giggle and later referred to himself as Mr. Who. Afterward, we all were taken to Blom's restaurant by the Artists Association. Talk about high cotton!

Tomorrow is our first performance, and we're all shaking, including Cookie, but she tries to hide it. Beanie's in charge of the scenery, nearly two tons. We all had to help bring it out of the ship. The Det Nye Teater furnishes the lights and the furniture. I learned how Professor Butcher got his nickname, Beanie. When he was a kid he hung out with a boy named Porky, and that was that.

September 13, Tuesday. We're exhausted and too excited to sleep. Eight curtain calls! Eight! What a night! This morning Mr. D., following Dr. Cooke's ground plan, arranged the library furniture onstage for the first act; then he hurried off to get a bite to eat. When he returned just before curtain to review his stage, he discovered that the furniture has been rearranged. "Why?" he demanded of the stage manager. "Because this," explained Mr. Stage Manager, pointing his finger to the new configurations of chairs, tables, and desks, "this is Ibsen's plan." Under the disapproving glare of the stagehands Mr. D. moved the furniture back to the Howard plan, then sat on the sofa to discourage any further moves by Ibsen.

Out front, Dr. Anne Cooke waited at the door of the theater with her practiced curtsy to welcome the royal family. Crown Prince Olaf escorted her to their seats, and asked, "Dr. Cooke, are you nervous?" With the voice that we know as that of "Queen Anne," she answered, "Not at all, not at all."

Our excitement edged close to hysteria. The 750–seat house was packed. The light cues were coming in two languages; the curtain went up. All went well until act 4, when in the crucial scene where the idealist Gregers (Graham Brown) is explaining self-sacrifice to the child, Gregers's collar bottom popped off, allowing both wings of his celluloid collar to expose his Adam's apple. A silence gripped the stage. Gregers articulated something about the necessity for repair and repaired into the wings, abandoning Hedvig (Marilyn Berry, a freshman from Alabama), to improvise Ibsen for the royal family. When Gregers returned, his collar still winging it, they finished the scene. Attempting to ease Anne's distress, the crown prince leaned over and whispered, "And how do you feel now, Dr. Cooke?" She closed her eyes, tightened her lips, and shook her head. Nonetheless, we did it! Eight curtain calls! Eight!

September 14, Wednesday. Widely reviewed and they liked us. Critics point out that we know little about how Norwegians produce Ibsen. For example, traditionally the role of the bachelor Gregers is played by a dashing handsome actor, while that of Hjalmar is played by a less attractive male. In our production, the casting had been reversed. For Norwegians it must have been like seeing Gary Cooper play the villain. Several mentioned that the child Hedvig is usually played from her first-act entrance as a girl with the mark of doom upon her; Marilyn Berry played her as a normal cheerful girl, and they loved her. One reviewer called *Duck* "a freshly vacuumed Ibsen." Our six performances'll be SRO.

September 16, Friday. Tonight after our show, the University of Oslo gave us a dinner dance, and the vice-chairman said this was the first time he had ever met Negroes; we were amazed. Some wanted to know if there was a distinction between American whites and Negroes. When we said yes, they replied that Negroes are the more popular Americans because they see fewer of us.

September 17, Saturday. Our last full day in Oslo for a month. We made a tour of the folk museum and saw the Viking boats that sailed to Greenland, floating in the air like gulls. Our last performance of *Duck* tomorrow.

September 18, Sunday. Following the matinee today we rushed to our ferry for Copenhagen. Only the five principals took curtain calls. They ran up the gangplank still in curled beards and Victorian costumes. At 8 A.M. we woke up in Denmark.

September 19, Tuesday. What a friendly people! The press discovered our Hilmar Jensen (his grandfather had been a Dane), so they put in the headlines, "The Danish-American Jensen welcomed to Denmark with his fellow students." We toured Elsinore and Mr. D. thought he glimpsed Hamlet's ghost on the ramparts. Tomorrow, *Mamba's Daughters!*

September 20, Tuesday. This time fifteen! Fifteen curtain calls! At the last call, suddenly from the blackness beyond the stage we sensed people rushing up the aisles. Presently twenty-four bouquets came flying across the footlights. It was difficult to hold back our tears. Shauneille Perry especially was relieved because she had been shocked by being spit on as she was going onstage! Cookie had failed to warn us that the Danes spit on the costumes of the actors for good luck.[6]

The critics praised the show. One wrote, "The Howard Players showed us what impressive results university education in dramatic art can lead to. They are amateurs, and most of them do not even intend to go on the stage." Well, now some of us are thinking, maybe we will go on the stage.

September 22, Thursday. Yesterday at a reception held by one of the newspapers, a drama critic was talking to Dr. Cooke. The critic asked her if she liked eel. She fainted right into the china—kerplunk! They took her upstairs and called a doctor. Then we found out that just before our trip, she had had surgery for intestinal trouble and had developed adhesions. She'd been feeling strange all along, and the eel did it. Then we learned that Cooke's father had died in Gary, Indiana, two days before we had sailed; she had flown out to the funeral services and come back the same day to take us on the train to New York. Zaida Coles said it: Queen Anne is royalty.

September 24, Saturday. Shauneille is upset with Mr. D. (In *Mamba's Daughters* she plays Lisa, the granddaughter who returns from New York to Virginia, all dressed up.) Owen failed to get Shauneille a costume in Washington, and after he told her on Tuesday that he would get her one, he didn't. So on opening night she had no costume. He told her, "Wear your own best dress and I will replace it." In the scene, Gilly the villain knocks Shauneille down on the floor, and her dress got torn and dirty. It's the only dressy dress she brought, and she had to wear it to the Royal Danish Ballet to see *Gazelle*. Mr. D. better do something when we get to Sweden.

September 27, Tuesday. Two-and-a-half hours by ferry to Malmö. When we left Denmark, over 100 people brought flowers to say goodbye. From the deck of our ship, we started to sing the spiritual from *Mamba*, "Goodbye, Sister, going to leave you in the Hand," substituting

"Goodbye, Denmark" for "Sister." Immediately the Danes joined in with us, singing "Goodbye, Players." We were so overcome that we finished the song with quavers in our voices and tears in our eyes.

When we arrived here at Malmö, we were tired and I guess we showed it. Professor Cooke took us to task. "This is a new country. Perk up. You must be lively, young American people." So we "perked up." When we docked, the local fire-department band was playing "Carry me Back to Old Virginny." There weren't many people to welcome us—the cultural attaché and some others.

As we came off the boat, a Swede said, "Ver is Hedvig? Ver is Hedvig?" Marilyn said, "I am Hedvig." Poor Marilyn, she's so shy, but the man embraced her, saying, "Ah, Hedvig, what country do you like most in Scandinavia?" Marilyn said, "Skälling." Everyone laughed, but Anne didn't.

September 29, Thursday. Malmö has a famous modern theater where they produce Eugene O'Neill. We went to the university at Lund, founded 300 years before Columbus; there the students threw hats in the air to acknowledge our performance.

September 30, Friday. All day on the train to Stockholm. Rushed to the Hotel Christinaborg to change clothes and off to the American embassy for two hours of cocktails with the chargé d'affaires, Cummings, and his wife. Then back to the hotel at 10:00 P.M. to unpack and drop dead. So much for touring.

October 1, Saturday. Stockholm is not pleased with us. They did not give us a professional theater; we played in a school auditorium outside the main city center. We had such a poor attendance that they wanted to cancel, but we went ahead with maybe fifteen people in the audience. There may also have been a lack of publicity, but everybody agrees that after the enthusiasm of the Danes and Norwegians, the Swedes are cold; they're even formal to each other. Maybe that's why they've put us in a hotel instead of taking us to their homes. Or maybe it's racism. . . .

October 4, Tuesday. Played the university at Uppsala. Again, their caps flew into the air, then we ran to catch the train back to Stockholm. Shauneille is more and more upset with Mr. D. Yesterday, to go to a reception, she had to borrow a dress from a Mrs. Ochermann. He just refuses to buy her either a new costume or a new dress.

October 10, Monday. Trondheim. Here we are living at the university in a coeducational dorm! The men love it! These students are a very special group, very sophisticated. They talk of the "charm of a beautiful brown skin." If that is being exotic, give it to me. There was one student who spoke no English, so his friends came to Marilyn and said he was in love with her. She said that she was married, and they said that doesn't matter!

We did a line dance with the students about an old lady with a stick. We can't speak the language except *tak* for "thank you." And guess who shows up here in the mountains of Norway? Someone from the magazine *Our World,* to follow us around and take pictures when we fall down on the ski slopes. They took one yesterday of four young men trying to put ski boots on Marilyn.

October 13, Thursday. We played *Mamba* tonight, and it happened! When Shauneille said she wouldn't wear her own dress one more time onstage, she and Mr. Dodson had it out. He told her to wear a national Norwegian folk-dance costume! For a Negro folk drama! He said that was all he could find. She had enough sense not to. It would have had her look like an idiot. Some of us think he is spiteful and narrow-minded. Excellent performance anyway. The Norwegians stay up all night. Seems like we can't get to bed before 1:30 A.M.

October 14, Friday. Mr. D. looks worried. He'd gotten a letter from his sister Edith, who had an operation. She'd sent him the insurance papers to sign. Anyway, he went with us to tour the cathedral, climbing up all those spiral stairs.

October 15, Saturday. This morning we packed and crated costumes, then rehearsed for the revue that we put on tonight for the students. Group singing. John Bandy was the emcee. Pretty good performance considering only one rehearsal. Walked home. Light snow falling from the sky. Millions and millions of stars. I saw the Northern Lights. The students tell us that there is a rainbow sometimes. We're going to the dance tomorrow night, our last night here.

October 16, Sunday. A busload of us went up the mountain where the sun had melted the snow. Went to the waterfalls. The lodge had an outdoor water closet. One does not sit long. Oil lamps. We are to leave tomorrow morning at 7 A.M. A Negro named Griffin from Chicago on a Fulbright is studying Norwegian folk music here. Trondheim was better even than Copenhagen.

October 19, Wednesday. Oslo. Back at the Det Nye Teater unpacking. Shauneille's bought her new costume, a two-color affair, according to whatever light is on it, but Owen hasn't paid her for it.

October 21, Friday. *Mamba* opened tonight for a six-day run. Butcher didn't make the opening; he's sick in the hotel after coming back from seeing his wife in France, so our stage manager, Stewart Street, took over the role of Gilly.

October 26, Wednesday. Our last show today. Went to Blom's. We met Anne Brown, the original Bess in *Porgy and Bess*. She's married to a Norwegian ski-jump champion who's very friendly.

October 27, Thursday. Some of us went to the National Art Gallery and fell in love with "The Madonna" and "The Girls on the Bridge" by Edward Munch. Mr. Nilsen of the National Gallery showed us a new book that has just come out, *The Negro in the Theatre* by Edith Isaacs, and there were photos of *Mourning Becomes Electra* at Howard directed by Mr. D.!

October 28, Friday. Oslo, cold as can be. Ice. Zaida went to town to buy a sweater, but forgot that yarn is rationed. Marilyn had better luck. A Dane in a Norwegian university volunteered to take her to a shop and buy her one, a beautiful gold. It has probably taken his two weeks' allowance. He asked her when she got back to send him an American flag. We will never forget the graciousness of these people. Americans have a lot to learn.

November 5, Saturday. We are on the boat sailing to Bergen and our last performances will be at the National Skene, Norway's oldest theater, the one in which Ibsen first produced *The Wild Duck*. We gave two shows in Stavanger, and in the third act, the door of the set fell down. The scenery's showing signs of wear.

November 6, Sunday. The hotel here in Bergen is cold and no hot water. We saw a Norwegian adaptation of Saroyan's *Time of Your Life*. Not bad. A lot of American films and plays are showing here.

November 7, Monday. In Scandinavia, to show that a theater is sold out they hang a red lantern outside. So it was last night in Bergen. We return to Oslo now and prepare for Germany.

November 10, Thursday. Oslo. We leave at nine tomorrow morning for Hamburg. An old woman with a bouquet of flowers approached Bill Brown as he was packing the set and said, in broken English, "Will you give this to one of your girls?" She was one of the families who wanted to have one of us in her home, but she was not selected. Bill was so moved he kept the flowers himself. Mr. D. went shopping and bought a set of antique green glasses. He paid eight dollars apiece for them and says that he'll hand-carry them.

November 11, Friday. We left Norway on the 9:00 A.M. train. At the Oslo station, a man from the Hansa Brewery came looking for Dr. Cooke. It seems that she had attempted to take a beer stein yesterday from the restaurant as a souvenir, but they caught her. The man from the brewery gave her a box of six steins.

November 13, Sunday. Hamburg. We arrived at 5:00 A.M. Saturday, and nobody here knew we were coming, but nobody. No American of any installation had heard anything about any American players! We are supposedly under the joint sponsorship of the Office of the U.S. High Commissioner for Germany and Special Services of the U.S. Army. Good ol' USA. Every place we had been, somebody had been there to meet us. We got off the train in Hamburg, and those bastards had gone off for the weekend. Only Mary Nelson speaks German. The Hotel Continental put us up for two nights, the second night on credit. Hamburg is bombed out. Dr. Cooke's afraid to let us go far because we don't know when somebody might show up and we will leave for Berlin.

November 14, Monday. At last: the Military Air Transport (MAT) came and got the scenery in a big truck and went zooming down the autobahn. We are all on the train with the shades pulled because we're passing through Soviet-occupied territory.

November 15, Tuesday. Today a tour of Berlin by bus and a visit to the Russian Tomb of the Unknown Soldier. We went to the Sports Palace to hear Dvořák's *New World Symphony* (with its Negro themes) played by the Berlin Philharmonic. It was cold as ice; all the Germans were huddled together. Everybody and everything is so gray and grim. When we catch sight of a Negro American soldier, we wave, and he smiles.

November 18, Friday. We performed at the Titania-Palast last night, a concert stage about the size of Carnegie Hall. Most of the theaters have been destroyed. When the reviews came out and we got the translations, they were positive, except one from *Die Welt* where the critic wrote: "Many of the younger members of the audience are said to have been disappointed that not all the actors looked coal black or chocolate brown; nevertheless there was a high degree of civilization (*Zivilisierheit*) which was expressed even in the voices of the speakers."[7] This was a shock; in Denmark and Norway, there had been so little discussion of race. The Germans played up the color, but their students' association held a reception for us. They were a friendly relief.

November 19, Saturday. The Army flew us to Munich in a troop transport. We had to sit in bucket seats and felt like paratroopers. In Munich, which doesn't seem as bombed out as Berlin, we played in the Kammerspiele. Was fur ein theater! (I hope I got it right.) Magnificent!

November 20, Sunday. We took the bus out of Munich a few miles to Dachau. There were writings on the walls. They had statistics — Yugoslavs, Greeks, Turks, Arabs, Communists, as well as Catholics and Protestants who didn't cooperate. The man who was our guide talked like a circus barker, and he said, "Believe me ladies and gentleman, the Germans did not know this was going on." Then they showed us the railway tracks and how could they not know? The thing that really got to us was the ovens they had made for the children. We got back to Munich in time to see the opera *Fidelio* at the Prince Regenten Theatre.

November 21, Monday. Arrived at 7:00 A.M. in Frankfurt. We performed for American soldiers at the Althoff Bau Zoo, an outdoor arena.

November 24, Thursday. Thanksgiving. We are eating turkey with the Army in Kitzingen. The last few days have been mad. Performances for soldiers in Mannheim and Kitzingen. They loved us. After the last performance yesterday, we sang our alma mater and took the set outside the theater and burned it.

Eighty-eight days, fourteen cities, four countries, and fifty-four performances. We're ready for home. Good-bye, diary.

Howard's 1948 "cultural exchange," not then a catchphrase in American foreign policy, did achieve cross-cultural results. If reviewers remarked about the race of the players in *Mamba's Daughters* but not in *The Wild Duck*, it suggests that if the Blacks appeared in stereotyped roles, the criticism too was stereotyped.[8]

On the Howard side, an ensemble of American artists who had never been outside the States experienced a world and a theater they had not known. A telling remark came from actress Marilyn Berry: "We were treated so dearly by the Norwegians. At that time, meat was rationed; they had it only once a week. They gave up their stamps so we could have meat. The trip and those people saved me from ever being a racist." And from the twenty-one who made the trip, several elected to attempt a professional career: Graham Brown, Zaida Coles,

Roxie Roker, Shauneille Perry, William Brown, and Marilyn Berry. All succeeded.

When the Howard Players returned to America, an editorial in the *Washington Post* declared, "The Howard Players did a magnificent public relations job for the United States, the more effective because it was not the purpose but a by-product of their tour. Their presence in Europe and the quality of their dramatic work provided a telling rebuttal to Russian propaganda. They appeared not as representatives of their race but as representatives of theater art. They served their country very well." Drew Pearson then presented Pres. Mordecai Johnson of Howard with the American Public Relations International Award.

Most important, the Howard tour inspired the U.S. State Department to request legislation that would enable the United States Information Service (USIS) to bring American dance, film, art, music, and theater to the world. Within months, legislation was passed that enabled Robert Breen and Wilva Davis to take *Oklahoma!* to the Berlin Festival, marking the first instance of American financial sponsorship of international cultural exchange. Breen later took *Porgy and Bess* to the Soviet Union.

The trip was for Owen an unqualified success. Chosen to direct *Mamba's Daughters,* he had embraced the music and spectacle in triumph. True, he had refused to deal with the currency of any nation, and had left the student discipline to Cooke and all the technical problems to Butcher. However, in public relations, Owen reigned. People liked him. He also served as raconteur on the long train rides and ferry crossings, and his stories inflated events when he returned home: Two tons of scenery grew to four; four simple flowers given to Anne became a Hawaiian lei. Instead of standing backstage on the opening night in Oslo, he was seated beside the crown princess. A good story is a good story, and the tale of the green goblets he had bought in Norway spiraled into a true cultural gesture:

> I carried those goblets all the way back to Washington, and the Scandinavians met us at the airport. The Norwegians had a station wagon jammed with every kind of liquor that you can think of—gin, vodka, the whole works—and all three Scandinavian ambassadors. "Shall we go to your house?" they asked me. (I had a big apartment.) So just a few of us—the press attachés, a few of the adult students, and three faculty members—all went to my house. I had fireplaces. They uncorked one bottle and

asked, "Where are the glasses?" I said to myself, "Not the ordinary glasses, but the ones I brought from Norway!" and I unpacked my precious antiques, and found none chipped or cracked. The Swedish ambassador filled his lovely green goblet. He said, "Min skäl, din skäl, alla vackra flickors skäl." He drank it down neat and flung it into the fireplace. Well, I just stood there frozen, unable to move; then the Danish ambassador did the same, and then the Norwegian did it, too. Finally, they said, "Dr. Cooke!" so she said, "Min skäl, din skäl, alla vackra flickors skäl." And then Beanie. The last glass was my glass. So I said with good cheer, "Min skäl, din skäl, alla vackra flickors aaaaaaaahhhh!" So there went my glasses. You should have seen them. They were absolutely perfect.

The story may be apocryphal, but Owen's bright vision of etiquette rings true.

17

The Black Prince of Denmark, 1950–52

Many young souls embrace a career in art. Years later, in the course of an evening's drinking, the older artist will recall a time when his or her career burst sunward in such dazzling light, rose so rapidly in the public eye; when all barriers seemed to vanish, and the creative harvests lay open for the taking. So many black writers, painters, and other artists of Owen's generation recount this odyssey of soaring. But as the evening wears on and the soggy gravity of alcohol soaks the wings, the artist free-falls back into bitterness, rending the veil with wry laughter: "They didn't want no dark shadows clouding their sun anyway."

At thirty-five Owen felt the brass ring had come around to his hand. Scandinavia had launched him. *Powerful Long Ladder* had been acclaimed.[1] Farrar, Straus & Giroux promoted *Boy at the Window;* enthusiastic reviews prompted the publisher to offer him a contract for a second novel. Owen "terrified" Howard University audiences with his American premiere of Camus's *Malentendu* (*Cross Purposes*). He had fallen "in love with Earle [Hyman] at Thanksgiving,"[2] and the next year would direct him in *Hamlet;* the State University of New York at Alfred had offered him a job; and Bates College elected him to honorary membership in Phi Beta Kappa.

"Kill time and you murder opportunity, stab every favoring chance, and insult providence."[3] In April 1951, Owen lived that homily. He sent his work schedule to Gordon to prove that he too had dedicated his life to art:

8:30 A.M.   bath and breakfast
9:00 A.M.   notes for class
10:00 A.M.   stagecraft seminar
11:00 A.M.   lunch
12:00 M.   playwriting seminar
1:00 P.M.   conferences on *Pelléas and Mélisande*
2:00 P.M.   summer-school plans for *Hamlet*
4:00 P.M.   shop for food
4:30 P.M.   home and write letters about summer festival and answer ones about *Boy at the Window*
6:00 P.M.   fix dinner
7:30 P.M.   rehearsals for *Pelléas*
10:30 P.M.   sherry with Earle [Hyman]
11:00 P.M.   write a letter and finish poems or poem
12:00 P.M.   work on lecture for Kenyon College next week bed — whenever possible

Following a coy production of Maeterlinck's *Pelléas and Mélisande,* with William T. Brown, Owen plunged into O'Neill's *Great God Brown,* a demanding drama; when it opened, he turned directly to the plays for the Howard summer theater. *The Silver Cord* he had directed in Atlanta, and it moved easily. Next, Butcher launched *The Importance of Being Earnest,* asking the actors to shower and wear clean linen for rehearsals so they might regard themselves as English gentry who never perspired. Finally, on the steps of Douglass Hall, Owen capped the summer with von Hofmannsthal's *Electra.* "We worked ourselves to a frazzle," recalled Carolyn Stewart, the actress who played Electra. "Owen had the capacity to transfer, to communicate a vision without making you feel violated; it became your vision. Whatever you made of it was yours."[4]

For the maiden production of his playwrights' workshop, Owen chose Theodore Paul Smith's *Boys without Pennies,* a ghetto drama about a youth who reaches out from a sordid slum for a dream. Drama critic Leo Sullivan felt Owen's direction assisted "the script no end. In fact, he betters the play at almost every turn, bringing freshness to certain tired phrasing and lack of invention."

On September 10, 1950, Owen read poetry at Bennett College, a

Baptist school for girls in Greensboro, North Carolina. Impressed, the school's president, David D. Jones, invited him to write a pageant to celebrate the college's twenty-fifth anniversary. Within six weeks, Owen had set down *Constellation of Women* and persuaded Sebree to design the production.

President Jones ruled over the college like a patriarch over his family. He knew the name of every girl, about 500 of them. His slogan: "Gracious living." His idea was to help these girls to become like white ladies; presumably, sooner or later, they would break down the barriers of segregation.[5] One might be tempted to scoff until one recalls that in 1961 the sit-ins began in Greensboro, led by those same genteel students. Owen cast nine women, made use of a speaking and a singing choir, inserted Sebree's choreography (he danced himself), and used original music by the resident maestro, Frederic Kirchberger. The pageant, a triumph; locals had not seen actors with drums enter from the back of the auditorium.

Muffled drums sounded for the Dodsons too. On December 30, Lillian, at the age of fifty-one, died of a heart attack. Owen wrote Gordon, "When Lillian died something went out—not like security in having a home so much—but security in the world because so much goodness went with her."[6]

The day of Lillian's funeral ranked among the bitterest in Owen's memory. Lillian and Lef had bought jointly the house at 469 Quincy, but Owen and Edith didn't know that Lillian had signed over her share to Lef. Right after Lillian's afternoon funeral, Lef came upstairs and told them to get out and take nothing but their things from Lillian's room. They weren't allowed to touch any of the furniture downstairs or upstairs on the parlor floor.[7] Owen's rage at being evicted from "his own home" burst forth in his second novel, *Come Home Early, Child,* in which Coin the young son goes to the funeral parlor and looks down into Horwitz's (Leftwich's) coffin:

> As he looked down into the sliced mouth of her death, he saw that she was really dead in the virgin green of her shroud. Shriveled up in whipped cream. She was gone as a snuffed-out cigar and the color of one. She looked chewed up, cancerous, utterly finished. She looked hard as pavement. He whispered: *Meni, Mene Tekel Upharsin.* She was dead after all. He took another big swig [from his pint of whiskey] and standing ten feet

tall, in a porous of joy, he spat the whole drink in her dead face. What was left in the bottle he poured over that mouth, on those hands that had commanded him as a child, at puberty, in adolescence. Then he tossed the bottle in her stingy coffin; without staggering, he left the foul funeral parlor like a man.[8]

When Lef set Owen's furniture in the street, she consummated a hatred decades old. As Owen noted, much of her meanness could be traced to the fact that "no one had ever charted the geography of her body; she was a vagabond to love." Few or none spoke well of the hard-mouthed spinster; Edith and Owen strove not to speak ill: the novel spoke for them.

The trauma of losing 469 Quincy was more spiritual than economic. Edith had her apartment at 270 St. Nicholas in Manhattan; Owen, his double splendor at 1813 Sixteenth Street in Washington. Patrick O'Connor, a poet and friend, remembered his own amazement when he first entered 1813: "In a long entrance hallway of the first-floor apartment were endless paintings, endless, and on the left were bookcases, groaning bookcases. The living room was upper-middle bohemia, the quintessential chic—chemical beakers, flasks, and containers—New York chic from the thirties and forties. Imagine that sight for a boy from the slums of western Pennsylvania."[9]

Actor Earle Hyman recalled, "I had never seen a place like it before or since. There were windows but no real light ever came in; it was underneath the sea somehow, a protected place where you could live out your dreams, always feeling that you could cut yourself off from the rest of the world. He was one of the most gregarious men I have ever known, but at the same time from his poems, I got a feeling of closing in, being alone. Both were true."[10]

Owen had admired the sixteen-year-old Earle in the role of Rudolph in *Anna Lucasta,* and for many years in letters Owen addressed him as "Rudolph." After Hyman had studied with Sybil Thorndike and recorded scenes from *Hamlet,* he invited Owen for dinner, and afterwards he played recordings of Sir John Gielgud and Maurice Evans, and then slipped his own in. Dodson exclaimed, "Wow! Who is that actor? He's the best one of all." At age twenty-four, Hyman was still an unknown, but Dodson cast him as Hamlet, the production to open at Howard in the summer of 1951.[11]

That same spring, Gielgud swept into Washington, D.C., playing in

Christopher Frye's *The Lady's Not for Burning*. When Hyman approached the actor for advice on how to play Hamlet, Sir John invited Dodson and Hyman to lunch. Owen said "Where?" because Blacks couldn't eat at Gielgud's hotel. Sir John was shocked. They met and ate at the bus station. Dodson asked if he might give a party for the English actor and Gielgud agreed.

In his glory, Owen prepared meticulously and jealously guarded his conquest. When Bill Brown, a student who helped him clean the apartment, asked if he might come to the occasion, Owen replied, "No, Bill, you don't want to come." His neighbor Kermit Keith, a professor of architecture, drove up with a friend and asked, "Can't I come in?" Owen said, "No, we have counted heads and asked the people we want and I don't know you that well. I'm sorry." Many were disappointed. Owen had asked twenty-four men. His friend Herbert Kee, who was not present, heard reports from those who were: "Owen asked all the pretty white boys in D.C. although not all were gay. At one point in the festivities, Sir John averred, 'I have known Mr. Dodson for years,' and Owen looked around at his friends as if to say, 'So there!' "

Although he had only one night free from his own performances, Gielgud offered to assist with *Hamlet*. Hyman recalled,

> I had three coaching lessons with him and wrote down every word he said. He was so generous. Gielgud drew several sketches for scenes, explained to me how to exit from a thrust stage without turning one's back to the audience. Owen had seen Sir John's Hamlet and knew it was the best he had ever seen, and he knew I worshipped him, so there could be no jealousy. I said to Michael Redgrave once, "What happens if you have seen an actor who was absolutely perfect in a role and then that role is offered to you?" Redgrave replied: "Copy, my boy, copy."
>
> My Hamlet was based on Gielgud's coaching, Owen's ideas, and the death of my mother, who died the week that rehearsals were to begin. She died on a Thursday; the funeral, Saturday, and I began rehearsals on Monday morning. When I got to lines like "To be or not to be," I just knew what they meant with the death of my mother. Owen would never say anything. He knew my mother, who had loved him very much; the last words she ever said were "How are the rehearsals going?" In some ways, at

twenty-four I knew more about Hamlet than I do now at fifty-six. Gielgud also, when I talked to him later about it, agreed with me. His first time, he thought, had been in many ways his best.[12]

At that time I lived with Owen and shared his apartment. He would cook our dinner between afternoon rehearsal and evening rehearsal and we would eat with Claire Leyba, Frederick Wilkerson, or Austin Briggs-Hall. In the heat of that summer I would be exhausted and fall in bed asleep, but Owen would wash all those dishes, and when I got up the next morning, everything would be clean. He knew everything that was going on. And he taught classes while directing. Incredible energy.[13] Also, I was looking for a substitute father; a great difference in our ages, Owen knew more and had done more. Extraordinary understanding.[14]

Owen appealed to friends, to strangers for favors. Next door on Sixteenth Street, David Amram, then a young history major from George Washington University, played French horn in the National Symphony. The sound of Amram's practicing floated over the back fence and gave Owen an "idea of something he thought would be useful," so he asked the young musician to compose an original score for a few instruments—French horn, oboe, flute, percussion. "The production of *Hamlet* was the most exciting theatrical project I had yet undertaken."[15]

They made every single costume (except the tights) but money ran out before the men could have complete blouses and jackets, so they went almost bare-chested. A professor from Carnegie Tech saw the production, said it was admirable, but wondered why the men went around with their tits hanging out. Dodson told her, "We designed the costumes to make them feel free."[16]

All performances sold out. Owen had gone on radio two weeks before opening; the commentator asked him, "How in the world can black people do *Hamlet?*" Dodson replied, "You come and see it." To Gordon he wrote, "No goddamned body here thinks Negroes can do anything but nigger parts. The truth really is that few Negroes, or Americans for that matter, are ready."[17] He cast his friends—Claire Leyba as Gertrude, Austin Briggs-Hall as Polonius, Carolyn Stewart as Ophelia, and voice and diction teacher Frederick Wilkerson as Claudius. On a sweltering July evening audience and play crammed together into Spaulding Hall.

Richard Coe reported Hyman as the most athletic Hamlet he had ever seen. Early on in the first act, Earle not only fainted after the Ghost had gone (most actors crumble) but fell straight over backwards. Said Hyman: "In those days, I could fall straight forward on my face or straight backward without injuring my head; it's a trick. I could not do it now."[18]

The actors entered from everywhere offstage and from the audience, even the Ghost. The King on the top level read his proclamation with the Queen down below. In the middle of the speech, Earle, dressed in his inky black, entered in a surprise-pink spot, and the audience gasped. He was in full control, and spat out with deadly calm, "A little more than kin and less than kind," sending a shiver through the whole theater. Owen wove a subtle sensuality into the closet encounter between Hamlet and his mother. When Earle placed his hands upon the Queen's shoulder and neck, her eyes closed, her mouth opened slightly and her head tilted. Claire Leyba remembered, "Owen would come and whisper to me sometimes in rehearsal a little sensuous thing here, one there. I began to feel that Gertrude was a real bitch."[19]

They had rehearsed with the swords and the King had warned Earle many times, "Watch that sword. Don't you stab me." Earle kept saying, "No, I won't," but opening night, Earle did stab him. Frederick Wilkerson turned and fled the stage, and Dodson had to grab him. It was only a nick, but Owen had to push him back onstage. The King said, "If that fool comes at me again with the sword, I am going to walk off that stage," but he returned to die his stage death.

For the final scene with the dead bodies, Dodson orchestrated all the extras with torches, and then they lifted Hamlet's body; the only sound, muffled drums and Horatio's final line. At the end of every performance, there was a tremendous ovation. The last night the business manager turned away 500 people. Then they added two more performances and put loudspeakers outside where people sat on the lawn and listened. In all that heat, no one coughed.

The honesty of Jay Carmody's review in the *Evening Star* reflected the paternalism of many whites who came to mock and stayed to praise:

> On the surface, it is lamentably mismatching play and players when any save the most gifted performers take on *Hamlet*. It is tradition that in any such case, both the greatest of dramas and

the most reckless of casts shall lose—with the audience a third loser. Well, tradition is being pleasantly interrupted at Howard this week when *Hamlet* is being played by a company of professionals and student performers under the perceptive and artful direction of Owen Dodson. This is not merely the most ambitious venture in the university's drama history, it also is the most interesting.

Neither Spaulding Hall's miniature stage nor the limited experience of even the ablest members of the company is permitted the implication that this is a mid-summer folly. Frankly, that is what this reviewer anticipated and never had he been more definitely wrong.[20]

The Scandinavian embassies attended and suggested that Dodson might bring *Hamlet* to Elsinore, but that he must first replace the weak members of the cast, and must get a production in a professional theater. To Owen, it all seemed inevitable.

A month after the play closed, with praise from the *New York Times*'s review still caressing his heart, Owen boarded American Export Lines' SS *Independence* and sailed for Italy, France, and, of course, Elsinore. He did not sense himself as an academic on the grand tour, but as an artist seeking the Grail.

Tourist Rome, Ruskin's stones, a series of postcards to Peggy, Edith, and Carl, the Sistine Chapel, and the grandeur of the Spanish Steps; then, after a week, flinging his pilgrim cape about his shoulders, Owen galloped north to Asolo to honor the grave of Eleonora Duse.

The last thing that Earle had said to him was, "Bring back sprigs from Duse's grave. It overlooks Monte Grappa, only a short distance from Venice." Owen had read all the biographies and could recite verse and chapter of her life—her legendary moments in *The Lady from the Sea,* her love affair with D'Annunzio, her encounter with Mussolini. Hyman and Dodson considered themselves charter members of the Duse Club, although neither had ever seen the great artist perform.

Owen ran his fingers over the marble slab, outlining her name and dates (1858–1924) and then walked the streets of the small town that Duse had loved. Wrote Owen: "That secret, silent woman twenty-seven years later had become my companion and my mentor in Art because somehow like Icarus, she had grown wings and flown into the eye of the sun where Apollo dwelt."[21] She was the artist who made art into a religion: "Il faut s'oublier . . . s'oublier . . . c'est le seul moyen!"[22] ("One must forget oneself . . . forget oneself . . . it's the only way!") Owen rarely could lose himself, but sometimes when he directed, sometimes when he told stories, sometimes in writing a poem, the goddess possessed him.

He returned to his train and rode for thirty-one hours to Elsinore. He wrote Gordon, "Alors, mon ami, mon espoir du théâtre. I'm still trying to follow in your footsteps. Tu reste, mon idole." He had saved the best for last: Paris. The rooftops, the chimneys, the art, *La Bohème!*[23]

Gordon Heath had found a true love: Lee Payant, a white actor from Seattle, Washington, six years his junior, whose talents complemented Gordon's own. Together the two had fashioned a life around a small nightclub, L'Abbaye, a club popular not only with American and Swedish tourists, but with the postwar French who enjoyed sitting on the floor, sipping cognac, and listening to folk songs accompanied by Gordon's guitar. L'Abbaye became a legend that lasted twenty-seven years. Its rituals were famous—no one applauded performances because children slept upstairs; to convey approval the patron must snap his fingers; no one could enter or leave or talk during a set (unheard-of courtesy for the French).

Dodson arrived at 45 Rue de Sèvres on September 18, and on the 20th took over the pension's dining room for Gordon's thirty-third birthday. Owen liked Lee, as who did not? And if Owen was jealous, it was not of Lee, but the idea of Lee, for at midlife Owen had no true love of his own.

Embraced by art and Gordon's bonhomie, Owen's ten days dissolved. Like a cat cozy in September's afternoon sun, Owen sauntered through Rodin's sculpture garden admiring Rilke's château, with its tall eighteenth-century windows that pulled the light into the statues. Rodin pleased Owen: he had made people larger, more romantic. Owen was fond too of wandering serendipitously through the open markets of Clignancourt, so much so that before he sailed home, he sent Edith a request to meet him on October 5 at the Cunard Line "with taxi fare."

Once home, he drew up his ideal cast for his Negro *Hamlet*, keeping Hyman, Leyba, Wilkerson, and Stewart, and adding Sidney Poitier, Ruby Dee, Fred O'Neal, Ossie Davis, Leigh Whipper, Lloyd Richards, and two students—Walter Hall and Graham Brown. These would be the cast for Elsinore.

A graduate of the Yale Drama School, T. Edward Hambleton,[24] reluctantly accepted the position of producer on the condition that Dodson raise $10,000 to open at the Brattle Theatre in Cambridge. If the play succeeded, they could move to New York and get the attention needed for Denmark. Owen was certain he could get the money from friends; even the NAACP would consider the project worthy. Friends of the Howard Players in Denmark expressed their support: "Artistically it would be an exciting experience for a European public to see Negroes playing *Hamlet,* good for Negro players to get this opportunity to visit Europe, good for the way in which the Negro problem is judged in Denmark, to see what high standard the Negroes can rise to in America."[25]

Hambleton drew up escrow agreements, share agreements, and production contracts, but remained cautious: "I have found that the most enthusiastic friends often have very little money, and that most organizations have immediate demands that provide no surplus for such risky projects as the theatre."[26]

Owen sent out enthusiastic letters to Jerry Tishman, Marion Ascoli, John Farrar and Roger Straus, Blevins Davis, and, of course, the Riesers. He included an original poem. It was poor, but even a good poem would have brought a poor response: Only the Riesers invested. In Owen's heart, however, the dream of a black Hamlet at Elsinore still soared. Suddenly a scheme offered itself. In 1952, Carolyn Stewart (Ophelia) had returned from a Scandinavian tour with a script by Kaj Munk, *The Word (Ordet, 1932).*[27]

Owen called Earle: "We're going to do it because it will get us to Elsinore." Owen asked Hyman to play the role of Jonathan, a demented son who believes that he is Jesus Christ. At the end of the play, when his sister-in-law dies in childbirth, Jonathan, through his childlike faith, prays for her resurrection, and she sits up in her coffin; Jonathan's sanity returns. Hyman's reaction after reading the script: "My God, it's a great part, but the audience will die laughing."

Owen scheduled the play for June 30, and rehearsals began. Owen's key image for Earle: "Crucify yourself." Carolyn Stewart took the part of the woman who dies, and Marilyn Berry played a young daughter. Owen changed the venue from Denmark to the American South. In the last scene, Jonathan is standing by the coffin of his sister-in-law. The daughter says, "Uncle, you can bring her back to life because after all, you were Jesus. You can do it, can't you?" And the uncle replies, "I'll try. If you believe I can, I can." And then he brings the woman back to life. In the last line of the play, the doctor says, "I never did trust those death certificates anyway." If there were any laughter from the audience, the whole effect would be ruined. Owen was in a quandary and reportedly prayed, "My God, why did you give me this? We can't do anything with it! But if it's the only way we can get to Denmark, we've got to put it on."

Rehearsals struggled on into the hot summer. The miracle would not happen. Suddenly, one night in rehearsal, Owen jumped up shouting, "I got it, I got it!" He pointed to Fred Wilkerson, the establishment preacher who stood at one end of the coffin, and instructed him, "Sing 'A Mighty Fortress Is Our God,' and let 'em have it with all the authority of the Lutheran hymn," and then he pointed to the evangelist preacher standing at the other end and told him, "And you, you get right back at him. Sing something and get down!" The actor thought a moment and then thundered forth, "I know His blood can make me holy, I know His blood can. . . ." That was it.

Recalled Hyman: "It was one of the greatest theatrical moments I can ever remember. When it came time for Carolyn to rise up from her coffin, the gasping, the tears! Even the doctor saying, 'I never did believe in those death certificates.' There wasn't a laugh. I have never known such total silence as in that theater at the moment that girl comes to life. Owen had pulled it off!"[28]

They had won the audience, but not the ticket to Elsinore. Through the next two years, Owen held fast until the break came. Patrick O'Connor, who had gone to Rochester, New York, to start an arena theater, offered Owen his professional theatre for Earle's *Hamlet*. The year was 1955. Owen approached his old scene-design teacher, Donald Oenslager of Yale, who agreed to design for no fee. Then he asked Alvin Koat to design costumes gratis; Koat also agreed. Ruby Dee, Ossie Davis, and Sidney Poitier expressed interest, but Earle's career had not stood still waiting for Hamlet. Broadway had seen him in *Climate of Eden* (1952); he had been the Prince of Morocco in *The Merchant of Venice* (1953) at City Center; at the Jan Hus Playhouse he had played the lead in *Othello* (1953); he had a strong role in a Columbia motion picture, *I Was a Prisoner in Korea* (1954). He had appeared twice with the American Shakespeare Festival at Stratford, performing in *Julius Caesar* and *The Tempest*. In the autumn of 1955 director Bobby Lewis offered Earle the Broadway role of a lieutenant in *No Time for Sergeants,* and the next year the lead in *Mr. Johnson.* As a result, Owen had no Prince for Denmark. The black *Hamlet* had become a dream deferred.[29]

18

Boy at the Window, 1951

... and he will be so as a boat baptized
for a brave journey.
                                        —*Charles Sebree*

On February 18, 1951, Dodson appeared on the ABC radio
program "Author Meets the Critics," a program heralding the release
of *Boy at the Window.* Owen sent a copy to Eleanor Roosevelt, who
pecked out on her own typewriter, "I look forward to reading this
book when I have the time." Anne Cooke managed, "It's a very little
book."

The critics discovered a novel with a black boy who behaved like
any white nine-year-old. The author had eschewed two clichés: sen-
timentalism and overt racial themes. When the novel was reissued
sixteen years later under the title *When the Trees Were Green,* a journalist
noted, "This is the life Dodson knew best—almost free of the 'propaganda' in every form. Because Coin's life isn't plagued by racial
attitudes, the book gives an unusual picture of the boy growing up as
a boy, not a sociological specimen."[1] In interviews, Owen made a special
point to mention racism, for to omit the topic would be, in the eyes
of some professional Blacks, to avoid his negritude.

When a critic called the book "autobiographical," Owen countered,
"How does he know?" Yet the book abounds in correspondences to
the author's boyhood. Edith tried to duck the question: "I can't read
it anymore. There's a lot of truth in it. Owen's imagination and truth
blended and flavored it."[2] In his notes for the novel, on an undated
page, he set down what he thought the novel should be about:

Middle class Negroes in America battling to keep a basic dignity and self-respect for their race and the country in which they live; struggling to keep normal, not to be pulled by the octopus suckers that have grown out of being black in America. A family that struggles against [becoming] neurotic because of race or fanatical for that race or attached to a cause like Communism as a cure for the disease of prejudice. They struggle to not be middle class or to imitate the dull respectable society in which they might be forced to live. [The] Chief character will be a young man's problems, set-backs, and growth in a difficult society from the late twenties to the present time. Three parts: Childhood, youth, manhood.[3]

In his early notes, Coin (the "boy") is sometimes called Owen, and his sister Bernice is first named Edith. On a piece of paper Owen drew a map of Berriman, with the neighbors' houses of his boyhood clearly identified. To friends he admitted that Coin was a self-portrait, and nowhere were the parallels more pronounced than in the chapters on his mother's death and funeral. The alchemy of Owen's feelings changed the prose to poetry; images that seemed to emerge from the unconscious, but that were consciously molded by the writer, reveal the root of his later life distress: his unresolved love for a mother who unwittingly had led her baby boy to believe that he would be able to possess her always. Early in the novel, the eight-year-old Coin emerges from his bedroom with something behind his back:

> "Mama," he said quietly, "here's a flower for your dress." He handed her a crepe paper rose about the size of a dinner plate. His mother looked at it and smiled. He knew it was all right.
>
> "Aren't you gonna put it on?"
>
> "Of course I'm going to wear it, son." She tucked it into the bosom of her dress.
>
> "That's the handsomest rose I've ever seen," admired Mrs. Quick, "just the prettiest that ever grew."
>
> "Oh it ain't real," Coin said shyly, wishing it were.
>
> "You put a real rose alongside it and I defy you to tell me which is which."
>
> Coin looked up at his mother who said quickly, "It's six in one hand and half a dozen in the other."
>
> The room looked different with his mother all dressed up in it. She was another picture. She was the one of all.

"Are you ready now, Mrs. Foreman?"

"Just about. I want to say goodbye to Popa."

[She opens the window and speaks to Popa below in his garden.]

"Goodbye, Popa," and she threw him the crepe paper rose. Coin watched the rose go down.

"Oh, I'm sorry, son, I didn't think."

"That's all right, Mama."[4]

But it was not all right, for the woman he wished to possess completely and forever not only chose his father, but would soon die, and there could be no surrogate. He would "eat his roses of love." Various women would mother Owen, but unlike Countee Cullen, he never allowed one to marry him. Edith, who resembled his mother, came as close to mothering as Owen could allow, but on occasion, in his rage, he turned on her, too, for in his child's heart he knew that his own birth had crippled his mother. (Shortly after Owen's birth she had suffered a stroke, paralyzing her left side.) This, coupled with his overwhelming desire to possess her, had caused her death.

By using the ninja principle that the safest place to hide is out in the open, he wove a bold motif into the novel to present his sexual dilemma, a stunted and guilty homosexuality. During his mother's funeral in the Baptist Church, Coin is unable to look into her coffin; the long ceremony drags on:

> There was a stir in the church as the names of the motherless were called off. Coin felt eyes on him from every direction and he took Woody's [Kenneth's] hand. It was thrust away. At that moment the tune of "Yes, We Have No Bananas Today," started.... The tune zizzed around in his head slowly, slowly, faint and sharp. He shook his head a little to get it out....
>
> Sister Sarah Russell, in the choir loft, rose, adjusting her book before her, opened her mouth "Yes, we have no bananas, we have no bananas today...."
>
> He knew he was going crazy. The *organ* [emphasis mine] took up the tune. The whole church heard the song that was running faster and faster in his head.
>
> "I love this 'Fleet as a Bird' song," Deaconess Redmond whispered to her neighbor. "They played it at Sister Sylvia Harris' rites and you should have learned the ..."

The two songs were racing in his head; they tangled with each other.

"Fleet as a bird that flies to rest, . . ."

"Yes, we have no bananas, we have no bananas today . . ."

"Fleet as a bird to the mountains, . . ."

"We got all kinds of onions

Carrots and bunions but . . ."

"Fleet as a bird to the heavens . . ."

With terrible effort, the sweat pouring off him in the cold church, he got up. Mrs. Quick rushed over with her bag and her bosom. He knew he had made a mistake. They would all be saying that he was beside himself with grief. He was *beside* [emphasis mine] himself all right. . . .

If his father really began to cry, he couldn't bear it. He'd run out and go home. The tune snapped on in his head. "We have no bananas today, we have no bananas today. . . ."

He must have been in a trance because Reverend Brooks was speaking quietly and Coin knew he'd be finished soon.

"I say, your children bid you [Sarah] goodbye, and farewell." It was a signal for a low moan through the church. . . . Coin knew he was expected to say the words [good-bye] but his throat burned and the tune went crazy in his head. Bananas were mixed with farewell. *The organ started vibrating; he could feel it in his behind* [emphasis mine]. [When the recessional finally began] all notes of the banana tune left him and he was caught up in the solemn meaning of age and death and the mournful celebration of them.

In his notes for the novel, Owen had jotted down, "Mama brings *Owen* bananas," followed by "*Owen* finds Mama not home, runs through the street yelling for her" (emphasis mine).[5] The author has boldly imposed the banana song upon the sacred terror of the mother's funeral, and, further, has juxtaposed it with "fleet as a bird to the heavens." In later poetry Owen becomes the "torn bird" (unable to fly, sexually maimed). This radical juxtaposition of incongruent symbols became Owen's literary signature: the likely-unlikely. The effect is at once comic, sad, and annoying, but it is the essence of Dodson's poetic imagery, a style that was his alone.[6]

In another chapter of *Boy at the Window* Owen literally came out of the closet. Coin's grade-school teacher reprimands him for his sassiness and places him in the classroom wardrobe, on the day his mother will die. The symbolically sexual images are deliberate:

> He closed his eyes and heard his mother talking. She was talking quick, real quick. She was saying dinner money, dinner money, dinner money for the house. Coin for the house Coin for a hole as big as a lemon Coin for a lemon as big as Coin for a hole as big as Coin. When he opened his eyes and peeked out the grate he spied Oscar [Nat, Jr.]. . . . Somebody was pushing the wardrobe door open. His heart began beating fast. What was Oscar doing there?
>
> "Coin, your brother's waiting to take you home." Her voice was very gentle and soft. . . . They walked down the hall, down the steps into the courtyard before Oscar said, "Mama's very sick."[7]

Owen had not been born in a satchel as his father had said. Had he looked upon his mother's nakedness, the portal of his birth—a thought so frightening, so attractive, so sinful he imprisoned himself, a closet penitent forever? Owen's gift remained that of a poet, and his images reverberate in ambiguities. Every Dodson had died by heart attack; he himself would, and "Dear Heart" remained his second-favorite address to friends ("Chile" was first). Owen may have been an artist who, consciously or unconsciously through his work, prophesied his death: "The organ swelled up: *When the Roll Is Called Up Yonder, I'll Be There.*"[8] The church organ, in addition to suggesting a sexual organ, may also have been his heart.

Images of Coin's blindness float like motes through the chapter about the mother's death: "The sunlight got in his eyeballs like splinters. . . . 'Don't rub your eyes, Coin. Don't rub the wood in.' " As we shall see later, Owen developed these images further in his chilling poem "Prisoners," but for the moment it is important to note that this young boy felt that his desire for his mother had caused her death; his male sexual impulse would forever be shunted from women and stunted toward men.

Woody taunts Coin about his self-crucifixion by calling him "Christoin." But finally Coin's pain and fear become so great that he psychically leaves his body: "He was *beside* himself with grief. He was *beside* himself all right" (emphasis mine).

He saw Undertaker Ward hammer up the gray ribbon crepe;

he ran away from the hammering up Berriman Street. Another
Coin popped out of him and ran ahead. After a while it came
running back into him, but when he spied his father coming
toward him leaning against the twilight-colored snow, one Coin,
then two then three, then a long line of Coins running behind
each other toward his father. Their feet hitting the pavement
together looked like seven boys tap dancing forward. [This would
become his poem for Duke Ellington as the boys tap-dance before
God.] Then they all folded into him like a pack of cards, and he
was alone on the white street with his father coming closer with
the question on his lips.

"How's your mother?"

The boys flew out of him again and all their seven tongues got
stuck tap dancing to the tune of *"How's your mother? How's
your mother?"* Coin finally answered, "Drinking orange juice."

Mr. Foreman nodded and said something, but the wind blew
his words away.[9]

Terror had overwhelmed him, crucified him, fixed him forever in
prepubescence. He would remain the boy at the window — neither
maturing into a homosexual as Gordon did nor fathering children as
Nathaniel, Jr., did.

Other "coin" soundings echo in Owen's poems. In his poem "Def-
inition," dedicated to Leftwich, he concludes:

> Fate is the collection plate
> of our sins and our loves — variety of coins
> stored away or stolen by those fakirs
> who blame the plus or minus of our condition
> on God or Devil or the sound of the sea.[10]

The name "Coin" is unique for a boy. Owen often repeated a "coin"
anecdote about Alain Locke. (These two aesthetes shared a passion
for art, a fondness for gay men, and a worship of their mothers.) Locke
kept ritual urns filled with copper coins about his apartment. On one
occasion he invited "Doug," a favorite philosophy student, to listen
to a recording of Isaac Stern. Locke told the young man to remove
all his clothes and sit by his chair. When the concerto was over, Dr.
Locke, still fully clothed, rose and picked up a pot of coins. In a
ritualistic gesture he let them rain down all over this boy's golden
body. He said, "Pick them up, pick them up. Take them home, take

them home." The boy put on his clothes and said, "Good night sir." Dr. Locke said, "It was a pleasure."

Estimates of Owen's love life by those who knew him ranged from busy to bleak. Gordon stated that Owen was not a man of casual affairs and was a poor lover. When Alex, one of Heath's lovers, decided to marry and have children, Owen confessed, "I had a dream about him [Alex]. He was very small and a root doctor had set him in a maze and he was running in burning roots of terror and suddenly he grew large and strong, stripped off his clothing and scratched his ear and a flower sprouted like a trumpet vine bloom and covered his face. Figure that one out."[11]

A root doctor is a medicine man who uses plant roots for healing. In this instance, Owen's dream informed him that the "burning roots of terror" that Alex had escaped represented Owen's own terror of (homo)sexuality. *Boy at the Window* was Owen's trumpet vine that saved his face, but exposed the rest of him.

Owen believed that "every single thing that happens to you is something you store in the back of your mind, unclaimed letters until you claim them. That is why artists and writers never rest; you are always waiting for a sound, a gesture, that will help remind you of something. The danger is that, like Hamlet, it can drive you mad, thinking too much, having too much inside until you explode—so many writers explode."

In *Boy at the Window* Owen exploded and claimed his "unclaimed letters" to a dead mother who had locked him into the closet. The novel was, if not the key to free him, at least a cry from behind the door. For Alain Locke, *Boy at the Window* "was a grand job. I was delighted and moved by it. I remember once writing about you as a writer in search of a style. In this book you seem not only to have found it, but to have located at last your proper medium—the poetic prose story."[12] Through the alchemy of his art, Owen had transmuted pain into beauty, into the "likely-unlikely," which not only expressed his sexual dilemma but became the benchmark of his literary style.

19

The Guggenheim Year, 1953

"My spirit is ready to break away from the academic and wing out into confusion," Owen wrote Gordon in the autumn of 1952. Dean Richard Barksdale of North Carolina's College at Durham had offered Owen $6,500 to head the Department of Drama. Although Howard was paying Dodson nearly $1,500 less, he refused to sink further into academia. Surely one of his projects would lift him into the art world. After all, PEN International had elected him unanimously to membership.[1] He had put together a second volume of poetry, *Cages of Loneliness.* He had begun his second novel of the Dodson family saga, entitled *A Bent House* because "someone had bent it." (Farrar, Straus & Giroux paid him an advance of $100 a month for ten months with possibilities of a second $1,000 for another ten months.) And *Hamlet* might open in Elsinore! In the higher stratosphere of dreams, *Bayou Legend* was finding its way to the motion pictures, to the desks of Dore Schary and George Skouras. *Boy at the Window* had already found its way to 20th Century Fox, and an outside reader, Jack Kerouac, revealing his own romantic view of Blacks, recommended the novel for production:

> You have written a great little book; would to God you would have made it longer. . . . There are not many like you around. As far as your being a Negro is concerned—Wright and all such fellows don't hold a candle to you. That's because you insisted on telling the full truth and not only bitterness.

I know you're a religious man. That being the case, I know you're capable of putting the world behind you and truly saying your kingdom is not of this world. . . . Forget all about money; make your living at what you are now doing, whether it's preaching or whatever; be humble as you have always been and tell your wife and children to be humble too. Address all your books to God as you have done in *Boy* and you will be saved. [Was this satiric?] All that matters is that I dig you and many of my friends dig you and the Kingdom of Heaven is in all our hearts. [Twentieth Century Fox had recently "made many Negro movies" but turned *Boy* down.] This is all, altho incomplete and poorly written, that I have to say to you. I remain you [*sic*] friend and admirer, in the bleakness of this mortal realm, and in pure delight of life.[2]

Owen's next encounter with the inebriated famous came through a letter from his composer friend Howard Swanson, who had met the poet Dylan Thomas. Wrote Swanson, "I told him by all means to look you up."[3] And Thomas did.

Recalled Owen: "We had a party at Robert Richmond's, head of the Institute of Contemporary Art. They had a kind of lowered living room where you came in, and a staircase, and before the staircase, a little walkway. Dylan saw me down there, and says, 'Oweeeen!' and he fell over the railing, but he was so relaxed that it didn't bother him. He got up and drank some more and began reading poetry and making the whole evening a wonder. I know that in those walls his voice is present, his presence and his mystery. Dylan Thomas, they say, was never drunk when he wrote but how can you be drunk all day and most of the night and get up and begin to write without that lingering thing? And his poems sound drunken and that is their glory. So many poets seem to be secretly knitting in a closet and not caring if you understand the emotions that only they have. Why should you have to figure poetry out?" The Welsh and the African-Americans shared an oral tradition: their poetry was conceived for the ear.

In the fall term of 1951, Dodson became acting department head.[4] (Cooke had sailed to Norway on a Fulbright Grant to study Ibsen.) He organized the annual spring Festival of Arts; he spoke at the alumni meeting of Thomas Jefferson High School; and on May 4, with Dorothy Porter of the Howard Library staff, he officially opened the Channing Pollock Theatre Collection, a gift from Helen Channing, daughter of the playwright.[5]

The following week at Catholic University, Owen directed a successful stage adaptation of Shirley Jackson's "The Lottery." When John Farrar learned of it, he attempted to persuade the National Conference of Christians and Jews to publish an article about this all-too-rare integration. That same week Owen read poetry to the wives of the Howard faculty, and perhaps this tender event keyed him to ask W. H. Auden for a Guggenheim recommendation. He needed to flee, to flee! Auden agreed: "I'll do what I can for you regarding the Guggenheim Fellowship, and let me warn you that the question in the form you fill out 'What are your ultimate aims as a writer?' is a trap and should best be left blank or else say 'to write as well as possible.' "[6]

To bless his summer production of *The Family Reunion* (another drama about maternal dominance) Owen invited the author to attend, but T. S. Eliot sent only his cordial good wishes. "I should be grateful if I might hear afterward of the success of the performances."[7] The critic from the Washington *Times-Herald* granted Eliot's request: "I wish to thank the cast and director for the sensitive, intelligent and generally painless reading they provide."[8] The reviewer acknowledged Earle Hyman's and Carolyn Stewart's professional talents, and one wonders what Eliot thought of his aristocratic English family played by Negroes. Other American universities would not use nontraditional casting until thirty years later.

On October 19, 1952, the poet-novelist Margaret Walker invited Owen to direct at the Diamond Jubilee of Jackson State College in Mississippi. Owen wrote her: "I have revised *Divine Comedy,* and it is now a play whose central core is a race riot. I do not think it would be acceptable in Mississippi at this time."[9]

Walker agreed and produced the Yale version. The Chicago *Defender* reported that "a standing room only crowd packed Jackson auditorium for Owen Dodson's verse play, stunningly directed by the author. The cast and the author were cheered as the curtain fell."

In the spring, to "keep his Shakespeare hand working," Owen cast James Butcher as Richard III and future novelist Toni Morrison as Elizabeth. He wrote Gordon, "I want the production to be melodramatic spit, but Richard's frustration must be explained and the high terrible truth of cruelty exposed with telling loudness." It was. Opening on March 11, 1953, *Richard III* packed the house every night "because our age understands evil."[10] He brought the play back for a spot in the summer program along with *Emperor Jones.*

While Owen waited to hear from Guggenheim, on April 8, in Andrew Rankin Memorial Chapel, Alain Locke, with Owen and sixteen other faculty members, founded the Howard chapter of Phi Beta Kappa.[11] Dr. Ralph Bunche, director of trusteeship of the United Nations, delivered the commemoration address. For years after, Owen wore his key proudly in his lapel rather than on his vest as Countee Cullen had.

On May 6, 1953, the good news arrived—a Guggenheim Fellowship beginning September 1 "for creative activity in the field of fiction." The stipend of $3,500, plus his sabbatical half-salary of $2,739, meant one thing to Owen—leave for romantic, inexpensive Italy. Owen had specifically chosen an island near Naples because of a line in a poem of Auden's: "Ischia—Whatever you charge shall be paid." Owen asked if he might rent Auden's house. The poet responded: "Your letter of June 25th has just reached me. Delighted to hear that you are coming out here. As to the house, I'm terribly sorry, but for the first time since I've had it, I'm staying in this fall till the end of November. If you wanted it after that for five months, I should be happy but I expect you want to get settled somewhere at once. Let me know."[12]

Owen seized it. Auden asked token payment, "two or three hundred lire a month."[13] Owen borrowed $500 from Peggy Rieser so that Edith might sail with him on the *Andrea Doria*. They would travel for a month, then Edith would go visit Gordon Heath in Paris, while Owen would sail to Israel to visit Sol Gordon. On the first of December, Owen would return to Ischia and move into Auden's house.

For a bon voyage celebration, Viola Scott invited all their friends to her studio on Fifty-seventh Street. The day before sailing, Priscilla Heath surprised Owen by arriving on Edith's doorstep. She had married Dennis Sutcliffe, a Rhodes Scholar teaching at Kent State; they had two children. Yet something of her love for Owen would not die. Later he wrote to her, "I had almost forgotten how lovely and wise and fine you were." She responded with such warmth and nostalgia that Owen wrote: "The sailing, the talking. It was an important time. For me, seeing you again, but also important as a history of ourselves. I looked back; you looked back. I was asking for nothing but only wondering (in a concrete sense) how our world would have gone under different circumstances. There is no change, or if there is change, it is not essential; we will continue along the paths we laid years ago."[14]

Later in his life, much too much later, Owen reconsidered taking the road not taken, but in 1953 he set his sails toward Italy. After eleven gentle days and nights the *Andrea Doria* docked in Naples, and Owen and Edith, ages thirty-eight and forty-four, like two children skipping out of school, dashed into their Roman holiday. Lodging at the Hotel Inghilterra in Baca di Leone, they climbed the broad Spanish Steps from Piazza di Spagna to Via Sistina, even traversing the distance beyond to the gardens of Villa Borghese. And the art! They feasted upon the Vatican past, and they devoured the contemporaries on the sidewalks of Via Babuino. Owen remarked to Edith how much Lillian would have enjoyed it. In Rome, the Dodsons were yet three, and with Kenneth, sometimes four. Only the shadows had shifted.

In Florence, they took a room in the Annalena, a pensione on 29 Via Fonderia where a number of artists lived, including a young aspiring novelist, Dennis Denitto. Their room had a low ceiling of great wooden beams, a marble floor, a magnificent armoire "the Medici must have used," and a window that looked out on a courtyard that seemed to whisper, "Yes, Edith, you really have escaped Brooklyn." The Annalena's hosts, Ulderigo Grassi and his mother Eloira, welcomed the Dodsons with such warmth that the guest-host contract quickly dissolved into one of "family," and the Dodsons ate dinner with the Grassis. After a few days of museums and concerts, Edith's departure for Paris and London evoked Grassi lamentations: "Yesterday I've begun a work I'd like to send you as a souvenir from me and I hope you'll like it, and of you I ask nothing but that you will help me to come to America. You are good and won't say no. Think of me as a brother because for me you are like a dear sister and my mother is called 'Mamma' by Owen." Then Mamma appended her appeal: "Try and help Ulderigo in what he's asking. Believe me, dear Edith, a secure job is really what we need badly."[15]

Edith and Owen pushed on to Venice, fed the pigeons in San Marco Square, resisted buying two ceramic commedia dell'arte figurines offered at too dear a price (Owen later sneaked back and purchased them); then, on October 5, Edith boarded the train to Paris, where Gordon and another dear friend, Ivory Wallace, a graduate student at the Sorbonne, were living. Edith, according to Wallace, "knew a little French; I taught her a little more. As for Owen, his knowledge of foreign languages was zilch. He knew it, so it never bothered him when I teased him about being tongue-tied. He did, however, pick up the good-morning-how're-you-fine-thank-you thing. Yet he butchered those tourist phrases to hell."[16]

Edith sailed home from Southampton on the SS *Liberté*. In her mailbox at home lay a let's-just-be-friends letter from a man who had been her lover for some time, George Wilbur Clark. A musicologist of some professional note, Clark kept a wife while he and Edith "kept company." (Apparently he lived as "George Wilbur" in the town, but "Edgar Rogie" in the country.) Then his wife died, and Edith believed that she would be the next Mrs. Clark, but he informed her he had decided to wed another woman who would be a better "step mother" for his daughter.

Owen held Edith's hand by letter, offering condolence, branding Clark a fool who would discover *again,* as he had in his first marriage, that he had yoked himself to a hausfrau with whom he could not converse about his passion—research in church and folk music. Some years later, Clark and Edith again took up their affair, which continued until his death in 1978, at which time Edith suffered the pain of being "the other woman" who could not attend her lover's funeral. Owen never forgave Clark for passing over Edith. Owen's friends, ignorant of the circumstances, interpreted his pique with Clark as possessive jealousy of Edith.

After his sister's departure from Venice, Owen traveled to Bern, where he sought out performances of his favorite oedipal dramas, *Hamlet* and Barrie's *Mary Rose*. After glimpses of Lucerne and Geneva, he returned to Florence. He had abandoned his plan to visit Israel, explaining to Edith that a better use of his time would be to study Italian. But the cancellation of his rendezvous with Sol Gordon in Tel Aviv left him petulant. When he met Gordon the next year, he wrote Heath, "Sol breezed in from Israel bearing gifts. He's married a third woman and is more laconic and devoted than ever. I don't pretend to understand him and take each situation in sequence. He still has his mopping kind of charm but little stimulation emotionally or spiritually. He's a twilight mirage."[17]

Owen registered at Berlitz ("my Italian swims uncongregated in the water on my brain").[18] He passed November outlining his book, attending the American Ballet Theatre, and reading Willa Cather, her dark-claret novels that "not only ran deep but often touched the bottom and told wisdom only the truly sensitive or hurt are capable of."[19] For his thirty-ninth birthday, he treated himself to a Segovia concert. All in all, he confided to Edith, "It's good to be in a country where one has met no slurs or insults but respect and kindness at every turn."

He had abandoned his pipe for Chesterfields (more than a pack a day), and he regularly drank two "slitty-eyed" martinis before dinner.

The *Principessa,* the ferry for Ischia, pulled away from Naples at 8:45 A.M. in weather like middle spring—the crossing, an easy four-hour spanking. In 1953, the tourists swarmed to Capri, while to the north her larger sister island, Ischia, nesting in the blue Tyrrhenian Sea, remained a hideaway. Barely remembering its last earthquake in 1883, Ischia had entirely forgotten Monte Epomeo's eruption in 1301. On its eighteen square miles of volcanic rock, artists and gays hid themselves away among the locals, the total population numbering under 10,000. Everyone in Forio, a small fishing village on the westernmost tip of the isle, knew Auden had rented his home to a black man. Auden's "houseboy" (Giocondo Sacchetti, age twenty-nine) shrugged, "I didn't mind. If he was white, it would have been the same thing to me."[20]

Sacchetti met the ferry. Owen stuttered his few words of Italian; Sacchetti, a slim man with melancholy eyes and a strong dimpled chin, took pity, and in English invited Owen to the Ristorante Di Filippe, named for its American owner, Philip Dakin, a fifty-year-old actor who in the 1940s had appeared twice on Broadway.[21]

Ristorante Di Filippe, with its veranda and sea-weary grace, dozed at the edge of the bay, a sea wall to the right, a fishing fleet to the left, and behind, Monte Epomeo. The same breeze that had caressed the Greeks twenty-five centuries earlier bussed the restaurant's peeling paint. Because he ate everything she set before him, Signora Francesca, the owner's wife, liked Owen at once. Philip liked him because he could speak of theater and art; Sacchetti liked him because "he was sensitive. He didn't like to see people unhappy. He laughed a lot, a gentleman." Owen, in turn, liked them all. (He would place each in his novel *Come Home Early, Child.*)

In the late afternoon, Sacchetti found a taxi, and, leaving the ocean behind, they rode along Cristoforo Colombo, then up the hill on Castellaccio, climbing to 22 Santa Lucia, a villa graced with a magenta spray of bougainvillea twisting up the white façade. Auden's dog Mose (found near a stream) met them with his companion, a black-and-white cat named Leonora.

Larger than Owen expected or needed, the house had three bedrooms, a large kitchen, a study, a studio, a dining room, and an indoor patio open to the sky. Behind lay a garden with giant cacti, great red-

and-white geraniums, artichokes, pomegranates, and citrus trees—lemon, tangerine, and orange—which Owen called breakfast-juice trees.

On the table, a pile of mail awaited him, manifestations of love from a dozen friends, but all of no help when Owen walked into Auden's study: "I sat down in desolation. I said, 'How can I write in the same room with the man who has written "The Age of Anxiety" with such perfect craftsmanship and whose longing is to win the Nobel Prize?' I had to exorcise Auden. So I took all his books and put them in boxes and cleared his table of everything and rearranged the furniture."

Owen wrote from nine in the morning to one in the afternoon; then lunch, followed by a walk either up the coast or to Bar Internationale to await the postman. The Internationale, also called Maria's Bar after its proprietor, belonged on a list of watering holes for artists who would one day be famous—the Ritz Bar, White Horse Tavern, Deux Maggots, Black Cat Café, Harry's Bar, Vesuvio's. In Owen's time the regulars included composer William Walton, painters Lello Fior and Eduardo Bargheer, and French singer Hughes Cuenot. Even the movie stars who had passed through signed the guest book—among them Clark Gable and Elizabeth Taylor. Auden, of course, had left his stamp, and the year before Owen's arrival, Truman Capote had etched Maria without sentiment: "Maria is a sawed-off woman with a gypsy face and a shrugging, cynical nature; if there is anything you want around here, from a house to a package of American cigarettes, she can arrange it; some people claim she is the richest person in Forio. There are never any women in her café; I doubt that she would allow it."[22]

Owen wrote Kermit Keith that Maria "not only excommunicated Truman Capote, she drove him off the island and dares him to return."[23] Owen's description of Maria rivaled Capote's:

> Most nights I go down to the one cafe here: Maria's. Imagine that wicked old bitch being named after the virgin. She has jet black hair which she wears in bangs and panels. Yes, it's dyed. She wears wooden mules, has the largest, squarest, flattest behind in the world. It's like a palisade. I think she wears a truss. She swears in five languages and is a procurer. If she doesn't like you, you're banished. Now I'm her favorite. Everyone goes to Maria's: beachcombers, sluts, poets, painters, novelists, journalists, local trade; loves are made and broken there. The ceiling is papered

with old copies of the covers of *Life, Time, Fortune* and the funnies. I usually sit under Chiang Kai-shek. Artists have exhibits there; it's the headquarters for the numbers racket and the lotteries. By the way, the new word for "pounce" is ZUMZUM.[24] ["Pounce" was Owen's private verb/noun for dalliance.]

Only there five days, Owen left for an overnight holiday in Naples to admire Ingrid Bergman in Rossellini's production of the Claudel-Honegger play *Joan of Arc of the Fire:* "I don't know when I've seen such soaring imagination. In the end when the fire had been lit, Joan tore her hands from the chains, lifted them to God, crying in an ecstasy of agony: 'Ecco, life is for the strong!' and she kissed the holy air about her." He also saw a shoddy production of *Turandot,* which he labeled "stewed Chinese fruit," and left after the first act.

A few days later, he returned to Naples for Rossini's *Cinderella.* Again, he took Sacchetti, and they bought tickets to see the popular blonde "Wandissima" (Wanda Osiris), a soubrette whose music hall fame rested on her plume fans, tons of rhinestones, and big spiral staircase. Sacchetti enjoyed the adventure but was puzzled: "Owen talked all the time about his sister; maybe he missed her, although he did not seem particularly homesick."[25] Sacchetti had been led to believe that Lillian was still alive and teaching. Indeed, in Owen's imagination she did live; he was writing about her every day in his novel *A Bent House.*

Christmas meant family. Sacchetti's mother and sister Rosa, with her two children, Vito and Assunta, had welcomed Owen into their home. Then on Christmas Day, Owen, with his savoir faire, gave "Mamma" a baby Jesus for the manger, a gesture that bonded him to the Italian family. (In his novel, he transformed Sacchetti's family into Fortunata's parents and kin.)

Winter chilled Auden's house; without a furnace, a kerosene heater, or hot water, Owen wrapped himself in his sweaters, typed with his gloves on. In the afternoons, he watched Sacchetti paint local scenes, watercolors that suggested the painter's interior landscape as much as the mountains and sea of Ischia. He collected bits of local color for his book, later renamed *Come Home Early, Child.* With no electricity after ten o'clock at night, Maria's bar closed, Owen retired, to arise at eight or nine. January passed.

In February, the sirocco swept across the Mediterranean, sifting Sahara dust down upon Ischia. With the sirocco came a bit of sunshine, an invitation from Gli Artisti di Forio requesting that Owen attend — "Costume e maschera sono obbligatori" — a "programma celebrano il carnevale."[26] For Mardi Gras, Owen slipped into red tights and donned a black cap. "Are you a demon?" asked Sacchetti. Owen laughed, "An angel in a black hat."

In *Come Home Early, Child,* the Mardi Gras soirée, set in the new home of Philip Dakin, degenerates into a Felliniesque bacchanal in which Coin, revolted by the advances of the gay men in drag, flees into the night, where the virgin Fortunata awaits him. They make love in the poppy field "drenched in rain." The "scar" where the man Franz kissed him on the mouth stops "burning." On the last page of the book, Coin "felt into his pocket for the stone Fortunata had given him, the stone that shone in the dark and rolled in his pocket" (from Bates College?).[27] The final pages assert that he knew he had become a man, but the evidence suggests Coin's impotence with women.

The surrealism of the second half of *Come Home Early, Child* had become Owen's major literary effort to resolve his sexual dilemma, but unlike *Boy at the Window,* the fantasy spiraled out of control. When finally published in 1967, the novel served as one more Station of the Cross on his road to Golgotha.

At the end of March, Auden reclaimed his home; Owen moved to Via Monticchio 3, a small apartment that vaunted running water — "the only one on the island." The residence also gloried in a gas heater — "the only one on the island." The landlord, Romualdo Maniere, and his sister lived next door and declared Owen to be the best tenant they ever had, "including a Protestant minister from Holland. I never found a bottle of alcohol in the trash."[28]

Sacchetti, not a servant for two masters, abandoned Owen, who cooked his own meals or strolled down the beach to Ristorante Di Filippe. On April 27, stage director Robert Lewis, on holiday from the London opening of *Teahouse of the August Moon,* arrived to stay two weeks. Both men were alumni of Yale Drama School; both passionately respected Eva Le Gallienne; both had known and admired the artists Rose McClendon, Bruce Nugent, Richmond Barthé, and Paul Robeson.

Spring hurried in. Owen made notes on the Easter pageantry, finding it "pagan, terrible, and right." A photojournalist appeared one day in pursuit of "Negroes in Rome" for *Our World* (a competitor with *Ebony*). The photographer followed Owen about, catching his Negro in situ.[29]

Soon the summer heat returned. Owen emptied his desk, his novel unfinished. He packed, purchased several of Sacchetti's watercolors (the artist gave him twenty more to sell). Before Owen's departure, a journalist from *Napoli* wrote about him, "He is not from Uganda or Congo." To prove his internationalism Owen sang "Sul mare Luccica," "without one wrong note." Then the journalist asked him if he were king, would he leave Forio as it was or would he change its habits? Owen smiled. "My only order would be to keep out the tourists."[30] (Today the menus are all in German.) On June 9, Owen sailed from Naples for New York.

He resumed his life in Washington with his advance from Farrar, Straus & Giroux consumed, his novel incomplete, his apartment in shambles. Once again he became Owen the teacher, but for one glorious year, Europe had nurtured him as Owen the artist.

20

The Amen Corner, 1955–56

From the sixth floor of Edith's St. Nicholas Avenue apartment, Owen watched Harlemites wade through the August heat. For many months he had been living in Ischia with poverty, but island poverty — always the sea and the mountains, flowers and clean air. Now, in the dog days of summer, Louise Leftwich had died. Owen declared her funeral "a poor, frayed picked cliché of a thing" and tried not to think too hard about the memories of disaster; then in a burst of spite, he wrote the climactic scene in *Come Home Early, Child* where he poured whiskey on her corpse.

With the first breeze of autumn, Owen left Harlem for Washington. He had entrusted his home to his drinking buddy Kermit Keith, who had used Owen's place for guest rooms. In exchange, Keith had fed and walked Nell Gwyn, Owen's poodle, a twin to Keith's own.

Owen called Kermit from New York to say, "I'm back!" Keith said that he was on his way to Canada, and someone would bring Nell Gwyn around. When Owen got home, he found that Keith's guest had cooked in his pewter dishes and bowls, burning holes through them; worse, his great bas-relief made of popo wood ("The Death of D. H. Lawrence"), which had taken him seven years to pay for, had been painted black (it cost $500 to restore it). Nell Gwyn had been drinking from a seventeenth-century porcelain bowl and had lost her manners, doing her do under the bed.

Two neighbors welcomed him home: May Miller Sullivan, his land-lady at 1813 Sixteenth Street, and Georgia Douglas Johnson, who lived right through the alley in "Halfway House," the sign all faded, painted nearly sixty years ago. From the 1920s, both women had written poetry and one-act plays.

Owen knew Ms. Johnson when she had become eccentric and old—when one could see all the wrinkles in her chest above her bosom; when she took in lame dogs, blind cats, any kind of limping animal (the animals would sleep under the rose bushes, mixing the smell of manure and roses); when she took in stray people, artists who were out of money for long periods, like Zora Neale Hurston, or artists who were a little berserk (she knew how to soothe them). Owen recalled:

> Her house, a mess! When you entered the hallway, you knew you were entering another country; an old-fashioned hat and coat tree, coats that people had not worn in years. There were old pregnant television sets when they were huge. She had old radios, old hats and corsets, old pictures; a bust of her son who died. I never dared go into the kitchen. In the living room, there was a pathway through the Chicago *Defender* and the Pittsburgh *Courier;* she wrote a poem every week for the *Courier* up to a month before she died.[1] The last one she wrote: "We live too long." She wrote lovely poems. "I Want to Die While You Love Me" or "The Heart of a Woman Goes Forth in the Night." Full of lace-grief. She grasped the covers for a week in a coma. She held on so long, so tight.
>
> At her funeral, they asked me to read her poems and I prepared some and got there fifteen minutes ahead. The Episcopal priest said, "I see you are on this program to read some poems; that is not in this service. This service is a religious service. You cannot do that kind of thing." I replied, "These are her poems; this is her funeral; I am her friend." He said, "You do it before the funeral, and I'll carry on with the regular service." So I said, "All right, I am not going to fight you and God at the same time." I read the poems. I just touched her casket while I was reading them. They had dressed this old lady in surprise pink. They had put a fresh sweat band on her, one of those twenties bands.
>
> Off we went to the cemetery; I noticed that her son had a bag, and I wondered if he had sandwiches in it or a Coke, but this man whom I thought did not understand his mother, this man

before they lowered his mother's body, he opened this old bag, and took out roses from her garden and sprinkled them over her coffin.

The second neighbor, May Miller Sullivan,[2] while less eccentric, shone no less a talent. The daughter of Howard's pioneer sociologist, Kelly Miller, she often had hosted a covey of incipient writers. This elastic salon "founded" in the early forties lasted on into the fifties, and at various times included Dorothy and James Porter, Gwendolyn Brooks, Rayford Logan, John Hope Franklin, Franklin Frazier, Charles Sebree, and Toni Morrison, who read the first pages of her novel *The Bluest Eye* there.[3]

The Howard theater's 1954–55 season[4] needed a black play. In January, Cooke handed Owen a script by a young writer who had published a novel, *Go Tell It on the Mountain*. In those days, few knew Jimmy Baldwin's name. Owen took the play home. Here are Dodson's recollections of the entire episode:

"I read the play that night. It was about a storefront church and Sister Margaret, a woman preacher who had fallen in love with God, after she had loved a trumpet player, an earthy man of unhealthy nightclubs, and had let him go. Her husband comes back to die in her arms. She knows way down that she still loves him, and that the love of a man is warmer than the love of God. The play has so many depths, so many eddies, so many different kinds of plumbing, human revelations. Beautiful. It is Jimmy's best work.

"We put the play into rehearsal. The actors understood about storefront churches. They knew about the hypocrisy of preachers and their goodness, the deacons and the deaconesses and their sins and good works, and how they came to visit your sick and at the end of the visit, the deaconesses in white and the deacons in black-and-white shirts kneeled down by the bed and said, 'If it pleases you to take away the soul of sister Matthews (Sister Matthews would wail) it must be so, thy will be done.'

"About two weeks before rehearsal, I called Jimmy up. (Luckily his telephone was on. He was a telephone freak, as we will observe later on. His bills, or rather *your* bill, would run up to $100, $200, or $300 and there it was, and you took a loan from HFC to keep your life running.) Anyway, I told him to come down and see his play and to talk about what needed to be done. He said, 'I'll come tomorrow, but

I don't have any car fare.' That did not jar me, but it was to jar me later on—'don't have any money.'⁵

"I got the money together and telegraphed him. He knocked on the door, and I was not prepared for him. Somehow or other, I know that we in America especially place so much emphasis on youth, on conventional Hollywood beauty, whether black or white—the girls would like their boyfriends to look like Harry Belafonte. I opened the door and there was James Baldwin, destined to become one of the greatest writers of our age. It was a shock. I had never seen anything quite like it. He had a triangular head; seen from the front, it was triangular, from the side it was triangular; his hair stood up like leaves of grass; his jaws were sunken in; his cheekbones reared out; he was skinny; he had bowed legs; he was slew-footed. But he had one of the most beautiful voices I have ever heard. We in America all have that kind of thing, but if you are a decent person, you get over it in a minute.

"We sat down and began to talk, and it was marvelous talk and at the end, I said, 'I think this play is going to be something, but what is more important to me, I think I have found a new friend, and I hope you feel the same way because we both have the same folklore rooted in mysticism, wide and loud Baptist mysticism.

"I took him to Howard. I could control myself, but those students— when they saw him coming toward them, they all got busy doing something. Finally they got themselves together and realized that they were in the presence of someone who had written this play. They performed for him. After the rehearsal, we went home.

"He said, 'Is it too late to get some vodka?' and from then on he required a fifth of vodka every day. It didn't upset his equilibrium, didn't upset his mind, his thinking, his attitude. It was like a medicine, a manna; as he drank his vodka, his mind became sharper. I pointed out the things that needed changing. He said, 'Those can be done immediately. Then we can hear how it sounds. We can have a typewriter there and I can write some more.' We did that up until the dress rehearsal. We were all shaky. I myself was exhausted directing because Jimmy began to work at one o'clock in the morning when I was ready to sleep.

"Opening night—jammed. How did we get all those people in? Whoever heard of Jimmy Baldwin? Opening night. Jimmy said, 'Do we have enough vodka for afterwards, too?' I said, 'Yes, enough for after, too.' His mother, his brothers, his sisters, his family had assembled. Anybody in Washington who was interested in the theater was there, all of the critics, and Sterling Brown, Alain Locke, they were all there; they knew somehow through the blood that an event was going to happen, and that event happened. It was magnificent. At the end of the play the audience broke out in such applause, it was a rock-and-roll applause, and we pushed Jimmy to the stage. He knew how he looked; his eyes were bloodshot and bulging; an old crinkly nineteen-dollar suit. First he shook hands with the actors. He told me afterwards, he didn't know when he could bear to show his face to all those people. Finally he did and they rose, and the evening ended. The critics reported that here is a good man writing well.[6] Somehow or other, it made Jimmy almost cry.

"I had fried five chickens and made potato salad that day. The onslaught came in. His sisters offered to help; they were charming; I had cheese and they cut the cheese in wedges. (You know I can't bear cheese cut in wedges.) I said, 'Jimmy, let's take a turn around the block and we'll come back and eat.' When we got back, it looked like termites had gone through the place, rapidly. There was no chicken left, there was chicken bones. No potato salad, no anything. Luckily, the liquor had been hidden.

"After his mother and sisters left, I said, 'Where are your brothers going to stay?' He said, 'Why, here.' I said, 'Jimmy, there is only one bed in the front room, and my bed in the back.' He said, 'The front bed opens out, doesn't it? Five men can sleep on that bed, can't they?' They managed.

"I said, 'Where are you going to sleep?' He said, 'In the back room with you.' I said, 'Jimmy, I'm tired; I like to roll around in the bed.' He said, 'That's the only other place besides the bathtub.' Well, I got to the far corner of the bed, and every once in a while when he rolled in his sleep, I just felt bones. You know that sermon, 'Dry Bones in the Valley.'

"So it was over; the reviews were in. He was relieved and happy and we rejoiced, and I had to go to school the next day and teach my classes. When I got back, Jimmy said, 'I have done so many rewrites; don't you think it would be a good idea if I stayed around for a week and got those rewrites together so you could have a script that is not broken up?' I said, 'Yeah, I never thought of that.' So he started at one o'clock in the morning. A week after the play opened, I could hear those keys even when I was asleep; he was a worker.

"Then one day toward the end of the week, he said, 'I want to work on a short story called "Sonny's Blues." You know Sonny is a jazz musician, and I have a friend called Arnold who is a jazz musician, and I am kind of patterning the whole thing after him. I think it would help me with the story if Arnold came down for the weekend.' I was full of good cheer, and I said, 'Sure.'

"So Sunday, at the knock of the door, I opened it and there was Arnold, a nice boy. He had a great strawberry birthmark on his face that made him look extraordinary. It made him look startled all the time. But the thing was, the cab man kept bringing in bags: his guitar, his new instrument, and two footlockers. So I said, 'Arnold, I thought you were just staying for the weekend. Are you bringing some things for Jimmy?' He said, 'I came to stay.' I had to pay the cab. It was the first of one of those things.

"I didn't know how to take action in any way at all. What do you do? Arnold drank two quarts of milk a day. Jimmy drank a fifth of vodka a day. I had taken the summer off so that I had just my little savings to get me through. Why, the grocery bills were tremendous. Charm exploded everywhere. I guess that was why I just didn't think about it. We had parties and Jimmy read part of *Giovanni's Room*. He was afraid of the book, as afraid of that book as he became unafraid of everything else that he has written since. The book was personal, about homosexual love, about two people locked together in a room, very much like *No Exit*. No place to go and you couldn't get away from the other personality even if you left by the door. Marvelous.

"I forgot all about the quarts of milk, the vodka, the legs of lamb that would go in one meal. I was just taking money out of the bank and taking money out of the bank. We would talk for hours. We would talk about all those things that only two people who had something simpatico—childhood, mother, relationships, lovers, bewilderment, ignorance in action, white people, why we had failed in certain areas. . . . And his smooth, melodious voice went on, and when we were not talking, he smoked me out of the house.

"Well, it went on that way, the charm, the talk, the Fourth of July, sparklers, then Jimmy said, 'Arnold and I would like to go down to hear some advanced jazz.' So I said, 'Sure, go on down and hear it because my best friend, Harold Jackman, will be here tonight, and we'll be talking and have time to reminisce.' At two in the morning the phone rang and a voice said, 'This is Jimmy.' I said, 'Yeah, hope you enjoyed yourself.' He said, 'Had a wild time, and we've been drinking Scotch all night.' (You know Negroes kind of hold to that idea that if they drink Scotch it gives us a little class.) He said, 'We are ready to leave and we don't have any money.' I said, 'Why did you order the Scotch?' Well . . . So I went down there and bailed them out. I should have let them wash the dishes; it would have been a nice experience for one of his books.

"So it went on from one kind of extravagance—extravagance for a schoolteacher—to another, till I looked at my bank account and that was it. The end.[7] I had done the shopping, cooked the meals, washed dirty drawers, towels, everything. I had watched creation being done, and I had created nothing the whole summer. A friend of mine used to come around, Claude Green. He had a beautiful tenor voice; he used to sing. I said, 'Tonight, Claude (Jimmy and Arnold were in the front room), sing me something, the songs of Araby and tales of old Kashmir.' So he settled down and sang, 'When I come to the end of my journey. Weary of life, when that old battle is won.' And the words go on—'He will say, I understand, and repeat, well done. Well done.' It broke me up. I burst into tears. It must have been Irish tears. It was a flood. I rushed into the front room. I said, 'Get out! You niggers leave my house. I don't care whether you are going to be the greatest writer in the world, I am finished! Get out of here!'

"They said, 'Well, there's no place to go tonight.'

"I said, 'Tomorrow morning, first thing, just go. Go.'

"Shameful. But I meant it. My money was gone. So they made a little procession with their bags, their dilapidation. They went to the Dunbar Hotel. I guess when you sign in, they assume you are going to pay when you sign out, but I didn't care at that point.

"Then began the great game. Whenever I had to go to Howard and had to pass by the Dunbar, I would go a block or so out of my way so I wouldn't meet the guilt. One day I met Jimmy. Pleasantries. He said, 'We are hungry. Can't we come over for dinner?' I said, 'Oh yeah, sure, come on over.'

"So I sprinted home; I can't believe how fast I got there. I took all the cans off the shelves. I emptied the icebox. I must have been possessed. I put all that stuff under my dirty clothes in the closet. I left out just enough for dinner that night. I said to myself, this is a matter of survival! Survival!

"So they came to dinner, and once again I had missed their presence. The silence and the talent of the guitar of Arnold. Jimmy's talk — what he was writing — and how *Giovanni's Room* was finished. All those things, but I knew I couldn't renege and let them come back because I would be ruined.[8]

"So finally Jimmy left. He said, 'I know you have spent almost all your money; I am not so silly that I don't know that. I want to give you a token, and I will send it to you; it is a picture of me, painted by one of the great artists, a black artist [Beauford Delaney].' The picture came. It looked like Jimmy. I think he did it on purpose, just to haunt me. And there it was. The eyes, the cheekbones, the haunted look. I did hang it up.

"A year or two later, after his great success in the world, one day I got a call. His secretary, who had a Swiss French accent, said, 'Jimmy is fixing up his apartment, and he would very much like to have his portrait back.'

"I said, 'You tell Jimmy Baldwin when he wants his portrait back, he must ask for it himself.'

"The next time when I went to New York, naturally I called him. Who could resist a great artist and a charmer? He told me about writing *Blues for Mr. Charlie*. He said, 'From now on only you will direct my plays.' I said, 'Gee, Jimmy, that's very flattering.' He said, 'You will get everything back — twofold. You have cast your bread on the waters.' I was buoyed up because I could see those royalties coming in. 'To show you that I really mean it,' he went on, 'you bring your lawyer or agent and I will bring my agent and we'll have dinner at Sardis.' (He didn't say on me. I guess I looked the oldest one of group, so the waiter slipped it under my plate.) But we came to an agreement, not in writing, that I would direct *Blues for Mr. Charlie*, which was being read at the Actors Studio. So I said, 'Jimmy, I would like to read the first draft.' He said, 'You will, you will.' I never did.[9]

"The first thing I knew, Burgess Meredith was directing *Blues*. I called Jimmy, no answer. I wrote him. The answer was the equivalent of 'Fuck you.' He had promised me. I went to see *Blues for Mr. Charlie*. It was a mess — a loud, raucous mess. Neither the director nor the actors nor anybody understood what it was about. Later on at Howard we did it. We weeded out the long passages that made no sense. I am arrogant enough to say that we made it into a coherent artistic whole.

"So now he is destined to go down as one of the finest writers of our time, and, I want to add, one of the most captivating personalities. Jimmy has gone off now to Paris,[10] away from the struggle, away from the fight; he goes to Istanbul. . . . He has made more than a million dollars and he has never set foot in the heart of Africa, only Northern Africa, exotic, white Africa. I hope that this marvel of a man and a talent will come back with a compassion that I know he has and write all of the things that he can write about with soul, and not be treading the cobblestones of Paris or see the sunshine through the windows of Chartres Cathedral."

Baldwin's daring sparked Owen to rewrite *Come Home Early, Child*. In the summer of 1958 he gave the novel over to Farrar, Straus & Giroux. On August 4, John Farrar wrote, "I read it through and was impressed. What my partners will say I do not know." A week later his partners said no because the book split in the middle and also because it would be difficult to sell. Owen gave the book over to John Schaffner, a literary agent. One top publisher after another praised the poetry but found the story bled from realism in the first half into surrealism in the second. After a year, Schaffner wrote, "Since after all, this submission of your novel to the New York Graphic Society is the fifteenth, I do think you ought to consider seriously the criticism offered by these people."[11]

Owen could not, or would not, rewrite again. Pat O'Connor, as a personal commitment, took on the task of finding a publisher. However, even O'Connor did not succeed until 1976, when, through his editorship at Popular Library, he placed the novel before the public. Owen sent copies to all he knew, and possibly mailed one to James Baldwin.

He did write Baldwin and ask for the money he owed him on the phone bills; Baldwin wrote back that he had no money and said that, further, he was not treading the cobblestones of Paris as a caper, but was determined to be a writer, and if he failed, it would be his own responsibility.

Owen never forgave Baldwin his daring. Sebree had done it; Gordon had done it; now Baldwin had done it. They had made a dangerous commitment more wonderful than tenure at Howard; they had given their lives to the only God Owen worshipped—art. He understood this terrible truth, but he remained mired and never forgave his three friends their success. At age forty, he could not choose the road less traveled by.

21

Loss of Stars, 1956–62

"The night Coin Foreman was returned home from his wanderings, the Corinthian Baptist Church of Christ burned to the ground in a five-alarm fire. Along Berriman Street the news was flashed from open window to open window by popped-out heads and mouths and mouths working into the disaster gossip like fast scissors."

So began the first chapter of *Come Home Early, Child.*[1] The empyreal destruction of the historic Concord Baptist Church in downtown Brooklyn had inflamed Owen's childhood memory. He entitled the chapter "Summer Fire" and sent it to the *Paris Review,* where it won second prize for the best short story of the year (1956). Proud and competitive, Owen dispatched a copy to James Baldwin.

The first half of the fifties brought an end to the fighting in Korea, and an end to the lies of Sen. Joseph McCarthy. The Reverend Martin Luther King, Jr., led the Birmingham bus strike. The Warren Court declared school segregation illegal, and President Eisenhower sent paratroopers to ensure the integration of Little Rock High School in Arkansas. At the end of the decade, *A Raisin in the Sun* burst upon Broadway—the first play by a black woman playwright to reach the Great White Way.

Still, new black plays were hard to come by. The theater at Howard searched but found few. For the 1956–57 season, Anne Cooke directed *Bayou Legend* a second time; then Owen hit upon *Lost in the Stars,* the Maxwell Anderson adaptation of Alan Paton's *Cry, the Beloved Country,* with music by Kurt Weill. To generate student enthusiasm,

Dodson cast Todd Duncan, who had created the role of Stephan Kumalo on Broadway in 1949. Duncan agreed to act the part if Owen would direct him, because "when Rouben Mamoulian directed me on Broadway, he didn't direct me at all. He thought all niggers could act by instinct and rhythm."[2] Owen rehearsed Duncan privately for two weeks before bringing the singer to Spaulding Hall with the rest of the cast.

The success of a college musical demands the cooperation of the music department; unfortunately, in many cases, music professors consider musical theater a pop art and prefer that their students practice Bach or Beethoven. The Howard director of music, Warner Lawson, son of a concert pianist, was an elitist. Under his directorship the choir by 1951 had become the unofficial chorus of the National Symphony Orchestra in Washington.[3] Lawson forbade the playing of jazz in the music department, banning the saxophone completely. Gospel he excoriated. His approach to spirituals can be inferred from his remark to the National Music Society: "I work entirely from the point of view of diction and concentration on consonants rather than vowels." He belonged to those teachers who determinedly pulled Blacks up and away from rural or ghetto roots.

Lawson did consent to conduct Kurt Weill's *Lost in the Stars,* but when rehearsals began, he sent a letter to Owen stating that "our choir's schedule is so crowded that I don't believe that we will be able to carry this production off."[4] And so began a classic academic feud. As the years slipped by, each man recruited allies and kept accounts of slights and "bitchings."[5] Although he possessed a sense of noblesse oblige that on occasion dismissed foibles with a wave of the wrist, Owen grew more bitter with each Lawson encounter and ever more amazed at his own bitterness.

To relate the tangled history of how Lawson received promotion to dean of fine arts (a position for which Owen thought himself eligible), to retell how the two men fought over the creation of Howard's centennial opera, *Til Victory Is Won,* with Lawson refusing to conduct unless the sequence on Bessie Smith was removed; to recount the petty delays, each's failure to acknowledge the other's successes; to report the Iagos who came whispering of what the other had done and said— all of this and so much more—would be to set down a tale as destructive to their students as to both teachers. What began as a small splinter under the nail festered in the proud flesh. Lawson's failure to direct the music for *Lost in the Stars* may have been the onset of Owen's disaffection with all of Howard University. He began to accept assignments outside the college.

In the late forties, a small, dedicated group of artists under the leadership of Mary Averett-Seelye had founded a dramatic company, Theatre Lobby, at 17 St. Matthews Court, an alley off Rhode Island Avenue near Connecticut. The theater was little more than a room rented from the church. Drama critic Richard Coe described the artists as "a marvelous little group—precious but they knew what they were doing. George C. Scott did a couple of plays there." Over four successive seasons (1958–62) Theatre Lobby invited Owen to direct *My Heart's in the Highlands, Thunder Rock, A Moon for the Misbegotten,* and *Look Back in Anger.* No facilities, no money, high dreams, and talented actors—Owen's cup of tea.

In the June heat of those same years, Dodson directed plays in Jefferson City, Missouri (population 32,000, mostly white and Catholic), at Lincoln University, a campus of red brick buildings with white Georgian windows founded in 1866 by black Civil War veterans. Dodson directed two summer shows in seven weeks by bringing with him one or two actors and a technician from Howard who understood his style.

As he did at Howard, Dodson cast nontraditionally, using a white mother and father with two black sons in *Death of a Salesman.* For *Tea and Sympathy* he brought black actor St. Clair Christmas from Howard to play Tom Lee, and he cast a local white woman as Laura Reynolds. After some rehearsals, the actress still had difficulty when she entered the boy's bedroom to teach him how to make love. Owen came out of the auditorium saying, "Child, you have got to let your hair down." She took it literally, and suddenly the scene began to work—all this only a few hundred miles and five years from Little Rock, where "when they speak of this. . . ."[6]

Winona Fletcher, who designed costumes at Lincoln, recalled that Owen trusted whatever he saw: "He never complained over a costume. The summer we did *A Loss of Roses* (about a drug addict) Dodson had cast a young white woman, who was supposed to be nude under a fur coat while a husky black lad threw her on the bed and manhandled her. We were all concerned how this was going to go over in white, conservative Jeff City—how to make her look nude and still have something on. We discovered that she was the daughter of the chief of police, but her father came and was enthralled by the production."[7]

Since the Howard drama department's inception, Anne Cooke had been chair. In 1957, she retired to marry sociologist Ira De A. Reid, who taught at Haverford College. Owen ascended to the departmental throne with a promotion to full professor at a salary of $7,450, but at the price of abandoning his self-appointed role of the gifted rebel against the bourgeois queen-mother Anne. Now, if Owen overspent the budget, Owen the bookkeeper must fix it. Almost at once he began to drink just a tad more. The drama department's golden years had peaked.

The greatest and most compelling of his new responsibilities was the completion of a new theater, named for the nineteenth-century actor Ira Aldridge. Dean Lawson, Anne Cooke, and James Porter (dean of art), under the supervision of an architect, had designed a tripartite complex—the Fine Arts Building—centered on a 1,507-seat auditorium that would serve the arts generally and a little theater seating 314 for drama department use. Dodson, who claimed that he had not been consulted, encountered expensive design errors that had to be corrected—$54,000 to reset the tier of lights so they wouldn't shine on the heads of the audience. One mistake amused him—the marquee sign arrived with Aldridge's name misspelled as "Alridge."

In spite of delays, on December 20, 1960, the three departments moved into their new home; Dodson into room 1047 with its deep blue sign on the door that would remain for ten years: "Owen V. Dodson, Head. Dept. of Drama." One of his first acts was to turn the Green Room into a museum. Two long tables ran down the center, flanked by chairs and glass cases on either side to display memorabilia. Bright posters of *Medea, Amen Corner,* and *On the Town* adorned the walls as a departmental legacy to instill pride.[8]

To augment his vision, Dodson hired a dedicated teacher named Marian McMichaels. A white woman, she arrived in time for the opening of the theaters and over the next five years discovered worlds she had not suspected. Among other things she learned how to use makeup on black actors, how to teach diction to a polyglot body of foreign students. Dodson cast an East Indian woman as Gertrude in his 1964 *Hamlet;* she asked McMichaels, "Can I walk at the same time that I talk?"[9] Finally, McMichaels learned how pervasive the effects of

racism could be. "Most of our students—our American students—
are from the South, and they have never had even one decently trained
teacher. They can't read; they can't write. This tragedy will take two
generations to remedy."

Dodson typified Howard's double vision—on the one hand, mocking the ignorance of the country clods, but on the other, furiously
determined to teach them the best the world had felt and thought.
One way to do this was to reinforce tradition: The college required
women to wear skirts, heels, and stockings to classes—no slacks or
jeans except on Saturday. The homecoming queens all had long hair
and very light complexions. The medical students carried stethoscopes
in their jacket pockets. Every Friday, the fraternities gathered under
the trees to the sing the fraternity songs. According to drama major
Glenda Dickerson, "Against this class regimentation the Howard Players—those who were gay or dark or poor or who hungered for personal
expression—created their own elitism and gloried in their campus
image of bohemians. They would stroll and strut down the mall, looking
like performers from a circus—wearing outrageous costumes and partying all night."[10]

Owen as gentleman-rebel-in-residence encouraged the nonconform-
ists; he hired Shizu Cole, who had for a time designed for the Washington Ballet. Because of Shizu's dedication, Dodson moved from one
big costume show to another: "She would go out and spend her own
money to buy fabric. She loved to touch it and feel it. One day, the
door to the costume room was three-quarters open, and I heard her
say, 'Today I will talk about how to groom your pubic hairs to please
your lover.' I said, 'I have to hear this.' She went on, 'If you have kinky
hair, they might like it to snap back the way it is, but some people
like to braid it with a touch of oil.' Then Shizu talked about pulses:
'You have them all over, all around your organs. Now put your hands
down there. Don't you feel it? On either side. For the men, there are
pulses in their penis, and for women, there are inner and outer pulses,
but we must make them work for you, so get a bottle of good perfume,
and put a little bit on all the pulses because those pulses make the
scent explode.' " Her pubic purview certainly extended the conventional conception of cosmetics in Theater 101.

On February 20, 1961, the Ira Aldridge Theatre opened its doors
with García Lorca's lyrical drama *Blood Wedding*. Owen remembered
it as a "dream of an opening in a dream of a theater."[11] Kermit Keith

had designed a blue flag for the department with an insignia of Hamlet from Elsinore, the foil with the double guard. As the lights dimmed, down the aisle came a student, Noble Sissle's son, with Dodson following, and they faced the audience. Owen delivered a poem he had written, "How did you do it Ira Aldridge, how?" In his excitement, he reversed Aldridge's dates: born 1867, died 1807. Then, when he read the title of his poem, the audience laughed.[12]

In the audience sat four people who had created the tradition of the Howard Players (possibly the oldest collegiate playing group in America): Sterling Brown, who remembered the days when the college would not hire anyone to teach drama; Montgomery Gregory, who had held the players together all those first years; and, of course, James Butcher and Anne Cooke Reid. Alain Locke, for whom Owen wanted the theater named, had died. Said Owen: "*Blood Wedding* with its songs sung in Spanish convinced the audience that the department could do plays from any culture."

Without a break Dodson turned to directing Jean Anouilh's *Antigone*, a play of classic conflict — law and order versus individual freedom. He dedicated *Antigone* to the inauguration of Howard's new president, James Nabrit. Either by lucky hunch or by premonition, Dodson's choice presaged Nabrit's future role in university politics. The *Washington Star* reviewer found that Owen's direction "enhanced the reputation of Sophocles." Dodson, now master of his own playhouse, invited friends to come play. In May 1961 he brought Earle Hyman and Carolyn Hill Stewart to perform in a collage of pieces, *Charade*, including two scenes from *Hamlet*. The next season, to perform Marlowe's *The Tragical History of Dr. Faustus*, he invited Gordon Heath and Lee Payant from Paris.

The introduction of professionals into a cast of amateurs was intended to provide the latter with a close observation of artists at work; at the same time, however, by moving the professionals into the leads, Owen denied the students an opportunity to play the great roles. Gordon and Lee moved with the authority of classical actors, spoke with the golden tones of Shakespeare; they knew each other's nuances; they impressed. "How," asked a Howard actor watching Lee ascend the nine-foot staircase, "can he glide up those stairs without moving his feet?" On the other hand, when in dress rehearsal Gordon called out to the lighting booth, "Laddie, I need a bit more light here," Bob

West responded that Gordon should get his ass into the spot provided. The result—a mixed bag of adulation and resentment.

Such tensions are common enough in dress rehearsal, and Dodson as director should have moderated tempers, but he neglected his authority; Heath, albeit reluctantly, took over in order to get the show on. For the first time in his career, Dodson shunned his directing responsibilities. Perhaps his new position as theater head had swamped him; money and the business of money had always eluded Owen's attention. By 1965, the drama staff had grown to eight members. The new theater building required hovering attention and constant "fine" tuning. Bill Brown had resigned to go to Nigeria, and a new tech director, Carlton Molette, was brought in. Dean Lawson already complained that the theater overspent its budget. Directing productions at Theatre Lobby and at Lincoln University had taken a toll on Owen's energy.

All these things Dodson would normally have discussed with Gordon, but during the *Faustus* rehearsals he did not confide in his friend; he simply left Gordon to fill the vacuum. After the show opened, Dodson, in his cups, told Gordon, "Don't think I don't know that you directed the show." Was Dodson grateful, resentful, relieved, ashamed, or simply jealous of his students' respect for Gordon as an artist? All of the above? Whatever the answer, critic Richard Coe nonetheless found that "Owen Dodson, that ingenious talent who gives Howard's drama department so much of its glow, here has devised the most elaborate entertainment yet presented at the university."[13]

Dodson's sudden directorial insouciance did not stop with *Faustus* but lapsed over into his next show, *Defiant Island,* a historical drama about Henri Christophe, King of Haiti. A huge spectacle, a vehicle Owen ordinarily reveled in, opened two months after *Faustus* closed. Dramatist James Forsyth attended rehearsals and like so many others was struck by Owen's affability: "He nursed the production along and wasn't dictatorial. I had misgivings that Dodson was enjoying himself too much. However, the poet had such a love of life that to some extent, he was probably less physical than the best of producers should be."[14] Forsyth's diplomatic assessment might be translated as "Dodson was not running a tight ship."

Bill Brown had designed a splendid Citadel, but Dodson ignored the set's possibilities; according to Brown, "He never used the doors

I had provided for the actors."[15] Dodson enticed a professional, Clayton Corbin, to play King Christophe. The actor arrived with his lines learned but soon was upset with Owen because he didn't give him any direction. Some sea change within Dodson had occurred.

At this same time, Dodson, with composer Mark Fax, wrote a one-act opera, *A Christmas Miracle,* an unrelentingly grim story of a blind child whose house has been burned and whose infant brother is shot in the arms of his mother. Miraculously the child's sight is restored. The opera was performed on March 6, 1958, for an unsuspecting conference of teachers. Day Thorpe of the *Evening Star* noted that "it is questionable whether such untempered gloom can be the subject of a successful evening in the theatre."[16] What possessed Dodson to write such a pathetic tale of unrelieved horror?

Teaching by day and directing by night had consumed him, but abruptly the long-dormant poetry again erupted onto his midnight pages. On December 13, 1960, poet Richard Eberhart invited him to record his poems for the Library of Congress (a lesser honor than being invited to read one's poetry before a live audience in the Coolidge Auditorium, where Dodson would read in 1973). In the introduction to his recording, Owen remarked he had stopped writing poetry because he "couldn't keep track of his poems."[17]

As he read, death and dying rattled like the Horsemen of the Apocalypse through every one of the twenty-two poems until Eberhart remarked upon the obsession; Owen ignored Eberhart and pressed on, including in his reading "Summing Up for the Defendant," a new poem brimming with thanatotic anxiety:

> Tell me my marks, Examiner, I've waited an inch-worm time
> Seeing you raised, I think you are eternal God who bathed
> In the seven oceans at once like a leprous Moby Dick:
> Rattling up the waters, sizzling the air, eating the weather,
> Teasing Ahab, forgetting your sperm of men, regretting Michael.
> Tell me my grades in conduct, arithmetic, arthritis, human love.
> I must be graded A B or F and itch a torment or eat my roses of
>   love.
> Registrar, Judge, Examiner, Jehovah of my knitted world: here I
>   wish,
> Demand your juried mind to conference and huddle. Let go
> The water, the firmament, the harpoons of death, this circled court.

Clear my passport passage now or bite my leg half in two
Letting me stump away slimy on my ransom blood.

In a revision of the poem, Owen designated his left leg to be the one bitten half in two, the same paralyzed heart-side of his mother, the same side on which the word "DEATH" had been tattooed on Coin's arm. What had he accused himself of? What rites of passage could clear him?

He sent "Summing Up for the Defendant" to Priscilla Heath and to Tom Pawley, as if to say to these two old friends, "See! See what has been done to me!" But what *had* been done to him? On the surface, he had climbed to new pinnacles, yet his guilty heart told him he had been sentenced to arthritis, a metaphor for a crippled life. Nonetheless, his fierce spirit still demanded to have its passport passage cleared.

A few years earlier, Earle Hyman, Frederick Wilkerson, and Owen had visited Lotte Lenya and her husband, George Davis, in Rockland County. At midnight, Lenya sent George to bed because he had a bad heart. She then said that on the third floor were two bedrooms, plus Kurt Weill's old study with a couch that would make a bed, the very couch on which Weill had died. Owen reported, "I have never seen such a scramble. Earle and Wilkie ran up the stairs so they wouldn't have to sleep in the dead man's bed. Very funny. So I slept in the bed where Weill had died. Then I found out that he had died at fifty-one. This was a magic age for me. So many people whom I have known and admired, friends of mine, died at fifty or fifty-one."

Lenya and Davis left for Germany, and a short while later Lenya wrote Dodson from Berlin: "I think the Greeks were right in their saying: 'They wept—they recovered—they recalled'—only at the moment it seems hard for me to accept that George is no more. I miss his screaming at me (by screaming I mean George's way of screaming which was the gentlest and most persisting screaming), I miss his love for me and for everybody who was ready to accept it."[18]

George died at age fifty! Dodson became more obsessed with the significance of the half-century, an age he would reach in 1964. Hadn't Lillian, his father, and his mother all died in that span of years? Even Richard Wright, who died at fifty-two, Owen claimed as evidence. After all, Wright had died on November 28, Owen's birthday. And then, there was the case of his friend Jimmy Whyte, the gallery owner and historian. Whyte's abrupt death in August 1962 confirmed Owen's fears: At midlife no child of his would carry the Dodson name. (He never spoke of his older brother.) Although Cullen, Hughes, Van Vechten, and Locke had died without progeny, Owen demanded, "Clear my passport passage now." Was it for a son?[19]

In this same period Owen showed an intense interest in the third pregnancy of a friend of his, actress Alfredina Brown. Dodson wrote her a lovely, poetic letter dedicated to her unborn child. The letter had stars and glitter, shimmering pieces attached to it—a gorgeous note. Later, in the hospital, Dodson sent her a magnum of champagne. When she came home, he visited the house and went to the bassinet to look in. Recalled Brown: "He just stood there fifteen or twenty minutes. I couldn't believe it. Couldn't understand it. I guess Owen must have gone into his sun porch thirty times to check on that little baby. He was just thrilled with it. He was a loving man who would have made a terrible husband."[20]

In 1943, on his twenty-ninth birthday, Owen had written to his sisters that if he died, "there is no spokesman to defend my position; no wife, no brother, no one who would say: 'I understand his whole relation with the world and stars.'" Two decades later he succinctly expressed that agony in the poem "Hymn Written after Jeremiah Preached to Me in a Dream." The four verses, published by Robert Hayden in 1967,[21] can be read (with a little help from the deconstructionists) as a bitter struggle for heterosexual potency:

> Nowhere are we safe
> Surely not in love
> Morning ripe at three
> Or in the Holy Trinity.
> (My God, look after me.)
> Where does Grace abide,
> Whole, whole in surety?
> Or does sin abide
> Where virtue tries, in shame, to hide?
> (My God, have I no pride?)
> Shall I try the whole,
> Crippled in my will,
> Spatter where it falls
> My carnal-fire waterfalls?
> (My angel, in compassion, calls.)

> Secret, knotted shame
> Rips me like a curse.
> Unction in my dust
> Give me final thrust.
> (My God, consider dust!)

One need not belabor interpretation of the sexual images of the poem beyond pointing out the homonymic use of "whole," the punning with "hymn," and the fact that "unction," in order to be understood in the context, must be read as a verb.

"Clear my passport passage now or bite my leg half in two": the passage Owen demanded would not — could not — be cleared.

22

Not without Laughter, 1963–64

For lovers, Owen chose melancholy souls, seriously serious. But for companionship, Owen chose an actor who possessed the secret of infectious, mad, rolling-on-the-floor laughter: "A person and a dog would be coming toward us, and they would resemble each other, such an ordinary thing to notice, but we would be convulsed in laughter."

The man who tickled Owen's funnybone, Roscoe Lee Browne, had attended Lincoln University, where he had gained attention by twice winning the American Championship for the 1,000–yard run, and where, most important for Owen, he had met Kenneth, "who was like a princely light at some reception-cum-party for us all." When in his cups, Owen would often address Roscoe as "Kenneth." He told him, "I know that you are younger than I, but you are like my older brother."[1] Sometimes Dodson's fantasy life with Kenneth was as strong as his real life.

When Roscoe played in *Brecht on Brecht* at Washington's Arena Stage, Dodson offered him the use of his ground-floor apartment. Each morning they would chat over breakfast. One October morning Owen phoned Browne and said, "Oh, chile, I've something here, you have got to read it." Browne replied, "Owen, if you will just hang up, I have to shower and I'll be right up." Owen said again, "I have revised the poem and the door is open."

When Browne came up, Dodson from the kitchen called Roscoe "Kenneth." Browne replied, "It's a bit early for a drink." Then, as Browne walked into the kitchen, Owen said, "Roscoe . . ." and fainted.

Roscoe caught him and got him to a chaise longue and loosened his dressing gown and silk pajama top. Browne said, "Owen, can you hear me?" Dodson indicated that he did.

Browne called both the police and Freedman Hospital. Dodson told Browne, "I have a pain across my chest . . . up here." Roscoe told him, "Don't be silly, your heart's not up there," and they both laughed. Two ambulances came immediately, and everyone who came in the door knew Dodson.

He had a loss of color but no paralysis; still, he was hospitalized for two weeks. His doctor suggested very little but did say, "Too much drinking. Too much stress." Browne thought that Owen could generate real stress by hyperventilating when speaking about a play or a poem: "He would exacerbate it with a kind of sweet hysteria. I say 'sweet' because I always found Owen lyric. He was vulnerable, sometimes weeping on a word. He would say, 'Read me that poem again, Roscoe.' I would read it. The phrase could be 'Oh, Martha.' He would break into tears, and say I have never heard anybody say the 'Oh' before. Owen would then repeat the line, and it would be 'Oooooooooooh, ooooooooooooooh, Maa-artha.' I would tell him, 'Owen, you are diphthonging.' He would say, 'I am not.' I would repeat, 'You are diphthonging on a single syllable.' " (Perhaps Owen's diphthonging carried over from his *Rashomon* rehearsals, his delight in producing samurai cries for Roscoe.)

One evening shortly after his return from the hospital, Owen suggested that they take a walk. Recalled Browne:

I helped him up and we traveled farther than we had intended. Talking and laughing, we rounded a bend and were in shock. About six kids — all pockmarked with acne and passion — had an old man against the wall, and here we were, two more. Dodson could not run. We had laughed and talked ourselves right into a cul-de-sac.

The boys are saying, "Give it up, come on, give it up," and they are coming toward us. One had a knife and another some weapon in his hands. Owen looked at me and we both knew that we were to die. I looked to Owen and said *"Rashomon."* (I am given to spectacular, vivid, and instant appearance of madness.) Owen said, *"Rashomon?"* I said, *"Rashomon.* You stand absolutely still and make the sounds. I will make the motions. He knew

exactly what I meant because we had seen the movie together
[and he had directed the play]. Suddenly, Owen's "Oooooooh
Martha" transformed into "Death" by my hands as I danced
about on my racer's legs. The kids said, "Oh shit. We gotta get
outta here," and they almost knocked us down trying to get away.
Kids who do things like that are almost invariably cowards; they
are terrified of a truly ill person or pure madness.

We could hardly get home fast enough. I said, "Owen, can't
you walk any faster? They may be behind us." I was afraid they
would realize that they had been duped. When we got home, he
screamed to me, "You are just plain crazy, you are crazy!"

A few years later, in the angry-black seventies, Roscoe arrived at a
theater after an angry play had begun, and he slipped into a seat beside
Owen. The actors, angry in their mock racial militancy, surged toward
them, shouting threats in what they thought was a great, marvelous
confrontational moment meant to menace the audience's security.
Knowing that Owen could not bear watching unrelieved shouting and
accusations, Roscoe sotto voce made the *Rashomon* sounds. Owen
began to convulse, and gasped, "Chile, we better get out of here; they
may be behind us."[2]

Owen's "heart attack" came at fifty, the age he thought he would
die. It also came during a period of frenzied productivity: From 1963
to 1965, he wrote twenty-five theater reviews of performances at Arena
Stage, the Howard Theatre, and the National Theatre.[3] In the same
period, he directed twenty-one shows, often back to back.[4] While some
were one-acts, many originals required concentrated creative effort.

On Shakespeare's 400th birthday, April 16, 1964, Owen produced
his third *Hamlet*. For the lead, he chose St. Clair Christmas, a tall,
melancholy artist who had designed sets for Howard. This decision
Owen made in the summer. Shortly after he had announced his choice,
Christmas's mother appeared. A tall, stately woman who wore a fez
with great dignity, she could have played the Queen. She took Dodson
aside and said, "I won't see *Hamlet*. I won't live until spring. I'm dying
of cancer."

As with Earle, Owen became father-mentor to the actor, and he
moved St. Clair into his apartment. The death of St. Clair's mother
informed his performance, which was charged with the desperation of
his wish that she were there close to him: "These things help to make
a performance when you have to call on every resource that you have."

When *Hamlet* closed, Shakespeare's birthday brought a letter addressed to "Professor and Mrs. Dodson." The return read simply, "The White House." President and Mrs. Johnson would welcome them at a reception June 22 at 6 P.M. Owen turned to his friend Pat O'Connor and asked, "What do you think Edith will say?" Pat replied, "What will I wear?" Owen picked up the phone and called Edith, who promptly responded, "What will I wear?"

Edith came to Washington three or four days early; she went to the beauty parlor and had her hair straightened, but in hot and muggy April her hair came down, so she went to the beauty shop the next day and had her hair straightened again; by the third day she said, "They're going to have to take me kinky hair or not." Owen too had jitters. O'Connor told him to "buy a blue linen blazer and white linen pants, the best—we're not fooling around here—and white shoes."[5] He did.

They started ironing the linen in the morning, and put their clothes on three hours in advance. The clothes wrinkled, so they took them off again and were ironing to the last minute. They left for the White House early. Mrs. Johnson, gracious, and Lyndon, towering over everyone, received their guests promptly at 6:45 P.M. The American Shakespearean actors—Katharine Cornell, Maurice Evans, Helen Hayes—were there. The president looked quite uncomfortable, and disappeared into his study a couple of times; when present, he talked with John Mason Brown, a theater critic originally from the Southwest. After a while, Edith went up to the president, her head barely reaching midway on Johnson's tie, and said, "You've talked to these important people long enough. It's time you talked to me," and she told him everything about life at St. Nicholas Place in Harlem—the muggings, the peeing in the hallways, the drugs. All the while, the president bent down listening for a long time.[6] Owen was horrified that Edith had approached the president and had not let him get a word in.

The White House reception concluded a three-day program that included performances at Stratford, Connecticut, which the Dodsons did not attend, and an Elizabethan luncheon at the Folger Shakespeare Library, which they did.

On midsummer's eve at 6:30, as musicians played round dances on sackbuts and recorders, hostesses in Elizabethan farthingales ushered 200 guests into a sixteenth-century theater, where they imbibed punch. At 7 P.M., seated at Table G with eight other guests, Owen and Edith surveyed their menus: "Guests maie take their trenchers to the serving board to pick out that whiche they would eate. Let our guests helpe themselves bountifully and be mindful not to stumble. We beg that Ye throw no bones under the table."[7]

Folger catered an abundant fare: salmon, roast beef, capon, young pig, lobster, artichokes, French wines, and English ale. Edith and Owen must have winked at one another in recognition that forty years before, at 140 Quincy in Brooklyn, they had served the table of Mary Folger, whose brother, Henry Folger (president of Standard Oil), had founded the Folger Shakespeare Library. Now, four decades later, the "damnable Dodsons" were seated at the banquet table, "tranquil blossoms on the tortured stem."[8]

Three days before Christmas, Carl Van Vechten died. For his elegy Dodson wrote, "He sought to solve the racial riddle of his time by samples and examples."[9] The two men had shared a vision of racial respect and a gay sense of play. Van Vechten often closed his letters to Owen with a postscript that exotic gifts had been sent, if not in the mail, certainly upon the backs of swans that should arrive momentarily on Owen's windowsill: "Four golden slippers, jade apples, and a bowl with sapphire dogs to you!"[10] Owen too began to close his letters with "three casques of rubies, a brace of dolphins, and a thimble of brandy to you." Over the twenty-five years of their correspondence, the two sultans exchanged all the treasures of paradise. Cards arrived in memory of birthdays, cards for social calendars, cards for rendezvous, but Owen telegraphed the final tribute to Fania, Carl's wife: "Carl always knew about angels. Now we know that they taught him that excellence is the most pleasing gift of God."[11]

In the sixties Dodson had lost two mentors—Carl Van Vechten and Harold Jackman—who were both ravenous collectors of black cultural memorabilia. Dodson had divided his manuscripts, his letters, his photographs between two archives: the James Weldon Johnson Collection at Yale, and the Harold Jackman–Countee Cullen Memorial Collection in Atlanta. When Jackman died in 1961, Dodson wrote Van Vechten, "Only now I'm beginning to realize the shape and the size of the impact of Harold's death and the influence he had on the lives of so many. All the words like 'faithful,' 'gentle,' 'disciplined honor,' and 'loyalty' had meaning when he was around."[12] The deaths of Jackman and Van Vechten left Dodson as custodian of black artists' unrecorded legends, tales, and anecdotes. In his telling, Billie Holiday, Georgia Johnson, Alain Locke, Countee Cullen, W. H. Auden, and many others all lived again. "Well, chile," became his own "Once upon a time." He seldom engaged the eyes of his audience, looking above their heads, staring off into memory, never pausing or groping for words. The more he retold the tales, the more he wove and embroidered their narratives into a form. "Well, chile, my last look at Paul Robeson alive was in August of 1963, at the march on Washington, where hope and dream of love and freedom had been so ever high; I caught sight of Paul standing all alone.

"I had known him onstage—singing 'Old Man River'; singing in a cheap show like *John Henry* and making it a monumental experience; playing Othello, one of the greatest of our time, not because he was the greatest technically or as an actor, but somehow the force of his personality broke through the faulty craft. When he said, 'Put up your bright swords,' you felt that you better put up your bright sword because something might happen to you.

"As I stood listening to Martin Luther King's 'I Have a Dream,' I saw this huge man standing under a tree, all alone and a space around him as if no one dared approach him. Most of the young people there did not know who he was.[13] I first met him about 1940 in Atlanta, when Ira Reid's wife gave a party for Essie Robeson. It was an occasion. We had on tuxedos. Essie, with the silver just coming into her hair, was going around greeting people, and finally she came to Anne Cooke, who introduced me. Then Essie invited us up to Enfield, Connecticut, for a couple of days during Christmas just to talk theater.

"So Anne and I went up there through a howling snowstorm. We finally arrived, and Essie came running out to meet us at the cab door, and we took off our things. And she said, 'Let me take you to Paul and Paul, Jr.' So we went to the bowling alley. I knew I wasn't going to make a jackass of myself by trying to throw one of those big black balls, but Anne in her high heels rolled them, and she knocked those pins down; we had a magnificent time.

"A magnificent dinner, a ham. Then we talked about theater. Paul said, 'I have gotten away without everything; I have gotten away without dramatic lessons, I've gotten away without singing lessons; I have made a success. Now I am planning my last years. I am going to sing *Boris Godunov*. It's all in my head. I have the voice for it, but I need to sustain it.' Then right after that he said, 'Essie, we have been here all day in a blizzard. Where the hell's the Scotch?' We talked. Essie brought out her jewels from all over the world. I slept in Paul's dressing room. Do you know that great man snored so that I was awake for an hour?

"My next memory is when Paul went to see Earle Hyman's performance of *Othello* at the Jan Huys House in New York. Earle had gotten excellent reviews. The reporters were there (someone had tipped them off). Paul asked Earle to close the door and said, 'No pictures.' Earle said, 'Why not? I want my picture taken with you.' Paul said, 'No, it won't do you any good. It won't do you any good at all.' Imagine the kind of humiliation you felt for a man who had to say that, but he wanted to save someone who could be contaminated by the reputation the racists had stamped upon him.

"And there that day in Washington, he stood alone under that tree. I went over to him and said, 'Hello, Paul.' He said, 'Great occasion, isn't it?' He wasn't crying, but tears leaped out of his eyes because deep in his heart he knew he should be up there singing, singing what he had started a long time ago. The great march began with what they did to him at Peekskill. Let America be America again. I asked him if we should have some coffee, and he said, 'No. I came alone and I'll go alone.' He said he would take the train back to his sister's house in Philadelphia. He put his arm around me and we walked and then I said good-bye. The last time I saw Paul was at his funeral at the Abyssinian Church in Harlem. Chile, that was something."

Then that anecdote would be told, too.

23

Dangerously Black, 1964–67

In 1964, Dodson staged the plays of a new generation: Ted Shine's *Sho' Is Hot in the Cotton Patch,* and *Dutchman,* by a former Howard student, LeRoi Jones (Amiri Baraka).[1] Word spread quickly. The theater sold out. On opening night the Daughters of Isis,[2] a sorority in formal dress, and their dates in ties and jackets applauded scene designer Whitney LeBlanc's realistic depiction of a moving subway car. Following the performance, Owen placed two chairs onstage.

Jones recalled that, wearing his fatigues, he came running up the aisle at a half-trot, and, much to the embarrassment of the stiff and proper Howard bourgeoisie, repeated all the curse words that Owen had bowdlerized from his play. Dodson, instead of being upset, seemed to enjoy the shattering of decorum. Whitney LeBlanc, however, recalled that Jones told the audience that his play had been "fucked up" and then walked off, leaving Owen and Ted Shine with egg on their faces. Whatever the truth, the evening was a timely prologue to the new era in black theater. Owen was enough of a rebel—at least by the standards of his generation—that he could enjoy Howard's chagrin, but three years later, in May 1967, when Amiri Baraka shouted from the steps of the Department of Religion, "We want poems that shoot and kill / setting fire to Whitey's ass. . . . Let the world be a black poem," this Owen could not accept.[3]

The university that had anointed Langston Hughes in 1963 with an honorary LL.D. was not the same Howard in 1967 when Hughes died. The assassinations of President Kennedy and Malcolm X, the march on Washington, the founding of the Black Panther party, America's plunge into the Vietnam war, and the murder of Martin Luther King had ignited the Howard students; youth demanded an end to curricula they perceived as racist, an end to privilege.

Over the years, Howard's administrators had taken care that the school should have a conservative image.[4] This husbandry had paid off with increased budget appropriations from the U.S. Congress. The Appropriations Committee of the House of Representatives thus directly dictated Howard student life. For example, in 1964, the public-information officer at Howard ordered that the Confederate flag that had been draped over the marquee to advertise the production of *Purlie Victorious* be removed lest it offend some members of Congress. Nonetheless, the consciousness of the dashiki sixties pushed up and out. For the first time the students elected a homecoming queen who wore her hair in an Afro and did not belong to a sorority.

On March 2, 1967, Howard's centennial celebration began with Charter Day. James Porter unveiled his portrait of Congressman Louis Cramton, who as a member of the House Appropriations Committee had secured funds for the new Fine Arts Center. Pres. Lyndon Johnson spoke and renewed his pledge on civil rights. Former presidents of the college and their descendants were honored at a luncheon. The evening's banquet at the Sheraton Park Hotel culminated with songs by Marian Anderson.

As a major event for the centennial, Owen and composer Mark Fax, a graduate of the Rochester School of Music, planned to present their opera *Til Victory Is Won,* "a history of Black people from their enchainment in Africa until the martyrdom of Medgar Evers,"[5] but Howard never produced the complete opera. The difficulty stemmed partly from the battles between Warner Lawson and Dodson; partly from Owen's own erratic behavior; and, certainly, partly from the chaos created by the student revolution, whose flash point — Lyndon Johnson's manic war on Vietnam — had ignited a counterflashing. On March 21, 1967, thirty students "rose from their seats in Cramton Auditorium, marched to the platform and prevented General Lewis B. Hershey, director of Selective Service System, from continuing his talk about operation of the draft system."[6] Their defiance moved President Nabrit to declare, "While continuing to support academic freedom and freedom of speech, he would not sit idly by and see the University become a place of lawlessness and disorder. . . . 'We recognize the right of our students to participate in the civil protest. We place no restrictions on their right. But when they participate they do so as individual citizens, not as representatives of Howard University, and bear their responsibilities as citizens for such action.' "[7]

The Board of Trustees agreed unanimously. The administration's resolution made those who flouted campus laws subject to arrest by the FBI, which had jurisdiction over federal property. In the spirit of Antigone, the demonstrators saw themselves as warriors in a moral war with Creon, and they laid their ideals upon the altar of martyrdom. They hanged General Hershey, Dean Frank M. Snowden, Jr., and President Nabrit in effigy.[8] They demanded that the charges against those who had disrupted the general be dismissed. They stormed Nabrit's office to demand that ROTC and senior comprehensives be discontinued. They demanded more courses in black music and black history. They demanded that the administration rid the classrooms of its white teachers. They declared that unless the college met these demands, a strike would close all classes.

In the newspaper, students referred to the college as "the plantation" and to the administration as "Uncle Toms." Signs appeared exhorting students to "Join the Black Guard." They seized and occupied Cramton Auditorium and barred Dean Lawson from his offices. The James Porter portrait of Rep. Louis Cramton, hardly two months old, was slashed.[9] On May 26, four fires broke out in Douglass Hall. Nabrit expelled nineteen students.

The revolution stormed onto the stage of the drama department. In November, a high-school teacher had called to ask Professor Butcher if it would be safe to bring her white students to his production of *Simply Heavenly.* Perfectly safe, he assured her, but that same day in the nearby community, a white policeman had shot a black woman. Butcher recalled that during that evening's performance, "at intermission, when the side doors were open, some of the people came in and took over the stage. One woman said, 'Every white person here get out and everybody who thinks white.' Some people did get up and go. One of the actresses came to me and said, 'Those people are armed and that woman is carrying a gun.' I said, 'OK, we're going to cancel the show.' I went to the back and took the group of students through the side door out to their bus parked on Sixth Street. They got on the bus and some began to stone the bus, but they were able to get away."[10]

Angry and hurt, Owen rejected the student movement as a personal denial of his values, and the students who had worshipped him were shocked that he refused to support their protests. They did not know that a bohemian in the arts might be a political conservative. Eleanor Traylor, a young scholar and militant who was a close friend of Dodson, told him, "We know who you are and your resources. Why in the hell won't you join this holy walk?" He could not.

Some years later, Prof. Traylor recalled that "Owen felt the black-power movement to be a desecration of humanism. Racism was for white people. He was a paradigm of his generation, pledged to the finest social views that one could possibly entertain. His exasperation over the revolutionaries of the sixties because they lacked that generosity of spirit was not unique to him. Ralph Ellison shared it. A generation shared it. They never harbored racial hatred. The ugly look of bitterness was not upon them. These people opposed every kind of violence associated with racism and bigotry; it was their duty not to behave that way. They felt that education and enlightenment would bring understanding, and racism would go away, and white people would stop being mean and hateful. Owen more than most people possessed an aesthetic vision of life. He finally came into conflict with values he could not accommodate and at a time in his life when he was involved with himself. It was tragic for him and his students because he had been one of the honored ones."

If Owen had not been passing through the long dark night of his soul, he might have ameliorated the moral war between Creon and Antigone, but he had set his course to his own vision—world-class theater.[11] Ecumenical in his choices, he directed Baldwin's civil-rights drama *Blues for Mr. Charlie*—"It had a kind of ritual quality and at the end the audience stood up and cried"[12]—at the same time Owen insisted upon *Hamlet* and *Oedipus Rex*. He did not believe that history had outrun either him or the eternal verities, and he delivered his message at the Writer's Conference at Alabama A&M College:

> James Baldwin and LeRoi Jones are really sacrificing their talents and their art to try to . . . bring the art of insult to bear on the white population who is the minority group to us. They are conscious artists and they are doing this to shake people and say: "This is no calm river, this is no Indian Summer, now you listen to me!" More and more, people listen all over the United States

and Europe.... The only cruel thing about it is that we hope that five years from now, ten years from now, all of their works will be invalid because they are sacrificing themselves, their art to try to recreate the kind of society we can bear to live in.[13]

Dodson boozed as never before. Bill Brown, his technical director, admitted that "one day he came in a taxi and nearly fell out of the cab. I helped him into the office. He was incoherent. It was common to see him in that state from time to time."[14] In spite of his secretary Evelyn Lee, who covered for him and carried his decisions through, he neglected his duties. His scene designer, Whitney LeBlanc, remembered that once at a party, drunk Owen had tried to slip his hand into Whitney's trousers. "How much of that Owen remembered, I don't know. It was his first and only attempt toward my body. If Ted [Shine] hadn't intervened, I would have socked him. He would pull students out of my classroom to go off and deliver things, or an order I put in for lumber would be held up on his desk."[15]

Robert West, a student in Owen's directing class, confirmed the chaos: "The closer he got to an opening, the more frequent his trips to his stash. Sometimes he would be wasted, but he never missed rehearsals. As young bloods, we took Owen's seminar, the senior directing class. The favorite thing—to stop at the liquor store and get a half-pint of gin and a pint of orange juice and mix them and then go to class. The teacher was lit and his students were lit. In spite of that, I would not have passed up the value of that for anything in the world."[16]

One January night, alone on the street, Owen fell on the ice and broke both his shoulders. How he fell remains a mystery. Many assumed he was drunk, but he may have suffered a "spell."[17] Owen never discussed his fall or his broken shoulders; he continued his duties as department head.

Then abruptly he moved from the apartment where he had lived for eighteen years. (May Miller wished to sell her building, and the new owner wanted more rent.) On June 1, friends and movers installed him at 1707 Columbia Road, N.W.: two baths, a great foyer and living room, a study, and walk-in closets. With Edith sometimes ill, he prepared to care for her—their two bedrooms were on the same floor.

He continued to coax talent out of actors they didn't know they had. And he did it with designers, too. Carlton Molette affirmed that

Owen did not understand technical theater, but he would talk about what he wanted to see in terms of painters. In *Hamlet* he talked about Rembrandt lighting. He could evoke an image that made it easier.[18] Even under the regular attack of alcohol, his standards of art held, but resiliency lost in spirit became lost in mind, then finally lost in body. Robert West noticed that Owen "had a funny walk like a crab"; he went up stairs sideways, touching his knees with his hands. A bitter rheum had seeped into his knees, later into his hips. Resentment hardened into arthritis.

April deferred her cruelties until May 22, 1967, when Owen's friend Langston Hughes died. Owen left for the Harlem funeral. When he returned to Washington he learned that the day after he had left, a popular girl (with a minor in drama) had undergone an illegal abortion. Something had gone wrong; she bled; it would not stop. The boy involved, a drama major, fled—allowing her to die. Rumors begat rumors. Someone reported that the death had happened in Owen's apartment—not true. Someone else reported that when Owen heard of her death, he said "What is her life compared to Langston Hughes?" Not credible. Someone said Shizu the costumer had arranged for the abortion. In sum, the drama department, with its reputation for wild bohemians, stood convicted, and that onus fell particularly on Owen. A final rumor claimed that the girl's parents had threatened suit against the university unless Dodson were removed. The threat was unnecessary.

For some time, the administration had admonished Owen for missing Monday classes after weekend parties, for appearing in class intoxicated. Now they confronted him: he must submit to a complete medical and psychological exam by the Howard Medical School. He did. The doctors discovered that he stood five feet six inches and weighed 146 pounds; that he had cirrhosis of the liver; and that his blood pressure was 180/100. Psychologically, they found him fit but recommended that he enroll in the "troubled faculty" program. He would be given a special grant for one year to recover. He would be reexamined upon his return to see if he were fit to teach.

In July, Owen resigned as chair. Although his shoulders still pained him ("On damp or cold days they ache like Mary Magdalen . . . the doctor says this will be forever") he managed to scrawl a nine-page letter to Rosey Pool, a friend in England, to explain his resignation: "All that paper work and meaningless meetings and frustrations to one's programs—I had to make that decision and decide to concentrate on teaching and creation."

At fifty-four years of age, he could not collect a pension for another eleven years. He had to accept Howard's offer. To supplement a sabbatical for the 1968–69 school year, he applied to the Guggenheim, Fulbright, Ford, and Rockefeller foundations for travel in Europe. The first three turned him down. Dodson turned to his old adversary, Dean Lawson of fine arts (one can imagine how reluctantly); Lawson not only granted Owen a sabbatical at half-salary ($7,000) but strongly supported Owen's application to Rockefeller,[19] which granted Dodson $3,900 to study and observe styles of European theater. Additionally, Howard awarded him $3,492.60 for travel to London, Paris, and Italy.

The arc of Owen's life, from his Lincolnesque boyhood of poverty to his rainbow ascensions and Icarian descent—whether by design or happenstance—had fallen coterminously with the arc of a declining America. Although Owen could still boast of being vital, his creativity had peaked. Gordon Heath, in a letter to their mutual friend Rosey Pool, made his own assessment:

> It has always been impossible *not* to love Owen. I have gone through thirty years of loving him, but he doesn't achieve "his own terms," that's what I quarrel with. He has lusted after Broadway and the professional world of writing and the theatre incessantly, but he has been inexact, unspecific and wooly-minded intellectually, he had coasted on his adolescent images of life and art and his "promise" as one of the "new Negroes." He has not decided what his job is and limited himself to it.
>
> There are reasons for all that. His personal life has been chaotic and unlucky. He has experienced the most perfidious of treacheries, death has cut away his family and friends. And Owen has never been selfish enough to go on to his goals in spite of the human demands made upon him and in spite of his organized energy and determination, the finest edges of his mind have been rubbed down.
>
> It is probably too late for Owen to do anything about Owen. He has not gotten around to doing anything really well at the really first-rate level and a handful of silver and a ribbon to stick in his coat do not compensate us for our lost leader.[20]

An overly severe marking? For Owen's students and friends, yes, for they protected their images of him; but for the one who counted most, Owen himself, Gordon's rating may have hit the mark. He was down, but far from out. To sustain himself, Owen turned to friends—Dorothy Ross and Rosey Pool.

Anne Cooke Reid, Howard University drama department. Photograph by Robert McNeill.

James W. Butcher as Richard III, Howard University, March 1953. Photograph by Robert McNeill.

Owen directing *Hamlet,* Howard University, 1964. Drawing by Miroslav Gregory.

Charles Sebree, April 1972, Washington, D.C. Photograph by Camille Billops.

Camille Billops, Owen, and James Van der Zee, *Harlem Book of the Dead* authors, 1977. Photograph by Jeanie Black.

Edith Dodson on West Fifty-first Street, New York City, February 1975. Photograph by Mary Ellen Andrews.

Owen at 350 West Fifty-first Street, New York City, February 1975. Photograph by Mary Ellen Andrews.

Owen teaching at Frank Silvera Writers Workshop, New York City.
Photograph by Adger W. Cowens.

24

Rosey to the Rescue, 1967–68

On good-weather weekends Owen conjured dinners with the wife of Harlan Jackson, the painter who had served at Great Lakes with Owen. Jackson, one of the first black painters of abstract art, had married Dorothy Ross, a successful investor who had had two children by a previous marriage; she had bought an old house — weatherbeaten, multiroomed, totally amenable — in Easthampton on Long Island — a place to feel comfortable. In back, a large field bordered a country cemetery where a boulder marked Jackson Pollock's grave. Houseguests often included Edith, architect Percy Ifil and his wife Natsu, Ted Shine, and Whitney LeBlanc. Owen and Kermit Keith ranked high among Dorothy's favorite fellow drinkers — a trio from a generation awash in alcohol. Kermit would lecture about race history; Owen preferred to "perform" for Dorothy's daughter Susan, who admired him.

For Christmas the whole tribe might travel to Washington, D.C., with Owen managing to put up as many as ten people; for dinner, there might be twenty. Owen enjoyed cooking for guests. Like a piece of stage business created for an actor, dinner had to be "made something of," and lemon sole was a dish he could make something of. Candles always, including a man-high candelabra — "borrowed" once for a stage prop from the Franciscan monastery — perennially draped with red and gold Christmas balls. Once, in his holiday inebriation, Owen baked beans in a crock that had been used for turpentine. Confronted, he threw a temper tantrum.[1]

During this period, Edith began to notice a change in Owen: "After

Owen went to Washington to work, I didn't see him that much. I would call him and couldn't get any sense out of him and it dawned on me that he was drunk. It was years before I realized, 'He has been drinking heavily since the early sixties.' "[2] That same gloriously desperate period brought Owen a friend, the kind he most needed, a strong-minded woman who worshipped African-American poetry as only a European could.

In 1959, Rosey E. Pool had arrived at Wayne State in Detroit as a Fulbright Fellow, and after three months, under the auspices of the United Negro College Fund, toured thirty southern colleges reading and lecturing about black poetry. She began her tour at Howard, where she confessed to Sterling Brown that she feared her talks "would be carrying coals to Newcastle." He told her, "You're in for a big surprise. Just go and carry that coal and make a nice little fire with it."[3]

Pool, born in Amsterdam in 1905, had earned her Ph.D. and a D.Litt. from the University of Berlin. Later she had been a schoolteacher to Anne Frank, and after the war had made the first English translation of the famous diary. During the Nazi occupation, Pool had joined the underground, been imprisoned, and, while there, taught fellow prisoners to sing Negro spirituals — reasons enough for Owen to respect her.

Eleven years Dodson's senior, Pool, with her graying short hair, round body, and print dress with a single strand of beads, could have passed for a housewife from Manchester, England. What one might *not* see at a glance was her focused missionary spirit for the dissemination of black poetry. In Europe, she had already published two anthologies of Black American poems[4] and asked Owen's help in assembling a third, *Beyond the Blues*.[5] (When it appeared, he ordered 200 copies for the bookstore and thirty for himself.) Pool became the artist/intellectual mother Owen had never had. For Rosey, who possessed an enormous capacity for nurturing, the bright child in Owen proved irresistible.

With the same intimacy with which Owen addressed Gordon Heath and Lee Payant jointly in his letters (with an occasional note to Lee), Owen now addressed Rosey and her female companion, Isa Isenberg. Like a proud nephew, he let them know his triumphs. Like a lover, he shared his romantic moments: "I saw under a mimosa tree a long-tailed, long-billed blackbird playing with a tawny rabbit, and the sun was on them through the leaves, and once the bird was on the rabbit's back combing the fur. This is true. I have witnesses."[6] At once, he began to send Rosey poems from his new work, *The Confession Stone,* and nearly every card and letter informed her of his progress (and how wonderful his poems were).

Rosey for her part loved the new poetry and arranged for BBC-TV to broadcast part of *The Confession Stone* at Christmastime.[7] Rosey hoped to teach again in southern black colleges, but Isa worked in London as a radiologist, and Rosey wouldn't abandon her companion even though "there's an enormous job to be done at Livingston or Tougaloo or elsewhere. During the last fifteen years, Isa and I have grown so close together that neither she nor I want such long separations ever again if we can help it. Oh, Owen, I miss you, I miss you, I miss you."[8] Within the week Owen responded, "I'm happy that you and Isa will not be separated for long periods. Once you get someone you love, never let them go." Then plans abruptly changed: Rosey and Isa were on their way to Alabama A&M College in Normal, where Rosey believed she would be most useful. Owen, with help from Sterling Brown and the budget of the drama department, found funds to bring Rosey to Howard in time to celebrate her sixtieth birthday. She gave three talks, and after she left, Owen wrote, "The students still talk about you with affection and brightness."

On April 24, 1967, Dr. Rosey Pool sent *Dr.* Owen Dodson a congratulatory telegram in care of the 101st commencement exercises at Bates College; Owen would be mantled with an honorary doctorate of letters. Edith made the journey with him, and both basked in President Reynolds's warm encomium: "There is much that we owe to those few poets among us who can enable us to discover, in places we might not otherwise think to look, elements of ourselves and of our involved human condition."[9]

In the receiving line, Owen stood straight, keeping his elbows pressed close to his waist, for he was still recovering from his fall and could not yet easily raise his arms to shake hands. He gave President Reynolds a Sebree painting of a clown, and that may have been when he decided to leave his art collection to his alma mater—quiet, tranquil Bates—which retained the secure atmosphere he watched being destroyed at Howard.

His final productions before his sabbatical were three original plays[10] by Floyd Barbour, a young black writer whose religious themes appealed to Owen. The pièce de résistance, *Auto Sacramental,* was intended as a *St. Joan* turned inside out. Joan of the visions was stoned to death, then returned to discover that her "voice," her messenger, was evil, the Antichrist. Barbour arrived for rehearsals to discover that Owen, without consulting him, had changed the ending; Joan now accepted the grace of God: "He hadn't discussed it with me. The plays opened and received very good reviews. I went to Owen and told him that I had to take the plays off; I felt they were not my plays. Our encounter was very painful—two generations in conflict, with the black-power movement coming into play."[11]

The new year brought Dodson to Dartmouth College to read poetry at the Black Arts Festival,[12] where co-chairman Gary Houston said that "*even* [emphasis mine] Ivy League types are unaware of substantial black involvement and innovation in the fine arts." Richard Eberhart, Dartmouth poet-in-residence, introduced Owen as "the best Negro poet in the United States." (Owen used this tribute in all his résumés.) Two days following Dodson, Amiri Baraka (LeRoi Jones) read at the festival, and Eberhart wrote in the student paper that Dodson at fifty-three and Jones at thirty-one had been a program of contrasts: "It is of interest that he [Jones] denigrated the Jews, whereas Mr. Dodson during his reading said, 'They are magnificent,' extolling them as a minority group like his own. I regret that of the two poets only the controversial one has been talked about, which indicates the temper of our times."[13]

A week following Owen's honors, doctors told Edith she had a "weak heart" and high cholesterol. The doctors speculated that cholesterol caused the triple purple pouches under her eyes. (Edith refused cosmetic surgery, electing to keep her occipital dewlaps.)

On April 4, Martin Luther King, in his efforts to bring justice and peace to Memphis, received the fatal bullet. In May, the poor of America marched on Washington, set up their tents on the Mall. On a rainy afternoon under an umbrella held by another, Dodson read "Resurrection City":

> By the hundreds we dwell
> In the city called Resurrection, we built beneath
> The memorial to Abraham Lincoln:
> Their huts are triangular
> Humid tunnels; almost airless
> The rains have beaten them
> Into the mud. The mosquitoes feast.[14]

Then he launched into his new poem "The Ballad of Badmen":

> There's a band of men who roam this land:
> No one knows how many
> They have no leader
> They don't know each other;
> Each are marked like Cain
> Their scars show only in the brain, my God
> Their scars show only in the brain.

The poem's remaining five verses detail the psychopathic thrills of violence, concluding with astonishment at the public spectacle of greed:

> And they tore at the flesh,
> They cracked on his bones,
> Made signs of the cross
> And knelt pious knees to you and to me, my God.
> They prayed in the slime of the night
> For more my God, for more my God, for more
> My God, my god, my god for more.[15]

The Vietnam war raged on. King and Malcolm X had been murdered. On June 6, Sirhan Sirhan gunned down Robert Kennedy. Sensing Owen's despair, Edith wrote her brother: "Many times when we've talked of friends struggling to meet situations and make decisions I've said to you, do what you feel is needed for me. We are at such a point now, only the roles are reversed and I cannot wait for you to give me the go-ahead." She then recited a long litany of his recent accolades.[16] Certain that his sabbatical in London would better him, she promised to join him there for his birthday and to stay through Christmas.

Prof. William R. Reardon of the University of California at Santa Barbara invited Owen to direct at the Summer Institute for Repertory Theatre. Dodson's mission, along with a staff of ten, was to train forty black college teachers by presenting three plays.[17] Owen would direct *Morning, Noon, and Night* by Ted Shine. He arrived June 16 and moved into the rented apartment of Prof. Phil McCoy. Owen described his new surroundings in a letter to Edith: "Those eternal mountains all around truly and the Pacific Ocean where the bold surfers ride the waves. Half the boys have handle bar mustaches, hair parted in the middle and long as Jesus'. The girls have hips—they all mostly go barefooted. The new campus looks like it was designed under the influence of Frank Lloyd Wright—everything open to the sun—the weekends are free; if you do not have a car or motorcycle, the distances are long johns apart. This house has no TV so I read a lot at night."[18]

A suggestion of isolation, of loneliness. Edith worried. On Owen's recommendation, Reardon had hired Howard's designer, Bill Brown, and Lincoln University's theater director, Tom Pawley. When Pawley arrived on campus, he drove by Owen's apartment and found him in a stupor with four or five empty vodka bottles near the bed. Dodson came to, recognized Tom, and told him, "I'll be all right."

On the first morning, everyone met in the theater: the students, hushed, expectant; Professor Reardon in his thick scholar's spectacles, warm and welcoming. Reardon diplomatically inquired whether the students and staff wished to be called "Black," "Negro," or "Afro-American." They elected "Black." One of the more militant students, perhaps filled with recent memories of the poor people's march on Washington, advocated that they not be burdened with "educated speech."

Professor Dodson went through the roof: "You poor little black boy! You want plantation accents?" Owen put the young man in the position of being unable to defend *not* using the language of the educated. He insisted that Blacks use the language at its highest level. The students were a bit afraid of him because he came from a life they did not know.[19]

On a weekday afternoon after a rehearsal, the college television station invited Owen to read his poetry. Pawley drove Reardon and Dodson to the station. Reardon went inside but Owen stayed in the back of the car because he had urinated on himself. Pawley was shocked.[20] After the institute closed, Professor Reardon had to buy Professor McCoy a new mattress. Owen had lost control of his bladder.

Dodson missed only one class; in casting he fought for and won the best actors, and he worked them hard. For the first time he had nothing to do but direct, and he felt that it was his chance to do it right. He told Tom that if *Morning, Noon, and Night* was not a success, he was going to kill himself.[21] Whatever his anxieties, they eased with opening night. Santa Barbara drama critic Ronald D. Scofield wrote that the play and the production "provided the audience with one of the most compelling, exciting, amusing, and horrifying experiences in drama that have come this way in years."[22] The old master had not lost his touch.

After the closing of his show, Owen traveled to UCLA to read his poetry in concert, then on August 3 flew back to Washington and prepared to escape an ugly America. He wrote Rosey, "Talk of the fearful conditions at so many of our universities and at Howard, talk of murder, assassinations, treachery, and foul play, all will come with me."

At high noon on August 22, Owen set sail on the SS *United States,* arriving five days later at Southampton. Rosey and Isa met him at Waterloo Station. Could Rosey find him a producer for *Bayou Legend,* a publisher for *The Confession Stone,* an inexpensive apartment to be his base while he toured Italy, Greece, Scandinavia, and Russia to see theater? By coincidence or concurrence, two days after he arrived, Rosey and Isa sailed for Turkey, leaving Owen for the month of September in possession of their residence in Highpoint, a hilly area with flowers and trees. Their two small rooms with a kitchen and a bath delighted Owen; a balcony looked to the south toward a church steeple and to the west toward the Royal Free Hospital, where Isa worked as a radiologist. Owen set about buying theater tickets by the handful,[23] and then set about arranging to see Auden, Gielgud, and James Forsyth, whose *Defiant Island* he had produced.

James and Louise Forsyth owned a country house "older than Shakespeare's" in Haywards Heath, Sussex; there Owen spent three days stroking the pet sheep and admiring the view, Bunburying at its best. They talked art and theater, and Forsyth recalled that Owen spoke of James Baldwin and felt the militants had a cause: "He never spoke of homosexuality. He was surprised that my wife Louise and I still had sex because we seemed to him past 'a certain age.' He asked, 'Do you still mount her?' "[24]

Louise, who had devoted her life to settling refugees from the concentration camps, left for a memorial at Dachau and gave Owen a lift into London. She told him how the camp had been cleaned up to look like an English park. He wrote Rosey in Istanbul, "All hurts these days seem to hurt me in a personal way." Then he appended, "If you find Jimmie Baldwin tell him to bring me Santa Sophia."[25] The hurt and the competition still lingered.

When the women returned from Turkey, Owen moved into the

Continental Hotel at 30–31 Store Street and, typically, made friends with the manager's family so that they exchanged Christmas cards for several years. On October 5, Dodson flew with Rosey to Geneva for the World Writers' Conference (PEN), where, under Rosey's banner, he spoke of African-American writers. As a result, Dr. A. Rahnema invited him to Iran for the spring. On October 10, he traveled to Paris to give Gordon a Sebree rendering of the costume Heath had worn in *Garden of Time;* to Lee he gave two Japanese masks. After a brief visit he returned to London to receive Edith's four-page description of Cousin Rubie's funeral.

Because it hurt to walk, two weeks before his fifty-fifth birthday, on the advice of Rosey and Isa, Owen submitted to a pelvic X ray. Dr. P. Ahern of Middlesex Hospital informed him that he had a large cyst in his left femoral head, almost certainly due to osteoarthritis. There was, however, no evidence of loss of joint space. His right hip appeared normal. One week later, bad news came from elsewhere: a telegram informed him that Edith had been taken to Rockefeller Hospital with a heart condition.

Edith's letters to Owen in September and October had seemed obsessed with reporting trivia: "Up Tuesday morning 10/1/68 and at the dentist by 7:10 A.M. Left his office by 8:30 A.M. and had breakfast with my former supervisor Ethelbird Dandridge who lives in Riviton Apartments where the dentist office is located. Left Miss Dandridge after a breakfast of orange juice, melon, waffles," and on and on for pages. In each letter she repeated the date she planned to arrive in London, not her usual style. She had been holding on.

Owen called Edith's doctor in New York, who assured him, "No need to panic; until tests are completed, we won't know the cause." Cousin Edna calmed Owen by saying Edith was not in pain. Owen wrote to his sister, "I will come immediately if there is any difficulty. I think of T. S. Eliot's short line, 'Teach us to be still.'" He then announced that he was sending her a pair of gold earrings for pierced ears.

To calm her guest, Rosey took Owen on a long walk and impressed upon him that he was "the rock," and must not weaken. Truly touched by her concern, he wrote her, "You have sung me the greatest gift of all: the gift of friendship and love." Edith improved, but the doctors told Owen it would take five months to complete the treatment they were administering (cholesterol removal). He wrote his sister, "Remember, I am there every minute: absent but present. I will be home at Xmas to see you. I bought four puppets over 100 years old and at Christmas I will gather actors together and give you a production in your apartment." Together the Dodson children would play again, but not at Christmas and New Year's, for Edith would not yet be released from the hospital.

Six months remained of his sabbatical. His great leap for freedom had fallen short, but then the Dodson family had never allowed any member to leap too far for too long.

25

Limb from Limb, 1969–70

While Edith convalesced in the hospital, philanthropist Ruth Stephan invited Dodson to be poet-in-residence at her Poetry Center in Tucson, where she provided a cottage and a library of tapes, recordings, and over 2,500 volumes of poetry. Established at the University of Arizona, the Poetry Center, since its dedication by Robert Frost in 1960, "maintain[ed] and cherish[ed] the spirit of poetry." Owen chose March 16–30, 1969. (James Tate and Allen Ginsberg had just preceded Dodson.) Recalled Owen, "I had a little house, a maid, and a circular garden with an orange tree of bitter fruit. I could just walk out into the desert and come back, lots of cactuses—saguaro. Beyond were the giant mountains that had deep purple shadows when I took my walk in the mornings, and at sunset there were orange thrusts amid the purple; it was pagan. The students would call me up and ask to read their poetry to me."

On Tuesday evening, March 25, Owen in his hush puppies, gray trousers, and blue jacket read his poetry. Few African-Americans came to hear him, although the student paper had featured his photo. (Of the 25,000 students at the university, a mere 400 were black—mostly men, mostly athletes.) The next afternoon, Owen met students at a coffee hour held in his honor. A poet, Ron Welburn, remembered, "Owen voiced a general disapproval of what was then passing for poetry. He was an intellectual and the [late-sixties] movement was anti-intellectual. He was not drinking, no muscular disability. He didn't seem like that kind of individual."[1] All in all, Dodson heeded Ruth

Stephan's suggestion that he be prudent—for there was a blessing inside him.

Easter found Owen back in New York, painting eggs with Edith, Gordon, and Lee. (Edith received a day pass to attend the ritual.) Tales of student rebellion poured in from Howard. William Brown still acted as department chair, but he too fled at the end of the year. To avoid returning, Owen determined to earn money by other means. He sent out fliers advertising himself, and over the next five months he delivered lectures and poetry readings at seven universities, taking fees that ranged from $100 at Durham, North Carolina, to $350 at Ohio Wesleyan. He slipped away twice to Bermuda to stay with his friends the Stowes; he claimed the warm currents eased his arthritis.

Each letter to Rosey reiterated his plans to see her soon. Hadn't the Shah's own representatives extended him an invitation to Tehran? He would stop in England on his way home. However as the intensities of the Geneva writers' conference waned, Owen had to acknowledge that Middle Eastern velleity had not translated into obligation. He wrote Rosey, "I won't be coming to England. I want to, I wanted to, but I'll be artistic director for a pocket-sized theatre in Washington and at the Theatre 73rd off-Broadway in New York. If I am to make my mark as a director in New York, I must do it now." Neither position ever materialized.

In September 1969, his sabbatical money exhausted, he filed his report: "I explored over one hundred and forty plays, operas, picture exhibitions, memorabilia, and works of art in London, Amsterdam, Paris, Geneva, and New York." He had no choice but to rejoin Howard and demonstrate that he had bested the demon gin. However, the student rebellion still raged. Dean Lawson, to an even greater degree than Dodson, had not been able to face a radical public reevaluation of black culture. In 1969, someone hung a wreath on the Dean Lawson's door saying, "The Dean is dead." A year later he was.[2]

In the autumn of 1969, Owen met his class in theater history and criticism. The first day, everyone knew he had returned and was in full attendance. He came in and directed, "Let October in." They did not know what to do. He repeated, "Let October in." He sat down and no one moved. He said, "Open the window, chile. We can't have class with a stuffy room." On his left sat Clinton Turner Davis; on his right, Debbie Allen. He began with an overview of classical Greek and Roman theater, playing all the parts either standing up with his walker or sitting down—one of those rare moments when students stop taking notes. He carried on for an hour-and-a-half. They did not want to leave.[3]

To open the season, Owen consoled himself by directing two plays by Ted Shine—*Shoes* and *Idabel's Fortune*. In rehearsal, the denouement of the ghoulish comedy *Idabel,* when the moving men carried out Idabel's furniture, was not funny. During dress rehearsal, Owen carried on a running conversation with himself: "Something's not working, not working." Finally he told two actors playing the moving men to do a time shuffle step. They said, "What?" He repeated, "Do a time shuffle step as you carry out the furniture—like a chain gang." They shuffled, and he said, "Yeah, yeah, that's it. Rehearsal's over." At the opening, that business got a terrific laugh. Mr. "D." had won again.

Shine's plays turned out to be the last Dodson would direct at Howard. His magic moments could not compensate for class days missed or indemnify his inebriation. He hobbled on a cane or a steel walker. He wrote Rosey, "I'm going to see a bone doctor. There is something more than arthritis. I'm in pain every step I take, but I keep each commitment and will not give in." A month later, he wrote again, "My arthritis is a mess. I have three speaking and poetry engagements Thanksgiving week in California, one in Bermuda and I direct Anouilh's *Antigone* in Los Angeles during semester break. I long for England and you."[4]

Owen confided his arthritic pain only to Rosey and to James and Louise Forsyth, possibly because James, too, had been unable to walk from room to room without "signs of lightning in my thigh."[5] Louise directed Owen toward self-therapy by recounting that her husband suffered most pain when emotional stress was high: "It seems that you are your own best doctor for such a complaint; I mean that the patient knows best how to avoid as much pain as possible by not doing the things that set it up."[6]

In February, between semesters, Owen flew to Los Angeles to direct *Antigone*[7] for the Inner City Cultural Center (ICCC), located on Vermont Avenue in one of the city's poorer districts. Over a six-week period, 25,000 high-school students would be bused to the center to view classical plays.[8] The National Endowment for the Arts had placed inordinate pressure on ICCC: Could minority artists succeed in presenting the Greeks, the Romans, the French to a young audience that was skeptical because the program was tied to the English curriculum? Large numbers of kids came as an outing, an adventure, their first trip to the "inner city." Then, to see on stage actors of different colors (ICCC's policy was multiethnic casting). Executive director Bernard Jackson, an African-American, knew that ICCC was viewed as a test case.

A lot of attention is paid to black people who accomplish things that no one expects them to. We had to achieve within an area that was considered extraordinary for so-called Third World people to achieve in — the production of European classics. We had to prove ourselves by being better than whites are, let's say for example, at performing Shakespeare or dancing ballet.[9] Of course we can do it, have done it, but it is very destructive. We are then looked upon as exotic, and it causes so-called minority peoples to look at themselves in false terms, as being "less than" Europeans. Nevertheless, this is how we had to secure funding to begin, and Owen Dodson was our first choice.

But Jackson worried. As a black man working under white standards, Dodson suffered stress from being uplifted and debased at the same time, a stress he endured his entire professional life.[10] Would Dodson would be able to sustain his commitment? The center's general manager, Josie Dotson, gave Owen a concerned mothering to override the lightning in his hip.

ICCC had leased the old Fox movie theater nearby at Vermont and Washington. Its exterior, a 1920s Gothic façade; inside, the 900–seat auditorium had been redesigned, giving the old cinema stage an apron. Compared with the theaters at Bates and at Spelman, Owen found the Fox West Coast Theatre easy to work in. He cast interracially, using talent rather than skin color as his criterion. ("My cast looked like the United Nations.") Aldolphe Caesar played Creon; Susan Batson played Antigone. Batson was a high-strung, demanding actress, but Owen made the French classic live for his audience of hormone-ridden adolescents, and Batson won the L.A. Drama Critics Circle Award for best actress.

Owen did not stay to see his opening, for on Washington's birthday he flew to an appointment at the Harkness Pavilion of the Presbyterian Hospital in New York. Two weeks later, Dr. Marvin Shelton replaced Owen's arthritic right hip joint with a steel one. Owen wrote Rosey, who herself had been confined with severe anemia, "Tuesday is the day for the slicing; from then on no one can say I'm not made of steel."[11] Edith, now up and around (their symbiosis: one sick, the other well), attended her brother "like a lay nun," even unto trimming his toenails. Before the operation, Owen asked Dr. Shelton if he might have the flowers, the cards, and his sculpture from Benin in the operating room. The doctor said of course. Owen remembered the white ceilings: "I was raised up to them and disappeared into my friends, into the paint." When he viewed the X ray a few days later he exclaimed, "I have a Miro in my hip or perhaps a Calder. Anyway, my design is unique. Each day I take a few steps. Today I took twenty-two. The grace of God is no small thing."[12] Two days after that, they told him Kermit Keith had died.[13] In the middle of the night, when no one could see, Owen cried. To add to Owen's sorrow, two days before Kermit's death, James Porter, Owen's longtime colleague in the art department, died. The older generation at Howard was passing.

Owen took sick leave for the spring, intending to return in the fall, but then his left hip, too, began to show signs of deterioration, and it became clear that a second replacement would be necessary. This diagnosis gave Owen and the university the excuse they needed. Bill Brown wrote Mark Fax, then acting dean of the College of Fine Arts, "In a recent telephone conversation with Mr. Owen Dodson he informed me that it was still quite difficult for him to move about and that there was the possibility he would have to have another operation. In view of this information, I asked him what his intentions were for his scheduled return to Howard for the Fall Semester of 1970. Mr. Dodson replied that under the circumstances he felt he must ask for retirement on the basis of disability."[14] With the recommendation of Fax, in five brief days disability was granted before Owen could change his mind.

Over the years of his service, the university had contributed two dollars for each one Owen put away. However, this regular retirement pension would not be available for nine years, at age sixty-five. Some of Owen's bitterness with Howard spilled over into pension matters; yet, given the circumstances, he seems to have been treated as fairly as the accounting procedures allowed an artist to be treated. Howard did manage to free his retirement pension at age sixty-two.

With Dodson out of the way, Howard University decided youth would be served. The drama department hired three young bloods, all in their twenties, all Howard graduates—Glenda Dickerson, director; Robert West, tech director; and Sam Wright, acting head of the department. Wright, also a recent graduate of Yale, wore a dashiki, and his first political move was to paint the Ira Aldridge Theatre black. Ceiling, walls, stairs—black! Great for lighting control. Depressing for the audience.

Dickerson tried to build a bridge between the new generation and the old: "When I returned to teach in '69, I taught freshmen, a mix of students: vets from Vietnam; some hard radicals; some who had been in the old tradition. I was twenty-four and very green. Everything was challenged and criticized, a process entirely opposed to my training. You could not please that student body. The students thought that everything should be angry."

Light designer Bob West, returning like a young lion to trash the old and build the new, admitted he had made a great mistake. Theater technicians—the keepers of schedules and tools—abhor chaos, and West confronted increasing entropy. According to designer LeBlanc: "Things started to disappear; expensive equipment walked away." When William Brown visited the Ira Aldridge a year later, he received a shock: "My mouth flew open. The walls were black; the counterweight system was in shambles like spaghetti. I was so embarrassed. The lobby, the shop, the pictures, and the posters had disappeared. I said to myself, 'If Owen saw how the theater looked, he would die on the spot.' "[15] Sam Wright's term as department chair was hallucinogenic, chaotic, and brief. James Butcher flashed with anger at the memory: "The new acting chair was a disaster. His appointment was a direct result of student pressure. He turned out to be a hothead. A bright fellow and former student, he gave a lecture to the students on drinking and using drugs in the Ira Aldridge Theatre, and within a month, he was off his rocker."[16]

The cultural revolution had stormed the palace and driven into exile the elitists whose century-old system had been designed to ensure the advancement of the race, but in their assertion of black pride, the cultural nationalists destroyed a theater of international reputation, one that Anne Cooke, James Butcher, and Owen Dodson had taken twenty years to build.[17] Howard's theater acclaim had been more than a white amazement that Blacks could perform Ibsen; the theater had given its students a world perspective and a solid training in its theater crafts. Some good, however, did come from the black nationalists' ferment: their agitation created the climate in which future black artists would find work in mainstream theater and television. But this victory would prove to be too late for Owen's career.

26

The Confession Stone, 1970–72

Learning to walk with a steel ball in his hip, Owen spent the summer with Edith at 270 St. Nicholas Avenue, and several projects grew to fruition. Roger Straus, Jr., after digesting *Time*'s assessment that Dodson was "peer to Frost and Carl Sandburg," reissued *Powerful Long Ladder* in both hardcover and paperback, their old contract from 1946 still valid — royalties at 7½ percent. Owen sent Straus a bundle of new poems entitled *The Morning Duke Ellington Praised the Lord and Six Black Davids Tap-danced Unto,* but the publisher decided the "collection was not right for us and we must stand aside."[1]

Paul Kresh, vice-president of Spoken Arts, Inc., had heard Owen read his poems in 1968 in New Rochelle, New York, and on the memory of that evening invited Owen to write an hour's narration for a series of four or five film strips to span the Black experience from the ancient past to the present. He asked for a script written in verse rather than in prose, "to convey the kind of heightened emotional effect and excitement that only a great poet and playwright could give it."[2] Spoken Arts would pay the "great poet" $1,000. Owen wrote *The Dream Awake.* James Earl Jones, Josephine Premice, and Josh White, Jr., recorded the verse. Lloyd McNeill and his quartet played the music. Kresh released the record and film strip in August 1970.[3] Richard Coe wrote: "A rare collection — sensitive and compelling — Dodson's words are as pleasurable to hear as they are to read."[4]

No project held Owen's heart as long or gripped it as tight as *The Confession Stone.* In 1960, for the opening of the Ira Aldridge Theatre, he had published eight monologues under the title *Sung by Mary about Jesus*. The poems covered the three days from Good Friday to Easter Sunday morning. For the next decade Owen played with his Easter litany, adding modern touches to a biblical cast—the telegram, the telephone. His verse, certainly the leanest he ever wrote, was as simple as a pine board; he called it "involved simplicity," and it attracted several composers who saw the poems as lieder, although none composed an oratorio for the whole cycle. Owen wrote Priscilla Heath, "The music will breathe through the pores and enrich, and, I believe, give astonishment of pain and wonder."

The collection's title, Owen claimed, came to him in Italy when he saw a peasant woman kneeling upon a stone: "There is a rock most people kneel upon and talk to God when trouble strikes, and wrestle there with soul agonies." The immediate impetus to write the poems came from Joyce Bryant, who told Owen she had given up her career as a cabaret singer, which she had begun at the age of fourteen, to join the Seventh Day Adventists—the life of working for Christ.

Delighted with Bryant's stories, Owen promised to write a song cycle for her. He began in 1960 with Mary's "Oh my boy Jesus." Then the thing got a hold of him, and the next cycle was about the letters of Joseph to Mary and after that Pontius Pilate and Judas and then God. He added Martha, the sister of Lazarus, "because she was more folksy." By 1970, Owen had expanded *The Confession Stone* to include the whole royal family: ten letters from Joseph to Martha, eight entries from the "Journals of the Magdalene," three songs addressed to Jesus by Judas, four by Jesus addressed to God, a single response from God, and a closing lullaby by Mary, twenty-eight pages in all.[5] Dodson declared, "*The Confession Stone* is not a dramatic work but a literary one, but if you listen, it will become a dramatic work, for within each of the characters whirls a tempest."

Rosey Pool presented the collection to Paul Breman, a London book antiquarian and publisher of the Heritage Series of poets. He read the cycle aloud to friends, something he rarely did. On January 15, 1970, Breman and Dodson signed a contract for the first printing of 500 books. They sold. Barbara Mahone McBain stated in her review, "The songs are us. They remind me especially of the South of my childhood. The warm earthiness of us down South. And I suppose Dodson's people are Southern Blackfolks. Human folk. On the verge of sentimentality, but too profound."[6]

Dudley Randall of Broadside Press distributed a second printing of 500. Owen asked that the royalties be given to the Harold Jackman Memorial Committee, but twelve cents a copy did not swell their coffers. Breman discontinued the series, and *The Confession Stone* had the ill luck to fall out of print to become a collector's item.

Never had Owen been so aggressively proud of a work as he was of this cycle; for him, the poems resolved the tiff between him and his father, between him and God, and at the same time laid Owen back into the arms of his mother for the pietà. By the year of his retirement, he had hammered out the razor edge of his response to God; it is Jesus who addresses the Father:

> Father, I know you're lonely:
> talk to me, talk to me.
> We need not speak of Calvary
> or the lakes of Galilee:
> as my Father, talk to me.
> Notify my soul where
> You will be,
> send some message:
> answer me.
> I sign me, your son,
>   Jesus.

Then God sends his response:

> Dear my Son
> my One, my constant One:
> . . . .
> Your Father has not deserted Thee
> to gardens of Gethsemane.
> The stars are the tears We weep,
> the sun is Our Mercy,
> the moon is Our slumber.
> Sleep, Jesus, sleep.
> Mary is come with a bowl of wine.
> Sleep, Jesus, sleep,
> sleep, Jesus, sleep.
> Your father first, then God!

So God and Owen tried to work it out: the son would not speak of Calvary; the father would not deny the son. But not without laughter. One day Owen admitted to a friend, "I have gotten more yardage out of Jesus and God than anyone you know."

And mileage he got, beginning with a premiere concert in Carnegie Hall.[7] Edith, when she learned that composer Robert Fleming had arranged two of her brother's songs for contralto Maureen Forrester as the climax of Forrester's program at Carnegie Hall, telephoned the management and asked for the center box. When informed that the box had been sold on subscription, she said her brother must have that box or there would be no *Confession Stone*. That evening brother and sister sat center, applauding and weeping as the Canadian diva touched their hearts with Mary's lullaby to Jesus. They joined the ovation and then hurried backstage to congratulate Forrester, who embraced Owen.

In the summer of 1970, when Dodson left the hospital, he was offered his old dream, freedom to be an artist, and its corollary, freedom to starve. Exiled from Howard, he launched vigorous appeals, writing letters: "I'm available for readings, lectures, directing." Lincoln University in Pennsylvania invited him to lecture for a month—fee, $500. He earned $424 for reading his poetry at Allegheny Community College; he judged a drama festival at Grambling College in Louisiana, where his play *Divine Comedy* was performed. Then in August an old acquaintance from Hampton offered him a consultancy with the Harlem School of the Arts at 651 St. Nicholas Avenue, just a few blocks up the street from Edith's apartment. Dorothy Maynor, a retired concert singer and founder and director of the school, asked Owen to be artistic consultant to the Community Theatre Board. He would lead a staff of four: coaches of voice, acting, body movement, and speech.[8]

Suddenly, in October, he canceled appointments. He wrote Rosey, "I'm in N.Y. hospital for four days—they are testing to see why I have occasional blackouts. So far the tests show that I am 'A.' I'm very anxious to get back to my lecturing and structuring the drama end of the School of the Arts; besides the money is good and needed as my pension won't come through for some time."

With no ties to hold him in Washington, he hired the Mayflower Transit Company for the sum of nearly $2,000 to pack, move, and (he thought) unpack his household in his new two-bath, two-bedroom apartment at 600 West End Avenue, Manhattan. The movers dumped the furniture and boxes into his apartment and left Owen to sort them out; then the company billed him for an extra $90. Owen wrote that he had paid the full fee before the move; Mayflower went to court and obtained a judgment of $238.51. Owen said he could not afford a lawyer or afford to pay them. But before the marshal came to lay claim to Owen's carousel horses, he paid the sum, or perhaps Edith did.

To open his 1971 program at the Harlem School of the Arts, Owen took the easy way — directing an old favorite, Saroyan's *My Heart's in the Highlands*. In February he directed Odets's *Bury the Dead,* and in March, an original by Norman Riley, *Runaway People*. In May, he returned to *Medea in Africa,* using in the lead Marilyn Berry, his Hedvig from Howard days.

This time he cast the husband as white and the children mixed. Because Berry was very light and even lighter under the lights, she secured a book on African art and looked at hairstyles, bought dark makeup, and had a wig made with gold braided in. Owen came on his walker backstage: "Do you know what you look like on that stage?" He got very formal. "You look like a little black pickaninny." Berry replied, "Mr. Dodson, that is exactly what I am, a black pickaninny. I refuse to give up the makeup or the wig. An African woman with mulatto children needs to be dark." The play ran for three weeks, but with little publicity; the school had not yet discovered how to advertise in the community.[9]

Although no one in his productions at the Harlem School of the Arts recalled Owen complaining about the pain in his hips, some did recall that he drank a lot. Somehow he had driven himself to direct six plays for the school, perhaps hoping that work and vodka would kill the pain, but he lost the confidence of his actors. Alcohol allowed him to be eccentric, to rant and rave. "He called a dress rehearsal," recalled Berry, "the day of performance, and no one showed up but me." By July, when Owen staged Ted Shine's *Idabel's Fortune* and *Hamburgers Are Impersonal,* he had scheduled his second hip replacement for December.

That spring, Rosey Pool had been in and out of the hospital — mostly in — with leukemia. Blood transfusions achieved little success; her doctors then introduced an experimental drug that might produce new blood cells. She was discharged to go home. In June, Rosey had to return to the hospital for another transfusion. Then the drug seemed to give her a remission. She and Isa traveled to Paris and visited Gordon

Heath. Buoyed up on a wave of optimism, Rosey had begun work on Chester Himes's stories of the 1940s when the powerful drug she was being given for her blood deficiency decided to run amok and break down her white blood corpuscles.[10] She wrote that her condition was not favorable; the white blood cells "won't fight. I'm sixty-five." At the end of November, Isa wrote that Rosey was one day up and one day down, and that "I try to be brave."[11] With the turn of the new year, Owen and Edith promised Rosey a short visit in June after Owen's show closed.

Edith purchased inexpensive tickets on a charter flight, and on May 26, Owen, on two canes, waved down a taxi, picked up Edith, and arrived at the airport. The purser called out to the line of passengers, "Give me your passports." Owen replied, "What passport?" He had left it in the apartment. Assuring Edith he would catch another flight, he returned home, placed a glass of orange juice beside his bed, and (if he is to be believed) slept for three days. When, after a week, Edith returned, Rosey wrote Owen that she was bitterly disappointed that he had not come. "We loved Edith's visit, but miss you even more acutely." In the hospital, drugged and depressed, she closed the letter, "Dear Owen, please try to come."[12]

But he could not. A week after Edith returned from her flying visit to England, she was taken to the hospital with a stroke. Her speech was not impaired; however, her right arm and hand were limp and needed therapy. In late June, Owen again fell, sustaining a closed fracture of the mid-femur that was treated with a cast and pin immobilization. The Dodson symbiosis had broken down: brother and sister were both in the hospital at the same time.

Owen did not write Rosey for five weeks. Finally he sat down at the typewriter. His letter greeted both Rosey and Isa, but addressed Rosey in the third person: "How wonderful it is that Rosey is well enough to have made the new trip." He listed the plays he produced. He did not tell her of his injury. "This program left me joyously weary, and even though I long to see you, I believe that leaving my passport unintentionally behind was some part of a secret plan to make you rest."[13]

On September 22, 1971, Rosey died. Owen wrote Isa, "When your letter came—even before I opened it, I somehow knew. I am with you and remember that Rosey quoted, 'Canta che ti passa' ['Sing and it will pass']." A year later, Owen wrote an entry in his series of anecdotes about artists and friends, which he called *The Gossip Book*. He entitled the anecdote "Rosey":

> I was going to see a friend of mine who was dying. My bags were packed. Miss Dorothy Maynor called three hours before I was to leave for England and said she would like to talk with me. So I told her I was going to England, and it was inconvenient. She said nevertheless she wished to come, and so she came.
>
> She had on a brown dress—middle brown, and she sat in the middle of my red couch, and spoiled my decor. She really didn't have anything to say except that I had known her thirty years, and she was telling me the troubles of the school.[14]

After blaming Dorothy Maynor for his failure to remember his passport, he closed with, "I knew in my condition, I would not be able to get down those deep subways of London. I never saw Rosey again. She died!" Clearly Owen could not bear to watch Rosey die. A man possessed by fear, his account of the passport concentrated on trivia in order to suspend his horror. In December he felt the lightning flash in his left hip and he entered the hospital for replacement.

Rosey dead but two months, Owen summoned Isa to lay Rosey's ghost to rest by offering a biographical narrative to her spirit "with contributions by her friends." Paul Breman agreed to print a brochure with a full-page photograph of Rosey opposite a poem by Owen (another occasion poem and a poor one). To be bound in red cloth and tooled in black, the edition would be limited to 250 copies and published in 1974 on her birthday, May 7. Cost was thirty dollars in advance of publication or forty after—an impressive amount in 1972, particularly for poets and writers. Orders trickled in; yet Isa's enthusiasm prompted her to suggest that they might use the profits from the book's sales to award a poetry prize.

Owen had expected Hoyt Fuller, editor of *Black World,* to join the effort, and when it was clear the quota could not be met, Breman suggested that Owen write Fuller and ask him to devote an issue of his monthly to Rosey Pool. Owen replied, "I had sent him one of the brochures, and he never even answered. You know how it is in the U.S. now between the races, and the Jackson [Johnson] Publishing Company might just think that it would be improper to dedicate a whole magazine to a white woman, although she had done so much to encourage black poets here and abroad." Owen twisted every arm, pressing people to subscribe and, if they had known Rosey, to write a tribute. Some did—Gordon sent a sincere poem entitled "Coffee with Rosey"—but most black poets did not. Dudley Randall had cautioned Dodson that "many of us forget those who've helped us."[15]

In November Isa wrote Owen. Perhaps the price was too dear; did Owen think people might buy a cheap edition for ten dollars? Their mutual failure to find an interested public embarrassed them both, and they quietly dropped their correspondence. Owen wrote Forsyth, "Perhaps it is better to be far away from where someone you have loved has died because even now I don't quite believe that Rosey is dead—and of course, she is not."[16] But the memorial volume's failure said that she was.

In 1959, Owen had met Helen Armstead Johnson at the Virginia State Drama Festival of Negro Colleges. (In those days, Petersburg, Virginia, provided only segregated restaurants, so Johnson and her husband, Clifford, had invited the Howard theater cast home for spaghetti.) When Owen moved to New York City, Professor Johnson called upon him. Once she had to ring the bell and ring the bell. Then she could hear him shouting, "I'll be there! Hold on! Hold on!" When he finally opened the door, he collapsed on the floor. She declared that Dodson was never able to function after his knee and hip operations: "He fell after every one of them."[17]

In November 1971, Owen entered Columbia Presbyterian Hospital with a fractured femur; he claimed to have blacked out and fallen. Whether he fell from blackouts, arthritic pain, or vodka, he did fall with some frequency, and on three of those occasions he broke his legs. This time, Dr. Marvin Shelton treated his leg by intramedullary pin fixation, and it healed rapidly.

During his pre-Christmas days of convalescence at Presbyterian Hospital, Owen began to tape biographical sketches of artists he had known. Without pause or stutter, he recited for an hour at a time, spinning stories of Langston Hughes, Jimmy Baldwin, Paul Robeson, Alain Locke. Each vignette flowed onto the tape as a polished tale with a beginning, with suspense, with a climax. These tales came from "The Gossip Book"—sixty short tales of people he had known and observed, greatly embellished in the telling.

"The Gossip Book" served for Owen a dual purpose—potentially to make desperately needed money and to punish Howard for the meanness, the silliness, the stolidity of its faculty and administration. In an interview as late as August 1979, he told a reporter that his new book would cause "much gnashing of the teeth in such places as New York, Washington, D.C., and Los Angeles." And many believed him, querying him slyly, "How's the gossip book coming?" Owen baited the curious by recounting naughty histories—one of a dean of women whose finger checked the girls' vaginas to see if they had bathed. However, his Howard *Decameron* never materialized; the stories he wrote contained little malice toward either individuals or the university, and he did not publish them, but casually gave the memories away to cultural historians.

Like a griot, Dodson composed and arranged while he sang. Knitting tales together for one and sometimes two hours, he would bridge the gaps between stories, never allowing an opening for question, comment, or interpretation. His art and craft stemmed from black preachers, the studied rhetoric of his father, his own school training in recitation, and his sometimes-desperate need to be the center of attention. In the Thomas Jefferson High School yearbook, beneath Owen's graduation photograph, the editor wrote, "The speech of Webster, the head of Clay." The oral eloquence of Clay, Webster, and Lincoln had long inspired American schoolchildren, but as early as the 1920s schools' emphasis shifted from reading aloud to silent reading.

By the late 1940s, the demise of "listenature"[18] could be heard in the dry recordings of Robert Frost and T. S. Eliot. These poets rendered humanity's most powerful emotions with aridity, not only in reaction to the nineteenth century's tearing of passion to tatters, but also in reaction to the poet's change of office: no longer a public priest declaiming, the troubadour had become a private confessor, whispering. Only Carl Sandburg and Vachel Lindsay continued to sing their lines, and they were soon demoted to the second echelon of American poets. In the contest between popular and elite culture, Eliot won the Nobel Prize, while passionate expression fled to rhythm and blues and, later, rock music. Owen asserted that "so many poets in these obscure magazines, you can't figure out what they are about. I do not say that they are bad poems, but they write for their friends or themselves. Recently I reread *The Four Quartets* of Eliot, and I don't know what the hell they are about. I don't know where or what East Coker is. Ezra Pound is supposed to be a great poet, but when he gets into Latin and Greek, that is a terrible arrogance and indulgence on his part. No matter how much you discover what the Latin and Greek means, it does not add up to a meaning. However, in something like James Joyce's *Ulysses*, if you read it long and well enough, it emerges, it comes through."

Owen never abandoned declamation. Invited to read at colleges, celebrations of black history, and conferences, he captivated audiences by performing with emotion. Poetry consultant Josephine Jacobsen recalled Owen's reading at the Library of Congress: "He had planned to read a suite of poems dedicated to Duke Ellington, and he wanted a young dancer whose work he admired to perform while he read. That was a bit of a problem. This was strictly a poetry series, and there was no provision for the intrusion of another art form. Mr. Howland, director of our recording studio, accustomed to flooding quartets with a chaste illumination, was asked to provide 'a baby pink spot.' I really did quail at this request, but that—or its reasonable approximation—is what we got."[19]

On March 26, 1973, Owen and Edith attended a luncheon at the Library of Congress, held in the eighteenth-century-cum-Victorian lounge, a room whose lighting and furniture seemed imbued with the dust and patina of culture. Then in the evening the Dodsons taxied to the library itself and entered under the stone arch to the ground floor. There the pop of Edith's heels echoed on the marble floor, and Owen on his crutches clunked along behind, greeting those he knew.

The Elizabeth Sprague Coolidge Auditorium had been built in 1925 for chamber-music recitals but now served as a platform for poetry. The steeply raked house with a double aisle was softly lighted by tinted-glass fixtures of the twenties; a quiet green curtain bordered the proscenium but could not be drawn. Nancy Galbraith, special assistant in poetry, guided Owen to the back of center stage, where he waited for the house lights to dim. Then the double sliding doors parted for his entrance. The audience, including 100 black guests, most present in the auditorium for the first time, gave him more than a ripple of applause. Using only his cane, Owen moved to stage right and read several poems from *Powerful Long Ladder;* then the sliding doors parted again. Tall, graceful, bare-chested, the dancer,[20] wearing a tight-fitting velvet costume with a jeweled collar, earrings, and flashing cymbals on his long fingers, moved to Owen's Duke Ellington suite:

> The morning Duke Ellington praised the Lord
> The stars plus the moon shone out loud—

Six little black Davids
tapped danced unto:
Gabriel trumpeted up arthritic Michael:
Plus some Archangels who had slipped from grace
Into Hell when God rode like a roaring
General of peace into the universe.
Trumpets: Who whee, who wheee—
Duke's horns, all his brasses plus drums
Did a dip pip pip-a-de doo.
. . . .
The six black boys tapped dance up
        the marble altar praising unto
                God, our Lord and His Hosts.
Whoo-whoo wee, whoo wee.
Dip pip, pip-a-de doo
dip-a-de-doo.
Doo.

The Library of Congress Poetry Program had never seen anything like it. Jacobsen told Dodson, "Your reading was one of the most exciting and worthwhile things which have taken place since I have been poetry consultant—and incidentally one of the evenings most enjoyed by our audience." Bionic Owen had managed to dance again.

To read "Dip pip, pip-a-de doo" silently is to read it egregiously silent; performance is inherent, even in the poem's less prancing lines: "The stars plus the moon shone out loud." This device of the mixed metaphor is common enough in Owen's work to be a benchmark of his style. To a degree, this device makes his poetry unique, sometimes too much so. His likely-unlikely images are not intellectual enough to be conceits; if read silently they cause disruption, like stubbing one's toe in the dark. One gropes for the likely, but may stumble upon the unlikely. After many of these sore discoveries, one begins to move more slowly through the lines, that is, reading them aloud. Then, with some gesture of voice and body, the image lives.

Yet while Owen's oral virtuosity informed his literary poems onstage, his holding court offstage isolated him from intimacy. He talked; others listened. After his retirement, to hold his brief hour upon the stage, his dependency on readings and storytelling grew. He boasted that he did not usually drink before he performed, but when the applause died, the king, still draped in his accolades, found himself thirsty for listeners to supply the drug—attention—that he had to have. When refused an audience, he could turn spoilsport, as he did one evening on Columbus Avenue when he, Edith, and Camille Billops taxied to a buffet dinner at the apartment of Françoise Burgess, a French scholar fascinated by Black American writers. As Owen rocked through her door on his walker, a sheaf of poems poked ominously from his pocket; he asked his hostess for a vodka and tonic. Françoise, petite and charming, had planned her evening; guest balanced with guest, wine with entrees: clearly a salon evening of camaraderie in the arts. Her guest of honor, the black poet. Edith, recently recovered from a heart seizure, at once discarded her doctor's orders and lit up a cigarette, an omen of how accurately she must have divined her brother's mood.

Determined to render his poems aloud, Owen refused all offers to be drawn into conversation. Placing himself at the head of the small room, he announced that he had written new poems, and the gracious hostess encouraged him to read them. As he declaimed poem upon poem, Françoise attempted to divert him during his vodka-sipping pauses. Edith, wisely, did not intervene, for how much stress can a weak heart endure? Camille had left the room to hold a private conversation with Malwine Blunk, a German student studying Black Americana. Other guests drifted away, waiting for the buffet dinner to stem his torrent, but Owen continued reciting over his tray of coq au vin. By dessert time, Françoise's savoir faire barely concealed her fury, but breeding won out, and the guests all stumbled out into the night, Owen mumbling, cursing the taxi drivers who raced by.

For those whom Owen had regaled on many, many occasions with the wassail of his gleeful narrations, the evening had been a pesky rout, but still acceptable; he simply had had an off night. But for those like Françoise who enjoyed no intimacy of Owen's style, C'était plus qu'un crime, c'était une faute (It was more than a crime, it was a blunder).

When Owen could not capture a listener, he called one on the telephone. He confessed, "It is the same thing as setting up a sound unit—testing, testing. Getting reactions. I would like to be a poet who can be read aloud and understood. Perhaps it was my working in the theater that has made me a sound poet instead of a literary one. I am trying to emotionalize other people's emotion through my own emotion. I try to become the character; it becomes more objective. Not like my subjective love poems. My poems now are those of public speech."

The charges to his phone bill matched the sleepless hours of his friends. Right up to the end, he called to read new poems to friends, who wearied of his midnight calls, who tired of his speech slurred with alcohol, who had heard him read the same poem the night before. Peggy Reardon in Santa Barbara kept the phone on her side of the bed. Owen would ask at three in the morning for "Dr. Reardon, please"; she would pass the instrument across the covers to Bill, who in Christian charity would listen to Owen read for an hour. James Forsyth in Sussex responded to a four-in-the-morning ringing up with his best English pluck: "Your call coming clearly to us in the dark of the autumn morning was a dear and friendly gesture we didn't deserve."[21] One dear friend laid her phone on the pillow beside her head. As Dodson talked on and on, Vivian Robinson dozed, only to be awakened by Owen shouting, "Hello! Hello!"

"Yes, Owen," responded Vivian, "what do you want?"

"Chile," he asked softly, "who am I talking to?"[22]

27

Owen's Song, 1972–74

Amid Dodson's troubles, Fortune sought him out for blessings. Just when Dorothy Maynor dismissed him as theater consultant for "lack of funding," from out of the clouds another stipend descended. Theodore Gross, chairman of the City College of New York's English department, invited Professor Dodson to teach a creative-writing class on Monday from 2 to 4 P.M. As distinguished guest he would receive $14,010 for one class—a generous consideration.

Owen mentored them well, and the students wrote with talent. In spite of the fact that he could teach no classes in December because of his hip operation, the faculty recommended his reappointment for the spring, but alas, they assigned him to a class that met on Friday at 9 A.M.—a most uncreative hour. In late March, he informed Gross that he would be unable to teach for a month because of further hip surgery; he assured him, however, that "my students will be working in my absence on their long project and I promised them that upon my return, the few sessions that I missed would be made up."[1]

One more time he hobbled into Presbyterian Hospital, this visit for a low-friction arthroplasty of his left hip, performed again by Dr. Shelton. The technology of successful replacement of diseased joints involved a stainless-steel ball on a shaft inserted into the thighbone and cemented in place. The steel ball swiveled in a strong plastic socket attached with acrylic cement to the pelvis.

Owen returned to his job five weeks after entering the hospital, but his students complained that even when present he was absent—drinking again—and he was not rehired for the fall. But once again Fortune insisted, this time giving him a visiting professorship at York College in Queens. The immediate source of this largess was Prof. Helen Armstead Johnson, who secured Owen an associate professorship with a take-home pay of $977 a month. In Helen, Owen found a replacement for Rosey, someone to share his delight in gossip, his passion for theater. Every Sunday morning, he would call her with various complaints, compliments, and confessions. The more Owen loved Helen, the more Edith disliked her, and the more their contretemps amused Owen. For Thanksgiving, he invited Helen to dinner, but he didn't tell Edith, who opened the door and could only say, "Oh, it's you!"

Owen hired a limousine to chauffeur him to York College, but the distance from West End Avenue to Queens seemed to grow longer with each passing week. So weary did he grow that some days he did not find his way at all. He did not grade his papers; at the end of the semester, nearly all his students received an A. Sometimes his clothes were dirty. (This was before Edith moved in with him.) Professor Dodson had become an embarrassment.[2] At the end of the year, the administration let him go.

But Fortune flew right back. Seven years after Owen had written the opera *Til Victory Is Won*[3] to celebrate Howard's centennial, the massive three-hour work, in four segments and with twenty-one solo parts, swept onto the Kennedy Center stage in Washington, D.C. The Howard Choir sang (their director, Warner Lawson, who had opposed portions of the opera, had died). Three thousand people packed the house, and Owen somehow managed to "walk" out onto the stage, wearing dark glasses, to give a short introduction. Because he had never seen the opera performed, Owen was startled by what he had begun nearly a decade before. The reviews expressed dismay that only four weeks' rehearsal had been allotted, and that the stage was bare of scenery, but they praised the scope of vision and Mark Fax's use of spiritual and jazz motifs, and they lauded the Bessie Smith scene, the one Lawson had insisted be cut.

In August, Owen's former students Glenda Dickerson and Mike Malone assembled a collage from Dodson's plays, poetry, and stories. Glenda wrote him, "I hope you will not think it presumptuous of us to consider this piece a tribute to you, a living monument to the great and powerful ladder of words you have created to guide us in our search for the bird of freedom."[4] On October 24 *Owen's Song* premiered at the Colony Theatre in Washington, D.C., making an immediate splash. Clive Barnes, then of the *New York Times,* declared, "There is an infectious joyousness to the piece, a visual beauty and a swiftly poetic message. It has the essence of poetry to it, with a grandeur of concept and a simplicity of effort. It has a style of its own and trades in images. It is an unusually pregnant piece of theater, subtly suggestive of future possibilities."[5]

Robert Hooks agreed to produce it in the Eisenhower Theatre, and on the final day of 1974 *Owen's Song* opened at the Kennedy Center. The production pleased Glenda: "When the the cast came down off the stage and sang, 'Owen Dodson, this is your song. No hand can build freedom like your hand.' . . . how moved he was! He could not walk at that time but rose to his feet and stood there for the adulation of the crowd."[6] Kennedy Center wanted to tour the play, and he thought it was going to take off, but the producers could not come to an understanding. Instead, Dickerson brought it to the Harlem Cultural Center for three performances.

The good times, great and small, still rolled on. Between the years 1968 and 1974, nearly every major publisher in America issued at least one collection of African-American literature. The six-year flood brought Owen a pile of pin money, $50 here, $25 there, and $1.50 a line somewhere else. In all he published over seventy poems in thirty-three anthologies.

Then Fortune began to turn her back. An adaptation of his work *Bayou Legend,* at the Amas Repertory Theatre in New York,[7] did not fare well. Jack Landon, who played the lead, had written and inserted sixteen songs that extended an already lengthy play into an endless evening.

There were other desertions: Dodson, in a period of only a few months, watched several friends leave him. W. H. Auden died; Owen attended the memorial. Painter Karl Priebe died in Milwaukee; Owen attended the funeral. Actress Edna Thomas died; Owen attended the funeral. Writer Arna Bontemps died; Owen attended the memorial. Paul Robeson died; Owen attended the funeral. Milton Fried, his childhood "dear heart," died, but no one remembered to tell Owen. Then, on January 2, 1973, Owen's brother Nat, Jr., died in the Bronx. Owen refused to attend the funeral; Edith went.

Perhaps these intimations of mortality inspired Owen to tell his sister:

All these years I have never written you a letter saying that your grace and growth had been so good to me. I guess it is embarrassing for you to receive a letter of gratitude from your brother, but know that I love you and appreciate everything you have done, and that your faith in me is pride.

I also know that there is something in your heart and soul that has made me proud of our family and proud of you. Every time I write a book, although it may not say it is for Edith, it is for thee.

So, my dear, all that you have done for me I have not expressed, but it is here. Move along, walk along, love along, whenever you can.[8]

After living alone three years at 600 West End Avenue, Owen had demonstrated to his sister that he could not care for himself. Edith, now sixty-five and retired, with over thirty years of experience as a social worker, must have known that Owen would lose the battle of the bottle; still, she never hesitated to become his guardian. For his entire adult life, her brother had been her single greatest treasure, the Dodson family jewel, and she would not see him degraded. She found a penthouse apartment at 350 W. Fifty-first Street, and on June 1, 1974, they moved in together. The Dodsons' seventeenth-floor apartment (one of two on the roof) faced north, with privacy, sunlight, and from the balcony a view of the Hudson. Edith gave her brother the master bedroom, while, like a concierge, she slept in a small room across the hall.

This four-foot-ten-inch warrior met everyone at the door, and one might have as easily brushed past Genghis Khan as ignored Edith on the qui vive. Though tiny, she knew the secret: absolute self-assurance. As a young girl, Edith had been adorned with a marvelous set of buck teeth, and seldom smiled in photographs until later in life, after she was able to afford an orthodontist. Owen had assumed she would have few boyfriends, and few she had. Edith became for Owen "the only faithful one," playing Wendy to his Peter Pan—and now guardian mother to his bad child. For standing between Owen and his vodka, Edith became an object of his hatred—for a day or a week or sometimes more.

She inspected each visitor for evidence of vodka running, for Owen depended on runners. Like the Captain in O'Casey's *Juno and the*

Paycock Owen courted boon companions, Joxers who would bootleg a bottle in to their old buddy and stay to salute the world's "state of chassis." One, Walter Hall, had played the lead in *Bayou Legend* at Howard in 1948. A man of talents—carpentry, dancing, designing, acting—he had ended by living at the YMCA, surviving as he could. This Joxer brought Owen not only the comfort of the present but warm memories of past glory. One day Edith challenged the basket he carried into Owen's bedroom and insisted upon a customs inspection. Apples. Nothing but apples. Owen roared in fury: See! See! For days, he told everyone of the martinet across the hall. But even the most watchful eye must sleep, or sometimes leave to shop for groceries, and then it was that Owen's gold watch, his father's watch, slipped away in Joxer's pocket. In silent, slow attrition, Owen's treasures—rings, drawings, paintings, signed first editions—began to creep away.

Edith, with all her memories of Berriman Street poverty, had thought to harbor these treasures for an uncertain old age. Owen wavered between a potlatch prodigality and a foxlike cunning that promised bounty to the faithful after his death. But his present necessity pressed him: The Social Security Administration demanded a refund of $4,816.80 for overpayment. (He had failed to notify them of his employment at CCNY and at York College.) If he didn't return the money, they would turn the matter over to the General Accounting Office for collection.[9] Owen asked for a hearing; the decision was rendered: Owen was not guilty of deliberate fraud, but his professional status had enabled him to continue to earn considerable money, and he must refund the overpayment.[10]

At nearly the same time, Presbyterian Hospital pressed for overdue bills. The cost of three broken legs and two hip replacements exceeded the payments of Blue Cross, and unless he forked out $1,855.52, he would be subject to legal action. Even the Mayflower Transit Company, after four years, still pursued Owen for the fifty dollars they claimed he owed from the Washington move.

Owen assured his creditors he would begin payments when he resumed teaching at New York University in the fall of 1974, a position he was negotiating for but did not have. In the meantime, he snatched every chance to lecture or read—the Afro-American Summer Institute at Iowa ($500); Kalamazoo, Michigan, on the changing role of Blacks ($250); the Theatre Festival at Wayne State in Detroit (judge—$250); Negro History Week at George Washington High School, Alexandria,

Virginia ($600); and the National Conference of Afro-American Writers at Howard. Finally, he assembled a collage of tributes to *Owen's Song* onto a single page and announced: "Owen Dodson, Poetry Reading, $500 plus expenses. Dates Available." He appended his phone number.

In 1972, in similar desperate circumstances, Owen had written PEN, the world association of writers: "The hospital bills are tremendous. I managed to pay the doctor, but as of now I owe the Presbyterian Hospital $6,000 and more. I am not applying, of course, for the amount, but whatever your aid limit is for needy writers would be useful to me." PEN responded with a check for $500.[11]

When he read poetry with David Ignatow at York College and discovered that his $300 fee had been paid by Poets and Writers, Inc., he addressed a similar plea to Ms. Galen Williams, the group's executive director:

> Now my predicament is kind of tense because my position at York College terminates in June, and I have nothing lined up for the summer. Well, since your organization is called Poets and Writers, I thought I would ask you and your associates if they could suggest some kind of work that would help me, and for me to help young writers this summer and during the next academic season or speaking season, or whatever. So my dear Ms. Williams, I hope to meet you soon, and I hope perhaps with the magic you have, that you might produce a dove with money in its mouth. I did have a very successful reading of my poetry at the Library of Congress last March.[12]

On July 9, he reentered Presbyterian Hospital to have his right knee replaced with a titanium joint. At sixty, he was still five years short of a retirement pension. But there he was—a bionic poet writing strangers to produce a dove with money in its mouth.

28

The Gathering of Sons, 1973–78

Owen never lacked acolytes, young artists seeking a mentor, an idol, an agent—a father to nurture them. Owen would read and praise their poems and plays, write them recommendations, and into their hungry hearts pour his belief that art was "the only faithful one." In payment, these young men (and rarely women), nearly all of them black, fetched his mail, set his table, typed his letters, brought him Jamaican ginger beer while he sat enthroned upon his red-velvet sofa, reciting "all the higher algebra of pride: teaching of how to do, what not to do, with grace toward the chemistry of man."[1] Sometimes, like a grace note, Owen would drop a question on their plate, lamenting that he lacked a lover. Those few who answered yes, they would, Edith sent away, for she feared that they had come to fill their pockets. Those who answered no, they wouldn't, remained—indentured in their art.

One young writer, Raimundo Torrence, fresh from adventures in Africa, met Edith at the Community Church and followed her home to become one of Owen's unregistered pupils. Recalled Torrence: "Mr. Dodson encouraged me to have a spark, take chances, and become stronger. One day I took a book of poems of the sixties to his house: Nikki Giovanni, Ted Joans, Sonia Sanchez. I said, 'Listen to this.' He listened to a few and said, 'This is nonsense.' He went to the bookshelves and took down a big anthology and said, 'Read this and then you will understand what poetry is.' He showed me that poetry should last beyond the moment of fashion."[2]

Owen confessed that once at a banquet to honor Thornton Wilder given at the Polish embassy, he had stolen a spoon from the table. Later, he commissioned a jeweler to fashion the spoon into a ring with the spoon crest as the signet. One Christmas near the end of his life, he called Raimundo to sit beside him on the couch. He said, "Give me your hand," and he put the heavy silver ring on his finger, saying, "It's from a Polish friend of mine."

Hilton Als at age 13 came to 600 West End Avenue with a shopping cart because his teacher Imani Gibbs had informed him that Mr. Dodson was giving books away. Als carted off a complete set of Dickens. Two years later, he met Dodson again, this time waiting in the line for Tennessee Williams to autograph his memoirs; Als pressed on Owen a manuscript of his stories. Dodson noted Als's talent buried under purple prose, and wrote President Reynolds of Bates College, asking if he had a scholarship for his godson. Reynolds urged Als to apply, but he elected to remain in the city. Five years after Owen's death, Als wrote in the *Village Voice,* as part of a memorial for James Baldwin, "Owen was my champion, he wrested me from a most unmanly petulance by admitting, in no uncertain terms, that he loved me. It was the first occasion I have ever heard of in which men admitted such things, let alone to each other. Owen knew that and gave me 'Alas Poor Richard' to read. He said, 'Chile, all hell broke loose when Jimmy published that essay. But he had to do it. Sometimes I wonder if you'll ever say those things about me.' "[3]

Another novitiate, Glenngo Allen King, recalled: "My own father died when I was nineteen. Owen for me was like an art-grandfather. I felt I had come into his life during Act 5 of *King Lear.*"[4] One afternoon when a winter wind swept across the icy Hudson, Glenngo and two friends, Bill Castleberry and Marlene Tartaglione, pressed into the lobby of Owen's building, shivering to be buzzed in. The elevator crept up to the top floor, where they paused in the corridor before the sentinel at Owen's door—the enormous silver poster of the Alvin Ailey Dance Company. Edith pulled them inside and unwound them of scarves and coats.

Glenngo had promised his comrades a stage set for one principal actor, and they saw it—the carousel horses; the square, pearl-inlay piano that had belonged to General Howard; the mahogany bas-relief

"The Death of D. H. Lawrence" by Oliver Barrett. Owen had already taken his position stage left on his red-velvet sofa with his crutches parked behind him like banner staves. Glenngo, a force of flashing teeth and talking energy, introduced Marlene, a young poet with straight dark hair and lips outlined in black pencil, and Bill, a seriously handsome writer not yet twenty.

"We were nobodies," recalled Tartaglione. "We walked in, and we knew the man was erudite, but he had a warmth, an air of ancient weariness, an immense longing that could never be filled, a longing for God."[5]

They settled among the horses and read their poems. Owen nodded and encouraged. Edith brought them ginger ale. Then Owen read his recent poem about Billie Holiday, which ended,

> They stood the cops before your final hurt
> They snatched away relief from final pain
> They asked for curses, signatures, for photo looks
> approached your bed, and snitched your comic books.[6]

Yes, he had known Billie in the forties when Frank Harriott had been a journalist for *PM*. Owen had captured his young audience, describing Billie's voice as "so steady, so melancholy, elongated like an El Greco painting that had nothing to do with reality but everything to do with truth."

He told them how people waited half the night for Holiday to sing. Sometimes she didn't show up, sometimes she was absolutely on time, and sometimes she slipped down the microphone, and they would carry her out. Owen would look into their faces and say, "She was an immaculate artist. She projected the song, not herself."

Then he settled into the tale: "Billie lived at the Hotel Braddock. Today it looks like the asshole of all hotels; in those days, it looked the same. I had been invited by Karl Priebe to meet Billie to take her to the club and listen to her sing. I knocked on this door and a head came out, cold-creamed; the hair was a mess; like so many famous entertainers, she had a dirty old pink kimono, her giblets hanging all around and no girdle on. I asked for Karl, and she made some crack. I always had a white shirt and tie and looked like a college graduate. Every time we met during those three months, she used to call me 'the professor,' 'the schoolteacher,' or didn't remember me at all. They were all smoking pot. That shocked me. I never smoked marijuana.

Their spirits bubbled like just before Christmas dinner. Anyway, Billie got herself together and when she emerged from the bathroom—a marvel, a marvel.

"Once when we went up to her dressing room on Fifty-second Street, the room was very, very small; when I say small, I mean hardly any air coming in. She had pulled her dress up and evidently she had nothing on under the dress because I saw pubic hairs; she had an undertaker's fan and was fanning under there; she said, 'Sure is hot in here,' but when she came down, what a performance she gave.

"Once when Karl exhibited at Pearl Gallery, at the top of the steps as you entered was a small picture, a foot square, he had done of Billie. She came, had a glass of champagne and said she couldn't have any more to drink, she had to perform in an hour. Oh, that night, what a lady she was. As she was going out, she looked back and said, 'That's my picture on the wall.' 'Yes, it is, Miss Holiday,' said Pearl, who owned the gallery. 'Isn't that something,' she said. 'I like it.' She took it off the wall and put it under her great mink coat and walked out, with Pearl saying, 'Miss Holiday, Miss Holiday!' She said, 'It's a picture of me, isn't it?' and left.

"Billie loved her mother. When her mother died, she got to the funeral in the Catholic church about fifteen minutes late. She came down the aisle with Joe Guy, wearing her white lambskin coat, a black dress and a great big black arm band, and a gardenia in her hair. As she went down the aisle, she greeted Karl and looked at the 'school-teacher'; she greeted Joe Glaser, her manager, who had ordered so many cars and limousines there was no one to ride in all that fleet. Glaser stood on the sidewalk and said, 'That is Billie Holiday's mother in that church over there. Don't you wanta come to the cemetery with us? Don't you wanta comfort Billie?' 'God,' I said to myself, 'it's vomit time now.' Karl, Frank, and I attended the burial, but when she got back home, someone had broken into her apartment and stolen her fur coat and her gown and everything for her night life, her future heroin.

"This woman, who could not read or write music, wrote songs and could interpret the deepest passions, and in her work was involved with society. They threw her into the hospital. You could not come within four or five feet of her for fear you would give her some heroin or cocaine. They took away her comic books.

"I have been a big snob in my day, and it is a pity we learn so late.

I listen to her records; I hear her sing for the poverty-stricken, not for the Ph.D.'s. She was an Edith Piaf in her sensitivity, her quivering before life, her cursing what had damned her—poverty, neglect, a childhood of hopelessness that she overcame. That was the Billie I knew. She never tried to know me; according to her standards, I was never worth it."[7]

Staring down into their empty glasses, his young audience sat in silence. "Turn on the lights, chile," said Owen, and then it was time to step out into winter's evening. It had been a simple afternoon, a splendid afternoon. Tartaglione recalled: "If someone said to me, 'What to you was the most personal moment of glory?' I would answer it was when I read my poem. When I had finished, Owen just sat there; he just looked at me and said very quietly, 'You are a great poet.' That moment was one of personal glory, and I can die happy even if nothing else ever happens to me."

Once, after conducting a seminar at the Frank Silvera Writers' Workshop on Upper Broadway, Owen asked for assistance in descending from the platform. A slim, dark-eyed stranger glided forward, and as he eased Owen down the steps, the young man recited one of Owen's poems. This sudden burst of his own poetry from a stranger with splendid frontal diction startled Owen. He and Darryl Croxton had begun a friendship. Soon Mr. D. started making notes for another *Hamlet,* and Croxton undertook to direct a reading of Dodson's new oratorio, *The Morning Duke Ellington Praised the Lord and Seven Little Black Davids Tap-Danced Unto* (the poem had six Davids; the play had seven), subtitled "A blues, jazz dance and ceremonial entertainment."

Owen's inspiration had come from television one evening while watching Duke Ellington conduct his *Cantata to the Lord.* The plot was simplicity itself. Four black musicians—Dinah Washington, Bessie Smith, Billie Holiday, and Charlie Parker—attempt to enter heaven, but the Books of the Old Testament (the chorus) forbid them. Each of the sinners cries, "Don't judge me." But then they change and cry, "Yes, judge us. We been 'buked, and we been scorned. Yes, judge us!" Charlie Parker never says a word but plays his sax. One by one Jesus admits Billie, Dinah, Bessie, and Bird because their suffering has been transformed into the beauty of art. The opera ends with Six Black Davids (the ones he saw when his mother died) tap-dancing up and down the stairs before the throne of heaven, and the entire cast singing in an ecstasy of gospel revival—a brilliant vision.

Following a New York concert, conductor Everett Lee introduced Owen to Ellington, who said to send him the oratorio; yes, yes, he'd like to read it. But within two months, the Duke died. Owen turned the script over to Darryl Croxton for a reading (sans music) at the Frank Silvera Writers' Workshop. On January 12, 1976, Croxton assembled actors Mary Alice, China Clark, Barbara Montgomery, Cynthia McPherson, and Robert Christian. Owen praised the direction: "The music that you made with my words. How you made my words the energy of your faith and craft."[8]

Still in need of a score, Owen turned to a young musician, Roscoe Gill, who had directed the choir in Ellington's last Sacred Concert at Westminster Abbey. Gill, trained at Temple University and Juilliard, insisted that his own music was neither black nor white. But, unfortunately for the project, the text cried for gospel, for Owen had written out of the rhythms of the black church. On November 17, 1976, Croxton held a musical audition.

Jim Mapp, of the Playward Bus Theatre Company in Philadelphia, and his partner, Tyrone Collins, optioned the script. Owen signed a contract to rewrite and to direct *Duke*—projected opening, February 11 in Philadelphia.[9] Owen moved in with Mapp on JFK Boulevard and began work. He cast Beverly Kelch, his former student from Howard ('59), as Naomi and planned to use her daughter, dressed as a boy, as one of the seven tap dancers. Then one night without warning Mr. D. came down the aisle and stunned the cast by announcing that the play was off; there had been a disagreement between him and Mapp.[10] He returned to New York, angry and bitter.

A month after the collapse of *Duke*, Owen's bitterness surfaced at a reading sponsored by Victoria Sullivan at the Book Gallery on the Upper West Side. His program was humorless, all the poems centering on anger and death. Perhaps that bitterness seeped down into his leg, this time into his left knee until pain demanded surgery; again bionic Owen entered Columbia Presbyterian, this time without a private room. Several days after the operation, he wrote, "I'm writing half-propped up in bed with one leg in traction and a neat hole through my left ankle with a steel rod through it. There is a also a pulley that lifts my knee up and down like a play contraption." Owen emerged from the hospital to hear that one of his dearest friends had died—Peggy Rieser.

He once wrote her, "Although we do not see each other often I know you are there in Ravinia or somewhere comparatively near and

I feel your shawl of honest living and integrity about me."[11] (He had already written the line for his opera *Christmas Miracle,* but that did not mean it could not be Peggy's, too.) They had managed to see one another at least every year or two, Owen traveling to or through Chicago. Then one Friday in June, while Owen was writing a postcard to Croxton—"There is always something alarming about love, but friendship is forever our guardian angel"[12]—Peggy collapsed in her home; she died Saturday morning. Her family forgot to call Owen. Later, her son Leonard wrote him "You were one of her favorites."[13]

On the Fourth of July in 1976, Owen watched from his balcony as the tall ships glided up the Hudson; he pointed out the 130-foot topsailed schooner *La Amistad,* the ship he had written the play about nearly forty years before. Then he fled the summer heat to Bermuda, to see his friend Tom Stowe and to celebrate a wedding in their family. At the ceremony, a four-year-old boy crept into Owen's arms and whispered into his ear, "God made the world for you."[14]

In the spirit of bicentennial brotherhood, Coca-Cola and Westinghouse budgeted $300,000 for an hour-long television revue and review of African-American musical history. Gary Keys invited Owen to write a scenario. He produced a revue/pageant covering music from Africa through slavery to Diana Ross. In June they presented their package, *Sound of Soul,*[15] to the moguls of WNET-TV, with Lionel Hampton playing the vibraphone. Said Owen, "With their gray suits on, gray hair, gray minds, gray imaginations, they [WNET] said, 'No, it was too bitter.' And that nigger Lionel Hampton went right along with them. I'm going to find a way to smash his vibraphone."[16]

Owen and Keys didn't discard a good idea; they rewrote the piece into a stage show, and after two years *Sound of Soul* opened at the Ira Aldridge Theatre at Howard, with Geoffrey Newman directing.[17] Raymond S. Blanks, reviewer for the *Washington Afro-American,* complained that there was too much music and too little of Owen's poetry: "A voice like Dodson's, the poet/dramatist, does not have to play second fiddle to the music of Smokey Robinson. When Dodson's muse is permitted to sing, it is sweet and powerful like a preacher's sermon in a Baptist Church."[18] In the audience, Swiss ambassador Raymond Probst and Dr. Wolfgang Zorner, director of the Stadt-Theater in St. Gallen, Switzerland, liked what they saw and invited the company to give the European premiere.

On January 10, 1979, Edith and Owen flew to St. Gallen, where the show opened in the new fifty-million-franc theater. The critics commented on the dark and bitter side of the revue, but unlike the moguls of WNET they liked *Soul* the more for it. The show, on a double bill with the musical *Raisin,* ran two months before it moved on to Bern and then Geneva. Keys and Dodson, pleased by their success, returned and made further revisions, but American television still had no taste for the bitter history of black music.

About the same time, staff director Bob Morris of PBS Channel 13 proposed an hour-long special, *Owen Dodson: Poet,* with James Earl Jones: "In a word, it is our feeling that the mood of the country in general is closer now than ever before to the mood of Mr. Dodson's poems. Americans will be able to hear what he has to say, relate to his themes, identify with his struggles, and profit from his wisdom, as never before. It is an appropriate time to expose the American public to one of its most distinctive, though too little heard, poetic voices."[19]

In the patois of television, he ran it up the pole but no one saluted.

On Christmas in 1977, Owen's acolytes decked his candelabra with ornaments; the tree glowed in its sparkles; the gifts snuggled at the base of the tree (Owen rarely opened gifts in the giver's presence); a case of champagne chilled on the balcony; and a host of friends stood drinking and talking and talking. Owen had composed, and Edith had printed on special rag paper with red script, his Christmas poem. This season's feted guest was foreign-service deputy Louis Miniclier, an old friend from Washington. Miniclier, white-haired and hardly taller than Edith, dressed in a tux with a boutonniere, appeared every bit the diplomat. Owen, with a black patch—evidence of his cataract operation—raked wickedly over his left eye, upstaged his guest.

The soiree's special glow was provided by the expenditure of $1,500 —royalties advanced for the paper publication of *Come Home Early, Child.* Patrick O'Connor, a senior editor with Popular Library, had finally managed to bring out his friend's novel. The reviews were not many, but positive—one remarking that the literary world seemed to rediscover Dodson once every decade.

Hardly had the holiday ended than a ghost appeared whom Owen had not seen for thirty years: Ednah Bethea, now Mrs. Blalock, her figure still trim, her face fresh, had not suspected that her once-true love hobbled on cane and walker; she did see that he had trouble breathing. To her, he seemed "lonely and insecure." He was fussing, going out soon to "attend to things." Edith made them lunch of chicken soup and a salad. Owen told her that Woody King, Jr., had just opened *Divine Comedy* at the Henry Street Settlement under the direction of a former student, Clinton Turner Davis. Then came a phone call; someone read Mel Gussow's review from the *New York Times* to Owen over the phone. Dodson let out a few invectives.[20] Gussow had stated, "The play is flawed and somewhat fragmentary. At times the verse is windily poetic." However, the critic had gone on to call it "an intriguing play on a fascinating subject."[21]

In April, Owen and Edith flew to Seville, Spain, to visit Louis Miniclier, whose fevered letters told of his desperate heart condition. Hardly had Owen arrived at Miniclier's apartment at 5 San Gregorio when Miniclier died of an embolism. In the tiny European elevator the undertaker was able to stand the coffin upright.

A month after the funeral, Owen flew to Lincoln University in Missouri, where his friend Tom Pawley, now dean of humanities, had arranged that Owen be awarded his second honorary doctorate. Tom and Owen had been friends since they had roomed together at Spelman College in 1938. Owen had never approached Pawley or even hinted at an attraction, but now at age sixty-three and in his cups, Owen confessed. Tom was shocked. Owen concluded by saying, "I guess it would be pretty silly, wouldn't it, two old men kissing each other?" The matter never came up again.

Like Lear, "his knees corrupted and dismayed deep / in the naked earth beside impotent trees,"[22] Owen stumbled on, seeking his own Cordelia, a scion to comfort and care for him. He dreamed his fantasy into poems:

> I was courted by a lad
> whose body was made of gold.
> I polished it every night.[23]

He reached into his past to conjure friends who might still care. He dedicated a poem to Ted Shine:

> Take my hand while time still breathes;
> Hurry now hurry: Look take my hand
> Hurry now hurry: We shall be made of hope
> not manna, milk or honey, hurry now, hurry."

Some came running to care for him as best they could. Mercie Hinton, a young actor and friend of Croxton, made a valiant attempt. Hinton commented, "Everyone has to have a special friend, or a lover or a wife or someone you can share with. Owen was sad that he didn't have a lover. He would grab at me sometimes. I told him outright that I saw him as my grandfather, not even a father, and 'if we are going to continue, you cannot try anything sexually with me, you cannot make innuendoes, or I cannot come around again,' and he stopped.

"He wanted a sexual relationship, someone who would be with him all the time. The ones in the theater tried to use him. They would ask him to give them a production: 'I would love to play so and so.' He would try to ignore that for a while, but when he drank, it would come out. And then they would sometimes leave because they realized that he knew, or he would throw them out, or before Edith died, she would throw them out. Oh God, she loved her brother and protected him. She knew he was looking for someone and was willing to accept that person. She knew the thing that caused him the most anxiety — not having a special person."[24]

In his last collection of unpublished poems about the dispossessed, Owen scribbled one short lullaby:

> I wake up screaming
> Against the nibbling
> voices of decay.
> The world is deaf.
> Where is my son?
> Why did he die away?
> Go bye, go bye, go bye
>   bye bye

29

Just Go On, Chile, 1980–83

Frederick Wilkerson, the voice teacher at Howard who had played Claudius in *Hamlet,* was strangled in his New York apartment.[1] His murder swept Owen into a series of poems that slashed and burned. His subject—those sleeping in doorways and on subway benches, the city's desperate and poor. Poem followed poem. Although the series suffered from repetition of emotion, and many needed honing, Owen's passion seared them together in a manuscript he named *The Bag Ladies.* They received their first public hearing on a rainy April evening in Donnell Library at the eighteenth annual poetry-reading program hosted by Aaron Kramer, an East Brooklyn–born poet. The next day artist Penrod Scofield called. He was working on sketches of street people, the homeless, for a book. Muriel Rukeyser had promised to provide the text, but she had died. Would Dodson do it?

The two men soon discovered that their book had dramatic possibilities. To get a reading of the poems, renamed *Life in the Streets,* Owen turned to Glenda Dickerson, who had founded her own theater to exalt the spoken word—the Owen Dodson Lyric Theatre. In the winter of 1980, Glenda, while teaching at the Mason Gross Center for the Arts at Rutgers University, tried to give the poems a public reading, but couldn't arrange one. Scofield called her and said that they wanted the script back, and that they would drive out to Rutgers to get it.

Recalled Dickerson: "The next morning in a blizzard, the two of them, drunk as could be, drove out to Rutgers. Penrod Scofield is a big man, huge, a St. Nicholas person, and red as a beet with white hair. He came in my class and said, 'Give me my script or I am going to call the police.' I said, 'I don't have the script; it is at my house.' He said, 'Owen Dodson is in the car, and he wants to speak to you, and you better get your ass out there,' so I put on my coat and went out, and there was all this snow, and I started walking down the street; they rolled down the window of their car, yelling and screaming, two old fools, drunk. I refused to speak to them. That night Mr. Dodson called me and asked, 'What is the matter with you?' I said, 'What is the matter with you?' I changed my phone number."[2]

The production waited a year; then Paul Kresh, producer at Spoken Arts, approached Joseph Papp to include *Life in the Streets* in his series *Poets at the Public,* a weekly evening program in the Newman Theatre. Papp scheduled Owen's poems the week after Robert Penn Warren's seventy-seventh birthday celebration.[3]

David Amram's quintet wove the poems together, Scofield projected his drawings, Owen himself joined the readers, and Roscoe Lee Browne headed the cast. The performance sold out; friends flouted the fire laws, spilling over into the aisles. The evening, dedicated to Muriel Rukeyser, used poetry to gain empathy for the homeless, but the homeless remained adrift, and the poems were never published. But another poetry project appeared.

Camille Billops invited Dodson to write original poems for captions of the funerary photographs of Harlem's "picture takin' man," James Van Der Zee, who had recorded funerals in the 1920s, 1930s, and 1940s as part of Harlem life. (In those days few Blacks could afford to travel back down home for a funeral, so the relatives had a portrait made of the loved one in the coffin to show the style in which the deceased had been laid away.) "Right up my alley," responded Owen. "I've been going to funerals since I was a boy."

During the weeks of their work on the book, Owen would call and read poems to Camille. As the weeks passed, he became progressively drunker and drunker. One time he called at midnight and went into "Who are you? Where do you come from?" Billops told him, "You need to go to A.A.," and hung up. He called the next day, sober. She told him again that he needed to go to A.A. Then he read his "Allegory of Seafaring Black Mothers." She wept for the beauty of the poem.[4]

Owen's forty-eight lines adorned the black mother with jewels never worn before, his childhood images:

mothers milking nanny goats — telling the fortunes of
bees — grunting spells into the decks as they scrubbed
the ass of the ship
Then lo and behold a
new breed was born
How many mothers with their grit
with their bony and long dreams
have dared to splash with us out to sea?

Dodson belonged to a new breed, and, his tribute added, to employ Richard Blackmur's phrase, "to our stock of available reality." *The Harlem Book of the Dead* juxtaposed his poetry with photographs of the dead, and Billops tied them together with an introduction by Toni Morrison and a compelling interview on love, death, and God with Van Der Zee.

Owen's adversarial friendship with Billops survived several bouts. Once she rented a four-door Pontiac and took Owen, Edith, Vivian Browne, and Roscoe Gill to New Hope, Pennsylvania, to interview Harlem Renaissance artist Selma Burke. After a picnic on the lawn (Owen, who had had a couple of drinks before the ride to New Hope, drank some more) they filed into the house to ease Selma into a tape about a man she claimed to have been her husband, poet Claude McKay. Midway through the interview, Owen asked to be helped to the toilet. The task fell to Camille: "He was too woozy to stand alone, so I had to help him pee and he peed on my hand. I helped him put his 'johnson' back into his trousers, which he had also peed on. When he went back into the living room, he eased in so no one could see the stain in the front. I had thought that we were going to have these two great artists reminiscing together, but Owen was jealous."

While his body deteriorated, his artist's spirit flourished. In 1979, he wrote a translucent poem, a lyric with strong and deep religious undertones. Although claiming to deny the existence of a personal deity, all of his best work addressed God, sometimes obliquely, part of the paradox that suffused his life and art — the likely-unlikely. Nowhere was this more apparent than in the poem "Prisoners":[5]

I have a prison locked in me
Its bars are ancient alchemy.

Within that prison is another
Where imps and pimps sting in my brother.

Within that prison is a third
Where weeps alone the world's torn bird.

Within the torn bird's tears of course:
The splinters of the human cross.

They cry to me, they plead to me
"For pity's sake, come rescue me."

Their blood runs down all agony.

Can I reply: "I've lost the key.
I can't pick locks. Don't murder me."

I must retain serenity:
Kneading Sacred bread
Tasting Holy wine—
My prisoners locked within.
As their warden I begin:

My faith looks up to thee
Not to fail the world in me.[6]

The verse has all the simplicity of "Now I lay me down to sleep," while embracing the allegorical complexity of "Did He who made the lamb make thee?" The poem's double vision is offered in the first line. A prison is locked inside the narrator, making him at once a jailer and a prisoner. Within that prison is another and yet another like glass bottles placed one inside the other. Owen condensed into twenty lines his own soul's long, dark journey to redemption, the very essence of the African-American struggle to conquer pain by affirmation. He did it, not by direct reference but by resonance of image, by artful use of ambiguities whose translucence makes them seem effortless. The simplicity of the language and of the images, the easy and natural cadence of the lines, are witness to the poet's artistry. Like an old baobab on the dry plain, he bore fruit in a harsh season.

The mature years of Gordon Heath bore fruit, too. From 1947 to 1970, he centered his professional life in France and England, but then he returned for the role of Oedipus, a triumph at the Roundabout Theatre in New York. In the years following, he shuttled between Europe and America on a variety of assignments in film, theater and television (including the role of Hamm in Beckett's *Endgame* at the Roundabout). When in Gotham, he would drop by to visit the Dodsons. Although the Howard production of *Dr. Faustus* had not mortally wounded the intimacy between them, it had left them cautious. Owen's letters reported his theater productions, his poems; Gordon's, his acting assignments and L'Abbaye's celebration of its twenty-fifth anniversary in July 1974. Two years later, Lee Payant died of cancer and Gordon closed the club.

In 1978 at the Bonfils Theatre in Denver, Gordon had starred as Henry Christophe in *Defiant Island*. Owen flew to Colorado, intending to stay the week. After the performance, Heath improvised a small reception with the cast where Dodson could hold court, charming all with his anecdotes. After the guests left, Owen, now fueled by a bottle of Scotch, critiqued the production, the direction, and Gordon's performance with his usual acuity. He spent a quarter of an hour praising every element of Gordon's characterization. Heath went to bed. Owen went into the living room, sat in the armchair, and began a second bottle of Scotch. Minutes later, he launched into a drunken soliloquy, spitting out accusations against practically everyone he had ever known, claiming that all his lovers had failed him. The world had been ungrateful. He shouted at Gordon, "Get out! Get out!" He fell out of the chair onto the floor. Gordon, unable to lift him, placed a blanket over his body and returned to bed. At three in the morning Owen awoke and began packing his suitcase. Two hours later, crutches, baggage, and all, he left for New York. The next day, Dodson severed the artery between them: "What you said to me in Denver, I know was out of love. [Gordon had advised him to leave off drinking, that he was destroying himself.] You faced the window at one point saying 'We have not much time.' Remember in *Corinthians*—there is a time for everything. This is not the time, correction officer, to judge my mind, my heart or my actions or our time for friendship or the end. I don't want you to interfere. 'Whatever it is you predict for me / I hope I can bear it stoically.' I make no bargains. You must trust your inner feelings after fifty years. Go thy ways."[7]

From then on, he treated Gordon as an enemy, even snubbing him

in public. A half-century had passed since Gordon's mother had brought
them sandwiches, fried chicken, cookies at Camp Carlton—a wonderful place where the friends had sung in haunting diminuendo,

> Our boat is on the river: the hour's drawing nigh.
> And when the sun goes down, my dears,
> we're going to say goodbye.

Now they allowed the song to fade away to silence.

Owen raged on like Lear—a stubborn old man refusing rescue,
while crying out to others, "Hurry, now hurry" to rescue him. Some
of his cries flew back across the years to Priscilla Heath, his fiancée
from Bates College days. Their friendship had drifted. They exchanged
letters annually—Owen remembering that her birthday was sometime
in October. He made certain she received notices of productions,
speeches, awards; she had become keeper of his records, the old books,
the one who had known him since when.[8] In her letters, the valediction
"affectionately" had quietly supplanted "love."

Now in old age, he began calling, writing to Priscilla, seeing in her
an art-sensitive companion to ease his loneliness. She sent him a picture
of herself, adding, "It doesn't show that I have false teeth, mostly, and
arthritis in both thumbs. I guess you got the message when we talked:
I'm not coming to New York. It's useless for you to be 'interested' in
me, for any reason. In fact, I'd rather you didn't call again. The reason
I was so cordial at the beginning is that I thought you were my nephew."[9]

Cancer had struck Priscilla; she bravely called it "limiting health
factors, a euphemism I just thought of and will be careful to employ
about myself." She added, "Bobbie B. [Berkelman] said the artist can't
participate in life like other people. You have *The Dream Awake,* and
a long list of 'works.' I have two children I'm proud of, and who are
willing and able to communicate with me. I don't feel angry any more
that I didn't turn out to be a recognizable artist. Medication does
wonders. I feel better than I have for years, and I am lucky in my job."

Owen often called Priscilla at two in the morning or later. Her
daughter Sarah reported that her mother "was not only furious, but
frightened. Though she asked him to stop calling, he continued. He
would call and whine and complain about how miserable, lonely, and
misunderstood he was, how he felt victimized by things, how he was
financially bad off. My mother never said if she thought him drunk
during the calls, but she stated he seemed 'deranged,' childish, pouting,

sulky, and disagreeable. She was afraid that now that she was a widow [since 1964] with a small inheritance and a good job, Owen had designs either on her or on her money."[10]

Although Priscilla threatened to change her telephone number, she did not. Finally she wrote him, "Perhaps you've forgotten that technically, I'm still a cancer patient. For that reason and others, I am returning books, pin, and everything else that I have left. I have discarded the many letters years ago. I don't care what you do with mine. But I am asking you to return my Delta Sigma Rho pin [National Debate Society]. I gave you top billing on the *Garnet* editorial staff. I didn't want to; but you asked. Now I'm asking you to be generous. There's no point in your calling anymore, is there? I'm not the person you remember. I couldn't be if I tried."[11]

Owen did not find her pin. Priscilla thought he might have "sold" it. From Owen came surrender and apology: "At your wish I will not write or call you again. Perhaps Edith will call you when I die. I have not shown her your letter. I never meant to hurt you." She died March 27, 1983, three months before Owen, who possibly never knew of the demise "of the one who lov'd not wisely but too well."

But he did learn of the death of another beloved, St. Clair Christmas. Although their friendship had continued after Owen moved from Washington, D.C., St. Clair had taken Sandra Bowie as his fiancée, leaving a jealous Owen. Then suddenly on May 8, 1979, St. Clair died. The next Friday, Owen attended his memorial at Howard.

In November 1979, Owen finally reached retirement age, adding a welcome annuity of $5,545. With his disability pension from Social Security and his sister's pension, they managed with Edith's squirreling away any spare dollars. Like a married couple, Owen and Edith quarreled over money. When Edith tried to budget him, he would pull a print or a drawing from the closet and sell it, often at a giveaway price. When inebriated, he would give away signed first editions of Cullen, Fauset, Hurston, and Hughes, books and art. In the closet next to her bed Edith began to hide her books and paintings so he would not take them.

Mercie Hinton witnessed it all: "If someone came to the house Edith didn't like or trust, or saw them take something that she had not given them permission to take, she would tell them, 'Get out.' She was so forceful and had such a way, they would leave. Owen resented her for that. Sometimes, he would scream and yell for things, and she would be in her room and ignore him. The arguments they had were the ones that any two people whose lives revolve around one another sometimes have; it does not drive them apart because they are arguments of love. They both knew what would irritate the other."[12]

Edith weakened and had begun to make signs that she was approaching the end of her life. Once a meticulous and beautiful dresser, she had stopped caring. Once she had vigorously clipped items from three newspapers and several magazines for the Harold Jackman–Countee Cullen Memorial Collection; now the papers piled up in neglect. She gathered the letters Kenneth had written in college and furtively gave them to a friend for safekeeping because Owen might be jealous to know they had gone.

Between September 1981 and January 1983, she suffered three strokes. After two months' convalescence from her first stroke, Edith returned to the penthouse and resumed her guardianship and the combat it entailed. Her doctor warned her that she worried too much about Owen. She would not improve unless she moved out; if she did, she would live longer.

After a visit to the Dodsons, actress Carolyn Stewart, Owen's long-time friend, remarked that "Edith had the pain of a wife who has been beaten but when company comes, she pretends all is well." (No testimony has come to me that Owen physically struck Edith or any human being.) Nonetheless, her friends feared that the emotional beatings might stop her weak heart. To remove Owen from the combat, Ted Shine invited his old teacher to lecture at A&M College in Prairie View, Texas. The ruse worked, and on Armistice Day, Owen flew to Houston.

Owen seemed relieved to have escaped; he loved and respected Ted, wished to please him, and so he drank little, a glass of wine Ted might give him at night. At Ted's Friday-night party in his honor, Owen remained chatty and sober. On Tuesday, he met the drama majors. One, Teri Spivey, recalled, "Mr. Dodson was rolled into the theater in a wheelchair, and he looked like a living archive. The most vivid moment was when Dr. Shine introduced him. Dr. Shine is a very passive guy, doesn't show too much emotion, but when he introduced Mr. Dodson, he started crying. I said to myself, 'My God, this man must really be a symbol of something.' Then he read his work and the work was him, every little word, just like living history!"[13]

On Wednesday he met the English majors and read poetry. Then

Edith called. Yes, she was all right, but could he come back home? Owen canceled plans, and the next day Ted drove him to Houston. Before his flight, they lunched with Carlton Molette. When Owen rolled into the scene designer's office he saw the rendering of his production of *Long Day's Journey into Night* hanging on the wall and said, "I want that." Carlton started making excuses. Owen said, "I've been wanting that for a long time, now climb up there and get it down," and Molette did.[14] Before boarding the plane, Dodson persuaded Ted to buy several bottles of liquor "to take back to New York friends." That evening Shine called to see if Owen had arrived safely; the voice on the phone was by then blurred beyond recognition. Edith had her brother back.

Christmas for the Dodsons meant an elaborate dinner, but in 1981 the conspiracy of friends overrode Owen's objections (Edith was pleased), and Christmas dinner moved to the Hatch-Billops loft. Owen, in a pout, drank. With each refill of vodka and tonic, the conspirators reduced the liquor to barely a drop. Owen perceived their strategy, and like a miner panning an anemic vein, washed down one vodka after another. At last, when the table had been laden with victuals, Camille offered to help him out of the deep armchair, but the quicksand of his pout pulled him down. After coaxing and cajoling, Camille abandoned him for her own meal. Then others wheedled and pleaded. From the top of his eyes, he glowered and glared, so the guests shrugged and turned to their turkey. Edith rose quietly, filled his plate, and carried it to him. Embarrassed by her devotion, Camille brought him a tray, from which he ate.

After dessert and coffee, the hosts bundled Dodson into his coat and maneuvered him onto his crutches and out into the street, where they huddled against the north wind while a friend coaxed his old Plymouth to start. At last, creaking with ice and snow, the car pulled up to the curb. Edith slipped into the backseat while the entourage, pushing and shoving, hustled Owen into the car, slamming the door lest he fall back out. At that moment, Camille saw Owen's shoe lying in the snow. As the car pulled away, she managed to chuck his oxford into the backseat.

Before Christmas came again, in the last week of September 1982, in and out of intensive care three times with a seventy-three-year-old heart, Edith suffered her second stroke. Then in mid-November, so that she might come home for Thanksgiving, Owen hired a part-time nurse. At home, Edith walked about, her steps more and more decrepit. Sometimes she poised on one side of her room, holding onto the bed, then would scurry to get to her bureau before she fell. One day, as Mercie watched, she leaned against the desk and then toppled over. She said, "I'm all right, I'm all right." When he tried to help her, she swatted at him. She fought being helpless, even more than Owen had. She had been the eyes and ears for the house. Her stroke had affected one side of her brain, but she tried to appear more mobile than he did. Her taking care of him gave her validity—someone was worse off than she was.

Owen still attended the theater and offered criticism ever more acerbic: "Liv Ullmann in *Ghosts* acted as if she were Oswald's sweetheart instead of his mother, and Pastor Manders could only have been loved by a dog." He found Vinnette Carroll's *Your Arms Too Short to Box with God* "a noisy and shrill affair. Everyone had a mike. The gospel singing would have Jesus and His Father joking and slapping 'five.' " He himself began a new novel, *Parthenia MacBrown,* which opened with a "hilarious Tom Thumb wedding and ends with a crash of greed and disaster."

Having been denied his own Christmas in 1981, he decreed that the obligatory dinner would be held in the penthouse for 1982. Edith pleaded with him but finally acquiesced. Owen hired two boys to help. He invited a dozen guests, among them Helen Johnson. She recalled, "They had put chairs and two card tables in the hallway in front of the elevators to accommodate us all—fancy and elaborate, linen napkins and crystal. Edith had positioned herself in the doorway so she could look right out into the hall. Owen asked me to get him a drink. I felt terrible because I didn't want to fix Owen a drink, but I knew he would raise hell if I didn't. I went to the kitchen and made a small and watery one, and Edith said, 'I can't take any more.' It was a sense of resolution. She said, 'I have had all of this that I can take. I can't take any more.' Then she went on to say something about the drink. I didn't stay for dinner."[15]

The early hours had been fun. Owen read his poems from *Life in the Streets.* Then Edith became very weak and retired back into her bedroom, donned her nightgown and bathrobe and emerged to sit in the hall, waiting for everyone to be out so she could double lock the door. A sad way to end Christmas Day.

Edith would threaten, "I can move out and live in a room by myself," but she stopped talking about it after Owen returned from Texas. On January 4, Edith had an appointment with Dr. Edwards, but instead that morning the paramedics answered her emergency call. When they brought her into intensive care at New York Hospital, she looked at the young nurse, smiled, and said, "We made it, didn't we? We made it." She died at 5:19 P.M. of "natural causes."[16]

Owen placed a notice in the *New York Times:* "Dodson, Edith Kate. Beloved sister of Owen Dodson, died Jan. 4. She was a counselor and spiritual guide to many youths in her day, and a beloved brother to me, Owen Dodson."

"Beloved brother" echoed the lines he wrote for her birthday in 1940: "Be that brother in your sisterhood / Load my arms with memories."

At nine in the morning after her death, Owen, cold sober, dressed to meet with undertaker James McManus. Edith had left papers for the cemetery plot, but no will. She had wished to be cremated, and Owen chose one of the most expensive urns for her ashes—a gold-leaf or gold-painted urn.[17] About ten-thirty or eleven in the morning, cousins Doris and Edna Wilson arrived from Brooklyn. They were shocked at his decision to cremate—no Dodson had ever chosen fire over earth. The funeral director left to take care of business. About this time Owen began drinking and kept it up for four or five days, getting worse and worse; he wouldn't eat. Friends made the memorial arrangements—the Community Church of New York on January 18 at 5:30 P.M., so those who worked or lived out of town might attend.

The day of Edith's memorial, Owen phoned Mercie Hinton to make sure he was coming. When Mercie arrived, Owen had stopped drinking. While dressing, he called out, "Edith, we got to hurry, chile, we got to hurry. We have got to go." Mercie remained silent. He couldn't bring himself to say, "Edith is dead."

January 18 was one of the most bitterly cold days of the year, but 200 people attended. The organ played Handel, Bach, and Franck. Claire Leyba, Roscoe Lee Browne, and Owen read. Everyone watched to see how Owen would handle it. (Two days before, Owen had met with a friend, Sallee Hardy, and directed her about the bookshelves to find the quotations he needed.) At the service, he read with a young, resonant, clear voice, determined to bid his sister good-bye as she would have wished it, reading "Sorrow Is the Only Faithful One." He said, "I could not cry. She was my eternity."

He made no attempt to join the mourners at the reception in the church art gallery. Nor were the relatives invited to his home. Several close friends offered to accompany him; he refused them all and returned alone. That night he drank, and in all likelihood talked with Kenneth and Edith.

Into her funeral program Owen inserted this poem:

> There is a land of living and a
> land of the dead and the bridge is love
> The only survival, the only meaning.
> —In memory of Edith Kate Dodson

30

The Good-bye, 1983

The gossip ran that, with Edith dead, Owen did not have long to live. "The Vultures," as Owen named them, hovered, some perched on the casements, and a greedy one now and then swooped in to carry off a ring, a book, or even an etching. A small cadre of guardians sporadically shooed them off. Owen then sought a live-in companion—his first choice, Mercie Hinton, who recalled, "I said to myself, 'I am going to try and take care of him.' It worked for a while. I had my own apartment, so he gave me a key to his, and I would get up in the morning and dress two hours before I had to go to work, dress Owen, feed him, and get him ready for his day; then I would go to work. I would stop by, go shopping, then fix his dinner and then go home. This got so exhausting that I moved my clothes up to Owen's and would only go home on weekends to pick up my mail. I collapsed one day and called my friend Phillip and asked him to come and get me."[1]

Al Duckett appeared to be the companion Owen needed—black, a journalist, a childhood friend from Brooklyn. Duckett moved into Edith's room. To summon Duckett from across the hall, Owen would ring a bell beside his bed. One day, Al did not respond. Owen called and Duckett replied that he was eating. Owen told him to stop eating and come at once! He had been drinking, so Al cleared out all the bottles from under Owen's bed and hid the liquor. Enraged, Owen called the police and had Al evicted.

To entice new visitors and to woo old acquaintances, Owen posted rewards: upon his death, the loyal would inherit an Aaron Douglas print, or a Barthé sculpture, or perhaps the love letters of W. H. Auden (none ever found), or maybe his Austrian music box, which he verbally willed to the sons and daughters of several friends. He toyed with the greedy and the selfish, testing them. One man came to cut Owen's toenails, and all the time he snipped away, he spoke of how much he loved this painting and that vase.

If Owen tempted the demons, he rewarded the angels by bestowing books and prints upon them. Vivian Robinson, the president of Audelco, a black organization in Harlem dedicated to the preservation of its theater history, didn't visit him often because she didn't want him to think his gifts were the reason she came to see him. A couple of times when he offered her treasures, she told him, "I can't take it now. I'll get it next time." One day, he piled up all the books he wanted to give her. But Owen was drunk, so Vivian left them.

His last call to her was very late at night; he was a little incoherent. Vivian, tired, may have had an edge to her voice. Owen again insisted he had books to give her, and why didn't she come get them? She replied that she would when she had someone to help her. He responded, "My sister is dead, you know." Vivian answered, "I know." He kept repeating, "My sister is dead," and Vivian didn't know what to say. Finally, he almost screamed at her, "My sister is dead, you know!"

No day passed without evidence of his loneliness. Some nights Owen called Bruce Nugent, an artist of the Harlem Renaissance who was then living in Hoboken, New Jersey. Bruce was surprised because "we weren't close enough to have grown apart. We hadn't been in touch, but Owen almost broke down and cried, saying he needed friends."[2]

He did. Hinton stopped by one day, and there was an awful smell in the house. Owen was preparing a chicken. Hinton told him "That chicken is spoiled! Can't you smell it?" Dodson responded: "Are you sure?" Hinton threw the chicken out.

Owen's friend from Navy days, Sol Gordon, summoned a young man he had met in a mental-health workshop in Kansas. He judged Patrick Trujillo to be someone who could appreciate Owen and share his art experiences, someone who could cook and tidy up the house, someone youthful enough to be attractive but mature enough to avoid Owen's advances. Sol told Patrick he would pay his fare from Wichita, Kansas. If Owen liked him, he could make whatever arrangements from there on. To be with Owen did not mean to have sexual contact. On Wednesday, February 9, Trujillo, a slightly balding man in his twenties, flew to the Big Apple:

> I rang the bell, not knowing him or his surroundings. I heard him yell, "Come in." Owen was sitting on his red sofa. He said, "I know you have been traveling and must be tired, would you like a glass of champagne?" This was my first introduction. He said that there was champagne in the snow on the balcony. I brought in a bottle, and he opened it and poured us both a glass. (Sol had indicated that Owen had an alcohol problem.) We finished the bottle, and Owen was pretty drunk because he had already been drinking when I got there. I had to guide him back to his bed. He wanted to open another bottle and I said no, we had to be up early the next day and make our arrangements. Because I was a stranger he accepted that. I spent a week with Owen, a sort of trial. Owen was enthusiastic. I told him that I wished to return to Wichita and consider the job.

Trujillo called and said he was coming, but he did not say he was bringing two cats, one pregnant. When Owen awoke one morning, he thought he was having the d.t.'s — the pregnant cat had littered eight.[3] Later someone explained that Owen hated cats. In three days, an ad in the *Village Voice* had whisked those tabbies away.

Trujillo slept in a large walk-in closet behind Owen's bedroom. Owen wasn't using his urinal (which he didn't like), but they never discussed the problem. Each morning Patrick made breakfast and changed the sheets. Edith's room remained locked and Owen rarely entered it until his favorite cousin, Doris Jeffrey, came to help clear it. Entering Edith's room with a little more confidence, he told Jeffrey, "I can't break down, and I can't let go, because if I do, I will be a mess and won't be able to stop."

Without Edith to interdict the porters, Owen wrote twenty-five- and forty-five-dollar checks to Ben Miller, the liquor store around the corner. He would order three bottles and hide one or two. Patrick had no authority to stop him, but Owen did begin to eat again — chicken and vegetables — and Patrick saw to it that he took the medicine to inhibit his nosebleeds and to deter his fainting spells.

On a Sunday afternoon in late February, Opera Ebony presented a Black Heritage Concert to honor the songs and arias of black composers, playing thirty minutes of *Til Victory Is Won,* even reprinting the lyrics of the Harriet Tubman scene; however, they failed to send Owen tickets or to credit him with the libretto. Whereas once he had viewed human foibles with ironic good humor, now he raged. He felt that to omit him from the program was callousness unto barbarism.

Owen invited Trujillo to see *Porgy and Bess* at Radio City Music Hall. They dressed and rolled the wheelchair into the elevator. Trujillo parked Owen on the sidewalk while he hailed a cab. When the driver saw a cripple, he didn't want to take them, but Trujillo hurried Owen into the seat. The wheelchair had to be collapsed and placed in the trunk. The cabbie was shouting, "Hurry up, hurry up. Get in or get out!"

When they arrived at the theater, before Owen could get completely out, the driver started to ease away. Trujillo asked him, "Why don't you calm down? Take it easy—you see this man is handicapped." Owen began cursing the driver, "You're nobody; you're a fucking dog, you're nobody." He then gave him a nickel tip. In a foul mood, and partially intoxicated, Dodson began yelling in the crowded lobby for people to move out of the way. (He had learned that his wheelchair gave him license to jump lines, but public abuse was never his style.) Trujillo warned Owen that if he didn't stop yelling, he was going to park the wheelchair and leave. Once inside, Owen found the production frantic, "with so many mikes he thought the walls would crash in."

"Spring will spring me back," he once wrote in a letter, and indeed it did. He completed four chapters on his new novel; he announced he was beginning a song cycle for Edith, and he sent off three poems to Joe Weixlmann at *Black American Literature Forum.*[4]

On April 8, the Howard chapter of Phi Beta Kappa, which Dodson had helped found, celebrated its thirtieth anniversary. As early as February they had sent his invitation, but the fraternity was unwilling or unable to pay for a traveling companion. Owen could have met the expense but refused. Such slights, intended or imagined, caused him pain and perseveration about how Howard had neglected him and his work; nonetheless, he was possibly prepared to forgive everything if Howard awarded him a doctorate. (Beverly Kelch did submit the request that Owen receive the honorary degree.[5]) To help his case along, he phoned Michael R. Winston, director of the Moorland-Spingarn Research Center, to come to New York because he intended to deposit all his letters and memorabilia at Howard. (He had made the same promise in 1974 and then had withdrawn it.)

When Winston arrived, Owen greeted him from bed, treating Winston formally, as he always had. Owen pointed to the row of orange letter boxes beneath his desk and told him, "Pack up all these things and take them." When the task was completed and Winston prepared to depart, Owen said, "No, don't take them now. I have to go through these things one more time. I'll be back in touch with you. Will you have a glass of sherry? There's a bottle in the refrigerator."[6] He was not drunk.

With the same vacillation and procrastination, Owen denied his friends and heirs a legal will. Over the years he had written, in longhand and on legal-size yellow paper, several wills. Then he would make changes of executor, or change the beneficiary of his library, or his art. On June 8, under Owen's supervision, Trujillo made an apartment inventory. He tallied the paintings, the furniture, and so on. Then Owen dictated his will to Patrick, who took it down in longhand. They carried it to the bank, but they wouldn't notarize it. Owen tried a second bank; no luck. He went back to the house and took out his booze. He signed his last will and testament but it was unwitnessed by a notary.

On the day before Owen's death, a Sunday afternoon, Jerry Waters, working on a Ph.D. at Yale, dropped by with Michael Cummings, an artist. Trujillo let them in, and they "eyeballed" the living-room art and artifacts until Owen, assisted by Trujillo, shuffled in and eased himself onto the couch.

Seeing that Waters admired Richmond Barthé's sculpture "The Rugcutters," Owen told the story of how he bought it for $300 when Barthé was heavily into alcohol and low on money. Within a year, Barthé came to the realization that "The Rugcutters" was one of his more significant pieces. Owen had told him that he would never sell it back, but he would lend it. (Owen had two copies cast from a mold; he gave one to Edith, but he kept the original.)[7] Cummings noticed that Owen dwelt on what would happen to his collection after he died. He would have liked to give his things to Howard, but. . . .[8] He told his guests that Edith had kept flowers on the balcony; he used the tense that she "was going to be doing it," overlapping the past and present. To Cummings, "he didn't look like a sick man. He did seem large and overweight and seemed very full. He did have trouble walking. We were there about two hours, and he sat in one position; he held his cane throughout our stay. He had a suit on, and appeared very formal. He enjoyed gossiping. His voice rose and fell in volume, and he may have had a slight breathing problem. He would pause briefly, and then go on like a runner who wanted to entertain and who seemed comfortable in that role of telling us about the literary history. His words were unslurred and no scent of alcohol."

During the early-morning hours of June 21, Owen began calling friends. He was thought to be delirious or motivated by heavy drinking. Over and over, he pleaded, "Help me, chile, help me. Come now; not later, now. I need you now."[9]

The next morning, the first day of summer, Owen had an appointment with Richard Barnes, an attorney who was to clear Edith's estate and to write Owen's own will. Before Trujillo rose to make breakfast, Owen made at least two phone calls, one at six o'clock to his cousin Edna. (Her daughter Doris had left for Barbados and had asked Owen "to check on Mama every day.") Mrs. Wilson said, "Owen, why are you calling me so early?" He said, "I promised Doris I would. Are you all right?" "Yes," she said, "but I'm sleepy," and they both laughed it off.[10] His second call went to Mercie Hinton, who wasn't picking up, so Owen left his last message on the tape: "Hello, this is Owen. Hope you have a nice day in the rain." (He was piqued because Hinton hadn't come to see him lately.)

After Trujillo had prepared breakfast, he came to awaken Owen, who *had* been drinking heavily through the night, and he sat him up in bed and tried to feed him—toast, eggs, juice with seltzer. Owen didn't eat at all that morning. He kept saying, "I don't need you, I don't need any of these people around here. Just leave me alone." Trujillo left his food with him and returned to the kitchen to clean up the dishes.

Said Trujillo: "When I checked on him, the food was knocked over. I picked it up and cleaned it up, and took the dishes to the kitchen to be washed up. When I came back in, I found him on the floor next to the bed with his face down. I turned him over. He was dead. He had wedged himself between the bed and the table. It happened very quickly. I don't know if he had been trying to get out, or had rolled over and ended there."[11]

Trujillo called the paramedics, who, after trying to resuscitate Dodson, pronounced him dead. Trujillo called the coroner. The police came. They took some of his jewelry for safekeeping, but they did leave a list that was given to the attorney. Trujillo reported that "the coroner came in. She pulled the sheet that was covering Owen's face and said to whomever she was with, 'There are two ways we can go with this: we can call it a fatty liver or call it a heart attack.' There was no close examination."

The abruptness of Owen's death, and his cremation two days later, echoed like gunshots in a field of birds; sudden wheeling cries filled the sky. How had he died? Why had there been no funeral? Who was this man Patrick Trujillo? Both Hinton and Mrs. Wilson found it difficult to believe Owen had spoken that morning at six and was dead at ten. Some of Owen's friends whispered murder.

The police wanted Trujillo to leave the apartment. He told them, " 'No, you can't evict me! This man brought me here and employed me to work for him.' If they could have, they would have evicted me, but legally, they couldn't." McManus, the undertaker across the hall, came and dragged Owen's corpse off the bed and down onto the floor and into the black bag and wheeled him out. A day later he was cremated.

The legal authority of the blood-related cousins, Doris Jeffrey and Edna Wilson (who had been in contact with Owen and Edith over the years), was superseded by a closer blood tie, Virginia Staten, Nat, Jr.'s daughter. As a child, Mrs. Staten had known Owen but had not spoken with him in years. She had ordered Owen's cremation, which ignited the flames of rumor and gossip: How could the great funerary poet, who had loved the ritual of open coffins, within twenty-four hours of his passing have been cremated . . . and on the very day that he had planned to go to the lawyer to write his will. Again, some whispered of foul play.

Trujillo reported that Owen must have been up all that night. He had heard the TV going and said that "I would go in and check on him and he would say, 'I'm OK, just leave me, leave me and go to your room.' I thought that he was up because of the anxiety of having to go to the attorney the next day."

As the newcomer on the scene, Trujillo found himself spinning:

I've said this before and I don't feel bad about saying it. What if I had actually killed Owen, murdered Owen? It is a possibility, that kind of thing does happen. I am confident and glad in my mind that that didn't happen, but the point is, why didn't they check into the cause more closely than they did? Consequently, we don't know why he died, or if he had a heart attack. The coroner came in and signed the death certificate and that was that. I asked if they weren't going to do more than that, and she said, "Look, this happens to these people all the time." Maybe if she smelled the alcohol and the urine she could make a professional judgment. We don't know how he died, and we will never know, and that does not rest easy with me, knowing that. The whole thing was hard on me, and I lost a lot of weight. I couldn't just walk out. It meant more than that.[12]

As executor, Mrs. Staten gave Trujillo $150 to pack the contents of the house. With no crates or padding, he found it impossible. He claimed the $150 was for him to stay there and make certain the movers did their job. The movers packed the boxes unmarked, making an inventory impossible. The result: The artifacts of Edith's and Owen's life ended up on the concrete floor of a small cement-block warehouse in Brooklyn. The red-velvet couch and chairs, the carousel horses, General Howard's piano, lamps, bookcases, cartons of first editions, the brass beds, the oak desks, the paintings: all ended in a huge pile on the warehouse's damp, cold floor.

Soon accusations of pilfering and theft flew from mouth to ear. Where was the watch that Owen's father had left him? (It had been stolen several months before.) Where were the old coins that Edith kept in her room? (Doris had taken them for safekeeping.) Where was the Austrian music box? What happened to Owen's Phi Beta Kappa pin? His other jewelry? The manuscript for his new novel? His diaries and daybooks? No doubt demons snatched them.

On June 22 at the Trinity Crematorium, Owen at his private funeral was reduced to ash. Certainly, it offered none of the ceremony he had relished. Perhaps he didn't want it—he never firmly avowed burial—but his funeral anecdotes suggest that he might have wished to make a grand exit. The obit headlines in the major dailies were his[13]—unlike the gentleman in the *Harlem Book of the Dead:*

> I prayed that on the day I died
> Nobody else prominent would be dead
> The obituary page was supposed to be all about me today

Florence Mills, the greatest, died on my day.
Look-a-here Lord,
I was a faithful servant
Over many a money year.[14]

Howard University held its memorial service, and Pres. James E. Cheek declared, "For decades the name Owen Dodson represented the highest standards and achievements in drama. We were fortunate to claim him as a professor of drama. We shared him with the wider community and indeed the world."[15]

A week later at the Community Church in New York, 400 people attended a celebration of his life."[16] The organist played the same Handel, Bach, and Franck music that Owen had chosen for Edith. Two former students, Graham Brown and Ted Shine, spoke of remembrances. David Amram played his flute; Ossie Davis and Ruby Dee recited from *The Confession Stone*. The Reverend Donald Harrington praised Owen for his poetry, plays, teaching, knowing famous people, and setting an "I can" example for the youth: "He was one of the last of the great figures of that flowering of black culture we remember as 'the Harlem Renaissance.' "[17] The absence of Owen's body suggested a closing performance at which the star did not appear for his curtain call.

Later, in Evergreen Cemetery in Brooklyn, on a beautiful, crisp fall day, the urns with Owen's and Edith's ashes were placed in the grave with Lillian. There is no stone.[18]

There Are No Tears

How still grief can be
Photographing what has been,
Developing it all at once.
We hold the pictures
And can't see.
There are no tears,
No trombone sounds.
His heart is quiet;
A grain of sand.
His beach is not afraid
of the ocean anymore.
—Owen Dodson

31

A Personal Memory

Life, most of the time, is a bitter hope that
everything will be all right. Hold me in your arms and
tell me everything will be all right. Marriage, death,
all those things. You are not making a decision; you
go into them and hope they'll be all right.
          —Owen Dodson to James V. Hatch, 1982

Owen never made a formal decision about dying. He provided no will, no lawyer, no witness. He just sweated into the bitter hope that it would turn out all right. His biography, too: We drifted into it one evening, my curiosity and his caution loosened by two glasses of champagne. A young playwright had invited us to a reading of his new play. The occasion lay two or three blocks from Owen's apartment.

When I called at the Dodson flat, Edith opened the door, waved me to bend down, and gave me a kiss on the lips. At sixty-eight, her face revealed two Ediths: The lower portion radiated sensuality, her skin clear and soft, her full lips graced with a hint of mustache—an attractive and desirable woman; the upper portion exposed her karma, that of a woman who balanced the budget of their retirement incomes, a vigilant who protected her brother's reputation against young hustlers, against Owen himself. Thin blue halos, like suns in eclipse, encircled the dark pupils of her eyes, eyes engulfed in soft fold upon soft fold of purple melancholy.

She patted my arm and pointed me toward Owen, who sat wrapped in his velvet cape with his embroidered cap, his steel crutches gleaming against the red-plush sofa. His mustache was neatly trimmed, and he touched his new spectacles, which made his eyes large and luminous.

"Chile, ain't these something? Don't they make me look like Dr.

Eckleburg from what's his name's novel? I think they're kinda wonderful, don't you? Makes me seem wide-eyed with wonderment."

He refused my offer to hail a taxi and committed himself to walk the three blocks. His neighborhood was not the best, and I sometimes worried that he was an easy mark for hoodlums. As he swung along, he spoke to a sullen man who supported himself against an iron grate of a window, and to a woman slumped in a doorway, guarding her shopping bags: "How ya doin'?" Whether surprised by the greeting from an elegant gentleman, or by the sudden reminder that they still had the use of their legs, these street souls responded, "Evenin'. How you?"

When we arrived, two steep flights of wooden stairs confronted us. No elevator. Owen handed me the crutches: "I'll pull myself up by the hand railing." And so we began our ascent, step by step by step, with me close behind, braced if he should fall. He remained strong in his arms and even his legs, but the metal ball-joints in his hips never worked properly, and he shunned the physical therapist.

I introduced Owen to the playwright, impressing upon him his good fortune—he had in his audience an artist who had written or directed hundreds of shows, and who had led many talented writers to the discovery of their own genius. However, the attention of this writer, as it must be in any nascent talent, was absorbed by his own womb's issue. We filed into the rows of steel chairs to witness a play that harbored a curious emotional power, somehow self-imprisoned in an improbable story of Vietnam veterans in a bar.

When the curtain came down, the writer invited us to comment. The actors spoke of their characters, the audience complained of confusion, and then Owen spoke: "This play is about love, the love of two men, one black and one white, who become as brothers in Vietnam. But once in America, they cannot find a way to express this love, physically or verbally, so they fight."

The mystery revealed! I looked to the writer to enjoy the revelation upon his face: none. He hadn't understood because the play had come from a place within him that he dared not yet know. I didn't know, either, until years later when I finally grasped Owen's poem "Prisoners."

Later, we crept along the dark street to his building. "Wanta come up for a drink?" The elevator reached the penthouse. Immediately before us, framed posters—an Alvin Ailey dance performance, a huge kenti-cloth exhibition. In Owen's twelve years' residence there, none was stolen or soiled with graffiti. Some guardian spirit hovered over the hall until the day he died; then, within hours, the posters came down "to protect them from theft."

Edith had gone to bed. Owen said, "There's a bottle of champagne on the terrace and glasses in the cabinet. Bring them to the living room. I want to read you a new poem." I found half a bottle that had been recorked with a tonic cap. I poured two glasses and settled into a deep chair. At that moment, when I asked Owen about his family, writing a biography had never crossed my mind.

He told of his mother's stroke and how he had bargained with God for his mother's life. Oh yes, he had his enemies and the chief one was God. Then he murmured, "When I die, I would like to leave one memorable line . . . like Keats and Auden."

"You have," I told him. "Sorrow is the only faithful one." I particularly liked the last lines:

> Sorrow has a song like a leech
> Crying because the sand's blood is dry
> And the stars reflected in the lake
> Are water for all their twinkling
> And bloodless for all their charm.
> I have blood, and a song.
> Sorrow is the only faithful one.

As I got ready to leave his apartment, I suggested that we tape some of his memories in case he would like to write his autobiography. He agreed, and over the next year, on Wednesday afternoons, we taped thirty hours, and I began to glimpse the roots of his anger—the bitter year of his retirement from Howard University, when he had sought work in white schools. Repeatedly his applications had been returned to him, stamped with invisible names. While they would add the young militants Larry Neal, Amiri Baraka, and Sonia Sanchez to their staffs, the universities felt no need for a fifty-six-year-old black humanist to direct one more production of *Hamlet*.

Owen's career walked the very edge of theater history. Had he directed Baldwin's *Blues for Mr. Charlie* on Broadway, or had he set his black *Hamlet* onto the stage at Elsinore, his professional life could easily have been akin to that of Lloyd Richards. But these likely unlikelihoods arose five years before *A Raisin in the Sun,* a critical five years for a black artist in American theater.

Somewhere in the process of our taping he realized that he would never write his own life, so we sweated into the bitter hope that I would write his biography. The next year, I left to teach in Taiwan. While there I thought of the questions I would ask Owen and Edith when I returned. In his last card to me he wrote: "Spring will spring me back." And at the end of the letter, his pen ran out of ink, but the point scratched on, etching the final dry words into the paper: "I will not break." But the Examiner slammed the book shut, flinging Owen's breakfast tray all over the quilt and rolling Owen's body onto the floor.

I drifted into this biography, hoping with a bitter hope that everything would be all right. Now, a decade after interviewing his relatives, his friends, and his detractors, and after reading his poems, stories, letters, and plays, I realize that from the cruel paradoxes of his life, Owen wrenched his bitter hope into a song of celebration:

> Be it resolved resolved resolved resolved:
> Oh let it be the wheel of resurrection
> Upturning blooming waters from their souls:
> Oh let them splash flat-vertical and high
> To arc a rainbow in that triumph time
> When startled angels graduate, cum laude,
> From adoration to the bright divine:
> The indescribable, the only All.
> Watch wisely for Jerusalem, my dears,
> And every bleeding lamb from Ararat.

Notes

Abbreviations

Individuals: ACR = Anne Cooke Reid; CC = Countee Cullen; CVV = Carl Van Vechten; EKD = Edith Katherine Dodson; GH = Gordon Heath; JB = James Butcher; JVH = James V. Hatch; KD = Kenneth Dodson; OVD = Owen Vincent Dodson; PH = Priscilla Heath; PR = Peggy Rieser; RP = Rosey Pool

Dodson's Major Publications: BATW = *Boy at the Window;* BL = *Bayou Legend;* CHEC = *Come Home Early, Child;* CS = *The Confession Stone;* DC = *Divine Comedy;* HBD = *Harlem Book of the Dead;* PLL = *Powerful Long Ladder;* TGB = *The Gossip Book* (unpublished); TVIW = *Til Victory Is Won*

Research Libraries and Individual Collections: AFC = American Film Committee; CAHI = College Archives, Hampton Institute; ARC = Amistad Research Center, Tulane University; CCHJMC = Countee Cullen–Harold Jackman Memorial Collection, Atlanta University; GEBC = General Education Board Collection, Rockefeller Archive Center; HBC = Hatch-Billops Collection; JWJC = James Weldon Johnson Collection, Beinecke Library, Yale University; MF = Michel Fabre; MSRC = Moorland-Spingarn Research Collection, Howard University; NHC = Naval Historical Center, Operational Archives Branch; RAC = Rockefeller Archive Center; RB = Roderick Bladel; RR = Rosemary Rieser; RSF = Rosenwald Fund, Fisk University; UOSL = University of Sussex Library
All quotations from Owen Dodson are from interviews with the author between 1981 and 1982, unless otherwise noted.

Chapter 1: From Boydton to Berriman

1. Nathaniel Dodson graduated in 1891 from Wayland Seminary, now Virginia Union University.

2. Founders respectively of Tuskegee Institute, Tuskegee, Ala., and North Carolina College (North Carolina Central University), Durham, N.C.

3. Unsigned, "A Journalist," *The Crisis* 8 (September 1914): 222–23. Literacy was so esteemed that families often boasted that their uncle or cousin was the "fourth man to learn to read and write in our county."

4. Arthur P. Davis to JVH, July 25, 1985, Washington, D.C.

5. Blacks from Virginia, the Carolinas, and Georgia migrated north in such numbers that they became the majority of migrant African-Americans in New York.

6. Unsigned, *The Colored American Magazine* 2 (November 1900): 42.

7. Clay Lancaster, *Old Brooklyn Heights, New York's First Suburb* (New York: Dover Publications, Inc., 1979): 20. The Pierrepont Hotel was demolished; the Bossert, now a welfare hotel, stands in its place.

8. Breukelen had been granted its patent from the Dutch in 1646. By 1776, one-third of its population was black, "probably the highest proportion of slaves to total population of any county" in the North. Following the 1827 emancipation of New York slaves, Blacks flourished in and around Weeksville until the 1870s, when European immigrant labor flooded Brooklyn. Rita Seiden Miller, *Brooklyn USA* (New York: Brooklyn College Press, 1979): 9–14.

9. Following Appomattox, armies of Yankee schoolteachers invaded the South with missions to "establish higher institutions of learning for the freedmen when the majority of the emancipated millions knew nothing of the elementary subjects of learning." They built Howard, Hampton, Dillard, and Spelman. Miles Mark Fisher, *Virginia Union University and Some of Her Achievements* (Richmond, Va.: Virginia Union University, 1924).

10. "A Journalist": 222–23.

11. By 1920 nearly 500 "race" periodicals, many of them religious, nearly all weeklies, were distributed by mail. Illiteracy among Negroes had decreased from 70 percent in 1880 to 51 percent in 1890. Then it dropped to 44.5 percent by 1900 and to 30.4 percent by 1910. Press organizations were segregated. Frederick G. Detweiler, *The Negro Press in the United States* (Chicago and London: University of Chicago Press, 1922).

12. Frank Lincoln Mather, ed., *Who's Who of the Colored Race* (Chicago: Memento Edition, Half-Century Anniversary of Negro Freedom in U.S., 1915): 92–93. As chairman of the Executive Committee of the National Negro Press Association, Dodson supervised contacts with journalists in thirty-eight states and three foreign countries. Booker T. Washington wrote Dodson: "All of us owe you a great debt of gratitude. We appreciate it." Washington to Dodson, January 1910, HBC.

13. Nathaniel Dodson to Sarah Goode, February 12, 1896, HBC.

14. Manhattanites ridiculed the borough. Actress Ellen Terry wrote to

Henry Irving, "Brooklyn is as sure a laugh in New York as a mother-in-law in a London music hall."

15. Italians worked in construction; Jews owned and operated small businesses; Blacks worked in service jobs—mail clerks, porters, messengers, domestics (4 percent were professionals). Mothers and housewives did not work outside the home.

16. Edith knew little about her grandparents: "My mother's father was Alan Goode. He married at least twice—two sets of children. Mama was a product of the second set. My mother had a brother, Edward, and a sister, Mary, who was two years younger; both moved to New York, but only Aunt Mary, a rock of Gibraltar, kept in close touch." EKD to JVH, September 9, 1981, New York.

17. Edith did not concur with Owen's portrait: "They say that my father liked women. One time, my father was getting ready to go out and my mother decided that she was going, too. When my mother was all dressed to go she said to him, 'How do you feel, Mr. Dodson?' It was quite a dramatic moment." EKD to JVH, September 9, 1981, New York.

Chapter 2: 309 Berriman

1. Irene Richardson Garret to JVH, March 7, 1985, New York.

2. Joseph Janovsky to JVH, February 13, 1985, New York.

3. Harold Lewis to JVH, July 1, 1985, New York.

4. Edna Wilson to JVH, December 15, 1986, New York.

5. CHEC: 23.

6. The Elder Samuel White was called in 1847 from Abyssinian Church in Manhattan to organize Concord.

7. EKD to JVH, September 9, 1981, New York. In 1946, Richard Wright wrote from Paris asking if Owen had any news about the "dozens" in Harlem (a contest of verbal insults). Owen responded that he was not privy to the "dozens," but he referred Wright's request to Ira De A. Reid, an eminent sociologist.

8. Rev. Harten became the character S. Robert Blanton, the minister in his novel *Boy at the Window*.

9. Ruth Zwick to JVH, September 9, 1985, New York.

10. Recalled Owen: "My father taught us that we can't have clean socks every day because we can't afford that, so at night, instead of rolling your socks up, you open them and shake them and let the air get to them. I thought that was a wonderful little thing."

11. Edith Dodson and her cousins Edna Wilson and Virginia Staten designated Nat, Jr., as "a black sheep."

12. Cyril Bryan to JVH, March 2, 1985, New York.

13. Edith's account of the family's embarrassment is described in Owen's first novel, *Boy at the Window.* How bad was the Dodsons' "black sheep?" A relative opined that for the Dodsons, Nat, Jr., "was something in the closet, but today, he wouldn't have been in the closet." Ruby Jewell to JVH, July 7, 1984, Atlanta, Ga.

14. EKD to JVH, September 9, 1981, New York.

15. Leftwich may have been the child of an unwed mother in Boydton, Virginia. She appears in CHEC as the mean-spirited Lucy Horwitz.

16. From this maternal fountain flowed a series of "fictional" mothers and sons. The pattern evolved that the mother must suffer and die, while the son climbs on up the powerful long ladder to either gratitude and guilt, or crucifixion.

17. HBD: 8.

18. EKD to JVH, September 9, 1981, New York.

19. Untitled, HBD: 6.

Chapter 3: Thomas Jefferson High

1. Elias Lieberman, "Letter to the graduates of 1932," *Vista,* Thomas Jefferson High School annual. To an astonishing degree, he and a dedicated faculty created a generation of New York professionals.

2. The classes of '28 and '29 contributed money for an artist who labored two years to paint four panels on the steel fire curtain, fifty or sixty feet across—the muses in their togas—the classical enlightenment of Brownsville.

3. A generation later, Joseph Papp, founder of the New York Shakespeare Public Theatre, recalled how a black Caribbean mentor, Eulalie Spence, had laundered his tongue of his Brooklyn accent.

4. OVD to James Weldon Johnson, April 19, 1932, series 1, folder 129, JWJC.

5. James Weldon Johnson to OVD, April 21, 1932, series 1, folder 129, JWJC.

6. Cumulative grade averages, used for college entrance, came out much lower than they do today. Sylvia [Janovsky] Heimbach ('28) had the highest average in her class, and it was only a 91. Owen's cumulative average at graduation was 76.85. As the quality of education has declined, grade averages have inflated.

7. Henry Folger Cleaveland to JVH, September 23, 1984, New York.

8. OVD to Michael Fried, December 18, 1974, carbon HBC. Here is the voice of a Peter Pan who wished never to grow up. Owen's second-favorite form of address to friends was "dear heart." His favorite: "chile."

9. Owen emphasized that "the love that Milton and I had for each

other was not an abnormal love, but just the love of two boys who helped each other." "Abnormal" reflects his public persona.

10. Novel notes for BATW, Dodson files, JWJC.

11. GH to JVH, June 7, 1985, Paris, France.

12. Theodore Henry Shackelford, "The Three Hundred and Sixty-Eighth Infantry," *My Country and Other Poems* (Philadelphia: Press of I. W. Klopp Co., 1916–18): 34.

13. GH to Camille Billops, February 18, 1975, New York.

14. The City College of New York, established in 1847 as a tuition-free college, educated and trained the professional class that would administer New York City for four generations. From this school eight Nobel Prize winners graduated. (Gov. Nelson Rockefeller destroyed the free-tuition policy when the city threatened bankruptcy in 1976.)

Chapter 4: Here's to Bates

1. Under his directorship, 15,000 children enjoyed summer camps.

2. "Elm tree / for I see you / an oriental fan / against the blue." Owen's poem "Elm at Night in Maine" won the state poetry contest in 1936.

3. Rev. Oren Burbank Cheney had "recorded a vow in heaven" to build a Maine State Seminary. Himself a graduate of Dartmouth, he launched an institution in 1863 where "piety and intellect would not be separated" — the first coeducational college in New England, the second in the nation. Boston banker Benjamin Bates donated $100,000, and Cheney christened the seminary Bates College.

4. Mary Mitchell, a millworker, received a scholarship from the governor to attend Bates and became the first woman in the United States to graduate from a four-year college. Bates's radical concept of open admissions caused this bit of apocryphal dialogue: "How many college students have they down at Bates seminary?" "Five and a nigger and a woman." Milton and Jane Lindholm to JVH, September 26, 1984, Lewiston, Maine.

5. OVD to family, November 1932, HBC.

6. "One time when I was was walking up the stairs in the dorm I saw a bed coming down and thought, somebody's out of a bed. I walked into my room and my bed was gone." Milton Lindholm to JVH, September 26, 1984, Lewiston, Maine.

7. Berkelman, a Phi Beta Kappa graduate, had received an M.A. at Yale. When queried why he never got his doctorate in his first love, Shakespeare, he lifted a line from Lyman Kittridge: "If I were to write a dissertation on Shakespeare, who in this world would be qualified to test me?"

8. Roger Fredland to JVH, September 1, 1984, HBC.

9. By 1933 Mussolini had made clear his wish to "civilize" Ethiopia and to avenge the defeat of the Italian army at Adowa. Owen's awareness of international politics, and Africa in particular, had developed as an intrinsic part of discovering his own blackness.

10. OVD to family, January 11, 1934, HBC.

11. Literary Workshop to OVD, October 29, 1934, HBC.

12. OVD to family, February 6, 1934, HBC.

13. Gray W. Adams to JVH, February 23, 1985, Newburyport, Mass.

14. Arnold Kenseth to JVH, September 28, 1984, Amherst, Mass.

15. Like Miss Haversham in *Great Expectations,* the widow Mrs. Daboll never wanted to meet her young charge, but when he graduated from Yale, Dodson asked to see her and she agreed. Her suite at the St. Regis Hotel was very, very rich, and she was an ancient woman in a brocade gown who spent her days assembling jigsaw puzzles.

16. After passing the bar exams at Boston University, Carter enlisted in the Air Force, becoming one of the black pilots trained at Tuskegee; he rose to commanding officer in the 618th Bomber Squadron.

17. "Edwin Arlington Robinson" TGB, n.d., typescript HBC. Robinson died April 6, 1935.

18. Forty-eight years later, Ciardi recalled "Owen's enthusiasm in discovering the Italian language and how Owen went about saying 'architettonicamente' over and over, punching the dentals and rolling out the vowels." John Ciardi to JVH, September 4, 1984, HBC.

19. One would recall whether one "kissed or anything." They didn't.

20. Although Owen never challenged Priscilla's superiority in scholarship, he found satisfaction fifteen years later when the alumni membership of the Bates College Chapter elected him for "distinguished scholarly accomplishment in the years following undergraduate and graduate work." His initiation paralleled that of Benjamin Mays, who was also chosen for membership by Phi Beta Kappa of Bates fifteen years after graduation.

21. William Swallow to JVH, October 10, 1984, New Canaan, Conn.

22. Priscilla Heath, "Farewell, Sweet Love," *Western Review* 17 (Summer 1953): 305–20.

23. Arnold Kenseth to JVH, September 28, 1984, Amherst, Mass. For a time Priscilla Heath busied herself as a caseworker in Manchester, then married a Rhodes Scholar from the class of '37. But over the years she and Owen continued an "on-again, off-again" literary courtship.

24. Benjamin E. Mays, *Born to Rebel* (New York: Charles Scribner's Sons, 1971): 60.

Chapter 5: Divine Comedy

1. Oliver Wendell Harrington was born in Valhalla, New York, in 1912. Harrington's cartoon character "Bootsie" appeared in the *Amsterdam News*

in 1936 and was soon syndicated in black newspapers across America. The pudgy, cigar-smoking, baldheaded Harlem dweller provoked the same laughter and understanding nod in black readers as did Hughes's Jesse B. Simple.

2. The street slang in Dodson's early plays *The Shining Town* and *Divine Comedy* was probably borrowed from Ollie's accounts.

3. ACR to JVH, February 4, 1984, Washington, D.C.

4. Owen was one of four Blacks in the Drama School: Fannin Belcher, writing his monumental doctorate on the history of the Negro on the American stage; Shirley Graham (Du Bois); Anne Cooke; and Owen, the only one willing to act.

5. *Gargoyles in Florida,* typescript, HBC.

6. Leo Hamalian and James V. Hatch, "The Shining Town," *The Roots of African American Drama* (Detroit: Wayne State University Press, 1991).

7. OVD to EKD and Lillian Dodson, February 27, 1937, HBC.

8. GEBC, folder 2418, series 1, box 240, RAC. The General Education Board, established by John D. Rockefeller in 1902, had as its central mission the training of Negro teachers for higher education. By 1930, the GEB had come to recognize the importance of encouraging the development of artistic talents as well. The first artists to receive aid included Warner Lawson, Katherine Dunham, Lois Mailou Jones, Anne Margaret Cooke, James W. Butcher, Oliver Harrington, and Owen Dodson. Raymond B. Fosdick, *Adventure in Giving: The Story of the General Education Board* (New York: Harper and Row, 1962). The GEB archives and the Rockefeller Foundation archives are both located in Pocantico Hills, North Tarrytown, N.Y.

9. Barthé (a self-labeled "Creole" artist) sculptured the heads of John Gielgud, Katharine Cornell, Laurence Olivier, Maurice Evans, Judith Anderson. His black portraits included Rose McClendon, Langston Hughes, Jimmy Daniels, and Paul Laurence Dunbar.

10. Roger Starr to OVD, March 17, 1938, HBC.

11. Born in London on August 18, 1901, Jackman, with an M.A. from Columbia University, taught social studies in Harlem. Handsome, with distinguished features and silver hair, he occasionally posed for Schenley whiskey ads. With his sister Ivie, Jackman dedicated his time, talent, and money to promotion of artists, encouraging Jean Toomer, Claude McKay, Langston Hughes, Countee Cullen, Eric Waldron, Zora Neale Hurston, Gwendolyn Bennett, Carlissa Scott, Esther Popel, Owen Dodson, and many others.

12. Oliver Harrington to JVH, November 1, 1985, Berlin, Germany. Although Owen at Yale enjoyed more sexual freedom than he had at Bates, he did not advertise his preference. When homosexuals became gay and proud in the seventies, Owen did not join them.

13. Frances Gunner was executive secretary of the colored branch of the Ashland Place YWCA.

14. One may take satisfaction that forty years later (1979), Lloyd Richards, appointed dean of the Yale Drama School, produced August Wilson's prizewinning plays.

15. Ms. Clark became the first woman at Yale to be allowed to do both a set and light design. *Divine Comedy* was her first production, which enabled her to join the designer's union, the beginning of a professional Broadway career that lasted thirty-five years.

16. OVD to Lillian Dodson, December 6, 1937, HBC. William Corrigan, who played Cyril, recalled "High platforms, fast scene changes, and many follow spots. One false step, one way or another, and you stepped into blackness." William Corrigan to JVH, April 6, 1986, New York.

17. Essie Robeson to OVD, April 5, 1939, HBC.

18. On April 17, 1917, Ridgley Torrence had initiated the movement toward authentic black theater with the production of *Three Plays for a Negro Theater,* and Owen hoped that his play might initiate a second black-theater coup.

Chapter 6: Garden of Time

1. ACR to JVH, February 4, 1984, Washington, D.C.

2. "I selected Franck's D Minor Symphony. When in the first movement the religious questioning theme brings in a lyrical note, probably one of the most profound and heartbreaking in any symphony I know, I noticed a huge black woman in a corner. She was so huge that her breasts touched her belly and she overflowed in her chair. Her hair was not combed and poked out—big tears were rolling down her face. She didn't bother to wipe them away; she just sat, immobile and sad, sad like her big twisted fingers and her old brown dress. Her eyes were half closed and although I knew she was not asleep, she was dreaming and the dreams made her cry." OVD to family, June 1938, HBC.

3. Ednah Bethea Blalock to JVH, January 4, 1986, Southern Pines, N.C.

4. JB to JVH, July 28, 1985, Washington, D.C.

5. Michael Yates to JVH, January 9, 1986, London, England.

6. Whether Owen's version of the initial meeting is factual, an elaboration on a second meeting, or a fabrication, there is no way to know.

7. For a splendid description of Cochrane and the production, see Gordon Heath's autobiography, where, in retrospect, Heath praised the Scots director.

8. KD to EKD, April 21, 1937, HBC.

9. OVD to EKD, April 21, 1939, HBC.

10. Oliver Harrington to JVH, November 1, 1985, Berlin, Germany.

11. Owen included the refrain in his first book of poetry, *Powerful Long Ladder*, under the title, "Circle One," and dedicated it to Gordon Heath.

12. Bone, "Garden of Time," *Variety,* May 19, 1938. The tragic-mulatto theme has ever pleased American public taste.

13. Shirley Lola Graham, eighteen years Owen's senior and with an M.F.A. from Oberlin, had found her way to Yale Drama School after teaching at Morgan State, directing the Federal Theatre Project in Chicago, and composing an opera (*Tom Tom,* produced at the Cleveland Stadium before an audience of over 10,000). On a Rosenwald Fellowship at Yale, Graham did not pal around with Owen but chose a more mature scholar, Fannin Belcher. Years later, Owen said that Graham had been a true artist and accomplished more than Cooke had.

14. Margaret Bailey to OVD, May 8, 1942, Dodson files, JWJC.

15. "Winter Chorus," *Life and Letters To-day* 26 (September 1940): 251–52.

Chapter 7: Southern Exposure

1. JB to JVH, July 28, 1985, Washington, D.C.

2. Six years after the school's founding, John D. Rockefeller began donations. So essential were his efforts that the seminary was christened Spelman, Mrs. Rockefeller's maiden name.

3. Richard Long, *Artist and Influence* 8 (New York: HBC, 1989): 80.

4. Born in Cattaraugus County, New York, Florence Mathilda Read graduated from Mount Holyoke College in 1909, became secretary to the president of Reed College in 1911, and then for seven years worked with the International Health Board of the Rockefeller Foundation; in 1927 she became and remained president of Spelman College until her retirement in 1953.

5. In 1927, President Read hired Kemper Harreld to teach music and in 1928 Anne Cooke to teach drama. In 1929, she induced the Harmon Foundation to exhibit the work of Negro painters and sculptors. With Morehouse's president, John Hope, she merged Spelman into Atlanta University Center, sharing faculty, curriculum, and students.

6. Spelman's tradition in the histrionic arts had begun at the turn of the century when Mrs. Adrienne McNeil Herndon, a black teacher-actress in the Department of Elocution, had immersed her students in Shakespeare recitations. Richard Long, "Theatre at Atlanta University," *The Atlanta University Bulletin* (September 1974): 22.

7. OVD to family, July 4, 1939, HBC.

8. OVD to Alain Locke, August 1939, Locke file, Dodson correspondence, MSRC.

9. JB to JVH, September 23, 1987, Washington, D.C. After graduation and a stint in the Army, the fullback remained in Paris to open the Haynes Bar at 3 Rue Clauzel, the first soul-food restaurant in Europe. Haynes acted in films, married a Frenchwoman, and in 1986 died in Paris.

10. OVD to Alain Locke, August 1939, Locke file, Dodson correspondence, MSRC.

11. OVD to CVV, July 31, 1939, JWJC. Owen did manage to retype *Garden of Time* and send off a copy to Van Vechten, who told him that the play "in reading at any rate, doesn't quite come off."

12. OVD to Alain Locke, August 1939, Locke file, Dodson correspondence, MSRC.

13. W. E. B. Du Bois note to OVD, n.d., HBC.

14. Atlanta for the artist could be a grave. The Christmas after Owen had gone into the Navy, Prophet wrote him, "Sometimes I feel a sort of desperation coming over me. I will not speak of *here,* for I could give you but a pathetique tableau, as it grows more hopeless day by day." Elizabeth Prophet to OVD, December 1, 1943, HBC.

15. Dr. Lucy Clement Grigsby to JVH, October 29, 1985, Atlanta, Ga.

16. Recalled Douglas: "For me to come to Atlanta, Georgia, after living all my life in Europe as a free spirit, was the most traumatic, destructive experience a person could go through. I would leave the campus and go downtown and the people would say, 'Nigger, don't drink at that fountain,' and I would scream at them in Italian, *'Lasciatemi in pace! Io, vado dove voglio! Non ho bisogno della tua 'permissione,' imbecille!'* ['Leave me alone! I go where I please! I don't need your permission! Imbecile!'] It exhausted me. I was in trouble because I wouldn't sit at the back of the bus. White people: 'Doesn't she know her place?' Black people: 'Why is she bringing it to our attention?' I was screaming for help, but the horror that surrounded that campus had frozen those black people in ice. Not one ever mentioned the horror that I saw fresh and every day. Anne Cooke and Billie Geter were exceptions."

17. Owen saw him as a marked man, perhaps suggested by the prominent hollow in the center of his forehead, the scar where a growth had been removed while in high school. From that time on, Kenneth had his photo taken only in profile.

Chapter 8: Kenneth

1. Kenneth grew wise in the ways of the street and, later, the night life of Harlem; he pushed out into the world that Owen depended on him to explain.

2. Louise Leftwich to KD, n.d., JWJC.

3. Michael Alexander to JVH, February 18, 1987, New York.

4. Ruby L. Jewell to JVH, July 7, 1974, Atlanta, Ga.

5. "Six O'clock," *The Poetry of the Negro 1746–1949,* Langston Hughes and Arna Bontemps, eds. (Garden City, N.Y.: Doubleday & Co., Inc., 1949): 172.

6. "Poems for My Brother Kenneth," *Powerful Long Ladder* (New York: Farrar, Straus & Giroux, 1946): 63.

7. Thomas Pawley to JVH, December 14, 1983, HBC.

8. Unpublished poem, HBC.

Chapter 9: *Farewell Atlanta*

1. Countee Cullen had adapted Euripides's tragedy to colloquial English ("It never rains but what it pours") with the intention of casting Rose McClendon in the star role; however, before the play could be performed, she died. Countee Cullen, *The Medea and Some Poems* (New York: Harper Brothers, 1935).

2. OVD to CC, March 23, 1940, ARC.

3. In a press release dated April 19, 1963, for *Medea in Africa,* Dodson wrote, "As conceived by the American poet Countee Cullen, and rewritten by Owen Dodson." Ida Cullen, the widow and grail bearer for the dead poet, attacked Owen for assuming coauthorship. Owen then billed the play as an adaptation from Euripides directed by himself.

4. Two examples of parsimony and accounting: The comptroller of the General Education Board sent a letter to President Read asking about a *one-cent* discrepancy in the last two reports. On another occasion, Morehouse President Benjamin Mays demanded that a student pay his library fine under the threat that the Morehouse College faculty would hold a special meeting on the matter. Amount due: eleven cents. Benjamin Mays to Marion Cox, February 17, 1941, HBC.

5. He trained a chorus to recite the tribute on April 4, 1940. "Miss Packard and Miss Giles," PLL: 28.

6. Charles Sebree to JVH, February 4, 1984, HBC.

7. Dodson files, CCHJMC.

8. OVD to EKD and Lillian Dodson, September 22, 1940, HBC.

9. "Iphigenia," PLL: 94.

10. OVD to EKD and Lillian Dodson, December 1, 1941, HBC.

Chapter 10: *Anchors Aweigh*

1. OVD to Malcolm MacLean, April 3, 1942, CAHI.

2. Arthur P. Davis to JVH, July 25, 1985, Washington, D.C.

3. Gordon never entered military service, but left abruptly for New York City.

4. Commander Downes informed Owen and other young faculty that within the year Negroes could become naval officers, a position they had never occupied.

5. OVD to CVV, n.d. (Summer 1942), JWJC.

6. The New York City Co-ordinating Committee for Democratic Action, whose sponsors included the Reverend Adam Clayton Powell, Walter White, and A. Philip Randolph, reprinted the atrocity stories in a separate pamphlet: "Nazi Plan for Negroes."

7. "The Decision," PLL: 96.

8. National Personnel Records Center, Department of the Navy, St. Louis, Mo.

9. Named after the black hero who had been a pilot on the Confederate transport *Planter*. He ran the ship out of Charleston Harbor on May 13, 1862, delivering it to the Union squadron.

10. Lt. Dennis Denmark Nelson, U.S.N.R., "The Integration of the Negro into the United States Navy, 1776–1947," Master's thesis, Howard University, 1948: 105.

11. Charles Sebree became a major player in Owen's life. Born on November 16, 1912, in White City, Ky., Sebree at age four had been literally the only child in that tiny town; he had amused himself by sketching pictures in the dirt with a stick. At age twelve, Charles and his mother migrated to Chicago, where a teacher, Mrs. Honan, recognized his talents and placed him in the Burke Grammar School. At age fourteen, one of his paintings, "Seated Boy," was purchased by the Chicago Renaissance Society and used on the cover of the society's magazine. He began to attend the Art Institute and on April 10, 1935, his first one-man exhibition opened at the Randolph Galleries on North Michigan Avenue; over the next decades several major collections bought his paintings.

At the war's end, he taught theater design for the American Negro Theater in New York and there directed Harry Belafonte in his first major role, in Sean O'Casey's *Juno and the Paycock*. In 1953, his play *Mrs. Patterson* introduced Eartha Kitt to Broadway. Sebree never surrendered the soft honey of his Southern drawl; indeed, he carefully cultivated the poor-country-boy image. Even in his sixties he would say in a voice not unlike Gary Cooper's, "I guess yawl could call me a painter."

12. Painter Norman MacLeish, brother of the poet Archibald, had gotten Sebree onto the roster of WPA painters, where for a monthly salary of ninety dollars he was contracted to bring his paintings regularly into the WPA office. However, Sebree sold outside the WPA. When the assistant director, Florence Arquinn, called Sebree out on the carpet for not de-

livering work, he suddenly shouted at her, "Don't you dare call me a nigger!" All work in the office stopped, typewriters silent. "I won't allow you to call me a nigger!" he yelled, and stormed out of the office, leaving Mrs. Arquinn hurt and deflated. John Carlis to JVH, October 30, 1988, New York.

13. Ibid.

14. OVD memo to Lt. Comdr. Daniel W. Armstrong, December 8, 1942, JWJC.

15. Owen's productions: *Robert Smalls*, December 16, 1942; *John Paul Jones*, January 6, 1943; *Booker T. Washington (Climbing to the Soil)*, January 13, 1943; *Lord Nelson, Naval Hero*, January 20, 1943; *The Ballad of Dorrie Miller*, February 7, 1943; *Everybody Join Hands*, March 21, 1943; *He Planted Freedom* (General Armstrong, Sr.), April 1943; *Old Ironsides*, April 7, 1943; *Don't Give Up the Ship*, May 5, 1943; *Freedom the Banner*, June 6, 1943; *Tropical Fable*, July 7, 1943. Some productions were repeated on other dates. Typescripts, JWJC and HBC.

16. OVD to CVV, December 22, 1942, JWJC.

17. Charles Sebree to JVH, February 4, 1984, Washington, D.C.

18. OVD to CVV, June 3, 1943, JWJC.

19. Charles Henri Ford accepted "On the Beach" and "Metaphor for Minorities" for *View*, although he would have preferred "something more queer." Boston's *Common Ground* accepted "Black Mother Praying," and the socially conscious *Christian Century* published "Some Men Climbing."

20. Typescript, HBC. Also published in *Theatre Arts* magazine, September 1943.

21. Brooklyn-born Sol Gordon, Owen's junior by ten years, had graduated from Thomas Jefferson High School. Gordon met Owen at a USO performance in the Metropolitan Opera House. Involved with Jewish issues, he invited Owen to a pageant that inspired the poem "Jonathan's Song," which Owen dedicated to Gordon in PLL. On a copy in the Moorland-Spingarn Collection, the poem is dedicated to "M.J."

22. Typescript, HBC. Also published in *Callaloo* 7, no. 2 (Spring–Summer 1984).

23. W. H. Auden to OVD, September 3, 1943, JWJC.

24. In his later years, Owen enlisted the poem in his war with God: the mother had hurled a harpoon into the God who had permitted war and racism.

25. Nelson, "The Integration of the Negro into the United States Navy, 1776–1947": 105.

26. The Navy paid dearly for segregation. On July 17, 1944, two transport vessels loading ammunition at Port Chicago Naval Base on the Sacramento River were engulfed in a gigantic explosion shattering windows

twenty miles away. The blast killed 320 sailors instantly, and two ships and the large loading pier were annihilated. Several hundred others were injured and millions of dollars in property lost. Of Navy personnel who died, some 200 ammunition loaders were Blacks. Three weeks after the disaster, 328 survivors were ordered to return to work but 258 refused. They resented that only black men were assigned to labor battalions charged with doing dangerous and heavy work. Moreover, although all the men had been trained at Great Lakes Naval Training Center, apparently none had been instructed in safe methods for handling ammunition. Fifty Blacks were singled out, charged with mutiny, court-martialed, convicted, and handed sentences ranging from eight to fifteen years. Only through the intervention of Thurgood Marshall on behalf of the NAACP were these men later freed. Lester B. Granger, "Racial Democracy—the Navy Way," *Common Ground* 7, no. 2 (Winter 1947). Also Robert L. Allen, "The Port Chicago Disaster and Its Aftermath," *The Black Scholar* 13, nos. 2, 3 (Spring 1982).

27. "Administrative History, Bureau of Naval Personnel," Part 4, "Training Activity," Vol. 2. Department of the Navy, Naval Historical Center, Washington, D.C.

28. Ibid.

Chapter 11: Angels on His Shoulder

1. OVD to PR, June 8, 1943, HBC.

2. Leonard Rieser, Jr., to Errol Hill, September 10, 1985, Dartmouth College, N.H.

3. In the South, Rosenwald built 5,000 elementary schools for black children. So pervasive was his influence that many rural people thought that Mr. Sears or Mr. Roebuck or, as rumor spread, Mr. Montgomery Ward was a Negro.

4. OVD to Edwin Embree, August 28, 1943, RSF.

5. The library had two books by Blacks: Bontemps's *Drums at Dusk* and Johnson's *God's Trombones*. Van Vechten sent books and in turn requested that Owen send him copies of all his plays and poems for the newly inaugurated James Weldon Johnson Collection at Yale.

6. On the home front, Edith had attempted to join the war effort by taking a job with the USO in Utah, but she soon returned to care for Lillian.

7. He read Woolf's *Orlando* and *To the Lighthouse*. He also managed Roi Ottley's *New World A-Comin'* and Rebecca West's *Black Lamb, Grey Falcon*. He read Pearl Buck's *The Exile* and *Fighting Angel* and sent her

his poem and the China play; she responded that his China play was "in places beautiful, all of it good, and 'Black Mother Praying' was moving."

8. OVD to Edwin Embree, September 27, 1943, RSF.

9. After two years, the Navy called him into the hospital at Kingsbridge and examined him in the middle of the winter. Finding no symptoms of hay fever, they stopped his pension—eleven dollars a month.

10. OVD to PR, November 30, 1943, HBC.

Chapter 12: New World A-Coming

1. Frank Griffin telegram to OVD, April 12, 1944, Dodson Correspondence, JWJC.

2. Lillian Dodson to OVD, June 25, 1944, Dodson Correspondence, JWJC.

3. A design nearly identical to the one Du Bois used in 1913 for his pageant *The Star of Ethiopia*.

4. The American Committee of Jewish Writers, Artists, and Scientists invited Owen to speak June 19, 1943, on "The Negro Salute to the Fighting Jews of Europe." When the rift between Blacks and Jews broke out in the late sixties over control of New York schools, Owen was heartbroken.

5. *The People's Voice* 11, no. 2 (July 1, 1944). Had Owen achieved his Madison Square Garden pageantry in a non-racist America, his next step could have been an opportunity to direct an epic film.

6. Auden lived on a low bluff south of the Brooklyn Bridge opposite Lower Manhattan. In 1953, several blocks of the northwest corner of the Heights were razed for the construction of the Brooklyn Queens Expressway, and "the menagerie" disappeared forever.

7. W. H. Auden to OVD, February 25, 1944, HBC.

8. Humphrey Carpenter, *W. H. Auden, A Biography* (Boston: Houghton Mifflin Co., 1981): 325.

9. Carpenter, *W. H. Auden:* 3.

10. "No one will do for the narrator in my oratorio but you." Auden to OVD, February 25, 1944, HBC.

11. That weekend, the host poet played out his own private agenda. Auden had resigned his young lover, Chester Kallman—fourteen years his junior—into the arms of a younger suitor. When the Auden-Kallman "marriage" had broken up, Auden at thirty-four felt old. In replaying the Strauss libretto for Owen, Auden relived and possibly relieved his own heartbreak. Auden had admitted that he imagined himself in the role of the aging Marschallin in *Rosenkavalier,* sadly agreeing to resign her lover into the arms of a young rival. Carpenter, *W. H. Auden:* 313.

12. OVD to PR, February 11, 1944, RR.

13. Kalamazoo *Gazette,* July 7, 1943.

14. Many other Caucasians, feeling the same magnetism ("nigger lovers"), unable to withstand the social ostracism, had become "nigger haters." Negrophiles and negrophobes, two sides of the same coin. On the other hand, Blacks exhibiting a preference for whites were dismissed as wanting to be white. In the convolutions of racism, Priebe had the courage to assert his preference; and Owen in his ecumenicalism remained his friend until Priebe's death in 1976.

15. In 1928, Edwin Rogers Embree (1883–1950) took over the Rosenwald Fund's presidency from its founder. He had been educated at Berea College, a pioneer college in nonsegregated education. For a time he had served as director of the division of human biology at the Rockefeller Foundation (where he had befriended the black biologist Ernest Just), but, finding Rockefeller too conservative, Embree moved to the Rosenwald Fund and took a personal interest in his protégés, who loved him grudgingly when he was generous and bad-mouthed him spitefully when he was not.

16. The so-called common man who reverentially or derisively alludes to the power wielded by corporations has only a vague inkling how elaborate those connections are.

17. Slesinger letter to David Stevens of the Rockefeller Foundation, March 22, 1944, Record Group 1.1, folder 390, box 200, series 200, RAC.

18. Los Angeles, Mobile, Beaumont, and Detroit. The American Film Committee (AFC) created the Committee on Negro Mass Education (who is to be educated?), with its first meeting to be held on March 11, 1944. Its members were all black: Charles S. Johnson, Arna Bontemps, Horace Bond, Grace Townes Hamilton, Frayser Lane, Ira De A. Reid, and John M. Ross.

19. Charles S. Johnson to OVD, April 3, 1944, Dodson Correspondence, RSF.

20. OVD to Leonard Rieser, June 1, 1944, RR.

Chapter 13: Democratic Vistas on Film

1. OVD to EKD, July 21, 1944, New York.
2. Typescript, HBC.
3. Abram Hill to JVH, July 17, 1985, New York.
4. "Owen gave me emotional support and my start in the theater." William Greaves to JVH, February 15, 1988, New York.
5. Sadie Brown Amperado to JVH, April 30, 1985, New York.
6. Owen had little or no fund-raising experience. The selection of a Negro in 1944 perhaps indicated the board's progressive outlook, but their

choice of an artist rather than an administrator showed poor judgment and, in light of what happened, suggests the project was never credible.

7. In 1946, when the books of the AFC were audited, the Marion Ascoli Fund contained $3,700, with no record of other deposits. After thirty-five years of inflation, Owen had added an additional zero to her donation.

8. OVD to PR, October 3, 1944, RR.

9. Typescript, HBC.

10. Arna Bontemps to Langston Hughes, May 6, 1946. Charles H. Nichols, ed. *Arna Bontemps–Langston Hughes Letters, 1925–1967* (New York: Dodd, Mead & Co., 1980): 207.

11. Ibid.: 176.

12. He had joined the committee because he had thought they were going to be a production company; when he learned that they were only throwing out ideas and writing letters, he resigned.

13. Bontemps to Hughes, June 1945. Nichols, *Arna Bontemps–Langston Hughes Letters, 1925–1967.*

14. Donald Slesinger to Edwin Embree, September 7, 1945, AFC, RSF. They also hoped to start a second project, a feature film about the life of James Weldon Johnson.

15. Michael Alexander to Embree, September 17, 1945, AFC, RSF.

16. Jan. 7, at 3:00 P.M., in the series "New World A-Coming."

17. Owen Dodson, "Color, USA," *Twice a Year,* nos. 14–15 (Fall–Winter 1946–47): 355.

18. Slesinger to Embree, July 22, 1946, AFC, RSF.

19. Embree to Slesinger, telegram, July 29, 1946, AFC, RSF.

20. Read by OVD, October 24, 1946. "Edwin R. Embree," *Phylon* 7, no. 4 (Winter 1946).

21. OVD to PR, October 5, 1946, RR.

Chapter 14: *Powerful Long Ladder*

1. "Countee Cullen," TGB, typescript, HBC.

2. *Theatre Arts* magazine, August 1946.

3. OVD to Lena Horne, September 10, 1945, Countee Cullen letters, ARC.

4. "Hot Spots," an adaptation of Owen's film script "Where You From?" aired on January 23, 1945. On February 11, Race Relations Sunday, "They Knew Lincoln" dramatized John Washington's authentic story, starring Georgia Burke and Canada Lee. Owen's unsuccessful attempt to establish his own radio series, *St. Louis Woman,* by reusing characters and ideas

from his *Doomsday* play, had no relation to the Cullen-Bontemps play of the same name.

5. Gordon Heath, narrator for Pearl Primus's dance company in *African Celebration* at the Roxy Theatre, suggested to the choreographer-dancer that she commission Dodson to write a sound track. Owen did, and she put his fourteen short poems into rehearsal — an ensemble of verse nodding in diverse directions to black history. Owen recalled, "At her opening, some critic said, 'Miss Primus, why do you have all that talk that we have to listen to and watch you dance at the same time?' So without consulting me, she cut it all out. I never heard my words spoken from a Broadway stage."

6. Owen cast Marion Douglas as Ophelia, Austin Briggs-Hall as Polonius, William Greaves as Laertes, Dorothy Ateca as Gertrude, and P. J. Sidney as Claudius; Charles Sebree designed sets and costumes.

7. OVD to GH, September 21, 1944, HBC.

8. GH to JVH, June 5–7, 1985, HBC.

9. John Farrar to OVD, April 2, 1946, HBC.

10. Letter to OVD signed "A," n.d., HBC.

11. Jessica Nelson North, *Poetry: A Magazine of Verse* 69 (December 1946): 175–77.

12. "Ideas Fused with Fire," *New York Herald Tribune Weekly Book Review,* March 16, 1947: 12.

13. Alfred Kreymborg, "Lyrics in Black and White," *Saturday Review of Literature* 30 (February 1, 1947): 175–77.

14. OVD to Richard Wright, September 27, 1946, MF.

15. Alain Locke to OVD, September 1946, Alain Locke Collection, MSRC.

16. OVD to PR, November 29, 1946, RR.

17. Blevins Davis, from Independence, Mo., a childhood friend of Harry Truman, had married the widow of a railroad baron; the widow died shortly after the wedding, leaving Davis a millionaire.

18. OVD to PR, February 10, 1947, RR.

19. OVD to PR, February 18, 1947, RR.

20. OVD to PR, April 30, 1947, HBC.

21. Candace H. Wait, secretary at Yaddo, to JVH, September 24, 1985.

22. OVD to CVV, June 13, 1947, HBC.

23. Richard Coe to JVH, June 21, 1984, Washington, D.C.

24. *Botteghe Oscure* (Rome, Italy) 2 (1948): 280–81.

25. *The Tiger's Eye* (Westport, Conn.), October 1948: 14. The journal flowered for nine issues (1947–49); its quality rag covers enclosed work by Anaïs Nin, Boris Pasternak, Kenneth Rexroth, Paul Goodman, Van Wyck Brooks, Jorge Luis Borges, Marianne Hauser, Jackson Pollock, Mark

Rothko, Willem de Kooning, Alexander Calder, and Isamu Noguchi, to name a few.

26. Ibid.: 17.

27. Ruth Stephan, the only heir of Charles Walgreen (successful Chicago drug-chain founder), suffered from the image of the poor little rich girl. A blond, willowy woman, she wrote delicate poetry, published two biographical-historical novels based on the life of Sweden's Queen Christina, and founded the Ruth Stephan Poetry Center at the University of Arizona. Her long spiritual pilgrimage through three husbands, a residency in a Zen Buddhist ashram in Kyoto, and a patronage to the Freedom Schools throughout the South (she marched at Selma) ended on April 8, 1974, in an apparent suicide. John J. Stephan, "Ruth Stephan (1910–74): A Tribute," *Yale University Library Gazette,* April 1976.

28. Arna Bontemps to Owen, August 26, 1947, HBC. In February 1949, *Ebony* published a photograph of Owen among the other "big names" in Negro poetry that Hughes and Bontemps had assembled in their anthology.

29. Erika Duncan, in "The Literary Life," *Book Forum* 3, no. 3 (Fall 1977): 432, states that "she [Marguerite Young] spoke lovingly of Owen Dodson who dedicated to her a book about black preachers in the South." The "book" mentioned is Owen's poem "Funeral Sermon for a Dead Poet."

30. February 1949, Rankin Chapel, Howard University.

31. Dodson's work appeared in Sterling Brown et al., *Negro Caravan* (New York: Dryden Press, 1949); *Negro Digest* (August 1951); and Langston Hughes and Arna Bontemps, eds., *The Poetry of the Negro* (New York: Doubleday, 1949). He had been translated into Japanese — Hajime Kijima, ed., *Lift Every Voice* (Tokyo: Mirai-Sha, 1952) — and soon into Dutch — Rosey Pool and Paul Breman, eds., *Ik Zag Hoe Zwart Ik Was* (I Saw How Black I Was) (The Hague: Bert Bakker/Daamen, 1958).

Chapter 15: Howard University

1. St. Clair Price to OVD, April 25, 1947, HBC.

2. GH to OVD, November 25, 1948, HBC.

3. OVD to PR, September 25, 1947, RR.

4. In 1909, biologist Ernest Everett Just, then on the English faculty, organized the College Dramatic Club. By the 1920s, this group had evolved into the Howard Players, directed by Montgomery Gregory and Alain Locke (later Sterling Brown and James Butcher). The "sudden" creation of a theater department has complex causes: (1) Blacks with advanced degrees from northern universities in theater arts were available to teach;

(2) Congressional appropriations for Howard nearly doubled in 1947 and again in 1949; (3) Classically educated faculty were present.

5. ACR to JVH, April 12, 1986, Washington, D.C. For several years, Roxie Roker played in the TV series "The Jeffersons."

6. JB to JVH, July 28, 1985, Washington, D.C.

7. Roxie Roker to JVH, October 18, 1985, Los Angeles, Calif.

8. Richard Coe to JVH, June 21, 1984, Washington, D.C.

9. Charles Sebree to OVD, November 1947, Dodson unprocessed files, CCHJMC.

10. OVD to PR, February 25, 1948, HBC. In August, Sebree won a fellowship to Yaddo and rented his studio to Walter Hall, a student of Owen's (the star of *Bayou Legend*). When Sebree reclaimed his residence, he accused Hall of having stolen some of his paintings. Dodson made a countercharge: Owen had given a series of eighteenth-century prints to Sebree for framing. When they did not reappear, he asked Sebree where they were. "Where?" responded the astonished Sebree. "I framed them and left them inside your office door."

11. Jay Carmody, *The Evening Star,* May 8, 1948, B-22.

12. In 1950, Wilson Lehr, Owen's friend from Yale, gave the play its most elaborate production at Hunter College, using the classically trained actress Osceola Archer. Dennis McDonald, in the May 27, 1950, issue of *Billboard,* praised the effort but found the experiment "commercially doubtful." *Bayou Legend* received a puppet production in 1952, and Cooke directed it a second time in 1957. Shauneille Perry directed the show for Amas theater in New York in 1975. Aside from its publication in 1971, an impressive list of impresarios have turned it down. Published script: Darwin T. Turner, ed., *Black Drama in America: An Anthology* (Greenwich, Conn.: Fawcett Books, 1971): 205–95. Typescript, HBC.

13. Charles Sebree to OVD, April 9, 1948, CCHJMC.

Chapter 16: Wild Duck Flies Home

1. ACR to JVH, February 4, 1984, Washington, D.C.

2. Drew Pearson, "Washington Merry-Go-Round," *New York Times,* August 7, 1949.

3. Owen Dodson's scrapbook, newspaper clipping, n.d., n.p., MSRC. The choice of *Mamba's Daughters* favored a European audience who recognized the DuBose Heyward name (*Porgy* the novel had been translated into German, Danish, and Dutch). Also in 1948 few full-length plays by black authors had dramatic values sufficient to compete with Ibsen's play. Finally, the cast size of the two plays had to be nearly the same. On the

other hand, black writer Theodore Browne's 1937 play about John Henry *(Natural Man)* might have filled the bill.

4. This composite journal relies heavily upon diaries kept by Shauneille Perry and Zaida Coles. Other material is taken from interviews with Anne Cooke Reid, James Butcher, Marilyn Berry, William Brown, and Roxie Roker, and from interviews with and letters from Owen. Accounts in periodicals and newspapers are footnoted.

5. Owen Dodson, "The World Seemed Wide and Open," *Theatre Arts* 34 (March 1950): 105–6.

6. Anne Cooke, "The Wild Duck Comes Home," *Record of International Exchange, Department of State* 6, no 2. (March–April 1950): 2.

7. *Die Welt,* November 19, 1949. Translated by Kate Garretson.

8. Bergit Hammer at the age of sixteen saw *The Wild Duck* and recorded this in her diary: "This afternoon I went to see *Vildanden.* It was great seeing colored people performing that play, and they were good, I found them almost better than the Norwegian actors I saw at the National Theatre. Some of them seemed more at ease in their roles. Hedvig, for example, seemed stiff and quiet when Evy Engelsborg played her, and nothing like what I had imagined her to be when I read the play. Marilyn Berry, on the other hand, showed a more natural fourteen-year-old, merry but yet tragic. The others also played well."

Chapter 17: The Black Prince of Denmark

1. Owen had assembled a second book of poetry, "Cages of Loneliness." It was never published.

2. OVD to GH, April 3, 1951, HBC.

3. OVD to Richard Wright, September 23, 1946, MF.

4. Carolyn Hill Stewart to JVH, September 27, 1987, Washington, D.C.

5. Frederic Kirchberger to JVH, August 5, 1985, Boulder, Colo. The faculty were all black except for Kirchberger (the music teacher) and his wife, Marianne Hauser, who had recently emigrated from Alsace-Lorraine. The Bennett students could not attend concerts at a nearby white girls' college. Hauser called upon the white college to share cultural events but was refused. Then came her revenge: "The Budapest String Quartet, who were mostly European refugees, was booked to play at the white college in Greensboro; I wrote them. They said they could not cancel their commitment at the white college, but they would be happy to come over to Bennett and give a free concert. The news got out and my few white friends called me up and said, 'Would it be possible if we came to Bennett to listen?' I said, 'Of course, at Bennett we do not segregate.' " Marianne Hauser to JVH, July 11, 1985, New York.

6. OVD to GH, April 3, 1951, HBC.

7. Edna Wilson to JVH, December 15, 1986, New York.

8. CHEC: 206–7.

9. Patrick O'Connor to JVH, November 11, 1984, New York.

10. Earle Hyman to JVH, September 24, 1981, New York.

11. Earle Hyman to JVH, November 11, 1981, New York.

12. "Owen Dodson and Earle Hyman on *Hamlet*," *Artist and Influence*, 3 (New York: HBC, 1985): 61.

13. Earle Hyman to JVH, September 24, 1981, New York.

14. Earle Hyman to OVD, September 18, 1953, HBC. "You are flesh of my flesh, blood of my blood. You are the brother and father that I never really had."

15. David Amram, *Vibrations: The Adventures and Musical Times of David Amram* (New York: Macmillan Co., 1968): 86. He had previously composed for the Howard production of *Pelléas and Mélisande*.

16. "Earle Hyman," from TGB, typescript, HBC. The bureaucracy did not help. Dodson had to ask Cooke, as chair of the department, for requisitions. Then she had to get the dean's signature. After that, it went to the Budget Office, then to the treasurer, and he signed it. Then Owen could go downtown and get the material.

17. OVD to GH, November 22, 1952, HBC.

18. "Owen Dodson and Earle Hyman on *Hamlet*": 64.

19. Claire Leyba to JVH, May 21, 1987, New York.

20. "Howard U. 'Hamlet' Best of Its Drama Offerings," *Evening Star*, July 21, 1951: 14.

21. "European Tour—Eleonora Duse," from TGB, HBC.

22. Eva Le Gallienne, *The Mystic in the Theatre: Eleonora Duse* (London: Bodley Head, Ltd., 1966): 116.

23. OVD to GH, July 6, 1951, HBC.

24. T. Edward Hambleton cofounded the Phoenix Theatre in New York with Norris Houghton.

25. Froke Jakobsen, M.F., to Mrs. Sampson, Copenhagen, January 31, 1952, CCHJMC.

26. T. Edward Hambleton to Owen, November 27, 1951, CCHJMC.

27. Munk, a Lutheran cleric, was murdered by the Nazis. Mrs. Munk gave the play to Stewart, who brought it to Owen. Carolyn Hill Stewart to JVH, September 22, 1987, Washington, D.C. (Owen's premiere preceded Carl Dreyer's film by three years.)

28. Earle Hyman to JVH, September 24, 1981, New York. Richard Coe of the *Washington Post* wrote, "a stirring, impassioned final scene, excoriating the faint-hearted." The Danish Embassy wrote, "The performance of Kaj Munk's 'The Word' last night at Spaulding Hall was tre-

mendously impressive. I have never been touched this deeply by any play or acting as I was last night." Erik Jensen, commercial attaché, letter to Mordecai Johnson, July 1, 1952, HBC.

29. A small memento lived on: Kermit Keith of Howard's Department of Architecture visited Elsinore and on the castle walls discovered Hamlet's "sign," resembling a fencing foil with the tip buttoned, and the blade overlaid by curling double S's. Keith fashioned the figure into book plates for Owen, who promptly adapted it to every play program he directed.

Chapter 18: Boy at the Window

1. Donald Fitzhugh, "Washington Book World," *Sunday Star,* May 7, 1967.

2. Edith Dodson to JVH, September 9, 1981, New York. The novel's autobiographical correspondences are evident in the first notes, which Van Vechten insisted that Owen deposit in the James Weldon Johnson Collection at Yale.

3. Notes and manuscript, BATW, folder 11, 1946–51, JWJC.

4. BATW: 83–84.

5. Notes, BATW, JWJC.

6. The recent use of the likely-unlikely for discontinuity (destruction of narrative) by such poets as Ann Lauterbach and John Ashbery is an entirely separate style with another purpose.

7. BATW: 106–7.

8. Ibid.: 121.

9. Ibid.: 112.

10. PLL: 99.

11. OVD to GH, July 21, 1953, HBC.

12. Alain Locke to OVD, January 30, 1951, scrapbook 2, Dodson Papers, MSRC.

Chapter 19: The Guggenheim Year

1. John Farrar was president of PEN.

2. Jack Kerouac to OVD, December 29, 1950, HBC. Quoted with permission from Sterling Lord Literistic, Inc.

3. Howard Swanson to OVD, February 24, 1952, HBC.

4. Owen was appointed acting department head from September 1, 1951, to June 30, 1952.

5. Channing Pollock (1880–1946) was born in Washington, D.C. His most famous play was *The Passing of the Third Floor Back.* Owen had

met Helen Channing through Carl Van Vechten, and the daughter had told him she wished to deposit her father's books and files in a school that would appreciate them. Dorothy Porter to JVH, April 11, 1986, HBC.

6. W. H. Auden to OVD, October 18, 1952, JWJC.

7. T. S. Eliot letter to OVD, July 21, 1952, HBC.

8. Washington, D.C., *Times-Herald,* July 25, 1952.

9. OVD to Margaret Walker Alexander, January 7, 1952, HBC.

10. OVD to GH, November 22, 1952, HBC.

11. Fisk University and Howard were the first black institutions to be granted charters. (Phi Beta Kappa had been founded in 1776.) Kenneth M. Greene, secretary, Phi Beta Kappa, United Chapters, to JVH, September 13, 1985, HBC.

12. W. H. Auden to OVD, July 15, 1953, JWJC.

13. Giocondo Sacchetti to Jo Neal, December 25, 1984, Ischia, Italy.

14. OVD to PH, April 13, 1954, HBC.

15. Ulderigo Grassi to EKD, December 7, 1953. Trans. Sigrun Müller, HBC.

16. Ivory Wallace to JVH, September 6, 1986, HBC.

17. OVD to GH, December 8, 1954, HBC.

18. OVD to EKD, November 1, 1953, HBC.

19. OVD to EKD, November 21, 1953, HBC. At that time the critics had not yet suggested that Cather was gay.

20. Sacchetti to Neal, December 25, 1984, Ischia, Italy.

21. Dakin, gay and a monied scion of a wealthy Wisconsin family, had fled to Ischia and married Giocondo Sacchetti's sister, Francesca.

22. Truman Capote, "Ischia," *Local Color* (New York: Random House, 1950): 67–68.

23. Sacchetti claimed that Auden didn't like Capote, "who all the time would ask me in town, 'When can I see Auden?' It was not my problem; I told him, go and see him if you want to, but Auden didn't want to see him." Sacchetti to Neal, December 27, 1984, Ischia, Italy.

24. OVD to Kermit Keith, December 13, 1953, HBC.

25. Sacchetti to Neal, December 1984, Ischia, Italy.

26. Invitation, Dodson Collection, box 27–1, folder 18, MSRC.

27. Is he like Bigger Thomas in *Native Son* (as restored by Arnold Rampersad) "polishing his night stick?" Other Dodson symbols echo in the final chapter. "Death" has been tattooed on his *left* arm, and it only stops itching and burning when his sister Bernice (pregnant by an unknown man) tells him that they will one day live together. "He felt his father's watch ticking time against his heart." CHEC: 221.

28. Romualdo Maniere to Neal, January 1985, Ischia, Italy.

29. "Negroes in Rome," *Our World* (May 1954): 36–39. The article included novelist William Demby, sculptor John W. Rhoden, and soprano Evelyn Mack.

30. Undated clipping, scrapbook 1, Dodson Papers, MSRC. Trans. Sigrun Müller.

Chapter 20: The Amen Corner

1. Georgia Douglas Johnson died on May 28, 1966.

2. May Miller Sullivan wrote a number of one-acts reprinted in Kathy Perkins's *Black Female Playwrights* (Bloomington: Indiana University Press, 1989) and in Elizabeth Brown-Guillory's *Wines in the Wilderness* (Westport, Conn.: Greenwood Press, 1990).

3. Toni Morrison credited Sebree as the "key person in my writing. Without his encouragement, I never would have written *The Bluest Eye*." Toni Morrison to JVH, April 3, 1986, Albany, N.Y. On December 1, 1954, Sebree's fantasy-drama, renamed *Mrs. Patterson,* opened on Broadway, starring Eartha Kitt.

4. Anne would direct *Taming of the Shrew* and in the spring *Iphigenia in Aulus.* Butcher's assignment was *Summer and Smoke;* Owen's, *Finian's Rainbow.*

5. Owen the storyteller "improved" upon events, or perhaps he had forgotten that Baldwin was then at Yaddo (March 1955). In any case, Baldwin did express to Dodson that he wished to work on the play during rehearsal.

6. "There's a Good Writing Man in This Corner," *Washington Daily News,* May 13, 1955: 43. " 'Amen Corner' Worth a Look," *Washington Post,* May 13, 1955: 44.

7. Owen's salary was $5,478, paid over ten months.

8. Owen did let him come back later in the summer for three weeks while he was away. (Baldwin had his own key to the apartment.)

9. Baldwin never promised Dodson the directorship of *Blues for Mr. Charlie* in writing. He should have. Owen could have saved the play.

10. Owen recorded this in 1971.

11. John Schaffner to OVD, May 26, 1961, HBC.

Chapter 21: Loss of Stars

1. CHEC (New York: Popular Library, 1977).

2. Mamoulian, an Armenian born in Russia, had his initial success with Heyward's play *Porgy,* followed by Gershwin's *Porgy and Bess.*

3. Warner Lawson began his studies in Hartford, Conn., at the age of

five. With a B.A. from Yale and an M.A. from Harvard, Lawson traveled to Berlin and studied with Artur Schnabel. He came to Howard in 1941. Eileen Southern, *Biographical Dictionary of Afro-American and African Musicians* (Westport, Conn.: Greenwood Press, 1982): 239.

4. Lawson may have canceled to take his choir on a South American tour.

5. Light-complexioned Lawson had been born to wealth. Owen's family, dark and poor, did not fail to note the reasons for Lawson's arrogance.

6. Many actors considered Owen the best director they had ever worked with. Toni Morrison recalled, "Owen understood the play [*Richard III*] in a most extraordinary way. He was first rate. Our desire to please him onstage was enormous. He could have been another Peter Brook. Maybe he was." Toni Morrison, April 3, 1986, HBC.

7. Winona Fletcher to JVH, May 26, 1985, Bloomington, Ind.

8. Clinton Turner Davis to JVH, August 20, 1986, New York.

9. She noted that a senior in her "Introduction to Theatre" course asked her what she meant by "answer either (a) or (b)," a question that suggested an unfamiliarity with academic exams. Marian McMichaels to Constance Welch, March 26, 1965, and July 30, 1965, in the collection of Roderick Bladel.

10. Glenda Dickerson to JVH, August 16, 1985, New York.

11. OVD to GH, February 21, 1961, HBC.

12. JB to JVH, September 5, 1987, Washington, D.C. The speech and poem are three typed pages, HBC.

13. Richard Coe, *Washington Post,* March 10, 1962.

14. James Forsyth to Bert Stimmel, March 8, 1985, Sussex, England.

15. William Brown to JVH, April 9, 1986, Baltimore, Md.

16. Day Thorpe, "Howard U. Opera Based on Miracle," *Evening Star,* March 7, 1958.

17. *Literary Recordings: A Checklist of Archive of Recorded Poetry and Literature in the Library of Congress.* Item 275, Dodson, Owen. T 3212, December 13, 1960.

18. Lotte Lenya to OVD, December 28, 1957, HBC. George Davis died in December 1957.

19. Owen had certainly been childlike. Easter 1962 found him in Meridian Park with a basket of Easter eggs. As he passed through the park he was saying to all the children and sundry, " 'Christ has risen! Christ has risen.' " James Forsyth to Bert Stimmel, January 1985, Sussex, England.

20. Alfredina Brown to JVH, April 9, 1986, Baltimore, Md.

21. Robert Hayden, ed., *Kaleidoscope Poems by American Negro Poets* (New York: Harcourt, Brace and World, 1967): 122.

Chapter 22: Not without Laughter

1. Roscoe Lee Browne to JVH, April 7, 1986, New York.
2. Ibid.
3. All published in *Washington Afro-American,* HBC.
4. From 1961 to 1966 Owen directed *Antigone* (April 25, 1961); *Charade* (May 15, 1961); *Bad Seed* (July 5, 1961); *Rashomon* (July 29, 1961, and again in December 1961); *The Tragical History of Dr. Faustus* (March 8, 1962); *Sign of Jonah* (March 24, 1962); *Defiant Island* (April 26, 1962); *Morning, Noon, and Night* (December 6, 1962); *Medea in Africa* (April 10, 1963); *Long Day's Journey into Night* (December 5, 1963); *Easter Resurrection Play* (March 22, 1964); *Hamlet* (April 23, 1964); *Dutchman* (October 21, 1964); *Sho' Is Hot in the Cotton Patch* (October 21, 1964); *Air Raid, Happy Journey, Til Victory Is Won* (January 31, 1965); *Blues for Mr. Charlie* (November 4, 1965); *Sandbox, The Academy, The Return* (February 17, 1966); *Threepenny Opera* (April 28, 1966); *Oedipus Rex* (October 19, 1966). These, plus writing twenty-five reviews for the Washington paper, plus teaching, guest lecturing, and writing poetry and the opera *Til Victory Is Won,* might have driven anyone to a heart attack or to drink.
5. O'Connor also ordered Edith to Hattie Carnegie's to buy a pale-blue linen dress with hat and gloves and shoes to match. Patrick O'Connor to JVH, November 11, 1984, New York.
6. Ibid.
7. The menu, "A Midsomer Nightes Feaste," HBC.
8. "On Hearing a Symphony of Beethoven," Edna St. Vincent Millay.
9. "Carl Van Vechten," written for the CVV Centennial, Cedar Rapids, Iowa, June 14–17, 1980, HBC.
10. CVV to Owen, June 24, 1942, HBC.
11. OVD telegram to CVV, December 23, 1964, CVV and OVD folder 52–64, JWJC.
12. OVD to CVV, August 1, 1961, CVV and OVD folder 52–64, JWJC.
13. William Branch, who saw Owen and Robeson at a rally in Washington, states that it was not the year of King's "I Have a Dream" speech but a Washington rally the year before. Owen the storyteller placed his tale at a more dramatic event.

Chapter 23: Dangerously Black

1. Jones never took a class from Dodson, but he knew him. Owen refused to refer to Jones as "Baraka," as he refused to address any of his students by their "African" names. He referred to Ntozake Shange as "Nagasaki."
2. Owen claimed that the theater had been sold out to the Church of the Atonement.

3. Owen made a specific attack on the "artless" young black playwrights in "Playwrights in Dark Glasses," published in *Negro Digest* 17, no. 6 (April 1968): 30. He found they lacked universality and suggestiveness, and had no love of the language.

4. Howard had evolved into a college for professionals, a leadership class who perpetuated an elitism of class and color that left many of the darker and poorer students furious.

5. Program note, Kennedy Center, April 12, 1974, HBC. His initial title, *Lift Every Voice and Sing,* personified his generation's vision of black pride: onward and upward. Warner Lawson found the anthem title unacceptable.

6. Rayford W. Logan, *Howard University: The First Hundred Years* (New York: New York University Press, 1968): 509.

7. Ibid.: 509.

8. Ibid.: 510.

9. Dorothy Porter to JVH, April 11, 1986, Washington, D.C.

10. JB to JVH, September 5, 1987, Washington, D.C.

11. James Butcher commented, "I don't think that Owen had any greater dedication to world theater than Anne or I did. I caught hell from students as much as Owen."

12. OVD to GH, November 20, 1965, HBC.

13. "Proceedings of the General Session," Writer's Conference, May 29–30, 1965. Rosey Pool, Dodson Files, folder 18, box OD, CCHJMC.

14. William Brown to JVH, April 9, 1986, Baltimore, Md.

15. Whitney LeBlanc to JVH, October 15, 1985, Cerritos, Calif.

16. Robert West to JVH, December 14, 1985, New York.

17. As early as 1952 Patrick O'Connor reported, "Sometimes when I visited him, he lost control. Not like epilepsy. He wasn't violent, but would speak gibberish. Edith said that it was booze. I said, 'Absolutely it is not. He does it without drink. He becomes another person.'" O'Connor to JVH, November 11, 1984, New York.

18. Carlton Molette to JVH, April 10, 1986, Baltimore, Md.

19. Dean of Fine Arts Lawson wrote: "The conflict between his own creative work and his onerous job as department head proved to be too much." Telephone conversation, May 27, 1968. Summary by N.L. (Norman Lloyd), director, Rockefeller Foundation. Dodson File, RAC.

20. GH to RP, September 24, 1963, MSRC.

Chapter 24: Rosey to the Rescue

1. Susan Gardner Brooks Ross to JVH, December 16, 1986, New York.

2. EKD to JVH, September 9, 1981, New York.

3. Rosey Pool, *Freedomways Magazine* 3, no. 4 (Fall 1963): 512.

4. Rosey Pool, ed., *Ik Zag Hoe Zwart Ik Was* (I Saw How Black I Was) (The Hague: Bert Bakker/Daamen, 1958), and *Black and Unknown Bards* (Lympne Kent, England: Hand and Flower Press, 1958).

5. *Beyond the Blues* (Lympne Kent, England: Hand and Flower Press, 1962). She awarded five pages to Langston Hughes and eight to Owen.

6. OVD to RP, July 12, 1960, MSRC.

7. At 6:15 and 10:45 P.M. on the BBC, December 27, 1964.

8. RP to OVD, September 4, 1963, MSRC.

9. Read by Pres. Thomas Hedley Reynolds at the graduation ceremony on April 24, 1967, at Bates College, "for a distinguished academic career; for imaginative contributions that have helped many see themselves more clearly and their fellows more honestly." *Bates College Bulletin*, 11, 64 series (June 1967).

10. *Oranges, Auto Sacramental,* and *The Bird Cage,* December 7, 1967.

11. Floyd Barbour to Sallee Hardy, July 26, 1984, New York.

12. January 10, 1968, Dartmouth College, Hanover, N.H.

13. Richard Eberhart, "Another Poet," Letters to the Editor, *Dartmouth News,* January 11, 1968.

14. "Resurrection City," *The Dream Awake,* recording SA 1095 (New Rochelle, N.Y.: Spoken Arts).

15. "Ballad of Badmen," *The Forerunners,* ed. Woodie King, Jr. (Washington, D.C.: Howard University Press, 1975): 64.

16. EKD to OVD, August 6, 1986, HBC. Edith had graduated with her master's degree in education from New York University, as well as with a certificate for working with the hearing-impaired from Gallaudet University in Washington, D.C.

17. Loften Mitchell's *Land Beyond the River;* Ted Shine's play *Morning, Noon, and Night;* and C. Bernard Jackson and James V. Hatch's civil-rights musical *Fly Blackbird.*

18. OVD to EKD, June 21, 1968, HBC.

19. William R. Reardon to JVH, October 13, 1985, Santa Barbara, Calif.

20. Thomas Pawley to JVH, April 15, 1985, Jefferson City, Mo.

21. *Morning, Noon, and Night* opened on July 24, 1968.

22. Ronald D. Scofield, "Brilliant Realism, Negro Theater Group Offering Compelling," *Santa Barbara News Press,* July 7, 1968.

23. He saw James Roose Evans directing *Richard II;* new plays, *Spitting Image* by Colin Spenser (a play about homosexuals having babies), followed by *The Latent Heterosexual;* he returned to Shakespeare's *The Merry Wives of Windsor* and *As You Like It,* then to *The Relapse, The Advertisement, The Dance of Death,* and "the Ring Cycle"—four hours of Wagner for four nights that Owen predicted would turn his hair white or perhaps to

gold. He cooked kidney stew for himself and watched *St. Joan* and *The Forsythe Saga* on the telly. OVD to RP, September 11, 1968, UOSL.

24. James Forsyth to Bert Stimmel, March 8, 1985, Sussex, England. Owen's question to Forsyth about his sex life seems uncharacteristic of him.

25. OVD to RP, September 7, 1968, UOSL.

Chapter 25: Limb from Limb

1. Ron Welburn to JVH, February 25, 1985, New York. In his letters Owen complained of arthritis, and how "plus" the Arizona climate had been for it. His health had improved, although his cholesterol was up to 184 from its usual 140.

2. Lawson died on June 3, 1971.

3. Clinton Turner Davis to JVH, August 20, 1986, New York.

4. OVD to RP, September 27, 1969, RP.

5. James Forsyth letter to OVD, October 8, 1969, HBC.

6. Louise Forsyth to OVD, November 12, 1969, HBC.

7. Jean Anouilh's *Antigone* opened on February 13, 1970.

8. The first year the operation had been directed by Andre Gregory and a largely white staff. The second year C. Bernard Jackson, black director of ICCC, set out to find someone of color who had a distinguished academic background acceptable to the Office of Education and to the National Endowment for the Arts.

9. "There is nothing wrong or extraordinary with Marian Anderson singing German lieder, but to put it into the perspective of 'Isn't it amazing?' is to debase the whole people. Whites performing black material are seen as elevating black music. (Dvořák's use of the Negro themes in *The New World Symphony* was seen as making them significant.) These songs did not need to be validated within the black community." C. Bernard Jackson to JVH, October 16, 1985, Los Angeles, Calif.

10. That he was seen as a "special" Black meant that Owen was being debased. No wonder he once told Katherine Biddle, who asked him for some Negro poems, "I don't feel Negro today." Owen's stipend for the month, $1,500, encouraged him to believe that he could survive by directing, lecturing, and reading poetry independently of Howard.

11. OVD to RP, March 2, 1970, UOSL.

12. OVD to James Forsyth, March 26, 1970, HBC.

13. Kermit Keith, associate professor of architecture, was born on June 23, 1928; he died on March 30, 1970. Owen dictated a poem, "For Kermit," over the telephone; it was read at the funeral.

14. William T. Brown to Dean Mark Fax, June 25, 1970, carbon, HBC.

15. Brown to JVH, April 9, 1986, Baltimore, Md.

16. JB to JVH, July 28, 1985, Washington, D.C.

17. The 1970–71 season exemplifies the change in command. The plays produced were *Being Hit, Ornette, B. S. Black, El Hajj Malik, The Blacks, In the Wine Time,* and *Kuatoka.* Aside from the Genet play, nothing of classics or world theater.

Chapter 26: The Confession Stone

1. Roger Straus to OVD, December 11, 1970, HBC. Owen later changed six Davids to seven.

2. Paul Kresh to OVD, November 15, 1968, HBC.

3. *The Dream Awake,* recording SA 1095 (New Rochelle, N.Y.: Spoken Arts).

4. Richard Coe, "Dodson Disc," *Washington Post,* October 2, 1970.

5. The evolution of the cycle extended over nearly fifteen years. Robert Fleming composed two songs from *The Confession Stone* for contralto Maureen Forrester, who recorded them on her album *A Charm of Lullabies* (Westminster WST-17137). Dodson pressed Pool to ask Benjamin Britten to set the entire cycle to music.

6. Barbara Mahone McBain, "The Confession Stone: Song Cycles," *Black World* 20, no. 12 (October 1971): 90.

7. The performance at Carnegie Hall was held on February 2, 1968.

8. Owen packed the board with his friends: Osceola Archer, Alice Childress, Ming Cho Lee, St. Clair Christmas, Chuck Davis, Earle Hyman, Ulysses Kay, Robert Lewis, Dorothy Ross, and Perry Watkins.

9. Marilyn Berry to JVH, May 26, 1985, New York.

10. RP to OVD, October 10, 1970, UOSL.

11. Isa Isenberg to OVD, November 28, 1970, UOSL.

12. RP to OVD, June 10, 1971, UOSL.

13. OVD to RP, July 16, 1971, UOSL.

14. In the spring of 1972 Owen directed his last two plays—Edgar White's *Mummer's Play* (March 3, 1972) and Martin Duberman's *In White America* (April 7, 1972)—for Harlem School of the Arts. Dorothy Maynor dropped Owen as her theater consultant, citing lack of funding.

15. Dudley Randall to OVD, July 23, 1972, HBC.

16. OVD to James Forsyth, December 11, 1971. A biography of Rosey Pool is in progress, written by Dutch scholar Anneke Schouten-Buys.

17. Helen A. Johnson to JVH, January 30, 1986, New York.

18. The term "listenature" is borrowed from Diane Ravitch. For a century, declamation entertained both black and white Americans. Then the intimacy of radio, the close-ups of cinema, and the effortless conver-

sationalism permitted by the microphone drove declamation and elocution from the stage. Rap, with its driving rhythm, predictable rhyme, and lack of pianissimo is black youth's very loud cry to be heard.

19. Josephine Jacobsen to JVH, Johns Hopkins University, Baltimore, Md. In 1967, poetry consultant James Dickey initiated the policy of presenting two poets on the same bill; Owen shared the evening with Lucille Clifton. During Jacobsen's two-year term, she invited more black poets to read than had any previous consultant.

20. Dancer David Bryant lived with Owen for a short time on 600 West End Avenue, sharing the rent. Then, according to Owen's "The Gossip Book," Bryant borrowed money from Owen's friends, which led to quarrels. Bryant left and Owen changed the locks on the apartment.

21. James Forsyth to OVD, June 19, 1971, HBC.

22. Vivian Robinson to JVH, July 28, 1984, New York.

Chapter 27: Owen's Song

1. OVD to Theodore Gross, March 23, 1972, copy HBC.

2. Helen A. Johnson to JVH, January 30, 1986, New York.

3. TVIW opened on March 4, 1974. Previously conductor Everett Lee had led the Baltimore Symphony Orchestra in excerpts; the composer, Mark Fax (who also wrote some of the lyrics), had conducted songs from the opera at Howard, but he died without seeing the whole opera staged.

4. *Owen's Song* opened on December 31, 1974. The "bird of freedom" reference is to the epigraph for PLL. The composers were Dennis Wiley and Clyde J. Barrett.

5. Clive Barnes, "*Owen's Song* at D.C. Black Repertory Company," *New York Times,* November 1, 1974.

6. Glenda Dickerson to JVH, August 16, 1985, New York.

7. *Bayou Legend* opened on January 10, 1975.

8. OVD to EKD, June 26, 1973, HBC.

9. William J. Rivers of Social Security Administration to OVD, November 9, 1973, HBC.

10. "Notice of Decision," Department of Health, Education, and Welfare, Social Security Administration, Bureau of Hearings and Appeals, January 26, 1974.

11. Barbara Rice Jones for PEN to OVD, August 16, 1972, HBC.

12. OVD to Galen Williams, Poets and Writers, Inc., February 24, 1974, HBC.

Chapter 28: The Gathering of Sons

1. "Allegory of Seafaring Black Mothers," HBD (New York: Morgan and Morgan, 1978): 14.

2. Raimundo Torrence to JVH, March 17, 1985, New York.

3. Hilton Als, "Fathers and Sons," *Village Voice,* January 12, 1988.

4. Glenngo King to JVH, November 15, 1989, New York.

5. Marlene Tartaglione to JVH, November 28, 1989, New York.

6. "For Billie Holiday, Finally, Lady, You Are Gone from Us," *Black America Literature Forum* 18, no. 1 (Spring 1984): 5.

7. His tale seems based partly on experiences with Holiday, partly manufactured, and partly taken from William Dufty's series that ran in the *New York Post* in June and July 1959.

8. OVD to Darryl Croxton, January 12, 1976, Croxton.

9. Elaine Wells, "O. Dodson Writes, Directs, Ellington Opera," *Philadelphia Tribune,* January 24, 1976: 15.

10. Beverly Kelch to JVH, June 23, 1984, New York.

11. OVD to PR, July 13, 1956, RR.

12. OVD to Croxton, March 3, 1976, Croxton.

13. Leonard Rieser to OVD, June 14, 1959, HBC.

14. OVD to Croxton, July 23, 1976, Croxton.

15. Their script shares its title with Phyl Garland's history of black music.

16. OVD to JVH, June 26, 1976, HBC.

17. Previews began on December 8, 1978.

18. Raymond S. Blanks, "*Sound of Soul* weaves dance, music and poetry," *Washington Afro-American,* December 30, 1978.

19. "Owen Dodson: Poet," a typed proposal from Bob Morris for PBS Channel 13, n.d., HBC.

20. Ednah Bethea Blalock to JVH, January 4, 1986, Southern Pines, N.C.

21. Mel Gussow, "*Divine Comedy* play of Father Divine," *New York Times,* January 18, 1977.

22. "King Lear and the Fool," *Black American Literature Forum* 18, no. 1 (Spring 1984): 5. "Impotent trees" may have referred to himself.

23. "Lady-O" written in the winter of 1980. Typescript, HBC.

24. Mercie Hinton to JVH, March 13, 1985, HBC.

Chapter 29: Just Go On, Chile

1. "Voice Coach Frederick Wilkerson Slain in N.Y." *Washington Post,* April 9, 1980.

2. Glenda Dickerson to JVH, August 16, 1985, New York.

3. *Life in the Streets* was performed on May 3, 1982, in the Newman Theatre by Roscoe Lee Browne, Mia Dillon, and Gloria Foster, with the David Amram Quintet.

4. Camille Billops to JVH, February 8, 1986, New York.

5. "Prisoners," *Black American Literature Forum* 14, no. 2 (Summer 1980): 51.

6. "Now hear me while I pray / take all my guilt away / O from this day / be wholly thine." "My Faith Looks up to Thee," a black church hymn (1830).

7. OVD to GH, March 9, 1978, HBC. An account of the Denver incident appears in Heath's autobiography.

8. Priscilla Heath, for Black History Month in 1976 (she was librarian at Clemson College), displayed all of Owen's pictures and books. As for her own creative work (her novel was never published), she wrote Owen that her children more than compensated.

9. PH to OVD, November 17, 1974, HBC.

10. Sarah Sutcliffe-Hetman to JVH, September 22, 1984, HBC.

11. PH to OVD, August 3, 1980, HBC.

12. Mercie Hinton to JVH, March 13, 1985, New York.

13. Terrence Spivey to JVH, December 4, 1989, New York.

14. Carlton Molette to JVH, April 10, 1986, Baltimore, Md.

15. Helen Armstead Johnson to JVH, January 30, 1986, HBC.

16. Death certificate, New York City, no. 156–83–100137.

17. Edith was cremated in the Trinity Church Crematory on January 6, 1983.

Chapter 30: The Good-bye

1. Mercie Hinton to JVH, March 13, 1985, New York.

2. Bruce Nugent to JVH, February 21, 1984, Hoboken, N.J.

3. Patrick Trujillo to JVH, June 5, 1986, New York.

4. "King Lear and the Fool," "For Billie Holiday, Finally, Lady, You Are Gone from Us," and "The Star," *Black American Literature Forum* 18, no. 1 (Spring 1984).

5. Beverly B. Kelch to Owen D. Nichols, Board of Trustees, Howard University, July 7, 1983, copy, HBC.

6. Michael R. Winston to JVH, July 24, 1985, Washington, D.C.

7. May Miller received the second. Barthé never quite forgave Owen for denying him the original.

8. Owen's dismay over the destruction of "his" theater and theater library at Howard remained unabated.

9. Dodson called his old Navy buddy Bob Boyd at five or six in the morning, fearing for his life. Boyd called 911 from the Bronx but couldn't get the police.

10. Edna Wilson to JVH, December 15, 1986, Brooklyn, N.Y.

11. Patrick Trujillo to JVH, August 11, 1986, New York.

12. Trujillo to JVH, August 5, 1986, New York.

13. The *Chicago Tribune, Chicago Sun Times, Washington Post, New York Times, Washington Afro-American, New York Post,* and (he would have liked this) *Jet Magazine.*

14. HBD: 23.

15. "Howard Pays Tribute to Famed Owen Dodson," *Washington Afro-American,* July 2, 1983.

16. Owen's memorial, July 11, 1983.

17. Eulogy written by Donald Szantho Harrington, minister emeritus, the Community Church. Owen might have groaned, "I don't know why they think I'm the last Negro alive from that mess [the Harlem Renaissance]."

18. Main section, plot 732. When they arrived at the grave, the holes for the urns had not been dug. It was lunch hour. Then, when they started, it was the wrong grave. (Owen would have enjoyed the telling of it.)

An Owen Dodson Bibliography

Theater Participation

Owen Dodson's participation in the theater as an actor, director, set designer, and writer:

Nov. 9, 1933 — Bates College 4A Players, *Ile,* actor
Mar. 8, 1934 — Bates College 4A Players, *Macbeth,* actor
Apr. 1935 — Bates Baptist Church, *Deep in Your Heart,* writer-director
Apr. 21, 1935 — Bates Baptist Church, *The Terrible Meek,* actor
Nov. 7, 1935 — Bates College 4A Players, *Allison's Lad,* director
Dec. 12, 1935 — Bates College 4A Players, *Candida,* director
Apr. 30, 1936 — Bates College 4A Players, *Granite,* actor
May 1936 — Brooklyn College, *Including Laughter,* writer
June 13, 1936 — Bates College, *Trojan Women,* codirector
1936 — Yale Drama School, *Fashion,* actor
Mar. 28, 1937 — Yale Drama School, *Ascent of F6,* actor
Feb. 16, 1938 — Yale Drama School, *Divine Comedy,* writer
June 28, 1938 — Atlanta University, *Outward Bound,* actor
July 5, 1938 — Atlanta University, *Divine Comedy,* director-writer
? 12, 1938 — Atlanta University, *Three Faces East,* actor
Feb. 10, 1939 — Howard University, *Divine Comedy,* writer
Apr. 15, 1939 — Talladega College, *Amistad,* writer
May 17, 1939 — Yale Drama School, *Garden of Time,* writer
June 20, 1939 — Atlanta University, *Kind Lady,* director
June 27, 1939 — Atlanta University, *Once upon a Time,* actor
July 11, 1939 — Atlanta University, *Little David,* actor
July 11, 1939 — Atlanta University, *Smokey,* actor
July 19, 1939 — Atlanta University, *Our Town,* actor
Nov. 3, 1939 — Atlanta University, *Allison's House,* director
Dec. 1939 — Atlanta University, *No More Peace,* director

Mar. 15, 1940—Atlanta University, *Medea in Africa,* director
May 8, 1940—Atlanta University, *Mary Rose,* director
June 18, 1940—Atlanta University, *What a Life,* set design
June 25, 1940—Atlanta University, *RUR,* director
July 2, 1940—Atlanta University, *School for Scandal,* actor
July 9, 1940—Atlanta University, *Pygmalion,* set design
July 17, 1940—Atlanta University, *Mamba's Daughters,* director
Nov. 1, 1940—Atlanta University, *You Can't Take It with You,* set design
Dec. 8, 1940—Atlanta University, *Devil and Daniel Webster,* director
1941—Tuskegee Institute, first prize, *Gargoyles in Florida,* writer
Feb. 7, 1941—Atlanta University, *Time and the Conways,* director
Mar. 14, 1941—Atlanta University, *Outward Bound,* set design
June 18, 1941—Atlanta University, *Tovarich,* actor-set design
June 25, 1941—Atlanta University, *My Heart's in the Highlands,* director
July 2, 1941—Atlanta University, *Elijah's Raven,* actor
July 9, 1941—Atlanta University, *Silver Cord,* director
Nov. 21, 1941—Atlanta University, *Cherry Orchard,* director
Apr. 24, 1941—Atlanta University, *Family Portrait,* actor
June 25, 1942—Hampton Institute, *Kind Lady,* director
July 23, 1942—Hampton Institute, *Divine Comedy,* writer-director
Aug. 14, 1942—Hampton Institute, *Hedda Gabler,* director
Oct. 30, 1942—Hampton Institute, *Pygmalion,* director
Dec. 16, 1942—Great Lakes Naval Training Station (GLNTS), *Robert Smalls,* writer-director
Jan. 6, 1943—GLNTS, *John P. Jones,* writer-director
Jan. 13, 1943—GLNTS, *Booker T. Washington,* writer-director
Jan. 20, 1943—GLNTS, *Lord Nelson,* writer-director
Feb. 7, 1943—GLNTS, *Dorrie Miller,* writer-director
Mar. 21, 1943—GLNTS, *Everybody Join Hands,* writer-director
Mar. 24, 1943—GLNTS, *Lord Nelson,* writer-director
Apr. 7, 1943—GLNTS, *Old Ironsides,* writer-director
May 5, 1943—GLNTS, *Don't Give Up the Ship,* writer-director
June 6, 1943—GLNTS, *Freedom the Banner,* writer-director
July 7, 1943—GLNTS, *Tropical Fable,* writer-director
June 26, 1944—Madison Square Garden, *New World A-Coming,* writer-director
Aug. 4, 1944—Howard University, *Mourning Becomes Electra,* director
1944—Atlanta University, *Everybody Join Hands,* writer
Jan. 7, 1945—WMCA radio, New York City, *Hot Spots USA,* writer
Mar. 7, 1945—American Negro Theater, *Garden of Time,* writer-director
July 23, 1945—Hampton Institute, *Outward Bound,* director
July 26, 1945—Hampton Institute, *Hamlet,* director

Dec. 9, 1947 — Howard University, *The Glass Menagerie*, set design
Feb. 3, 1948 — Howard University, *All My Sons*, director
May 4, 1948 — Howard University, *Bayou Legend*, writer
July 1, 1948 — Atlanta University, *RUR*, director
Mar. 7, 1949 — Howard University, *Great God Brown*, director
June 22, 1949 — Howard University, *Silver Cord*, director
July 20, 1949 — Howard University, *Electra*, director
Sept. 13, 1949 — Det Ney, Oslo, Norway, *The Wild Duck*, stage manager
Sept. 17, 1949 — Copenhagen, Denmark, *Mamba's Daughters*, director
Sept. 28, 1949 — Malmö, Sweden, *Mamba's Daughters*, director
Sept. 29, 1949 — Lund University, *Mamba's Daughters*, director
Oct. 1, 1949 — Stockholm, Sweden, *Mamba's Daughters*, director
Oct. 1, 1949 — Uppsala University, *Mamba's Daughters*, director
Oct. 2, 1949 — Svenska Institute, *Mamba's Daughters*, director
Oct. 10, 1949 — Trondheim University, *Mamba's Daughters*, director
Oct. 21, 1949 — Det Nye, Oslo, Norway, *Mamba's Daughters*, director
Nov. 16, 1949 — Titania-Palast, Berlin, Germany, *Mamba's Daughters*, director
Nov. 19, 1949 — Munich, Germany, *Mamba's Daughters*, director
Nov. 21, 1949 — Althoff Bau, Frankfurt, Germany, *Mamba's Daughters*, director
Nov. 23, 1949 — Army base, Kitzingen, Germany, *Mamba's Daughters*, director
Feb. 14, 1950 — Howard University, *No More Peace*, set design
Mar. 28, 1950 — Howard University, *Boys without Pennies*, director
May 13, 1950 — Hunter College, *Bayou Legend*, writer
Oct. 30, 1950 — Bennett College, *Constellation of Women*, writer-director
Jan. 23, 1951 — Howard University, *Cross Purpose*, director
Apr. 30, 1951 — Howard University, *Pelléas and Mélisande*, codirector
July 18, 1951 — Howard University, *Hamlet*, director
Feb. 12, 1952 — Howard University, *Alcestis*, director
Mar. 14, 1952 — Augusta, Georgia, *Bayou Legend*, writer
Apr. 28, 1952 — Howard University, *Lottery*, director
June 30, 1952 — Howard University, *The Word*, director
July 23, 1952 — Howard University, *Family Reunion*, director
Oct. 23, 1952 — Jackson State College, *Divine Comedy*, writer
June 24, 1953 — Howard University, *Richard III*, director
July 25, 1953 — Howard University, *Emperor Jones*, director
Dec. 3, 1954 — Miner College, *Guest in the House*, director
Mar. 4, 1955 — Howard University, *Finian's Rainbow*, director
May 11, 1955 — Howard University, *Amen Corner*, director
Mar. 28, 1956 — YMCA, Harlem, N.Y., *Divine Comedy*, writer

May 29, 1956—Washington, D.C., *Chitra,* director
Apr. 24, 1957—Howard University, *Bayou Legend,* writer
Apr. 26, 1957—Theatre Lobby, Washington, D.C., *My Heart's in the Highlands,* director
Nov. 7, 1957—Howard University, *Bury the Dead,* director
Nov. 1957—Theatre Lobby, Washington, D.C., *Thunder Rock,* director
Mar. 6, 1958—Howard University, *Christmas Miracle,* writer-director
Sept. 26, 1958—Theatre Lobby, Washington, D.C., *Medea,* director
Oct. 30, 1958—Howard University, *Noah,* director
Dec. 4, 1958—Armstrong H.S., Washington, D.C., *Dream Come True in White and Blue,* director
Feb. 17, 1959—Howard University, *Macbeth,* director
July 1, 1959—Lincoln University, *Cave Dwellers,* director
July 27, 1959—Lincoln University, *Hatful of Rain,* director
Sept. 25, 1959—Theatre Lobby, Washington, D.C., *Look Back in Anger,* director
Nov. 3, 1959—Howard University, *Medea,* director
May 2, 1960—Howard University, *Julius Caesar,* director
July 4, 1960—Lincoln University, *Tea and Sympathy,* director
Aug. 1, 1960—Lincoln University, *Death of a Salesman,* director
Sept. 23, 1960—Theatre Lobby, Washington, D.C., *Moon for the Misbegotten,* director
Feb. 20, 1961—Howard University, *Blood Wedding,* director
Apr. 25, 1961—Howard University, *Antigone,* director
July 5, 1961—Lincoln University, *Bad Seed,* director
July 29, 1961—Lincoln University, *Rashomon,* director
Mar. 8, 1962—Howard University, *Dr. Faustus,* director
Mar. 24, 1962—Yale University, *Sign of Jonah,* director
Apr. 26, 1962—Howard University, *Defiant Island,* director
Dec. 6, 1962—Howard University, *Morning, Noon, and Night,* director
Apr. 10, 1963—Howard University, *Medea in Africa,* director, tour
Dec. 5, 1963—Howard University, *Long Day's Journey into Night,* director
Mar. 22, 1964—Howard University, *Medieval Easter Resurrection Play,* director
Apr. 23, 1964—Howard University, *Hamlet,* director
Oct. 21, 1964—Howard University, *Dutchman,* director
Oct. 21, 1964—Howard University, *Sho' Is Hot in the Cotton Patch,* director
Dec. 27, 1964—London BBC TV, *The Confession Stone,* writer
Jan. 31, 1965—Bermuda, *Til Victory Is Won,* writer-director
Jan. 31, 1965—Bermuda, *Air Raid, Happy Journey,* director
Apr. 30, 1965—Howard University, *Til Victory Is Won,* writer-director

Apr. 30, 1965—Howard University, *Air Raid*, director, tour

Nov. 4, 1965—Howard University, *Blues for Mr. Charlie*, director

Feb. 17, 1966—Howard University, *Sandbox and The Academy*, director

Feb. 17, 1966—Howard University, *The Return*, director

Oct. 19, 1966—Howard University, *Oedipus Rex*, director

Dec. 7, 1967—Howard University, *Oranges, Auto Sacramental*, director

Dec. 7, 1967—Howard University, *The Bird Cage*, director

July 24, 1968—Santa Barbara, Calif., *Morning, Noon, and Night*, director

Dec. 4, 1968—London, BBC TV, *The Confession Stone*, writer

Oct. 23, 1969—Howard University, *Idabel's Fortune, Shoes*, director

Feb. 7, 1970—Baltimore, *Til Victory Is Won*, writer

Feb. 27, 1970—ICCC, Los Angeles, *Antigone*, director

Mar. 4, 1970—Kennedy Center, *Til Victory Is Won*, writer-director

Apr. 22, 1970—Howard University, *Til Victory Is Won*, writer-director, excerpts

May 23, 1970—New York City, *The Confession Stone*, writer

Aug. 1970—New York City, *The Dream Awake*, record and filmstrip writer

Nov. 15, 1970—Grambling College, *Divine Comedy*, writer

Feb. 21, 1971—Harlem School of the Arts, *Bury the Dead*, director

Mar. 27, 1971—Harlem School of the Arts, *Runaway People*, director

May 21, 1971—Harlem School of the Arts, *Medea in Africa*, director

July 28, 1971—Harlem School of the Arts, *Contributions, Shoes*, director

Jan. 30, 1972—Philharmonic Civic Center, *The Confession Stone*, writer

Mar. 3, 1972—Harlem School of the Arts, *Mummer's Play*, director

Apr. 7, 1972—Harlem School of the Arts, *In White America*, director

May 7, 1972—National Arts Club, *The Confession Stone*, director

Mar. 4, 1974—Kennedy Center, *Til Victory Is Won*, writer

Oct. 24, 1974—Washington, D.C., *Owen's Song*, writer

Dec. 1, 1974—Harlem Arts Council, *Owen's Song*, writer

Dec. 30, 1974—Kennedy Center, *Owen's Song*, writer

Jan. 10, 1975—Amas Theatre, New York, *Bayou Legend*, writer

Jan. 13, 1977—New Federal Theatre, New York, *Divine Comedy*, writer

Mar. 26, 1978—RACCA Arts Consortium, New York, *The Confession Stone*, writer

Dec. 8, 1978—Howard University, *Sound of Soul*, writer

Jan. 13, 1979—St. Gallen, Switzerland, *Sound of Soul*, writer

Jan. 14, 1979—Theatre Off Park, New York, *The Confession Stone*, writer

Apr. 1, 1979—Salle Patino, Geneva, *Sound of Soul*, writer

June 17, 1979—ICCC, Los Angeles, *Bayou Legend*, writer

Aug. 11, 1979—Bermuda, *Bayou Legend*, writer

Nov. 10, 1979—Opera Ebony, New York, *Til Victory Is Won*, writer

Jan. 10, 1980—Karamu, Cleveland, *The Confession Stone*, writer

May 3, 1982—Public Theatre, New York, *Life in the Streets,* writer-actor
May 22, 1982—Riverside Church, New York, *Til Victory Is Won,* writer
Feb. 13, 1983—Carnegie Hall Opera Ebony, *Til Victory Is Won,* writer

Published Drama, Fiction, and Poetry

Individual poems in periodicals and anthologies are not listed here, nor are Dodson's essays and theater reviews. For a bibliography of these and other items, see James V. Hatch, Douglas A. M. Ward, and Joe Weixlmann, eds., "The Rungs of a Powerful Long Ladder: An Owen Dodson Bibliography," *Black American Literature Forum* 14 (Summer 1980): 60.

Plays

"Sonata," *The Garnet* (Bates College), May 1935: 18.
"The Poet's Caprice," *The Garnet* (Bates College), December 1935: 12.
"The Ballad of Dorrie Miller," *Theatre Arts* 27 (July 1943): 436.
"Everybody Join Hands," *Theatre Arts* 27 (September 1943): 555.
"Bayou Legend," *Black Drama in America: An Anthology.* Ed. Darwin T. Turner. Greenwich, Conn.: Fawcett Books, 1971.
"Divine Comedy," *Black Theater USA.* Ed. James V. Hatch and Ted Shine. New York: Free Press, 1974, 322.
"Freedom the Banner," *Callaloo* 21, no. 7 (Spring–Summer 1984): 57.
"The Shining Town," *The Roots of African American Drama.* Ed. Leo Hamalian and James V. Hatch. Detroit: Wayne State University Press, 1990.

Fiction

Boy at the Window. New York: Farrar, Straus & Giroux, 1951; Tokyo: Hayakawa Shoko, 1961 (Japanese trans.); New York: Popular Library, 1967 (paperback); Chatham, N.J.: Chatham Booksellers, 1972; New York: Farrar, Straus & Giroux, 1977; New York: Popular Library, 1977 (paperback).
"The Summer Fire," *Paris Review* 12 (Spring 1956): 63.
"Lodge Sisters at the Funeral," *The Book of Negro Folklore.* Ed. Langston Hughes and Arna Bontemps. New York: Dodd, Mead, 1958, 594.
"The Summer Fire," *Best Short Stories from the Paris Review.* New York: E. P. Dutton, 1959.
"Train Ride," *Cavalcade: Negro American Writing from 1760 to the Present.* Ed. Arthur P. Davis and Saunders Redding. Boston: Houghton Mifflin, 1971, 396.
Come Home Early, Child. New York: Popular Library, 1977 (paperback).

Poetry

Powerful Long Ladder. New York: Farrar, Straus & Giroux, 1946; New York: Noonday Press, 1970 (paperback).

The Confession Stone. London: Paul Breman (Heritage Series, no. 13), 1970 (paperback).

The Harlem Book of the Dead. With Camille Billops and James Van Der Zee. New York: Morgan and Morgan, 1978; New York: Morgan and Morgan, 1978 (paperback).

Index

JAMES V. HATCH is professor of English at the City College of New York and editor of two anthologies, *Black Theater USA* and, with Leo Hamalian, *The Roots of African American Drama*. He has won an Obie Award for the best off-Broadway musical, *Fly Blackbird*, and the Grand Jury Prize at the Sundance Film Festival for the docudrama *Finding Christa*, which he wrote and directed with his wife, Camille Billops.